My Father

An American Story of Courage, Shattered Dreams, and Enduring Love.

D0061051

By Michael Bennett

ISBN: 0615553052
ISBN-13: 9780615553054

Author/Publisher Contact Information:
e-mail: B918@aol.com
phone: 443 386 5455

For Sharon

She opens her mouth with wisdom,
And a lesson of kindness is on her tongue.
She guards her household,
And never tastes the bread of idleness.
Her children arise and praise her.
Her husband lauds her:
Many women have excelled,
But you excel them all!

From A Woman of Valor
By Abraham

Chapter One

The fertile expanse of land now known as the Ukraine and the independent state of Moldova was for centuries home to hundreds of small, predominantly Jewish villages called shtetles.

Despite centuries of sporadic upheavals that included the killing and maiming of hundreds of thousands of their people and the expulsion of entire populations, the Jews of the shtetles managed to rebuild their remarkably self-sufficient communities over and over again. Extreme poverty notwithstanding, the shtetles had comprehensive social structures, which included services that literally encompassed life from before the cradle to beyond the grave.

The rabbis were the venerated central figures in the shtetles. These were modest men, who through years of Torah study and self-refinement became recognized for their scholarship and piety. With selfless dedication, they shepherded generations of Jews young and old, rich and poor, through the good times and the more frequent difficult times.

When the region came under the dominion of Imperial Russia in the early 19th century, metropolitan cities hosting large Jewish communities developed. One of the largest of these was located in the Ukrainian port city of Odessa.

When the Russians took possession of Odessa in 1789, it was little more than an ancient Turkish fortress overlooking the Black Sea. With the building of factories and shipping facilities, Odessa's importance as a seaport grew and the city became a major center of commerce.

Drawn by the burgeoning economic opportunities, large numbers of Jews from Galicia and Germany immigrated to Odessa and by 1892 the Jewish community had grown to about one hundred thousand, or more than a quarter of the total population. Many of the Jews that immigrated to Odessa were devotees of an ideological movement known as the "Haskalah," which roughly translated means "The Jewish Enlightenment."

Troubled by the secularizing impact the European Enlightenment was having on many Jews, a young German-Jewish philosopher named Moses Mendelssohn sought to stem what was a growing tide of assimilation. By providing his coreligionists with intellectual and philosophical tools drawn from the Torah itself, Mendelssohn hoped to strengthen Jewish identity amidst the material and other temptations of the times.

Rabbinic leadership initially supported Mendelssohn's efforts. However, most of the leading rabbis eventually came to oppose his approach, believing that it would lead to even greater assimilation.

After Mendelssohn's death in 1786, the Haskalah indeed became an anti-religious, assimilationist movement whose proponents, the Maskilim, argued that speaking Yiddish, wearing traditional Jewish clothing, and clinging to an "antiquated" religion with its cloistered lifestyle stunted intellectual growth and fueled anti-Semitism. They proposed that Jews retain only a few symbolic vestiges of their religion, and to keep even these practices hidden. Their slogan became "Be a Jew in the home and a man on the street." The Maskilim also openly sowed contempt for the rabbis, slanderously accusing them of controlling the ignorant masses through superstitions and irrational dogma for self-aggrandizement. A number of high officials within the Russian government, who were eager to drive the Jews away from their religion and convert them to Christianity, became benefactors of the Maskilim and facilitated government funding for schools where young Jews could be indoctrinated with Haskalah ideology.

The Haskalah movement gained traction throughout Russia, eventually becoming the dominant ideology in large urban areas, such as Kiev and Odessa. Jews in these cities became increasingly involved in the government, and many earned recognition for their contributions to the arts and sciences.

But despite such successes, Russian Jews largely remained pariahs and the objects of scorn at practically all levels of society. Ironically, anti-Semites commonly cited Jewish acculturation as evidence of a conspiracy to take over Christian society. And at times of widespread economic trauma or social unrest, the Jews in Haskalah dominated cities still became the prime targets of violent attacks.

Under Imperial Russian rule the independent state of Moldova was known as Bessarabia. A lush, but sparsely populated and mostly rural area, Bessarabia stretched from Austria-Hungary in the north to the Black Sea in the south and was bordered by the Dniester River to the east and Romania to the west.

Shortly after taking possession of the area in the early 19th century, the Russian government sought to consolidate its control over Bessarabia by encouraging Russian citizens to settle there. But lack of widespread response prompted a government program aimed at populating the province with Jews.

As a consequence of offering tax exemptions and land ownership—things long forbidden to Jews—Jewish settlement in Bessarabia dramatically increased. By the end of the century, the number of Jews living there swelled to almost a quarter of a million. Kishinev, the provincial capital, hosted the largest Jewish community, which by the beginning of the twentieth century numbered approximately fifty thousand, or almost half the population of the city. With dozens of Jewish schools, more than sixty synagogues, and several Jewish owned and operated factories, Kishinev was a city where Jewish life flourished. But despite the growth of their community and decades of economic integration and socialization, the Jews of Kishinev, like the Jews of Odessa, remained a quasi subculture amidst an only slightly submerged and ever-present anti-Semitism.

In 1903, anti-Semitism in Kishinev boiled over and the Jews there became the targets of an infamously vicious attack that later became known as "The first pogrom of the 20th century." On the heels of a spate of venomous newspaper articles, a blood libel, and following vitriolic sermons at Mass on Easter Sunday, an angry mob led by local priests menacingly marched through the center of the city calling for violent attacks against the Jews. Shouting the traditional battle cry of the anti-Semite, "Kill the Jew!" small groups of axe, knife, and club-wielding pogromchiks broke away from the crowd and stormed into the Jewish neighborhood.

The Jews shut themselves in their homes and listened in terror as the invaders rampaged through the streets. The horror lasted for two days.

When the rioting in Kishinev finally ended, the traumatized survivors emerged from their hiding places and filtered onto the streets of the city, the city that they had called home for generations which was now enveloped in a pall of destruction and death. Mangled and mutilated bodies lay everywhere; entire families were found lying butchered amidst the rubble of their destroyed homes. The wounded were carried to the small community hospital for treatment, while the dead were lined up in courtyards and alleyways to be identified by family members. The remnants of torn and defaced sacred Torah scrolls were tearfully removed from the rubble of synagogues for burial. Hundreds of homes, businesses, and synagogues had been destroyed and thousands of families made homeless.

In the wake of the pogrom, scores of Jews fled Kishinev. Many relocated to the nearby poor, rural village of Kalarash, the majority of the population of which was Jewish. Others stood fast and decried the lack of a Jewish response to the violence, calling for the formation of a self-defense force. Some, however, fought against the idea of a militia, arguing that it would only make things worse.

But the determination to finally fight back took root and soon grew into a nascent Jewish army led by a young man from Kishinev named Vladimir Zev Jabotinsky. Forty-five years later, Jabotinsky's revolutionary idea became the foundation for the Israeli Defense Forces.

In 1905 another pogrom struck Kishinev. This time, to the utter surprise of the attackers, the Jews fought back. Although they had no military training and few crude weapons, the newly formed defense force repulsed the brunt of the assault.

Enraged by the audacious Jewish resistance, about twenty young attackers set out for Kalarash to settle the score; en route, the gang met up with about one hundred like-minded locals who eagerly joined in the murderous mission.

When the mob entered the village they immediately began to attack. Within twenty-four hours dozens of Jews lay dead—seventeen were burned alive in one structure alone—and a majority of the homes and businesses were in ruins.

The violence against the Jews that year was by no means limited to Kishinev and Kalarash. Similar attacks took place in shtetles and cities across Bessarabia and the Ukraine. In all, about six hundred and thirty-nine pogroms occurred throughout the region that year.

The wide scope and the coordinated timing of the attacks, combined with the outright refusal of government officials to intervene, made it clear that the violence was officially sanctioned. To the Jews this meant they could no longer look to the government for protection, and that more attacks were likely. Shock waves of fear went through every Jewish enclave in the region, precipitating large-scale emigration.

During the years of the eastern European pogroms, the United States was in the midst of the industrial revolution. Consequently, there was a growing demand for labor, particularly cheap immigrant labor, and America's liberal immigration policy reflected an official desire to fill that need. From 1880 until 1924, when intense public pressure resulted in new laws restricting immigration, more than two million European Jews came to America; most of them were from Russia, few spoke any English.

These disoriented and hopeful souls sought help from charitable organizations, hundreds of which had been established by Jewish communities across the country. Most of the immigrants came with little more than they could carry, and had to make do with only the meager stipends these organizations could provide. The lucky ones joined relatives already living in America. Others moved into filthy and overcrowded immigrant absorption centers.

For most new immigrants hard work and sacrifice paid off with only modest gains. Many men, who were frustrated and depressed by the lack of progress and the ever increasing financial burden placed on them by their growing families, abandoned wives and children in search of an easier life. Some immigrants never found jobs no matter how hard they tried and subsisted on the charity of others. Too many became homeless. Some returned to their homelands. A rare few made it big.

Despite America's immigrant-nation identity, anti-Semitism was rampant. Many viewed the newcomers as an economic burden; carriers of disease, criminals, and a source of cheap labor that threatened to displace American workers. Consequently, regardless of the great need for unskilled and semi-skilled labor, Jews had a tough time finding work. Anti-Semitism, it appears, was an even more powerful force than greed.

Besides garden-variety bigotry, Russian Jews were the victims of additional strains of xenophobia. Coreligionists from other eastern European countries, such as Galicia and Lithuania, regarded them as crude and uncivilized; Western European Jews considered them intellectually and culturally inferior; and although American Jews contributed enormous sums of money for their welfare, many of those native Jews, including some in leadership positions, fought any effort to integrate Russian Jews into mainstream society out of fear of creating even greater anti-Semitism. Others were simply embarrassed by them.

Chapter Two

"The mission of the United States
is one of benevolent assimilation."
— **William McKinley. 25ᵗʰ President of the United States**

When sixteen-year-old Harry Boens came to New York from Odessa in 1906, he was fortunate to get a place to stay with relatives. He was even luckier to land a job.

There was nothing glamorous about waiting tables in a subterranean restaurant below Rivington and Allen Streets on Manhattan's Lower East Side, but the tips were decent and the nighttime crowd enjoyed hearing Harry play his accordion.

At six feet tall with blond hair, steel-blue eyes, and the jaunty walk of a confident, motivated young man, Harry was a standout amongst his landsmen. There was something aristocratic about him. To all who knew him, Harry Boens was going places.

The Ladyzhensky family fled from Kishinev to Kalarash following the 1903 pogrom. After the 1905 attack on Kalarash, Esther Ladyzhensky, the family matriarch, scraped together enough money to send her fifteen-year-old daughter, Dora, to America.

Dora, a petite, brown-eyed girl, was determined to make it in her new land. She hoped to one day meet a handsome boy, get married, and raise a family. She also hoped that one day her family back in Kalarash could join her.

After making her way to New York via Canada together with her uncle and cousin, Dora, her last name changed by immigration officials to Ledene, moved into a tenement on the Lower East Side, not far from New York's garment district.

Jobs in the needle trades were practically the only ones available to unskilled immigrant women in those days and in order to survive, everyone had to work; even young children.

Because of the cramped, airless, and generally deplorable conditions, garment factories were appropriately called "sweatshops." Dora went to work in one. For about five dollars a week, nine and a half hours a day, she sewed the collars on children's clothing.

When Harry Boens and Dora Ledene moved there, the Lower East Side had already become a jam-packed ghetto of mostly Jewish immigrants. Approximately half a million people lived within a one-and-a-half-mile radius, making it what historians have referred to as "the most densely populated slum in the world."

Tenements were usually four-to-six-story brick buildings privately owned and located on plots originally apportioned for single-family row houses back in the early 1800s. As new immigrants increasingly populated the area, the row houses gave way to multi-unit structures that would generate greater income for the property owners. Lacking occupancy laws, there were no restrictions on how many renters could be crammed into each unit. Some thirty-seven thousand tenements dominated the Lower East Side.

The typical tenement apartment consisted of a small front room, an even smaller kitchen, with no appliances, and a tiny bedroom in the rear with a window that opened to an airshaft—the only source of sunlight and ventilation. Each apartment occupied less than three hundred and fifty square feet.

In 1901, government action was taken to improve sanitation and water quality on the Lower East Side. Nevertheless, remaining sanitation deficiencies, poor nutrition, and overcrowding contributed to exceedingly high rates of diseases such as tuberculosis (20,000 cases a year—8,000 associated deaths), rickets, influenza, and diphtheria.

During the sweltering New York summers, tenements became stifling hothouses. To find relief, residents often slept on rooftops, fire escapes, or on water-soaked sheets. To keep warm during the freezing New York winters, families crowded into the small kitchens and huddled around coal or wood burning stoves. Building fires were more common in the tenements than anyplace else in New York.

Crushing poverty, crowded and squalid conditions of the Lower East Side predictably gave rise to a proliferation of criminal activity. The area was rife with tramps and bums, pickpockets, purse-snatchers, and nascent Jewish mobsters who extorted protection money from even lowly pushcart peddlers. Youth gangs were everywhere. According to some estimates, there were over two hundred of them on the Lower East Side at any given time between 1900 and 1930. Not surprisingly, prostitution was also rampant in the area. Allen Street, where Harry Boens worked, was the heart of the red-light district.

But not all aspects of life on the Lower East Side were gloomy or sordid. Some tenements were built with elaborate architectural appointments and owned by conscientious landlords who kept up their properties and treated tenants with fairness and respect. Although a large percentage of the immigrants were not observant, religious life thrived on the Lower East Side: more than four hundred synagogues operated in the area; scores of Talmud Torahs (schools for religious education of children) were set up and staffed by volunteers or meagerly paid teachers; groups of observant men faithfully gathered daily to learn the Torah, and as they had done in shtetles, the Jews of the Lower East Side organized a litany of charitable groups and organizations.

Harry Boens and Dora Ledene were married in 1913. They settled down in a first-floor three-room unit in a tenement at 178 East 2nd Street on the Lower East Side. Their new residence featured a washtub in the kitchen, and a toilet in the outside hall. The building was conveniently within walking distance of Harry's diner, as well as Dora's sweatshop.

On April 30, 1914, Dora gave birth to a baby girl, whom the couple named Clara. On June 11, 1915, Irving was born. Three months later, Harry left his family. He returned in 1917 and Dora gave birth later that year to the couple's third child, Philip. But Harry went AWOL again.

In August of 1920, Harry returned once more. However, the reconciliation lasted only six weeks. This time Harry left for good.

For Harry Boens, it seems, life in America turned out to be a depressing disappointment. He had left the cosmopolitan city of Odessa to escape the increasing anti-Semitism and expected this new land would provide him with unfettered opportunities to succeed. Instead, he was a despised immigrant and a working stiff in a dead-end job living in an overcrowded ghetto with a wife and three little children.

Harry was a romantic. After leaving Dora the second time, he began pursuing a career in music. The Yiddish theatre was flourishing at the time and he tried his hand at song writing, published a few pieces, but his career never took off.

After scraping together enough money to partner in a liquor store business, Harry moved to Brooklyn and bought an automobile.

But his business plans were ill conceived. Between 1905 and 1917 the country was embroiled in a contentious and sometimes violent debate over the epidemic of alcoholism. States across the country were banning the manufacture, transportation, and sale of "intoxicating beverages." With ratification by three-fourths of the states, in January of 1920, the United States Congress passed the 18th Amendment to the Constitution making alcoholic beverages illegal. Harry was out of business.

While Harry was on the lam chasing his dreams, his wife and children were becoming ever more destitute. With three children under five years old and no money to pay for a babysitter, Dora entrusted her little ones to the neighbors so she could work in the sweatshop to provide for their needs and pay the rent. But with the pittance she was paid, Dora kept sinking deeper into penury.

In May of 1921, five-year-old Irving and seven-year-old Clara were declared wards of the state of New York, removed from their mother's care, and placed in the Hebrew Orphan Asylum. Philip, because he was only three years old at the time, was allowed to remain with his mother for six more years before he too was sent to the orphanage. Irving Boens was the child that would become my father.

Until the later part of the 19ᵗʰ century there were no government-run social service agencies or programs in America such as exist today. Private charities were often the only sources of support to which immigrants could turn. However, the sheer volume of needy families put enormous strain on charities and handouts to the poor were rarely sufficient to fill even an individual's basic needs. Unable to survive, some families sought refuge in government-run poorhouses where they lived amongst bums, derelicts and the mentally ill. But this was not an option most people were willing to choose. Consequently, streets became home to a growing population of homeless children, the so-called Street Arabs; there were thousands of them in New York City.

It was during this period, the mid-1800s, that hundreds of privately run orphanages were established across the country.

Although high morbidity and mortality rates in the ghetto contributed to the problem, the majority of the Street Arabs came from families where men had simply cut-and-run; men like Harry Boens.

By 1905, the problem of desertion became so widespread, Jewish leaders organized The National Desertion Bureau (NDB). The NDB acted as a kind of Jewish FBI, tracking down deadbeat husbands and fathers across the country and beyond, forcing them to either reconcile with their spouses or provide support. One of the NDB's most effective methods was to publish wanted posters of deserters in Jewish newspapers across the country. Readers were encouraged to report anyone they recognized to local law enforcement. The NDB was a remarkably effective organization that helped thousands of abandoned immigrant women and their children.

Dora reported Harry to the NDB after his first desertion, when my father was just three months old.

Chapter Three

Founded by German Jews in 1860, the Hebrew Orphan Asylum (HOA) started with thirty children being cared for by a retired Hebrew School teacher and his wife in a rented house in the Chelsea neighborhood of New York City. By 1863, the number of children in the HOA had doubled and larger quarters were needed. With help from the city, the asylum moved to a larger facility on Third Avenue and 77th Street. Over the next ten years, the number of HOA's "inmates" increased ten-fold.

While the self-proclaimed elite of American Jewry—Jews of German extraction—considered the HOA a jewel in their charitable crown and despite seventy percent of its operating expenses covered by government subsidies, the asylum was in financial trouble and under threat of closure. Blaming the troubles on poor management, the HOA's trustees formed a search committee to track down a new superintendent. They zeroed in on a fifty-one-year-old German expatriate by the name of Dr. Hermann J. Baar.

An orphan himself since age ten, Hermann Baar was a self-made man. He had struggled and sacrificed to work his way through prestigious educational institutions in his native Germany, where he earned his Ph.D., and was recognized as a scholar in science, philosophy, psychology, history, and literature. After moving to England, Dr. Baar became a child educator and earned a reputation as an innovator. Retiring early due to health problems, Dr. Baar immigrated to America and organized a Reform Jewish congregation in Washington DC. He later moved to New Orleans, where he founded a similar congregation.

Stout, wearing gold wire-frame glasses and sporting a chin curtain style beard, Dr. Baar appeared the archetype of pedagogic leadership. And he was an ideal choice to head the HOA.

When he arrived at the HOA's 77th Street building in 1876, Dr. Baar, a devotee of the regimentation of German culture and the formality of British pomp, set about reformulating the orphanage based on those models. He intended to transform the institution into a kind of factory for fabricating Jewish ubermenschen.

Weekday mornings at Dr. Baar's HOA began at 6:00 A.M. with the clanging of the Rising Bell. By 6:30 the orphans had washed and dressed before another bell signalled inspection. As the children stood in rows, their arms outstretched, palms facing upwards, the toes of their boots touching ropes stretched just above the floor, the feared superintendent severely strode among the ranks, carrying a rattan switch. Anyone found to be unclean, unkempt, not toeing-the-line, or otherwise out of order was first sternly rebuked, and then switched across the palms.

The balance of the day consisted of breakfast, religious services, classes, lunch, more classes, calisthenics, dinner, and finally bed. No free time whatsoever was afforded the orphans, and with the exception of questions and answers during classes, they were not permitted to speak; they awoke in silence, ate in silence, silently marched to meals, classes and other activities, and went to sleep in total silence. The children were also forbidden contact with the outside world, including their closest relatives. Violating the rules meant immediate physical punishment.

Dr. Baar also established the HOA's military-style Cadet Corps and Marching Band, which became the pride of the institution.

Given the times, the HOA, under Dr. Baar's leadership, gained a reputation as the premier institution of its kind anywhere in the world.

However, to most, if not all, of the children living under his heavy hand, Dr. Baar was the warden of an intolerable prison. They longed for life in a home they could call their own, with a loving mother to nurture them and a strong father to protect and guide them.

As a result of the asylum's reputation for success and the massive influx of eastern European immigrants, the HOA's ranks swelled to the point of overcrowding and the waiting list to get in grew long. The need for a larger facility became pressing.

In 1884, construction was completed on the Hebrew Orphan Asylum's colossal new complex located atop an expansive hillside plot in upper Manhattan.

Facing Amsterdam Avenue and spanning from 136th to 138th street, the new facility was an imposing, Victorian, four-story, mostly red brick complex. The entrance featured an ornate portico with huge wooden doors and was topped by a soaring clock tower ringed by stone spires.

The Hebrew Orphan Asylum. 1906

The building housed what amounted to a small city that included facilities such as medical clinics, a three hundred-seat synagogue, ten dormitories (six for boys and four for girls), and enough classrooms to accommodate an entire public school. A labyrinth of dimly lit hallways and staircases linked all parts of the building. The rear of the property extended two blocks to Broadway—an unpaved road at the time—and featured a large field overlooking the Hudson River. Located in a rear corner of the field was a five-story brick structure known as the Reception House where newly arriving orphans were taken for processing before being admitted to the main building.

At the Reception House, children were subjected to a battery of pre-admission procedures. They were interviewed, stripped naked and examined; their heads were shaved; they were bathed, vaccinated, given new clothing, and assigned to their sleeping quarters in the isolation ward on the fifth floor. The entire process took about two hours. New arrivals remained in isolation for approximately six weeks while HOA staff monitored them for signs of disease or mental illness. If a health issue arose during that period, competent medical treatment was arranged.

Upon entering the main building, each child was assigned an ID number and given a set of institutional clothing, a green army blanket and a sheet to cover a wire mesh cot plus an additional blanket and sheet for warmth. Children were required to mark all of their items with their ID number.

The youngest orphans attended school in the main building while middle school and high school age students went to various public institutions throughout the city.

When Dr. Baar retired as superintendent of the asylum in 1899, the number of orphans in the HOA had grown to over eight hundred not including those in the foster care or boarding-out program.

During the two decades following Dr. Baar's retirement, in response to the progressive trend in childcare, some of Dr. Baar's more oppressive policies were relaxed or, in some instances, eliminated: orphans were allowed limited contact with relatives and were permitted to write and receive letters; girls were no longer responsible for taking care of the boys' dormitories; periods of free time were added to the children's schedules; uniforms were eliminated and replaced with civilian clothing, and the "no-talking" rule was substantially relaxed.

In 1920, the year before my father and his sister became inmates, the HOA appointed what would be its last superintendent—Lionel J. Simmonds.

Short, pudgy, balding, bespectacled, cigar-chomping Lionel J. Simmonds had grown up in the HOA during the Baar administration. Now, he lived in his mentor's spacious institution apartment.

In the years preceding his appointment, Simmonds functioned in various capacities within the HOA, including as head of the Cadet Corps, which earned him the title of "the Colonel."

Although he was a protégé of Dr. Baar, Simmonds' philosophy on institutional childcare differed significantly from that of the former superintendent.

Ostensibly, Simmonds believed children learned best from their peers, and that incentives and competition were more effective tools in modifying children's behaviour than fear of punishment and an oppressive administration. He eliminated Baar's system of military-style ranks and replaced it with one made up of counselors, captains, and monitors comprised primarily of the orphans themselves. He expanded the HOA's sports programs, added extracurricular activities, such as theatre and music, and also organized the HOA's first Boy Scout Troop.

But despite these improvements, life in the Hebrew Orphan Asylum under Lionel J. Simmonds was in one fundamental aspect even worse than it had been under Dr. Hermann Baar: corporal punishment.

Ever since Charles Dickens penned his famous works about the life of orphans, the image of a dark, foreboding institution run by a sinister headmaster became the stereotype of orphanages. Dickens' stories were fictional, but, at the time, they accurately reflected the plight of London's homeless children. While the HOA was not exactly Dickensonian, the castle-like appearance of the building, the harsh intake process, being torn away from family (no matter how dysfunctional) and forced into an institution with hundreds of strangers made for a profoundly traumatic experience for children. And when it came to abuse, physical as well as psychological, the HOA could go toe-to-toe with anything the early 19th century writer had conjured up.

Whether it was part of their sincere belief or simply an attempt to counter the well-earned reputation of orphanages, when drafting the HOA's bylaws the Board of Directors added explicit language forbidding the use of corporal punishment.

But regardless of official policy and public pronouncements by superintendents, including Lionel J. Simmonds, decrying its use, corporal punishment was endemic in the institution. Abuse became a sport to the counselors, captains, monitors, and others who dished out new and more imaginative methods of giving "lessons."

Simmonds himself often demonstrated his displeasure by punching, slapping, kicking, or otherwise abusing children for even minor infractions, such as showing up late for class or an assembly, the Colonel punished with exceptional cruelty children whose transgressions he feared would bring disrepute to the institution. Offenders of such things as petty theft were summoned to appear before Simmonds in the synagogue where in front of a large assembly of children, he would launch against the wrongdoer a humiliating tirade that culminated in a vicious beating.

Weekdays in the HOA began at 6:00 A.M. with the clanging of the Rising Bell. Children had to make their beds—tight enough for a tossed coin to bounce—wash, dress, and be lined up in double-row formation before the 6:30 bell rang. After a brief inspection, inmates silently marched to the huge dining hall where they took their designated seats. After everyone was seated, another bell rang, which was followed by a bellowing "ALL STILL!" Once the children were in perfect compliance, another bell signalled them to recite the blessing before meals.

The children were given thirty minutes to finish eating before another bell rang and another "ALL STILL" was hollered, after which the monitors made rounds making sure that no food was left on anyone's plate. Any one in violation was forced to finish their meal as a glowering monitor stood over them and the entire dining room watched and waited.

Another bell signalled everyone to recite the Grace After Meals and when that was completed, yet another bell rang and another "ALL STILL," marking the end of breakfast. A final bell rang for line-up followed by a silent march back to the dormitories.

Once back in the dormitories, everyone rushed to double check the neatness of their beds and their lockers before cleaning the bathrooms and showers then sweeping the floor in time for a second inspection, signalled, of course, by another bell.

School day had not yet begun and the children had already endured nine bell rings and three "All Still" announcements.

The cry of "All Still", like the ubiquitous bell ringing, was a sacrosanct demand that meant you had *better* freeze in place and stay absolutely silent or face immediate and painful consequences.

The penalty for violating an ALL STILL command could have been a slap across the face, a kick in the rear, or a sucker punch to the back of the head. It made no difference whether the violator was sick or simply didn't hear the call. People from virtually all levels of authority enforced this rule and monitors were especially eager to do so.

Punishments frequently went beyond a single blow to an individual. Children were often penalized collectively for various and sundry offenses, such as an unkempt dorm area or a missing and presumed stolen item that no one would fess up to.

Collective punishments included things like "playing coconuts," which involved lining up children front-to-back and having a monitor or a captain shove the last child's face into the back of the head of the one in front. All down the line faces slammed into the backs of heads, followed by screams, cries, and moans as orphans clutched their aching skulls or covered their bloodied noses and mouths. Another frequently employed form of collective punishment was the so-called "standing lesson." This involved a group of orphans standing side-by-side and holding pillows in their outstretched arms. The punishment could go on for more than an hour and anyone who moved or lowered his arms was cruelly beaten. Collective punishments could also include an entire dormitory of children marching single file past a gauntlet of monitors who struck them at random.

Kicking, punching, slapping, boxing of ears, assuming the angle, ridiculing, etc., etc., etc., it was all part of the unofficial culture of an officially banned policy of corporal punishment in an institution whose leadership often employed it. Reporting any of these abuses to higher authorities was useless, and could even result in another beating for having snitched.

Of course the abuse had a positive side: it was effective in maintaining control; fear usually does that. But it also created hatred, anger, resentment, and a yearning for revenge, as well as a behavioral pattern that often carried on long after the children left the orphanage.

As he looked through the fifth-floor window of the isolation ward down at the field below, my father became transfixed by what he saw: The body of a former HOA boy killed in World War I had finally returned home. The flag-draped casket rested on a bier surrounded by the entire orphanage; a contingent of soldiers stood at attention. Unknowing of what was happening; he was mesmerized by the sight. Haunting notes pierced the air as a lone bugler blew TAPS, the sound seemingly emanating from nowhere yet everywhere. It was the day he arrived at the orphanage.

❖ ❖ ❖

He was walking through an empty corridor, bravely trying to find his way to the room where he was told to go. If late, he'd get punished, like when he was knocked to the ground for disobeying the "All Still." He felt lost. Nothing seemed familiar; the hallways all looked the same. He was alone, but he tried to hide his fear anyway; maybe it would go away if he did that. All that he could hear were the echoes of his own feet striking the hard floor. He kept walking. His six-year-old senses on high alert; his eyes frantically scanning for movement; ears finely tuned for sound...any sound that might mean there was someone or something to help him. If he could, he would have willed help into existence. Walk faster! Maybe around the corner at the end of the hall there'll be people down there? As he approached the bend, a figure suddenly popped out and screamed an evil scream, a scream meant to terrify. Kids think scaring people is funny. The fright was so intense it became physical. His ocular muscles became spasmodic; his eyes crossed and remained fixed.

It took several days before a qualified ophthalmologist could come to the asylum's clinic and operate on my father's eyes...without anesthetic. The surgery was successful; he would not be permanently cross-eyed. However, now he needed glasses.

By all accounts, my father was a kid with a natural excitement, a kind and generous disposition towards others. Though not aggressive he wasn't shy either; spending the first five years of his life in the slum had made him self-reliant, even at such a tender age.

In the orphanage, being a skinny, curly-headed, four-eyed kid named Irving Boens made him the object of much ridicule and a favorite target of bullies. Under such circumstances there were two options: he could curl into a ball, close his eyes, and pray that everything would disappear, or he could learn how to avoid trouble, navigate the system, and defend himself.

At the age of seven my father was moved from the M1 (Male 1) dormitory, which was under the supervision of a matron, to the M2 dormitory with its alcoves, lockers, and monitors. It didn't take long before the ridicule and harassment started: Catcalls of, "Hey, it's Bones! What's rattling *Bones*?" and "Hi, *EEERRRVING BONES*" came from all corners of his new world. The name-calling hurt, and it made him angry; he started spitting at his provocateurs.

After repeated run-ins with bullies, my father accidentally discovered how to deal with them when a particular miscreant had set his sights on him. He started to walk away, but the bully kept coming. Fed up and feeling like he had nothing to lose and nowhere to turn, as the attacker closed in my father spun around and punched the malefactor square in the chest. The kid doubled over gasping for breath, falling to the floor in a sobbing heap. The result shocked my father. He had acted on reflex and hardly expected his punch to have such dramatic results. He began to feel empowered. He adopted the posture of someone nobody would mess with, and the next time someone even *looked* like they were going to start with him, he would let them have it first. After several such pre-emptive strikes, he earned a reputation and the trouble stopped. My father had discovered the universal truth that *inside every bully beats the heart of a coward.*

The only happy constant my father had in his life was his sister, Clara. Although their dorms were in separate wings and they attended different classes, they saw each other at mealtimes. She was his big sister and that felt good, he was her little brother, she loved him and worried about him. But knowing that they had parents made their being in an orphanage uniquely bitter.

When she could afford transportation, Dora came to the HOA on visiting days.

Two years after their admission to the HOA, my father and his sister were boarded out to a home in Little Ferry, New Jersey. Two months later, they were returned to the orphanage. Four months after that, my father was sent to a boarding house in Phoenicia, New York, where an incident occurred that would cause him to be sent back to the orphanage again:

He was given the chore of raking leaves; pile them up in a field where later they would be burned. Instead, he cheated, sweeping some of the debris under the porch where somehow they caught fire, almost burning down the house. My father admitted fault. It was a display of character he would repeat again and again throughout his life—taking responsibility for his actions.

Ten months after he returned to the HOA, he was boarded out again, this time to a family on Beck Street in Manhattan. Six months later, he was sent back to the orphanage once more.

Some of the moves were made at Dora's insistence either because she didn't approve of the foster family, or she wanted her son to be closer to her.

Orphans who were boarded out often had bad experiences that made them prefer being in the asylum. Many families who signed up to be foster parents were in it largely for the stipends they received and often neglected the children, or even used them to their advantage; the girls were especially vulnerable to this and were frequently relegated to the status of domestic servants. Clara was the victim of such exploitation more than once.

As the years slogged by, my father became more active in the HOA's extra-curricular activities. He joined the asylum's Boy Scout Troop and became active in sports, such as baseball (Babe Ruth visited the HOA one day), football, and swimming; and he joined the choir. His singing career, however, abruptly ended when adolescence made an ill-timed appearance. While holding a long note during a solo before the entire orphanage in the Warner Gymnasium,[1] his voice cracked, sending the audience into roaring laughter.

Although the HOA's religious affiliation was Reform, Reform Judaism was much more observant then than it is today. Besides having a kosher kitchen, HOA children attended daily twenty-minute services in the synagogue. Sabbath services lasted about two hours, during which Lionel Simmonds delivered a sermon while wearing a black robe, as the HOA's ordained rabbi silently watched from his seat on the stage. Each boy attended bible study classes and was given a Bar Mitzvah. At the conclusion of every Bar Mitzvah ceremony, Simmonds addressed the boys with the declaration "Today, you are a man," after which he handed each one a fountain pen to mark the occasion. The ceremony so lacked meaning the children offered their own declaration of, "Today, I am a fountain pen!"

After completing lower school in the asylum, my father attended P.S. 153 located on Amsterdam Avenue and 147th Street. Following the usual morning routine and final inspection, he walked together with other HOA children to school. It was during one of these morning treks that my father had his first experience with death when a classmate wandered too close to a busy street and was struck and killed by a passing car. Seeing his

---

1   The facility was named in honor of Jack and Harry Warner of Warner Brothers Studios, who donated the money for the gymnasium's construction.

little friend's lifeless body lying in the road was an agonizing image that stayed with him throughout his life. And, unfortunately, it was far from the only time that he would come to know violent death.

Making the switch from elementary school to junior high school isn't easy for most kids. For HOA children the challenges were even greater. Being labeled an orphan carried with it a stigma that was impossible to escape. Despite great efforts to hide their status by referring to the asylum using code names such as "the H" or "the Home," other students would inevitably uncover the humiliating truth. And being a *Jewish* orphan was the ultimate degradation.

But HOA kids did not shrink in the face of anti-Semitism: they confronted it. And when one of them was attacked they closed ranks.

The journey from the HOA to P.S. 153 meant going through a mostly Irish neighborhood called Vinegar Hill. As troops of HOA kids made their way through the area, they were frequently met with taunts of "Hey Kikes!" and other equally repulsive invectives. Members of Irish gangs that proliferated in the predominately poor neighborhood tried to start fights with HOA kids, but the assailants quickly learned that these were no pushover *nebbishes*, and, other than occasional epithets, the attacks quickly stopped.

The one thing in their lives to which HOA children looked forward was summer camp. Every year, orphans old enough left the Amsterdam Avenue complex and embarked on a journey aboard buses, subways, and trains until they came to an old Indian trail in the Ramapo Mountains of New Jersey. They hiked along the path until reaching the shore of Lake Stah-hah-hee and then crossed in rowboats to the HOA's campgrounds. The boys' area was called Camp Wah-kee-tahn, the girls', Camp Wee-hah-hah. For three weeks HOA children went swimming, canoeing, hiking, and played a variety of team sports; they learned survival skills, teamwork and independence; they barbequed hot dogs and ate toasted marshmallows while sitting around campfires listening to adventure stories from the popular summer counselors.

But at the end of their brief respite the children returned to regimentation and abuses of the HOA.

Harry Boens became a wanted man. The National Desertion Board had been provided with his photograph and a tip that he was in California.

Harry had indeed moved to Los Angeles, where his cousins Sam Fengel and Rose Merman were living. As the founder of a new Yiddish newspaper in L.A., Harry must have been shocked to receive a request to publish his own wanted poster.

When the NDB caught up with him, Harry was courting a woman named Rose Kalisher. Rose was from a wealthy, prominent California Jewish family. She was also some twenty-five years Harry's senior.

Harry had big plans. He was going to marry Rose and use her money to grow a real estate empire. The fact that he was still legally married to Dora was a minor glitch he could solve by filing a petition with the court and placing an ad in the local newspaper.

But now that his whereabouts were known, Harry was facing possible extradition to New York for desertion. To make matters worse, the HOA had also located him and was demanding money to support his children. Harry was stuck. He had to face the music and return to New York to settle matters.

His cigarette habit climbed to five and a half packs a day.

Meeting his father in 1930 for the first time since he was five years old was a bewildering experience for my father. He was thrilled on the one hand but angry on the other, as he blamed Harry for his plight as well as of his mother and siblings. He wanted to ask Harry one simple question: "Why?"

Harry took his children out for ice cream, a movie, and a photographer for a family portrait. He told them about life in California and promised that when they graduated from high school, he would bring them west to join him. My father was thrilled. There was a life worth living outside orphanage and beyond the streets of New York City.

Clara, Harry, Philip, Irving

In a meeting with Lionel J. Simmonds, Harry promised to contribute to the support of the children, which in fact he did, eventually covering all of their expenses in the orphanage.

He also had a hearing with NDB officers, but their attempts to convince him to reconcile with Dora were fruitless. Harry wanted nothing more to do with his wife. He resented her for reporting him and returned to California.

On May 18, 1931, the California Superior Court In And For The County Of Los Angeles granted the petition of one Harry Boens to change his last name and those of his minor children to 'Bennett.' Later that year, Harry divorced Dora through legal default[2] and married Rose.

Before starting high school in the fall of 1931, my father and his brother, Philip, were boarded out to another foster home. This time, it was to a couple who lived, according to the HOA social worker, "in one of the exclusive residential sections of the Bronx," in a fancy new building, "complete with doorman and elevator," on the Grand Concourse. In her report, the social worker wrote, "The rooms on the second floor are large, sunny, and artistically furnished with paintings and statuettes. The boys are to have one of the rooms facing the street," and that the lady of the house seemed to be "an intelligent, americanized woman." After the children had been living there for a while, the social worker reported the woman was complaining "that her laundry bill has risen due to the fact that Irving changes his shirts daily."

For high school, my father attended Evander Childs, located on Gunhill Road not far from the Grand Concourse.

With a new last name that wouldn't draw ridicule and the promise of a future in California, my father

---

2   Harry's petition and newspaper ad satisfied the court's requirements, but it is unclear whether Dora ever knew that Harry had divorced her.

became energized. He had always been a good student, but now he excelled. Even his vision improved and he was able to dump the Harry Potter glasses he'd been saddled with since he was six. Although a freshman, he made the high school swim team.

Harry wrote him frequently, and he visited Dora every weekend.

But despite the fine living arrangements in the Bronx, its close proximity to school and his weekend visits with Dora, my father longed to be closer to his mother. In response to his request, and with the permission of his foster mother, he was moved to a new foster home on Audubon Avenue in Manhattan.

1933 was a good year for my father. He was a senior in high school, his team won the city swimming championship, and it was only a matter of time before he would start a new life in California. Eager to head west, he wrote Harry asking if he would pay for an accelerated learning program at a private school. Harry agreed and my father attended the exclusive Hamilton Institute for Boys. Harry also told him that he had made arrangements for him to attend the University of Southern California at Los Angeles, and promised him membership in an exclusive beach club.

Meanwhile, Clara had graduated from high school the year before and was doing her mandatory year at the HOA's pre-release preparatory program called The Friendly School for Girls. She had fallen in love with an HOA boy named Bernard "Bud" David Rosenzweig, whom she planned to marry. Bud, an auburn-haired, well-muscled, tough kid, who had once slugged Superintendent Simmonds after the Colonel slapped him for being late to an assembly, was admitted to the asylum when he was thirteen years old after his mother succumbed to the Spanish Flu. Bud, who was four years older than Clara, was sharing a rented apartment with a friend and attending City College, which was across the street from the HOA.

As with all the HOA's wards, before my father was released to Harry's care, a social worker was dispatched to confirm that he was going to a financially stable environment. The orphanage representative reported back from California that Harry had apparently done well since his move there, writing that he had a "very sumptuous office," and that she had overheard a conversation "between Harry and Pola Negri[3] with whom he was arranging a certain stock deal."

After completing the course at Hamilton, my father returned to the HOA, where he was handed an envelope from Harry that contained a ticket for ship's passage to California, a hundred dollars, and a list of duty-free perfumes to buy for Rose.

After a tearful meeting with Dora and goodbyes to his friends and younger brother Phil, who had become a well-liked junior counselor that the kids nicknamed "Jaunty Bennett," my father packed his meager belongings and set out on his long awaited journey.

It was a glorious end to what had been a sad and traumatic childhood. My father was on top of the world. He had overcome the adversities of a broken home; the trauma of a regimented and too often abusive institution; the pain of being ridiculed and bullied; the humiliation of being labeled an orphan, and the insecurity of being bounced from foster home to foster home. He was going to start a new and promising life in California with his wealthy father and attend a university in view of becoming a person of stature; someone people respected—a doctor or a lawyer.

---

3   Pola Negri was a world famous actress who had been brought to Hollywood from her native Poland by Samuel Goldwyn.

June 9, 1933, two days before his eighteenth birthday, was my father's day of liberation. He walked through the Hebrew Orphan Asylum's great wooden doors, under the soaring clock tower, past the ornate portico, beyond the iron fence and onto Amsterdam Avenue for the last time. Clara was waiting for him in the taxi that would take them to the dock where he would board a steam ship headed for the California Coast. At the dock, he said his goodbyes to his beloved sister, boarded the ship, and never looked back.

Chapter Four

*"Far away there in the sunshine are my highest
aspirations. I may not reach them but
I can look up and see their beauty, believe in them,
and try to follow them."*
— **Louisa May Alcott**

Being out on the open ocean on a floating city, my father was able to put the long dreary past behind him and daydream of his new life. The meals on the ship were fit for a king. His private cabin featured its own electric ceiling fan, which the porter advised him not to leave on at night or he would get sick. When he awoke the next morning with a head cold, he kicked himself for not heeding the advice. Unremarkable as the incident was, my father took the lesson to heart. Like after his bad decision to rake the leaves under the porch in Loch Sheldradke, he sought to learn from his mistakes and to blame no one else for them. Such had become his way.

When the ship passed through the Panama Canal, he marveled at the man-made waterway and a mechanism that could rise and lower huge ships eighty-five feet through a series of watertight locks to create a route eight thousand miles shorter than it would be otherwise. He was even more impressed than when he used to watch from the orphanage windows as the George Washington Bridge connecting New York to New Jersey was being built. "This is what could be accomplished through man's ingenuity and when people work together," he used to say.

Arriving in San Francisco almost a month later, my father walked down the gangplank carrying all his possessions in a single suitcase.

Harry waited for him, dressed in a custom tailored, double-breasted three-piece suit, complete with a white carnation in the lapel, a gold watch chain, dangling at just the right angle across his lower vest and ending in a fob of the Ten Commandments, and two-tone, cordovan wingtips. He was surprised to see how his son had blossomed into a handsome young man. But the first item on the agenda was to head to a clothing store; no son of his could be seen wearing coarse and clumsy institutional clothing.

My father's eyes practically popped out of his head when he saw Harry's cream-colored, 1932 Stutz, its huge chrome headlights and grill gleaming in the sun. The orphanage kids dreamed of the legendary automobile; he couldn't believe that his father actually owned one!

After a trip to the department store where Harry bought his son a new wardrobe that included fine cotton shirts, a silk tie, V-neck sweater, white slacks, and black-and-white saddle shoes—perfect college attire— they headed to Fisherman's Warf for an elaborate meal, before checking in for the night at the St. Francis Hotel.

The next morning, following a continental breakfast, they checked out of the landmark building and waited for the valet to bring the Stutz around.

Father and son headed south for Los Angeles.

As they crossed over the Golden Gate Bridge, my father alternated between looking at Harry, relaxed and dignified as he casually grasped the polished hardwood steering wheel, a cigarette burning in the long-stemmed holder clenched between his teeth, and gazing at the amazing scenery around him—the blue pacific to his right, the hazy mountains and majestic cliffs to his left. It was better than a dream come true.

Although it had only been a month since he left New York, the Lower East Side, the HOA with its monitors and bullies and regimentation, the foster homes, and even the orphan's clothes he had just jettisoned had already become the dusty memories of another lifetime.

The big Stutz made the five hundred mile drive down Pacific Coast Highway a breeze. With only brief stops for food, gas, and cigarettes, they arrived in Los Angeles in time for dinner.

Harry pulled the car up to the entrance of the Arcady Apartments, one of the most prestigious addresses in Los Angeles. The Carrera marble of the building's façade was brilliant in the light of the setting California sun. A red-jacketed white-gloved doorman greeted my father as he stepped from the extravagant automobile under the pure white awning. Clutching the only remnant of his previous life, the HOA suitcase, he stood beside his father as they rode in the opulent elevator to Harry and Rose's penthouse apartment.

As he handed Rose the perfume he had purchased for her aboard ship, my father was momentarily struck by her advanced age. But he was floating on air and of no mind to ponder the superficial incongruity. Besides, he could tell that Rose was good-natured.

While he unpacked his meager possessions in the guest room, Rose set the table for the supper she had already prepared. After the meal, my father showered and retired for the night.

The next morning, he awoke at exactly six o'clock, just as he had done for the last thirteen years. He washed, made his bed—tight enough to bounce a coin on—and dressed in the clothes Harry bought for him in San Francisco, which he had perfectly folded before going to bed the night before.

After breakfast, Harry took his son out to a small resort south of Los Angeles, where he handed him another hundred dollars and taught him how to play some of the games of chance. Before heading home, Harry gave him a tour of the city.

As they cruised down Hollywood Boulevard, my father was amused by the oddball characters and wannabe actors hanging out in front of the Chinese Theatre and on the corner of Hollywood and Vine hoping to be "discovered." The not-yet-famous John Carradine strolled down the sidewalk wearing a black top hat, cape, and carrying a walking stick. Trying to crush any budding thoughts his son may have of one day joining the ranks of these "losers," Harry repeatedly intoned in his thick Russian accent, "Fricks! A buncha fricks!"

It turned out that Harry's office was indeed "sumptuous," as the HOA social worker had described, and it was located at 408 South Spring Street in Downtown—the prominent Continental Building, the tallest building in Los Angeles at the time. He took his son with him there every morning, where my father watched Harry conduct his newspaper and real estate businesses.

At the end of each workday, the two made stops at Harry's favorite hangouts—clubs and bars frequented by other Russian immigrants who had also ventured west. As he entered the cheesy establishments, Harry's cronies greeted him like royalty; kissing his hand as a devout Catholic would do upon meeting the Pope. My father felt embarrassed.

Harry convinced his son to take what he called a premed course at the National School of Physiotherapy, which was located in a ramshackle two-story house on Western Avenue. It was a far cry from the sprawling campus of USC that my father had envisioned, but he trusted Harry. After all, Harry literally *wore* the Ten Commandments, and he had made good on his promises thus far. And, as he often heard Harry, when conducting business, say, *"My woid is my bond."*

For the next year, my father learned how to twist, bend, and massage arms, legs, and backs in preparation for the ultimate goal of medical school at USC.

Later that year, Bud and Clara arrived in L.A. and moved into in a rented bungalow. The Depression was in full swing and jobs were scarce. But Bud had learned auto mechanics while he was back in New York and his skill and affinity for cars made him marketable even in tough economic times.

Both Bud and Clara had begun a personal reinvention before they were married and in preparation for new lives in California: Bud changed his last name from Rosenzweig to Rowe, and Clara changed her first name to Claire.

⊕ ⊕ ⊕

"Was ever book containing such vile matter
So fairly bound? O that deceit should dwell
In such a gorgeous palace!"
— **William Shakespeare**

When he completed the course at the National School of Physiotherapy, my father expected to finally enroll in USC. But Harry had other ideas for his son's future.

California real estate was cheap and few people had money during those depression years, which created golden opportunities for Harry who had access to Rose's fortune. He had already planned his next business venture—a gas station, which my father could run while Bud took over the mechanic operation in rented facilities across the street. Instead of spending years in an expensive school with no guarantee of success, Harry wanted his son to work for *him*.

It was the second disappointment coming from Harry and my father was beginning to get edgy. But again he put his feelings aside and went along with the plan. What choice did he have anyway?

Harry set up an office with an oversized desk for himself in the back of the old, run-down gas station in East L.A., while my father went to work cleaning and polishing the long neglected property. It may have been a lonely little service station when they took it over, but my father intended to make it the best one around.

Months went by, but despite steady growth Harry refused to invest any of the profits into the business, and the salary he was paying my father and Bud remained negligible.

My father was becoming more suspicious by the day of Harry's motives. Bud, more cynical by nature, had already figured Harry out and quit the project after securing a job with Chrysler at their Plymouth plant in Maywood, California.

After Bud left the operation, my father confronted Harry about his promise to send him to college. Harry told him that he wasn't cut out for a college career; that his future was in business.

Long ago my father had learned to hold his tongue in the face of disappointment. Although he wasn't a cynic, after all that he had been through in his young life he knew very well how to accept not getting what he wanted; he usually didn't get what he wanted. But this was more than that; this was *his father* who had pulled a bait-and-switch on him.

Going to college was the goal of many orphanage children. It was their way to a better life and it was my father's dream. He wasn't going to rationalize away Harry's mendacity again, not this time. Besides having no tolerance for bullies, my father could not stand a liar. Harry was too arrogant to notice, but he had lit the fuse on a powder keg that was soon going to blow up in his face.

My father came to the painful realization that Harry was a fraud. He had brought his children out to California for selfish reasons. He cared more for his Stutz, his lavish lifestyle, and his well-bred image than he cared for his children. His generosity was a con job. Harry wanted to use his children; exploit them, reap the benefits that he felt were inherently deserved from grown children. Harry had not changed. He was the same person who twenty years earlier had selfishly abandoned his wife and children and thereby subjected them to a life of poverty, institutionalization and foster homes. "My woid is my bond," indeed.

He called out Harry on his abandonment and neglect. Harry defended himself by responding, "I supported you!" *"In an orphanage?"* my father fired back, his blue eyes blazing. That it would turn out was just the opening salvo.

After the confrontation, my father packed his meager belongings in the small HOA suitcase, left the Arcady Apartments, and moved in with Bud and Claire.

Having gone through the orphanage together, Claire and my father were exceptionally close. Married and starting her life with Bud, Claire wasn't as intensely affected by Harry's duplicity as my father was. But she was equally disgusted with him, as well as angry and hurt by the pain and disappointment he had caused her little brother.

My father felt like a kid who could only gaze longingly through the candy store window. Claire and Bud supported him in his pain and loneliness.

By all accounts Sam Fengel was a hard-working, decent guy. He was nothing like his cousin Harry; he had no pretenses.

Sam was a peddler of medical supplies who neither relied on nor trusted anyone other than himself. Every year he drove the length and breadth of the U.S. visiting doctor's offices and small community hospitals selling cotton balls, tongue depressors, and anything else he could buy in bulk and sell at a profit.

Sam had a unique sales strategy: he worked backwards. In the wintertime he headed east. When the weather turned warm, he doubled back west.

Never married, Sam lived in a one-room apartment so overstuffed with junk the family called it "Sam's Cave."

Sam had a gimpy leg and driving his old sedan across country was getting increasingly more painful. He'd been pondering hiring a driver for some time. After my father's blowup with Harry, Sam offered him the job.

Bud was an excellent driving instructor and eager to help. My father admired Bud's tough-guy image and independence, and Bud appreciated his brother-in-law's character, commitment to principle, and especially his loyalty. In fact, when Bud got a speeding ticket and had the option of paying the fine or spending the night in jail, my father, pretending to be Bud, bedded down for him in the local lockup. After a couple of weeks of lessons, he was ready to drive on his own and began preparing for Sam's winter run east.

My father enjoyed driving Sam and thought the whole enterprise an exciting adventure. He was amazed at the size of the country and the diversity of its landscape. From the deserts of the West to the farmlands of the Midwest to the Rockies, America was a grand country. And despite his hardships my father was grateful to be born in America, although he remained pained by what Harry had done and he still yearned for a college education.

Other than nearly going off of a cliff after hitting a patch of black ice in Fargo, North Dakota, the trip went smoothly. That is until they arrived in Illinois.

With its plethora of medical facilities, Chicago was a large sales market that usually took Sam a week to cover. On his first day there, my father met a local guy who had a female friend he thought would be a good match and suggested a double date. My father was game and got Sam's permission to use the car. While he was driving everyone home at the end of the evening he sensed that something was wrong. When he looked in the rear-view mirror and noticed that his passengers seemed comfortable, too comfortable, he realized what was bothering him: all of Sam's medical supplies were gone!

Fearing Sam's reaction, my father devised a plan. He returned to the hotel and parked the car, leaving it unlocked.

The next morning, when the two arrived at the car to begin their workday, feigning shock at the "discovery" that all the supplies had been stolen, my father pointed to the unlocked door: "Somebody must've broken in!" It wasn't exactly a lie, but Sam didn't believe it and accused him of selling everything and pocketing the money.

My father's denials and his turned-out pockets meant nothing to Sam who fired him on the spot, giving him however train fare back to L.A. Despite the circumstances, my father, once again, blamed no one but himself for his predicament; he shouldn't have gone out that evening, and he should have told Sam the entire truth.

Back in L.A. with Bud and Claire, my father tried his hand at a variety of odd jobs, one of which was with a double-talking, carnival barker/con-artist selling junk furs who, after trumpeting a line of gibberish to get peoples' attention and draw a crowd, proclaimed his goods to be "genuine Russian *Chaserai*"[4] at flea markets and anywhere else he could set up shop.

His life had become nothing like what he had dreamed when he left the orphanage, and his anger with Harry was growing.

⚜ ⚜ ⚜

"In the little world in which children have their existence whosoever brings them up, there is nothing so finely perceived and so finely felt, as injustice."
— Charles Dickens

In the days when my father was working at Harry's gas station, a young lawyer named Sherman Grancell came in looking for someone to fix his dented fender. Bud expertly took care of the repairs and Grancell, my father, Bud and Claire became regular friends. After his return from the disaster with Sam Fengel in Chicago, my father explained to Grancell everything that happened with Harry and asked if he had any legal options. Grancell, who was just starting out in law at the time, brought the matter up with the senior lawyers at his firm.

While a father's obligation to support his family was long established in American law, there was no precedent for someone suing a parent for college tuition. The senior lawyers at the firm were intrigued by the case and gave Grancell the go ahead.

---

4   Yiddish for "junk."

My father was not a vindictive person. If anything, he was easily placated when wronged, provided the wrong-doer acknowledged his or her mistake. But Harry's history of neglect and how it so adversely affected the whole family combined with his reprehensible scheme to exploit his children were beyond ordinary forgiveness. Harry was a liar and a bully and my father knew how to deal with both. On January 22, 1935, attorney Grancell filed suit[5] on behalf of my father against Harry Bennett alleging abandonment of his wife and minor children, asking for back child support payments of $250 per month, sufficient monies for a college education (including tuition and fees, books, and transportation to and from college), attorney's fees and, since he was still legally a minor, for my father to be freed from Harry's dominion.

If Harry resented Dora's reporting him to the National Desertion Board, the summons informing him that his son had filed a lawsuit must have driven him into a mad Russian lather. He probably snapped his long-stemmed cigarette holder in half and ground his lapel carnation into powder. He hired local lawyer Harry G. Sadicoff to represent him.

The Los Angeles Times caught hold of the story and published the first of several articles in bold headlines, "SON SUES FATHER FOR EDUCATION FUNDS."[6]

Concerned that a jury might be biased against a son suing his father, Grancell requested a bench trial. My father, using his birth name, had the suit filed as Boens v. Bennett. The case was assigned to Judge Arthur Coats in Los Angeles Superior Court. Trial date was set for Thursday, February 14th, but subsequently moved to Friday the 15th due to a crowded court calendar.

---

5   The suit was initially filed two weeks earlier but was thrown out on a technicality. Grancell re-filed the suit on January 22, 1935.
6   L.A. Times January 19, 1935.

During the trial, my father and Claire, who was pregnant with her first child at the time, testified as to Harry's history of abandonment, their mother's suffering, and how Harry had promised his son a college education and his daughter a job in San Francisco. Bud testified in detail about Harry's gas station scheme and his refusal to even recognize his children in the way a father would be expected. Harry's extravagant lifestyle and evidence of his wealth, which was estimated at $1.5 million (about $23 million in 2011 dollars), were also detailed to the court.

Harry testified that he had never made promises of a college education to his son and that he simply could not afford to pay for one as his holdings were being greatly exaggerated. Furthermore, Harry said, his son was "shiftless and dishonest," and not suited for a college education. He insisted that it was his children who had rejected *him*. Harry even brought some of his Russian cronies into court to testify in support of his self-serving, outrageous, and defamatory claims. Sadicoff argued that the children were not in his client's custody during the time they were in New York and therefore Harry could not be held responsible for their maintenance.

After deliberating over the weekend, on Monday, February 18th, Judge Coats announced his decision: He awarded my father $150 per month during the period of his minority to be deposited with a court appointed guardian; he further ordered that Harry pay all costs necessary to "procure an adequate supply of clothing and other furnishings, as well as adequate transportation facilities to and from college and in and about college and for the payment of college expenses, tuition, and books." Moreover, buying none of Harry's soap-opera testimony and angered by his behavior towards his wife and children, the judge delivered a scathing denunciation of Harry, saying that his refusal to furnish his son with funds to attend college was "on account of selfish reasons pertaining to the defendant alone and without any regard whatsoever for the welfare of said Irving Boens." And to top it all off, Coats ordered Harry to pay Grancell $450.00 in legal fees. Harry had received a royal Bolshevik beating at the hands of a good ole American judge.

Freshman attorney Sherman Grancell had made law.

Defense attorney Sadicoff immediately announced that he would be filing an appeal.

The next day, the Los Angeles times published an article with the blaring headline, "YOUTH WINS BATTLE FOR EDUCATION."

My father had prevailed, but he wasn't gloating; he had after all sued his own father. Nevertheless he didn't regret what he had done. He was fighting for his sister, brother and mother as much as he was fighting for himself because he felt it was the right thing to do.

It took two years for Harry's appeal to reach the Second Appellate District Court.

In a four-page ruling, the court upheld the Superior Court's decision insofar as child support from the time my father came to California until he reached the legal age of maturity. The appellate court also ruled that Judge Coats was correct in awarding legal fees. The bulk of the court's decision addressed the matter of forcing Harry to provide for a college education. Knowing that their ruling would establish law and have national impact, the justices took special pains to carefully consider the issue and elaborate on it.

In the decision, Judge John White writing for the court stated that they could find no case law on the matter of "requiring a father to send his boy to college," and had only the School Code of the State of California,

"[which] imposes upon parents, guardians or other persons having control of any child between the ages of 8
and 16 years the duty to send such child to a full-time
school."

Judge White went on to state:

"The alien philosophy that the child is a creature of
the state finds no countenance in the American system
of government; and when the child has reached the age
of 16 years the courts are not authorized to substitute
their judgment for that of the parent as to whether the
best interests of the child are served by sending him to
college, teaching him a trade or preparing him for a business career in a practical way. It is not only the privilege but the duty of parents to supervise the intellectual
as well as the moral development of their children. The
father is under no legal duty, after his son has attained
the age of 16 years, to send the later to college, no matter what the father's financial circumstances may be.
True, many a father does it at a sacrifice to himself and
the other members of the family, but he does so voluntarily. No doubt the trial court had such instances in
mind, but, after all if a father sees fit to content himself
with a common school and high school education for
his son, the law ordinarily will require no more of him.
A father, unless his parental authority has been taken
away by the courts, is the one to decide the extent of the
education of his child beyond what is provided by the
school system of the state."

Judge White concluded:

"The son's ambition in the direction of a liberal college education is in itself commendable, but upon the
facts now before us, the father cannot be forced to grat-

ify that ambition without making an unwise exception to a good rule."

Harry had won insofar as overturning the lower court's ruling on forcing him to pay for his son's education, but only as a matter of law. On the matter of character, the court subtly referred to Harry as a fatherly deadbeat, and to my father as "commendable."

Harry wasn't satisfied. He petitioned the California Supreme Court to relieve him of the burden of past child support and attorney's fees as well. The case wound up being remanded to the lower court for retrial on those issues.

My father felt that although he had lost the battle over tuition he had nevertheless won a moral victory, which he had. He had stood up for his principles and fought it all the way through. He had fought for justice for himself, for his mother, and for his siblings, and that, no matter what the outcome, is always a win. He had told the truth. Harry had lied.

Harry may have gotten his neck out of the noose of having to pay for his son's college education, but in so doing he had brought shame and disgrace upon himself.

In light of the Supreme Court's decision on the single issue of college tuition, there wasn't much reason for my father to retry the case and attorney Grancell advised him as such. Harry, with little to gain and facing a higher legal bill, wanted to avoid another trial. Consistent with his deceptive ways, he offered some conciliatory words to his son. My father saw through Harry's act, but he chose to take Grancell's advice and agreed not to retry the case. Sadicoff told the judge that father and son had reconciled and motioned for the case to be dismissed. In reality, no reconciliation had taken place. My father wanted nothing whatsoever to do with Harry, and Harry disinherited his son.

When he wasn't working at various odd jobs or looking for work, my father spent a lot of time with Claire and Bud, whom he was still living with. On weekends they often went horseback riding or to the beach. He developed a circle of friends and had an active social life. And he finally landed a steady job selling women's apparel, wholesale.

On November 1, 1937, Claire gave birth to a baby boy, whom she and Bud named Wayne David.

No longer waiting for Harry's illusory promises to be fulfilled, my father had taken charge of his own life. He left the women's clothing business for a warehouse job with the Century Distributing Company, which sold carpet and linoleum. He met a girl, fell in love, and became engaged.

But the girl's father wasn't supportive. He had concerns about his future son-in-law's ability to provide for his daughter, suggested that they defer marriage and offered to put my father through college. But my father, jaded by the experience with Harry, didn't want to do it, so the couple eloped. The girl's father had the marriage annulled and the relationship ended.

My father's brother, Philip, meanwhile, had been discharged from the HOA and married Pauline Adler, who had her own heartbreaking story of poverty and homelessness. With all the tumult happening with Harry in California, Philip and Pauline decided to remain in New York for the time being.

Philip was the most sensitive and politically active of the three children. Like his older siblings, his experiences in the HOA made him a lifelong champion of the underdog and a mentor to children in need. Perhaps that's what motivated him to become a communist.

With no end of the Depression in sight and disillusionment with the government at an all time high, the

Socialist movement was gaining popularity in America. Jewish people in particular were attracted to the phenomenon and a disproportionate percentage of members of socialist groups, such as *The Workman's Circle,* were Jewish. Philip wound up getting involved with the movement and attended group meetings in private apartments and the like, eventually becoming something of a spokesman for the cause.

But his affinity for communism faded when he realized his naïveté and he eventually came to denounce the philosophy.

Philip and Pauline eventually moved to California where Philip pursued a career in social work and operated an after-school youth center. They had two children, Jill and Richard.

With Germany's invasion of Czechoslovakia in March of 1939, widespread war in Europe was on everybody's mind and American officials began quietly preparing for the possibility of U.S. military involvement. In May of that year, Adolf Hitler formed an alliance with Italian dictator Benito Mussolini and in August, Germany invaded Poland. In April of 1940, the Nazis next invaded Denmark and Norway. By then, everyone pretty well knew that despite America's declaration of neutrality and strong opposition at home to becoming involved in the war, it would not be long before the first American soldiers joined the battle lines in Europe.

President Franklin D. Roosevelt signed into law the Selective Service and Training Act on September 16, 1940, requiring all male citizens from the age of 21 to 35 to register for the draft beginning October 16th. Thirteen days later the first United States peacetime draft lottery was held in Washington DC. Blindfolded, the secretary of war, Henry L. Stimson, drew the first slip out of a large glass container and handed it to President Roosevelt who announced the number.

My Father with Wayne circa 1939

On March 1, 1941, my father received a letter from the President of the United States that began with the word "Greeting" and ended with "...you must report for your pre-induction physical examination as directed." He had been selected in the first draw. On March 14th, he was inducted into the United States Army at Fort MacArthur, California. Conscription was for twelve months.

Chapter Five

Assigned to the 40th Infantry Division 115th Quarter-master Regiment based at Camp San Luis Obispo, California, my father went through basic training and soon became the acting sergeant-in-charge of the Division motor pool, aka the Chief Dispatcher. After six months with the 115th, he was reassigned to the 7th Infantry Division Medical Detachment stationed at Fort Ord, Monterrey, California, where he became sergeant-in-charge of the infirmary.

On Sunday, December 7, 1941, while my father was standing in line for lunch outside of the Fort Ord mess hall, carrying a three-day pass that he intended to use the next day to visit Claire, an announcement came over the loudspeaker system: "THE JAPANESE HAVE BOMBED PEARL HARBOR. ALL LEAVES ARE CANCELLED." It was approximately two and a half months before his scheduled separation from the army.

On the evening of Thursday, December 11th, a report came in that a Japanese submarine had lobbed an artillery shell at an oil refinery near Santa Barbara. In response, the entire 7th Infantry Division was mobilized and, moving out under blackout conditions, began patrolling the California coast from Santa Barbara to San Jose. My father's unit took over the Portuguese Hotel in Santa Clara, establishing their headquarters there, while the rest of the Division took over the Libby McNeill Cannery near San Jose.

After weeks patrolling the coast, the Division was moved to Camp San Luis Obispo to begin training in the Mojave Desert in preparation to join with General George Patton's tank corps in confronting German Field Marshall Erwin Rommel's forces, which were thundering through North Africa.

After extensive desert warfare training, and a night during which he shared his sleeping bag with a very large tarantula, in February 1943, my father received orders to report to Fort Bliss in El Paso, Texas. He had been assigned to the 5th Cavalry Regiment of the 1st Cavalry Division. Most of the 1st Cavalry Division's mounted units had already been eliminated or converted into mechanized cavalry or infantry units.

The commander of the 1st Cavalry Division was a thick-necked, gruff-speaking, career military man by the name of Major General Innis P. "Bull" Swift.

A longtime cavalry soldier who enjoyed riding his dappled-gray stallion around Fort Bliss, General Swift became infamous among the troops for charging up on unsuspecting young men and shouting "WHAT'S YOUR NAME SOLDIER?" Snapping to attention, the usually trembling draftee would barely be able to squeeze out the answer from his constricting throat before Swift, atop his snorting and clamoring steed, would bark back, "GET YOUR HAIR CUT SHORT AND MOVE IN ON 'EM, SON, WE'RE GOIN TO *WARRR!*" and then gallop off in-search of more quarry.

While stationed at Fort Bliss, my father underwent intensive combat training in such disciplines as, artillery, heavy and light machine guns, chemical warfare, demolition and explosives, grenade, rifle, pistol, sub machine gun, as well as hand-to-hand combat.

In May of 1943, the entire 1st Cavalry Division was mobilized for deployment to Australia in preparation to confront the Japanese juggernaut rampaging through the Southwest Pacific.

On June 6th, my father was promoted to Staff Sergeant. Five days later, he turned twenty-eight years old.

After arriving by train in San Francisco on the foggy morning of June 20th, he boarded the SS Monterey and steamed out of the harbor into San Francisco Bay headed for Australia. As the converted luxury liner passed under the Golden Gate Bridge and came under the escort of a U.S. Navy destroyer and a blimp overhead, most of the men felt sad as the reality of leaving home and not knowing if they would ever return began to sink in. For my father, it was a moment flooded with complex emotion:

As the Golden Gate Bridge slowly faded into the distance, my father, leaning on the deck-railing of the ship, gazed at the massive steel structure and recalled the time that he had crossed it in Harry's Stutz. He thought about how he was just a naïve eighteen-year-old who had been lied to and betrayed by his own father; the "father" who had abandoned his wife and left his children to be raised in an orphanage and foster homes; the father that he had sued. And he thought about Claire and Phil and Wayne, and if he would ever see them again. And he thought about Dora, and he wondered...

At the end of twenty-eight days of zigzagging[7] across the Pacific, the SS Monterey arrived in Brisbane, Australia,

---

7   During the war, ships zigzagged as an anti-submarine maneuver.

on July 12th. After disembarking from the ship, the men were loaded onto waiting trucks and driven eighteen miles north to an area called Strathpine.

At Strathpine, each man was handed five blankets and instructed to march fifteen miles on a given azimuth to a location where they would build a camp. Upon arrival at the site, the men were provided with saws for cutting down trees and rope and parachute material for setting up tents.

On the first night in Strathpine, as my father bedded down in his tent shivering from the frigid night air, he understood why he had been given the five blankets. He also began to appreciate that learning to cope with his hard life-experiences were now to his advantage. The loss of privacy that comes with living in barracks and the regimentation and discipline that are part of army life can be very difficult for many people; some can't cope at all. But for my father, communal living and regimentation had been his lot in life. He had lived those inconveniences and hardships and frustrations and worse since he was five years old and he knew how to survive them. After two weeks of camp building, marching, and drills, he was selected as one of fifty men to train with the 1st Australian Commando Battalion.

At the conclusion of commando training, he returned to his platoon at Strathpine and began engaging in combat maneuvers and training with 37mm cannons. It was during one such training exercise that he drew the attention of General Swift, who had relocated there together with the Division, as well as with his horse. After watching him use a whistle to signal his men in simulated, coordinated attacks, and rigging up ropes and harnesses to maneuver the heavy weapons across a gully, Swift called out my father and told him that he was going to recommend him for Officer Candidate School (OCS). However, in August, before he would attend OCS, my father was loaded onto a truck and driven to a remote area in Southeast Queensland called Canungra.

Located at the base of the regional mountains, the Canungra Commando Training School was designed to provide intensive training to all combat units on landscape closely resembling that where the men would eventually see action. From heavily wooded mountains to brush covered plains and dense jungle, Canungra had just about everything in the way of rough terrain. The camp itself was austere; there were no buildings, electricity, or running water. And being at a high elevation, the nights were even more frigid than they were at Strathpine.

The soldiers at Canungra trained twelve hours per day, six days a week for three weeks, followed by a six-day "Mountain Exercise," during which the men were provided only rudimentary survival equipment, no navigational tools, and only minimum rations. At the conclusion of the course, my father stayed on at Canungra for two more weeks for additional specialized training. He successfully completed all of the courses with high marks.

After returning to Strathpine in mid-September, he rejoined his unit and for the next couple of weeks continued to train and engage in combat maneuvers.

Due to the need for additional firepower in the Southwest Pacific Area, heavy weapons units were formed in each regiment and designated as D and H Troops. My father's unit, a heavy machine gun platoon, was assigned to D Troop of the 2nd Squadron 5th Cavalry Regiment.

At this point, my father had been in the service for more than two years and his mind had become focused on his training and, of course, the war. He missed Claire and Bud and Phil, and his little nephew Wayne, and he missed his adopted state of California. Thoughts of the HOA and Harry didn't enter his mind anymore. That is until mail call one day.

As was his wont, my father returned to his tent, sat on his cot, and began opening his mail. Claire was good about writing and he most looked forward to her letters.

In the context of a letter sent to him by a cousin in California were the following words: "I was sorry to hear about your father's death." At 53 years old, Harry had died from pulmonary edema—a build-up of fluid around his lungs likely brought about by his five-and-a-half-pack-a-day smoking addiction.

At first, my father was troubled as to why Claire or Phil hadn't informed him of Harry's ill health, let alone his death. Then again, it was no secret how he felt about Harry and perhaps Claire and Phil surmised that given the circumstances, it was better to say nothing rather than deliver upsetting news. However, reading of Harry's demise elicited no tears from my father. He surely felt some sorrow, but mostly he felt indignation. *Pursing his lips and mildly shaking his head, he put the letter back in its envelope, tossed it on his cot, and left for another exercise.*

On October 3rd, my father received orders to report to OCS. Two days later he began a sixteen-week course in the 2nd class of the army's newly established Officer Candidate School at Camp Columbia near Brisbane.

On the first day of OCS, as the men lined up on the parade ground the commandant of the camp briskly walked into the area while another officer bellowed "ATTENTION!" Facing the assembly, the commandant, a tough, no-nonsense officer, introduced the men to OCS:

"Rip off your stripes! Rip 'em right off! You are now officer candidates, which is the lowest form of animal life. If the latrine orderly orders you to jump, *you better jump!*"

The commandant went on to explain that the men would be subjected to intense training and that he expected perfect compliance with the rules and with discipline. If a man successfully completed the school, he would be offered a commission as an officer; if not, he would be washed out of OCS and returned to his unit, in disgrace.

After the commandant completed his introduction, the officer in charge of Training, Advising, and Counseling, also known as the TAC Officer, addressed the candidates.

Contrary to what the title seems to describe, an OCS TAC officer in no way resembled a college guidance counselor. Strict disciplinarians and administrators, TAC officers were typically like marine drill sergeants but with even meaner dispositions and greater authority, and for very good reason—they were training men to lead other men into combat.

Pacing up and down the line of candidates, the TAC officer delivered his address in one long, intimidating rant, which began with "If you are asked a question, there are only three answers, YES SIR! NO SIR! AND I DON'T KNOW SIR!"

He went on to "explain" the rules of OCS: Any instruction that was not perfectly complied with would result in a demerit, or a "ding," so many dings and you would be washed out and sent back to your unit; there would be no drinking and no women; there would be no gambling and no fighting; bunks were to be made perfect and tight, boots, spit-shined; reveille was at 6:00 A.M., fall out for assembly at 6:05 A.M.; heads were to be shaved to within one quarter of an inch with no hair on the neck; there would be no exceptions to any rule and even the slightest disrespect shown to an instructor would result in being washed out and sent back to your unit.

In concluding his harangue, the TAC officer stopped pacing, faced the assembly, and shouted, "WELCOME TO OFFICER CANDIDATE SCHOOL, DISMISSED."

⚜ ⚜ ⚜

My father was athletic before he entered the service and after all the training he had undergone thus far, he was in the best shape of his life. Even though the OCS program was tougher than anything he had thus far experienced, his performance was strong and determined, and he excelled in all areas of academics as well. However, on one occasion he slipped. At inspection one morning, the TAC officer was taking his usual stroll through the ranks when he stopped behind my father:

"BENNETT".

"YES SIR!"

"You gambled and you lost. DO YOU KNOW WHAT I MEAN?"

"YES SIR!"

"WHAT DO I MEAN, BENNETT?"

"I SHOULD HAVE GOTTEN A HAIR CUT WITH NO HAIR ON MY NECK, SIR!"

"ONE DING," the TAC officer shouted.

My father wasn't overly given to vanity, but there was one physical characteristic that had been the bane of his existence since he was a child—his curly hair. Today curly hair on men is fashionable; it wasn't back then. Although his reputation as a fighter prevented most of the other orphans from saying anything about his hair within earshot at least, my father nevertheless was very self-conscious of his curls and he tried every conceivable method of grooming to try to hide them. This was the reason why he attempted to cheat on the OCS' hair requirement. It was a dumb move that he regretted. When recalling the incident decades later he seemed to still feel a little embarrassed.

At the end of training, the officer candidates were ordered to fall out for the graduation ceremony. While marching to the parade ground, to everyone's shock one soldier was yanked out of line and washed out. Over the four-month course, about half of the candidates were returned to their units.

On January 24th, 1944, my father was discharged from the regular army to accept his commission as a second lieutenant and thereby declared "An Officer and a Gentleman."

After a brief celebration in Sydney, he returned to Strathpine and continued training for another three weeks.

During the period of December 19th through February 25th, the 1st Cavalry Brigade was moved to Oro Bay, New Guinea. My father arrived there on February 22nd.

My father:

"When I arrived in New Guinea, I received orders to report to General Swift's headquarters. After reporting to his headquarters, General Swift said to me the following: 'When an officer candidate is commissioned, we send him to other units for reasons of discipline. However, your commanding officer has requested you return to your platoon with the 5th Cavalry. You can reject it if you want.' I said, 'No, sir, I've trained those men, they know me.' General Swift replied, 'Ok, if it doesn't create a discipline problem.'

On February 27th, the 2nd Squadron of the 5th Cavalry Regiment, about eight hundred men, received orders to gather their gear and report to an assembly area on the beach at Oro Bay. Sitting just offshore were three World War I vintage destroyers and two newer class destroyers. The men were told that they would soon be ferried out to the waiting vessels for a military exercise. All weapons were collected and bulk loaded onto the ships.

The men proceeded to board small landing craft that everyone referred to as Higgins boats, which transported them out to the waiting destroyers.

As the Higgins boats bobbed in the water alongside the huge vessels, the men scaled up thick rope ladders onto the decks. My father's platoon was assigned to one of the World War I destroyers, the USS Humphreys.

Onboard the Humphreys, the men were ordered to proceed below deck to their quarters, which was located in a converted boiler room.

Once everyone was accounted for and all the equipment had been loaded, the convoy moved out of Oro Bay and headed east before slowly turning north toward the Bismarck Archipelago.

After several hours out to sea, the officers on the Humphreys were summoned to the ship's map room. In the center of the room on a large table was a mockup of an island. The men were then informed that this was not an exercise. They had been moved out on secret orders as a reconnaissance force whose objective was to determine the enemy strength on the island of Los Negros in the Admiralty Islands, and, if feasible, seize and secure the Momote airstrip approximately one hundred and fifty yards inland. If they met heavy resistance, they would be withdrawn and evacuated back to the destroyers.

Once the ships arrived at a staging area about five thousand yards from the eastern shore of the island, the men would be ordered to scale down the rope ladders into Higgins boats that would take them to a rendezvous point about thirty-seven hundred yards from the landing site. Each boat would carry thirty-seven men and would be manned by three navy personnel—a coxswain and two gunners. Once they reached the rendezvous point, the boats would cruise in a circle while the destroyers and the air force bombed and strafed the landing area, to be followed by a flare signaling them to proceed to shore.

The assault would take place in four initial waves at five-minute intervals, followed by an ongoing shuttling of men and materials from the destroyers to the beach. Each officer was provided maps of the island and briefed on enemy dispositions, terrain, weather, etc. My father's platoon was assigned the number 2 boat of the first wave.

Gathering the twenty-four men of his platoon around him in the ship's converted boiler room, my father briefed them about the mission. He urged everyone not to try to be heroes and to work together, each man doing his job and looking out for the others. He told them to clean their weapons and to check and recheck their ammunition and gear, then to get some rest; it was going to be a two-day journey.

Although anxious about going into combat, my father felt confident. He had taken the training of the last three years seriously in anticipation of the coming day and was now more than ever glad that he had done so. His ability to maneuver in amphibious landings and survive in jungle combat conditions had become automatic. Emotionally, he had learned survival early in life. His focus in combat would be on the objective, his men, and staying alive. The desire to kill was not part of my father's make up, but because of the training, killing was now second nature to him.

My Father talked about his training and how it prepared him for combat in a 1999 interview:

"…and…uh…ya' know, BARs and Tommy Guns, stuff like that. But, ya' know you… you're limited in the training session because you don't want to hurt anybody; you're not supposed to kill anybody. But the dry runs… they give you a whole lot of dry runs…in other words you maneuver without ammunition but you have your guns and you squeeze off rounds and you hit the dirt, and all that sort'a stuff…and…uh…so what that does, it makes it automatic, you get an automatic reaction when you actually get into combat because the training, the dry runs, ya' know exactly what to do. The minute you hear a burst, you hit the deck, see, and you look around, and ya' get up on your knees…got your gun out in front of ya', and when you start advancing, ya' have your gun stuck right into your belly…butt of the gun…you're firing from your middle, not from the shoulder, see. What ya' do…it helps you to jump to the location where the fire is coming from instantly. See, ya' just jump, jump-to-the-right jump-to-the left, and so on… you fire at targets of opportunity; you don't know where they are, but if a target of opportunity pops up, that's where you go."

In order to get a perspective on the military campaigns that my father took part in and to better appreciate America's victory over Japan in World War II, some discussion as to the conditions that led up to the war and both the Japanese and American war strategies and tactics are helpful. And because of the role that he played in my father's life, it also becomes relevant to discuss in some detail the man who led America to that victory, General Douglas MacArthur.

Before the attack on Pearl Harbor, Japan had for years been engaged in military efforts to conquer East Asia. Japan had few natural resources, and the warlords, who were ostensibly under the control of the "divine" Emperor Hirohito, but who were in actuality controlling policy, were hell-bent on conquering every resource-rich or strategically important part of the region to solve their economic woes and feed their insatiable desire for power. In furtherance of its imperialistic goals, Japan had built up a gargantuan military machine consisting of naval, air, and ground forces.

America had long recognized Asia's enormous economic potential and strategic importance and during the years leading up to World War II, the U.S. was competing with Japan in the region over these interests. All of this made for a confrontation between the two countries an increasing likelihood. But few believed that Japan would be so bold as to launch a military attack against the United States itself.

Japan's warlords, hoping to get the upper hand on what they viewed as an inevitable war, recognized America's military weakness, which was due in large part to its commitment to the conflict in Europe. With few military resources in the region and much of the nation's pacific naval fleet at one location—Pearl Harbor—a unique opportunity existed for Japan to strike. From strictly a military perspective the Japanese strategy was shrewd.

However, what the warlords in Tokyo did not calculate well was how ferocious and determined America's response would be to such an outrageous, unprovoked act of aggression. When President Franklin Roosevelt addressed the country following the attack on Pearl Harbor, his statement that December 7, 1941, would be "a date that will live in infamy" was a prescient testimonial of the nation's united resolve to defeat Japan, as well as the prowess of America's military leadership.

Even before World War II, General Douglas MacArthur had earned a reputation as one of America's most brilliant military strategists and battlefield tacticians. He also understood Oriental culture and mentality arguably better than any of his contemporaries. MacArthur had grown up in a military family and had spent much of his childhood in the Philippines, where his father, a highly decorated veteran of the American Civil War, was the Military Governor. He was a graduate and former superintendent of the United States Military Academy at West Point, an experienced combat veteran and military commander from the time of the Spanish American War.

After serving in the Philippines in the 1920s, and later as U.S. Army Chief of Staff, General MacArthur resigned from active duty in 1937 and was serving as Field Marshal of the Philippine Army when President Roosevelt recalled him to active duty in 1941, prior to the Japanese attack on Pearl Harbor, appointing him Commander of United States Army Forces Far East (USAFFE).

On the day after the attack on Pearl Harbor, as part of the second phase of their operation, the Japanese launched an assault on the Philippines.[8] MacArthur ordered his forces to withdraw into the Bataan Peninsula on the main Island of Luzon. He relocated his headquarters to the nearby volcanic island of Corregidor inside bombproof shelters which had been constructed by the U.S. military just after the turn of the century.

After weeks of suffering Japanese aerial attacks, following orders of President Roosevelt, MacArthur was evacuated from Corregidor and taken to Australia where he re-established his headquarters and led the build up of Australian military forces. Determined to liberate the Philippines from whence he was driven

---

8   The same day, Japanese forces also attacked Malaya, Hong Kong, Guam, Wake Island, and Midway Island.

out, MacArthur became famously quoted for a speech he made to the exiled Philippine leaders in which he vowed, *"I Shall Return."*

General MacArthur's strategy for defeating an adversary with far greater military resources hinged on isolation and incremental reduction of the enemy through naval and air attacks. By, in MacArthur's words, "hitting 'em where they ain't" and "let 'em die on the vine," MacArthur waged what is referred to as a classic War of Attrition, hoping to stop Japan's advance throughout the Pacific and neutralize the threat to Allied Forces while using a minimum of his own, already insufficient resources. To these ends, MacArthur designed a plan to attack and occupy outlying islands that possessed terrain suitable for establishing airstrips and natural harbors capable of hosting large warships. If successful, the strategy would create an umbrella of protection for his advance to the Philippines and, eventually, facilitate an attack on Japan itself. In so doing, MacArthur would also be putting enemy strongholds of resupply within striking distance of Allied air and naval power, which he would then use to reduce those strongholds.

It wasn't a completely unique concept; the Japanese had been using a comparable strategy and employing similar tactics in their advance throughout the Pacific. However, there was one essential difference: Japan's strategy was almost exclusively offensive; they were relying on superior forces to capture and permanently occupy islands where they could establish air and naval bases to further their expansionist goals. This narrow strategy left the Japanese military defensively vulnerable.

America's war goal was to defeat the enemy in order to protect sovereign peoples or restore the territorial integrity of occupied countries, not to increase its own possessions. To ensure success, America had to permanently eliminate the threat posed by Imperial Japan.

In its purist essence, the war in the Pacific was a struggle between good and evil.

Japan's main foreword base and the place of its largest concentration of military resources in the Southwest Pacific Area (SWPA) was Rabaul.

Located on the northeast coast of New Britain island, Rabaul was a heavily fortified, volcanic harbor and inland airbase where the Japanese, since capturing the area from Australia in early 1942, had built some three hundred miles of underground tunnels and amassed vast numbers of planes, ships, quantities of ammunition and supplies, as well as about one hundred thousand troops.

In making Rabaul their center of operations in SWPA, Japan was able to eliminate the need to resupply its forces from its mainland, thousands of miles away.

Japan had also been using Rabaul as a staging ground for its warships to invade outlying islands and for launching air strikes that disrupted Allied supply lines and cut lines of communication. Moreover, the Japanese base at Rabaul threatened Australia, New Zealand, and even Hawaii.

Despite the attack at Pearl Harbor and America's declaration of war on Japan, throughout 1942 America's priority remained the war in Europe. President Roosevelt and the Joint Chiefs of Staff wanted Japan's increasing hegemony stopped and, like most Americans, they wanted Japan punished. But neither Roosevelt nor the Joint Chiefs were willing or ready to go on the offensive in the Pacific. (Some have argued that the reason behind this policy was, at least in part, due to Anglo-Saxon partisanship toward America's European roots.)

As Japan's conquest of the Pacific gained momentum, in March of 1943, America's war strategy began to change, although Europe remained the priority for the allocation of military resources. A plan was preliminarily approved that involved thirteen objectives in the Pacific, one of which was the capture of Rabaul.

However, at the insistence of General MacArthur, the plan, dubbed "Elkton II," was revised. MacArthur felt that without significantly greater resources, an invasion of Rabaul involving ground troops would be a bloodbath for the Allies. MacArthur was right, and the Joint Chiefs gave him the go-ahead to instead isolate Rabaul and engage the enemy in a war of attrition. It was this insistence of General MacArthur's that caused my father to later credit him with having preserved his life throughout the war.

By January of 1944, ahead of schedule, MacArthur had achieved all but one of his objectives in isolating Rabaul. To completely seal off the enemy stronghold he needed to gain control of a vital corridor in the Bismarck and Solomon Seas, and he chose the Admiralty Islands to achieve this final objective.

The Admiralty Islands consist of a chain of eighteen islands situated about two hundred miles northeast of New Guinea and about three hundred and fifty miles west of Rabaul. The two largest islands in the Admiralty chain are Manus to the northeast and Los Negros to the southwest. Los Negros, to borrow a golfing term, is shaped like a dogleg with its wider end in the south and is the smaller of the two islands. It is separated from Manus by a small inlet called Loniu Passage, which connects Seeadler Harbor and the Bismarck Sea. The narrow northern end of the Los Negros dogleg is called Mokerang Peninsula.

Since occupying the Admiralties after driving out a small force of about one hundred Australian defenders in April of 1942, the Japanese had built airstrips and established garrisons on both Manus and Los Negros, keeping their larger concentration of troops on Manus.

Both Manus and Los Negros have natural harbors. Seeadler Harbor, the largest, lies on the east coast of

Manus and extends south along the western side of Los Negros. Because of its size and depth, Seeadler was well suited to accommodate large warships and was therefore the most likely place for an Allied invasion.

Lying at the southeastern end of Los Negros is Hyane Harbor, a small and relatively shallow anchorage. The harbor's entrance is guarded by two opposing landmasses that form a passageway of only about seven hundred and fifty yards wide and that could easily be used for defensive emplacements. Coral reefs further narrow the passage for large vessels to a mere fifty yards. Hyane Harbor was a highly unlikely place for an Allied invasion, which to General MacArthur made it ideal.

The military intelligence of the enemy's forces on Los Negros was conflicting. Reconnaissance aircraft had reported that the airstrip was in "disrepair and overgrown with weeds" and that the island appeared deserted. Other intelligence indicated that there might be as many as forty-five hundred enemy troops hidden on the island.

MacArthur was appropriately cynical of most military intelligence reports and instead largely relied on his own network of so-called "coast watchers." By sending in a large reconnaissance force to Los Negros, as opposed to a full-scale invasion force, he would retain the flexibility he needed to rapidly withdraw the troops if they met heavy resistance, or, if there was minimal resistance, establish a beachhead and seize the Momote Airfield, the main objective on the island, before sending in reinforcements.

MacArthur convinced the Joint Chiefs of Staff to go along with his plan and the "Reconnaissance-in-Force" was scheduled for April 1, 1944. However, once his other objectives in the isolation of Rabaul had been met by the end of January, MacArthur felt that delaying the landing on Los Negros until April would unnecessarily give the Japanese time to figure out his strategy and reinforce their positions in the Admiralties.

On February 24th, General MacArthur issued orders to the 1st Cavalry Division to prepare a reinforced squadron to land at Hyane Harbor "no later than February 29th." The mission was code named Operation BREWER.

At the time, all American combat units in the area were assigned to the U.S. Sixth Army, commanded by Lieutenant General Walter Krueger. Krueger had formed an elite reconnaissance unit called The Alamo Scouts,[9] a precursor of today's Special Forces, and he put the Scouts to use for the first time in preparation for the Los Negros landing.

On the night of February 27th, a six-man team of Alamo Scouts approached the southern end of Los Negros in a rubber raft. After spending about a day on the island, the Scouts reported that the area between the southern coast and the Momote airstrip was "Lousy with Japs." However, the Scouts' description contradicted the earlier air reconnaissance reports and some discounted it as being more perception than reality.

MacArthur became deeply concerned about the unknown size of enemy forces on Los Negros as well as their known presence on Manus. If the size of the Japanese forces on Los Negros were significantly underestimated or if the operation's secrecy was compromised and they moved their forces from Manus to Los Negros, Operation BREWER could turn into a massacre for the Americans.

Hedging his bets, MacArthur ordered the landing of the BREWER task force to be preceded by extensive aerial and naval bombardment and for reinforcements to be prepared to mobilize from New Guinea on "a moments notice." To further ensure success of the

---

9   My father stated that he had been trained as an Alamo Scout, which I have no doubt is true. However, because I have not been able to confirm this through documentation, this part of his training has been left out of the narrative.

operation, MacArthur hastened it by arranging for rapid transport of the Reconnaissance Force from Oro Bay, New Guinea.

The vessels that were normally used to transport personnel in amphibious landings on a hostile shore were called LSTs (Landing Ship, Tank), which were capable of conveying large numbers of troops, equipment and supplies. But LSTs were slow moving and obvious troop carriers. If the Japanese spotted the bulky ships heading toward the Bismarck Archipelago, they would have time to reinforce their garrison on Los Negros as well as Manus. To address the problem, MacArthur conferred with Vice Admiral Thomas Kinkaid, commander of the U.S. Navy's 7th Fleet. Kinkaid was so unquestioningly loyal to the General the 7th Fleet was commonly referred to as "MacArthur's Navy."

In response to General MacArthur's concerns, Kinkaid dispatched a contingent of fast moving destroyers, which included the three modified World War I destroyers, to Oro Bay as transports for the Reconnaissance Force.

So that a decision as to whether to withdraw or proceed with the landing could be made on the spot, MacArthur decided to join in the operation.

In addition to the eight hundred men of the 2nd Squadron of the 5th Cavalry Regiment, the Reconnaissance Force included about two hundred soldiers consisting of artillery and antiaircraft supporting units, a medical detachment, a portable field hospital, a naval gunfire support party, and an air force liaison contingent.

After leaving New Guinea, the men of the Reconnaissance Force were treated to steak dinners, much to the chagrin of the navy personnel aboard the destroyer transports. When the meal was finished, my father went above deck to escape the cloud of cigarette smoke that was filling the converted boiler room. The ship was operating under blackout conditions and smoking above deck was strictly forbidden. A smoker for several years before the war, my father had quit when he arrived in Strathpine and instead used his cigarette rations to barter with the natives for coconuts, mangos, and laundering his uniforms.

Above deck, soldiers sat about cleaning their weapons, loading ammunition clips, and playing endless card games. Almost no one slept.

My father sat on the deck of the Humphreys together with his first sergeant, a young man from California by the name of Ostle K. Williams, whom he called by his nickname, OK. As they went over maps of the island and carefully reviewed their platoon's assault plans, my father wondered how his men would react when the shooting started. He knew these men well and had confidence in them. But this was going to be everyone's first real combat mission and he wanted to prepare for every eventuality, including the unexpected. But after trying to predict the unpredictable, he resigned himself to the fact that it would all boil down to the training, and how seriously each man had taken it.

As dawn broke on Tuesday, February 29th, the men of the Reconnaissance Force lined the deck railings of the destroyers and looked out over the Pacific waters under a dull-gray sky. Everyone had been on alert since the wake of an enemy submarine was spotted the day before.

The officers were summoned together again for what would be their final briefing.

Gathered on the bow of the Humphreys just beyond the overhanging barrel of the ship's big gun, the platoon leaders of D Troop huddled around Captain John Strong as he kneeled on the deck, a map of the landing area laid out in front of him.

Final Briefing before Los Negros Landing (Acme Newspictures)

Chapter Six

*"Take the first step, and your mind will mobilize
all its forces to your aid. But the first essential
is that you begin. Once the battle is started,
all that is within and without you will come
to your assistance."*

— Robert Collier

February 29, 1944. Tuesday
Heavy rain
Dull visibility
Muggy

As my father stood on the deck of the destroyer hold-ing his .30-caliber Springfield rifle, an officer's Colt .45-caliber pistol holstered on his right hip, he looked out over the mounting waves of the Pacific. To his right, underneath the low cloud ceiling, he could make out what looked like more than a dozen warships. To his left, five thousand yards in the distance, he saw the dark outline of Los Negros Island.

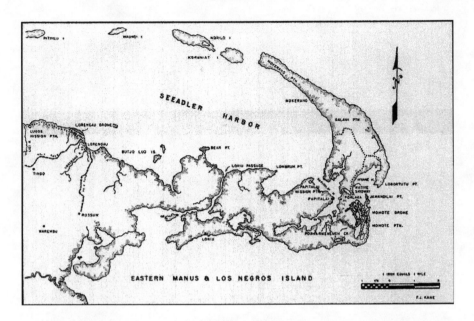

EASTERN MANUS & LOS NEGROS ISLAND

At 7:30 A.M., the Humphreys reached its rendezvous point and the ship's engines quieted. Within minutes the big guns of the destroyers opened fire, raining down five-inch shells on pre-assigned targets on the island. Huge muzzle flashes and thunderous explosions followed by thick black smoke belched from the ships' guns. The volume of artillery fire was so great; clouds of drifting black smoke partially obscured the island.

When the guns finally silenced, the soldiers turned their attention westward and watched as a group of American bombers came in low over the island. The men were too far away to see the actual bombs falling, but they were close enough to witness the brilliant flashes and the great geysers of soil and debris that rocketed into the air, followed by the dull *crumph* of the exploding ordinance.

The original plan for the pre-invasion bombing called for dozens of fighter-bombers to pulverize the landing area. But due to the low cloud ceiling, only a few of the aircraft were able to complete their missions.

When the bombing and strafing runs ended, naval guns resumed firing and the 2nd Squadron soldiers readied for deployment.

Twelve Higgins boats were lowered from their destroyer davits into the sea and the GIs, now loaded down with their weapons and full battle packs, climbed down the rope ladders into the bobbing landing craft. Once fully loaded, the coxswains throttled up the engines and the little boats roared out over the mounting waves to the rendezvous point.

While the craft circled in formation, the GIs cheered as naval shells screamed over their heads toward the island; they were thrilled that the enemy was getting pounded, and prayerful the bombardment would help ensure their survival.

At exactly 8:10 A.M., the naval guns ceased firing and a squadron of B-25 bombers approached from the south, dropping tons of heavy munitions around the landing area and further inland. After the bombers completed three runs, a flare was fired from one of the destroyers signaling the first wave to head to shore.

As the Higgins boats motored toward the beach, the destroyers opened up with yet more salvos from their five-inch guns.

While all of this was going on, unbeknownst to the men of the Reconnaissance Force, General MacArthur stood at the upper deck railing of the cruiser Phoenix watching events unfold.

As the first wave neared the island, mortar shells began hitting the water around the landing craft and machine gun fire opened up from both of the finger-like landmasses, Lobortutu Point to the north and Jamandalai Point to the south.

No longer cheering, scared, the soldiers crouched down on top of each other as the two navy gunners of each boat answered with continuous raking fire from their .30-caliber machine guns.

My father's voice:

"As we made our way to the beach, the coxswain of our boat had his head blown off."

A 25-millimeter round from an enemy machine gun slammed into the head of eighteen-year-old Albert Anthony Pinto, the first casualty of Operation BREWER. With no one steering the boat, the craft began to flounder. If not for one of the cavalrymen taking control, the number 3 boat would have rammed it.

After passing through the narrow entrance to the harbor, the Higgins boats turned left, hooking around Jamandalai, before veering right and heading toward three small jetties protruding from the beach.

As the craft skirted Jamandalai, sniper fire opened up hitting the gunner in the number 3 boat. The bullet ripped through eighteen-year-old Joe Chartrand's back and exited through his upper chest, just missing his heart. In a superhuman act of heroism, Chartrand managed to swing his machine gun around and fire a burst into the treetops, killing the enemy sniper who had shot him. Chartrand had originally been assigned to the number 2 boat but Albert Pinto, preferring the coxswain's position to that of the gunner's, convinced him to switch places. It was a choice that haunted Joe Chartrand for the rest of his life.

As the boats began to ground, the bow ramps were released and the cavalrymen hurriedly moved forward into about a foot of water and then onto the coral sand of the eight hundred-foot long beach. After climbing a small embankment, the GIs kept low and ran through waist-high kunai grass into an area strewn with coconut logs and palm fronds before fanning out toward their positions. Artillery fire from the destroyers continued to shriek overhead, deafeningly exploding about one hundred yards to the front.

**Feb. 29, 1944 Assault at Hyane Harbor
(International News Service)**

My father's platoon moved inland about twenty-five yards and took up a position to the left, setting up their guns[10] in support of the soon to be advancing rifle troops. It was 8:17 A.M.

As the second wave made its way to the beach, heavy machine gun fire opened up again, this time from both Lobortutu and Jamandalai, striking the bow ramp of one of the advancing craft. Four GI's were killed and the boats were forced to turn back toward the destroyers. An artillery barrage was quickly called in and five-inch shells were soon pulverizing both landmasses.

The men of the first wave held their positions.

---

10 The .30-caliber, water-cooled heavy machine guns were comprised of three parts: the gun, tripod, and coolant reservoir, which took approximately two minutes to assemble.

When the assault resumed, as each wave came ashore, the GIs hurried to positions about twenty-five yards to the front of the previous wave, leapfrogging ever closer to Momote.

While the 2nd Squadron was advancing on the airstrip, landing craft continued to shuttle in more men and supplies from the destroyers, as shore personnel quickly unloaded boxes of ammunition and grenades.

With the cavalrymen now holding their positions just east of the airstrip, two destroyers moved in and hosed down Jamandalai with heavy machine gun fire, while other ships pounded targets west and north of the airstrip.

Just above the right side of the beach ran a two lane, fifty-foot wide dirt trail used by the natives to drag their outrigger canoes from Hyane to Lemondrol Creek, an inlet of Seeadler Harbor. North of this native skidway and at the base of Mokerang Peninsula was a large coconut-palm estate called Salami Plantation. As the Reconnaissance Force reached the airstrip, sporadic enemy fire erupted from the area between the skidway and Salami. Another barrage of artillery was called in, which silenced that resistance.

By 11:00 A.M., less than two hours after the first wave had come ashore, the 2nd Squadron occupied the entire airdrome; some units had even advanced several hundred yards further to the west.

On the western and southeastern sides of the airstrip the Japanese had built dispersal areas where they parked their aircraft inside ten-foot high, U-shaped earthen bunkers. When the cavalrymen reached these revetments, they found that some of them contained the rusted remains of Japanese planes which had sustained damage from earlier Allied bombing raids. In others, they found intact aircraft hidden under camouflage netting. The airstrip itself was indeed overgrown with weeds and pockmarked with rain filled bomb craters.

As the units took up positions around the airdrome and reconnaissance patrols were sent to the north and south of the airstrip and the heavy jungle area of Porlaka further to the west, Brigadier General William C. Chase, commander of the 1st Cavalry Brigade, and Colonel William Lobit, commander of the 2nd Squadron 5th Cavalry Regiment, strategized on where to establish the perimeter.

The original plan called for setting up a perimeter encompassing the entire Momote airdrome. However, after seeing the terrain up close, General Chase had misgivings about defending such a large area with his relatively small force. When the patrols returned with reports of significant numbers of enemy troops in the vicinity, Chase ordered the Reconnaissance Force to pull back and establish a smaller perimeter on the eastern side of the airstrip until reinforcements could arrive, which was not expected for another two days. The final perimeter covered about two-thirds of the eastern side of the airstrip— from the base of Jamandalai Point to the native skidway as it turned west just below Salami Plantation—a total distance of about fifteen hundred yards.

During the afternoon, for the third time since the assault force landed, naval artillery and aerial bombardments pounded areas west and north of the airstrip and on Jamandalai and Lobortutu to further reduce the enemy threat to the perimeter.

At about 3:00 P.M., General Chase ordered the troops to begin preparing for the night. Machine gun platoons set up their guns near the revetments; foxholes were dug around the entire perimeter; outposts were established to the west, north, and south, and communication wire for sound powered telephones[11] was strung from foxhole to foxhole between unit commanders and

---

11   These were telephones that needed no external power source. They operated by way of a microphone that converted sound into electrical current.

the command post. Since they had no barbed wire to ring the perimeter, Chase ordered the men to dig in close to each other to reduce the possibility of enemy infiltration during the night.

But digging foxholes in the hard-packed coral sand with the short-handled army-issued picks was a grueling task. In some areas, even with persistent hacking and scraping only an inches-deep depression could be carved out.

After taking a position near a revetment in the southern sector of the perimeter about midway between the airstrip and the base of Jamandalai, my father instructed his men to set up their Final Protective Line (FPL). His four heavy-machine-gun squads placed their tripod mounted weapons fifteen yards apart—half the normal distance—and sighted them to fire about a foot above the ground toward the airstrip. After they were in position, my father walked the line of the emplacements and pushed a peg into the ground on either side of each machine gun to indicate the lateral limit that the weapon could traverse. The purpose of this was to create interlocking bands of fire as well as to ensure the safety of any forward positions. He reminded each gunner to wait for his order before commencing fire and what their rate of fire should be.

To the rear of the heavy machine gun positions mortar crews set up their weapons, registering them to lob shells about fifty yards beyond the front-line positions. When the shooting began, the interlocking bands of fire from the machine guns combined with the mortar barrages would create an impenetrable wall of steel and lead that would annihilate anything moving toward the perimeter. A few of the mortar crews registered their weapons to fire further west and north in order to drive advancing enemy troops into the interlocking bands of machine gun fire. The large guns of the field artillery units were positioned yet further to the rear and registered to fire on positions deeper into the jungle west and north of the airstrip.

At about 4:00 P.M. while organizing and preparing his position, looking through the rain draining off his helmet my father saw the unmistakable figure of General MacArthur standing together with Admiral Kinkaid on the eastern edge of the airstrip. Wearing his signature hat, gloves and a beige trench coat, the General appeared to be directing fire toward the west.

Since his days in the orphanage, my father had learned to respect authority; especially authority that was worthy of respect, and in my father's eyes General MacArthur was worthy of respect. He had studied the General's career and his battlefield strategy and tactics. In a sense he was a student of MacArthur. What he saw on that rain-soaked muggy afternoon of February 29, 1944, on the Momote airstrip, was an image that became forever etched in his mind. For the rest of his life my father referred to Douglas MacArthur as *"the bravest man that I have ever seen in combat."*

My father liked the heft, long-range power, and accuracy of his .30-caliber Springfield rifle. But after seeing the density of the jungle terrain and being warned to watch for Japanese snipers in the tops of palm trees, he started feeling uneasy about the bulky weapon. While it was still daylight, he walked over to the weapons depot and "liberated" a .45-caliber Thompson submachine gun.

While no one knew for certain what darkness might bring, the Japanese were known to favor nighttime attacks and the cavalrymen were anxiously anticipating just such an event.

With no barbed wire or antipersonnel mines to protect the perimeter, orders went out for the soldiers to remain in their foxholes throughout the night and to "fire at anything that moved." Any man leaving his fox-hole or moving around, given the circumstances, risked being shot by his own troops.

During nighttime, soldiers in the field worked on the buddy system—one man would sleep in his foxhole for two hours while his buddy remained on watch. However, with the uncertainty over the size and proximity of the enemy forces around Momote and the likelihood of an attack after sundown, all of the men were advised to stay alert the entire night. It wasn't going to be difficult to do.

At dusk, attempting to draw return fire so they could target the 2nd Squadron's positions with machine guns and mortars, the enemy began shooting from west of the airstrip. But the GIs held their fire. They had been trained in this tactic and refused to take the bait.

Just after midnight, the 2nd Squadron's outposts reported Japanese troops advancing from the jungle west of the airstrip and north from beyond the skidway. The outposts were quickly called in and everyone readied to fire.

Making no attempt to conceal themselves, small groups of enemy soldiers loudly charged the perimeter, tossing hand grenades and firing rifles. Pitch dark, the cavalrymen remained in their foxholes firing in the direction of the sounds and muzzle flashes and Japanese soldiers momentarily illuminated by flashes from exploding grenades. The machine gun units opened fire and raked the entire front of the perimeter.

The ferocious response destroyed the bulk of the frontal attack. However, at the northern and southern sectors, small squads of enemy soldiers managed to penetrate the perimeter. The infiltrators cut the cavalrymen's phone lines and lobbed hand grenades at individual positions. Japanese troops that had managed to survive the day's repeated bombardment on Jamanda-lai and south of the airstrip launched an attack on the southern area of the perimeter, near my father's position; desperate hand-to-hand combat broke out.

Another group of enemy soldiers that had swam down from Salami Beach wearing flotation belts and carrying grenades and swords silently crept up from Hyane and attacked the American's positions from the rear. An air force liaison officer in the southern sector who was caught sleeping in a hammock he had foolishly strung between two coconut trees was literally cut in two by one of the sword-wielding infiltrators.

After several hours of intense fighting, the cavalry-men overcame the fierce assault. However, infighting, sporadic enemy gunfire, and mortar strikes continued throughout the night.

March 1, 1944. Wednesday:
Light rain
Dull visibility

At daybreak, the bodies of more than sixty enemy soldiers were found lying in and around the perimeter.[12] A number of the "dead" Japanese soldiers were discovered to be playing possum, so the cavalrymen resorted to firing into the bodies whether they were dead or not. A few infiltrators who had managed to reoccupy their former pillboxes and dugouts and others who had strapped themselves to the tops of palm trees began sniping at the GIs. A small group of infiltrators were stalking General

---

12 Among the enemy dead was Captain Baba, the commander of the Japanese infantry battalion that had launched the attack. A document from the garrison commander, Colonel Yoshio Ezaki, was found on Baba's body; the official translation reads, "Tonight the battalion under Captain Baba will annihilate the enemy who has landed. This is not a delaying action. Be resolute to sacrifice your life for the Emperor and commit suicide in case capture is imminent. We must carry out our mission with the present strength and annihilate the enemy on the spot. I am highly indignant about the enemy's arrogant attitude. Remember to kill or capture all ranking enemy officers for our intelligence purposes..."

Chase's command post when the automatic machine gun fire of an alert cavalry officer cut them down.

Seven Americans had been killed overnight. More than a dozen wounded were carried down to the portable field hospital set up in an enemy dugout near the beach. Navy personnel that had remained ashore used the Higgins boats to transport the most seriously injured back to the destroyers. Lightly injured soldiers were treated and sent back to their units. The dead were buried in temporary graves east of the airstrip.

As they slouched in their foxholes eating K-rations and sipping tepid water from their canteens, the taste of the steak dinner they had been treated to en route to Los Negros no longer lingered in the mouths of the men of the 2nd Squadron,

Airdrops of blood plasma, additional quantities of rations, ammunition, and land mines were made during the day. Some packages drifted off-target and wound up suspended in coconut trees or captured by the enemy.

When patrols brought back reports of enemy forces still nearby, naval artillery hit the areas west and south of the airstrip and north of the skidway yet again.

As the shells struck the jungle west of the dispersal area, like a page out of the army manual, dozens of enemy soldiers were flushed out and made a suicide run at the 2nd Squadron's perimeter. A barrage of machine gun fire killed them all before they were able to cross the airstrip.

Throughout the day, the men of the Reconnaissance Force, which had now become an invasion force, further consolidated and fortified their positions. They laid newly arrived antipersonnel mines on the western side of the airstrip and to the north between the skidway and Salami Plantation. Still without barbed wire, they strung phone wire around the perimeter on which they suspended empty ration cans filed with rocks and chunks of coral to act as an early warning system.

At the beach, navy personnel continued to make runs to the waiting destroyers, bringing back more ammunition and supplies.

Just as it happened on the first night, at dusk, amidst continuing rainfall, sporadic enemy fire opened up on the perimeter. Squads of Japanese soldiers emerged from the dense jungle surrounding the airdrome and charged the American positions, firing rifles and lobbing hand grenades. Once again, infiltrators managed to penetrate the perimeter.

While the battle raged at the front lines, nineteen-year-old Navy Seamen Thaddeus Majusick, a gunner on one of the landing craft of the first wave, crouched in his foxhole near the beach and watched as a shadowy figure crawled on his knees and elbows from the skidway toward the ammunition dump. Having had no combat training and unsure of what he was seeing, Majusick froze. Seconds later, the ammo dump exploded in a massive fireball; the concussion wave was felt throughout the entire perimeter. Majusick spent the next sixty-seven years kicking himself over the incident.

After a two-hour bitter battle, things finally quieted down. With the exception of sporadic sniper fire and an occasional mortar round exploding within or around the perimeter, the night remained relatively quiet.

March 2, 1944. Thursday:
Heavy rain
Dull visibility

As the sun rose over the Pacific, the sleep deprived and fatigued soldiers of the 2nd Squadron set out to once again search the perimeter for infiltrators. Several were found; none surrendered. The rain finally began to let up.

At 9:00 A.M., six LSTs carrying the 1st Squadron of the 5th Cavalry Regiment approached the entrance to Hyane Harbor. As the ships passed by the guarding landmasses enemy machine gun and mortar fire erupted from Lobortutu. More naval artillery was called in, followed by bombing and strafing runs of eleven B-25s, which then also hit targets west of the airstrip.

Shortly after 1:00 P.M., General Chase issued orders for both squadrons to prepare to attack the entire Momote Airdrome.

Just after 3:00 P.M., the largest air assault yet began. B-25s, P-38s, and P-47s engaged in an hour and forty-five minute bombing and strafing attack on targets all around the airdrome; three bombs were mistakenly released on the eastern side of the airstrip, tragically killing two GIs and wounding four others.

While the bombardment was underway, due to a shortage of non-combat personnel, a problem that would plague the entire Admiralty campaign, soldiers of the 1st Squadron went to work unloading supplies and equipment from the LSTs. By 4:30 P.M. the ships were headed back out to sea, shooting their way past Jamandalai from were enemy machine gun fire was still originating.

When the air assault finally ended, both squadrons, more than fifteen hundred soldiers in all, advanced abreast—the 1st Squadron on the left, the 2nd on the right; they met no resistance. By 6:00 P.M., the entire airdrome was securely in the hands of the 5th Cavalry and the men were digging in for the night.

The 1st Squadron moved into positions formerly held by the 2nd Squadron on the eastern side of the airstrip, while the 2nd Squadron dug in on the newly gained western side. My father's platoon established a position near a revetment in the northwest dispersal area.

As the 2nd Squadron was setting up their section of the new perimeter, an occupied enemy foxhole was discovered on top of one of the revetments; a flamethrower squad was brought in to deal with the situation. A young private from

Columbus, Ohio, John Lauless, who had just arrived with the 1st Squadron and whose greatest fear was flamethrowers watched in abject horror as his nightmare became a reality. When the roaring stream of fire shot up the wall of the revetment and covered the opening of the foxhole, the Japanese occupant made a desperate attempt to escape the inferno. Emerging from his lair engulfed in flames and screaming a hellish scream, the human torch tumbled down the wall of the revetment. The body continued to burn and the acrid smell added to that of the putrefying corpses still littering the airdrome. After watching the gruesome spectacle, the cavalrymen resumed preparing their positions and digging in for the night.

Despite the heavy air and naval attacks, the arrival of the 1st Squadron, and the enlarged perimeter, the third night on Momote saw action similar to that of the previous nights. Sniping and periodic mortar attacks began at dusk, and, shortly after nightfall, more concerted attacks against the 2nd Squadron's positions emanated from the west and north. Crazed Japanese soldiers again making no attempt to conceal themselves came in lobbing grenades and firing into the frontlines. Once more, despite the beefed-up defenses, the perimeter was penetrated; phone lines were cut, and hand-to-hand combat raged. When the shooting stopped this time, nine GIs lay dead and twenty-seven were wounded. Two of those killed and two of the wounded were from D Troop—my father's unit. Private Lauless survived the night without meeting up with another flamethrower. However, his mere six-inch deep trench wasn't enough to protect him from the four enemy bullets that pierced his body. Lauless was treated and evacuated. His war had lasted only a night, but the trauma would remain with him for more than six decades.

Although the fighting of the previous three nights was intense, the relatively small scale of the attacks belied the true situation on Los Negros. The 5th Cavalry soldiers did not yet know it, but, based on later intelligence and operational reports, the airdrome was surrounded by more than fifty enemy installations; some one hundred more, manned by over four thousand enemy troops, which included Imperial Marines, infantry units, and antiaircraft and artillery batteries, were scattered throughout the island.

Documents taken off the bodies of enemy soldiers indicated that the Japanese commander of the Admiralties Garrison, Colonel Yoshio Ezaki, had expected an American invasion and had in fact been informed about the reconnaissance mission of the Alamo Scouts. But, as General MacArthur had surmised, Ezaki expected the landing to take place at Seeadler Harbor and incorrectly concluded the Scouts' mission as a diversion intended to get him to move his forces toward Hyane and away from Seeadler. Consequently, while eastern Los Negros remained significantly defended, Ezaki had kept the bulk of his forces in the northern and western areas and on Manus Island.

But the three days that the GIs had thus far spent in taking the airdrome had given Ezaki time to move reinforcements in to stage for a major counterattack, which captured documents indicated would take place on the night of March 3-4. The cavalry's reinforcements were not scheduled to arrive until the morning of March 4th.

March 3, 1944. Friday:
Intermittent showers
High, overcast ceiling
Visibility Fair

For the fourth day in a row, the morning was spent clearing out infiltrators, repairing lines of communication, consolidating positions, and shoring up defenses.

Knowing that a major counterattack was likely coming, the 5th Cavalry and its attached elements prepared for the worst. Extra ammunition and grenades were supplied to all front-line positions. Naval construction battalions, called Seabees (specialized troops trained in construction as well as combat), which had arrived aboard the LSTs, used bulldozers to dig trenches at strategic points along the front line, destroy Japanese pill boxes, and clear large fields of fire for the machine gun units in the western and northern sectors. All patrols were called off so that concentrations of naval artillery and aerial bombs could be placed on Salami Plantation and the Porlaka area west of the airdrome.

Although they were exhausted from three days of combat, not to mention the muggy heat, rain, and practically no sleep, the cavalrymen fortified their positions and focused on their jobs with renewed vigor and extra attention.

Late in the afternoon an American warplane flew over the airdrome and dropped leaflets with the following message:

"Soldiers of the 5th Cavalry:
On the 89th anniversary of the 5th Regiment, US Cavalry, the First Cavalry Division is proud of its oldest regiment. Your courageous, victorious conquest of the Japanese held Momote Air Field adds a luminous page to the regimental history. You have earned an honored seat beside your illustrious predecessors. This anniversary is not a celebration; rather let each of us make a prayer to Almighty God to care carefully for our comrades who gave their lives to achieve this victory. Your country, your Army, and your Division are proud of you, as am I—God Bless you.

Innis P. Swift, Major General, U.S. Army, Commanding"

Not everyone was impressed. Whether General Swift was aboard the aircraft or not, the GIs discounted his generous words while they were preparing for a large enemy counterattack.

The rain had stopped, but the sky remained overcast as darkness crept over Los Negros on the night of March 3rd. The soldiers remained quiet and anxious in their positions. The bitterness of the fighting of the three previous nights was very much with them.

Hunkered down in his foxhole, my father thought back to when he was six years old and he took that terrifying, lone walk through the cavernous halls of the orphanage. Back then he wasn't prepared for the moment that shocked his senses and caused his eyes to cross. But now, twenty-eight years old, and after three years of hard training, he was a combat officer who knew what to do. He sensed an attack was coming and that it would be on a scale unlike any of the previous ones. Any movement, any sound, any indication that the enemy was in the area and he would order his men to let loose a fusillade of fire that would obliterate anything in its path. No one was going to surprise him this time. No living thing would penetrate his Final Protective Line. The bastards could bring it on if they dared.

While the cavalrymen were tensely waiting in their positions at Momote, enemy barges were at work ferrying troops from Lorengau on the northern coast of Manus, down through the winding waters of Lemondrol Creek, and debarking them at Porlaka. They would reinforce the troops already there that had survived the previous three days of intense naval and air attacks by remaining below ground in bunkers and pillboxes, such as those at Jamandalai and Lobortutu had done.

Similar enemy troop movements were taking place on the western side of Mokerang Peninsula, where Japanese reinforcements were disembarking from barges at Salami Beach.

Back at Momote, at 9:00 P.M., enemy machine gun fire opened up from the direction of Porlaka and north of the skidway and grenades starting falling within the perimeter. The GIs had become accustomed to the enemy's disorganized attacks, but this one was different, it was clearly coordinated and of much greater strength. Under such intense pressure, limiting their response to preserve ammunition was impossible and the men opened up with everything they had. Withering fusillades of machine gun fire cut down wave after wave of enemy soldiers as they charged the front lines. Mortar teams fired incessantly and howitzers, positioned near the beach, boomed as the large shells struck with ground shaking force on Porlaka and Salami. But despite the GI's firepower and the enemy's massive losses the Bonzai attack was unrelenting.

A few enemy machine gun and knee mortar squads managed to penetrate the perimeter, where in the midst of the chaos they were spotted setting up their weapons and were killed.

A twin-engine enemy plane flew over the southern end of the airstrip releasing three bombs, but causing no casualties. Enemy artillery shells struck within the perimeter and rounds from Japanese knee mortars rained on the GI's positions.

The fighting continued to rage as a seemingly endless supply of suicidal Japanese came in again and again.

At 2:00 A.M. all of the perimeter phone lines went dead. With their ammunition running out, unit commanders resorted to yelling out for more, thereby risking disclosing their positions. Regardless of the raging battle, courageous Seabees hustled boxes of ammunition to the front lines.

After hours of fending off attacks, the cavalry-men continued to battle squads of enemy troops who were still attempting to assault the northwest sector of the perimeter. Several of the soldiers manning heavy machine guns climbed out of their foxholes and removed the hulking weapons from their tripods, firing them from the hip to get a better angle on the now disorganized enemy thrusts.[13]

But the attacks kept coming as groups of Japanese soldiers shouting and even signing and otherwise making no attempt at concealment charged directly into the FPLs.

With his platoon's ammunition running dangerously low and their position in danger of being overrun, my father ordered his men to fall back to their pre-arranged secondary positions while he covered them with bursts from his Thompson. The same scenario was playing out at positions on both his right and left flanks.

After his men had withdrawn, my father crawled out of his foxhole and began falling back. But as he started out, he could hear the shouting and jabbering of what sounded like dozens of Japanese soldiers closing in on his position. If he didn't find cover immediately, he would be killed. Coming upon a group of felled coconut logs near the revetment, he dove between two of them.

Getting captured by the Japanese meant being tortured and ultimately beheaded. And as an officer, the torture would be especially brutal and prolonged. *"I would rather die,"* he said to himself, as he withdrew his .45, chambered a round, and put the gun to his head. As he lay there in the dark prepared for the unthinkable, he heard the now familiar thump of a Japanese grenade being activated;[14] it landed next to his position and exploded.

---

13 Some have doubted that heavy machine guns could be fired this way. However, operational and intelligence reports clearly state that such was the case.
14 Unlike the elliptically shaped U.S. fragmentation grenades, which required pulling a pin and releasing a safety lever to activate, the Japanese cylindrically

Protected by the coconut logs, my father was uninjured by the flying shrapnel, but the blast rendered him momentarily unconscious. The invading enemy overran his position, leaving him for dead.

Regaining his senses moments later, my father recognized the distinctive chatter of American machine guns firing from the other side of the revetment, just yards away. Shaking off the fog in his head, he quickly realized where he was and what was happening. Still groggy from the explosion, he struggled to his feet and, keeping his head low, ran to his secondary position, which, it turned out, was also being occupied by soldiers from another platoon who were forced to withdraw there. A young corporal from Texas looked up at him from a foxhole and said, "Good of y'all to come to the aid of Texas!" Decades later, my father was able to laugh about the southerner's glib remark in that terrifying situation.

During a lull in the action, in a clearing about thirty yards to the front of a position held by a platoon commanded by Lieutenant Marvin Henshaw[15] of G Troop, an enemy soldier appeared wagging a saber with a battle flag tied to it. The sake-saturated man began screaming with drunken vehemence, "KILL THE AMERICAN DOGS!" He was immediately silenced with a burst of American machine gun fire.

By 3:00 A.M. the brunt of the Banzai attack had been repulsed, although mortar fire from beyond the airdrome and sniping from infiltrators continued throughout the night.

March 4, 1944. Saturday:
High, overcast ceiling
Visibility good

---

shaped grenades had a plunger on the top, which they often activated by striking the devices against their helmets.

15   On February 29th, while at the airstrip, General MacArthur awarded Henshaw the Distinguished Service Cross for being the first soldier of the Reconnaissance Force to land on Los Negros.

The traumatized GIs began slowly and watchfully emerging from their foxholes at 7:00 A.M. As usual, patrols were dispatched to rout out enemy infiltrators.

Naval artillery and airstrikes once again pounded Porlaka and Salami Plantation. Additional airstrikes and artillery barrages hit targets further to the north on Mokerang Peninsula, as well as the hilly Papitalai region west of Lemondrol Creek, which intelligence reports suggested was a stronghold of enemy forces and that the command post of Colonel Ezaki was located at Papitalai Mission.

At Momote, an hour and a half after daybreak, a group of some fifty enemy soldiers who had remained hidden in Porlaka emerged from the jungle and, apparently intoxicated, came marching down the Porlaka Road singing "Deep in the Heart of Texas." When the group brazenly attempted to charge the perimeter, they were cut down with machine gun and small arms fire from cavalrymen who had indeed trained deep in the heart of Texas.

As the morning wore on and quiet seemed to be holding, the GIs began to move about the airdrome. Although they had become hardened warriors, the men of the 5th Cavalry Regiment were struck by what they saw: The bodies of hundreds of enemy soldiers littered the perimeter. In front of the revetments in the northern and northwestern sectors, the dead were piled up in groups of eight to thirty. As testimony to their fanaticism, many of the fallen enemy were found with bayonets and scythes strapped to five-foot long bamboo poles and tourniquets tied around pressure points on their arms and legs to enable them to keep fighting despite loss of limb. During the night attack, a number of GIs were wounded by enemy fanatics wielding these primitive weapons.

On one side of the revetment that my father's platoon had occupied lay the bodies of sixty-eight Japanese soldiers. An eight-man squad commanded by Sergeant Troy McGill of G Troop had held a revetment to his right flank. During the nighttime attack, six of Sergeant McGill's men were killed. McGill held his position and ordered the remaining man to fall back while he covered his withdrawal, just as my father had done. But unable or unwilling to leave his position, McGill fired at the suicidal mass until his weapon jammed and then charged into the oncoming enemy, clubbing at them with the stock of his rifle. McGill was found the next morning with multiple bayonet wounds: he died several hours later. One hundred sixty-seven dead enemy soldiers were found in front of his position, and some one hundred additional dead and wounded in the jungle beyond.[16]

Intelligence reports later concluded that an infantry battalion of between six hundred and fifteen hundred enemy soldiers had attacked this sector of the perimeter during the night.

Twenty-eight GIs lost their lives and twenty-one others were wounded.

The fighting thus far had resulted in more than a thousand enemy soldiers killed in and around the airdrome and countless others in the surrounding jungle. Because of the constant threat of attack, the Japanese dead could not be buried and the decaying corpses remained where they had fallen. In the hot, tropical climate, the unbearable stench of death quickly engulfed Momote.

Reinforcements from the 7th Cavalry Regiment, the famed "Gary Owen"—named after an Irish drinking song of the same name and the former unit of the legendary Lieutenant Colonel George Armstrong Custer—came ashore at Hyane Harbor at 8:50 A.M. At the same

---

16   General MacArthur himself awarded McGill the Medal of Honor, posthumously.

time, B-25s and P-38s resumed bombing and strafing runs west of the airdrome and north of the skidway. B-17s dropped desperately needed ammunition.

While the 7th Cavalry's commanders were being briefed on the situation, more supplies and equipment, including vehicles and bulldozers, were brought in from the newly arrived LSTs. The Seabees began digging defensive trenches and clearing larger fields of fire in front of the forward positions, as well as burying some of the enemy dead in mass graves.

The 7th Cavalry took up front-line positions previously held by the 2nd Squadron, who, after five days and four nights of combat, were moved back to their original defensive positions to finally get some rest.

As the perimeter was being reorganized, a squadron of ten A-10 fighter-bombers attacked positions north of the airstrip. On the ground, eighteen 81mm mortars were moved into position in a center location on the eastern edge of the airstrip and registered to place mass fire one hundred yards forward of all front-line defensive positions. Two additional field artillery battalions were added to support both the 5th and 7th Cavalry positions.

By mid-afternoon, the airdrome had been transformed from a small perimeter held by the undersized Reconnaissance Force into a heavily fortified camp of more than three thousand troops, and it was teeming with activity.

Back on the eastern side of Momote, my father decided to pace off the entire length of the airstrip. It must have seemed strange to onlookers, a lone soldier striding alongside the five thousand-foot long airstrip in the midst of a war. But to anyone who knew him, the scene was not surprising. He had a keen intellect and a thirst for knowledge; the same qualities that caused him to do well in school and attend an accelerated program that enabled him to complete high school early so he could get started in his college career. But for Harry's broken promises, these were the qualities that would have seen him excel as a doctor or a lawyer. Pacing the Momote airstrip after an all night battle following four days of combat was right in line with my father's deep need to make sense and order out of an insane and chaotic world.

March 5-6, 1944. Sunday-Monday:
Light showers
Low clouds
Fair visibility

Over the next two nights, resistance at Momote returned to the scale of that prior to the big night attack. Small groups of from ten to fifteen enemy soldiers launched repeated assaults on the perimeter, lobbing grenades and charging the lines with their pole-mounted scythes. Infiltrators again managed to cut communication lines and, this time, tapping into them and impersonating American officers and issuing false orders. In one instance the subterfuge worked and a mortar platoon abandoned its position. In response, General Chase reminded everyone that officers are never to be identified in the field and he ordered all officers to adopt code names using L-sounds, which the Japanese had trouble pronouncing. Still a New Yorker at heart, my father gave himself the code name, *Lollapalooza.*

Eight GIs were killed and seventeen were wounded over those two days; two of the dead were from my father's unit.

The mangled bodies of seventy-nine enemy soldiers, killed as a consequence of American artillery, or perhaps through having committed Hara-kiri with hand grenades, were found in Porlaka.[17]

---

17 Operational reports mention this but are inconclusive as to the cause. However, my father told of the men having "...cornered about fifty Japs in a clearing

On the morning of March 6th, reinforcements from the 12th Cavalry Regiment arrived from New Guinea. Later in the day, after the Seabees cleared the land mines from the native skidway, elements of the 7th Cavalry advanced on Salami Plantation. After meeting little resistance, they established a beachhead.

Meanwhile, the 2nd Squadron's rest period ended and the men were ordered to advance to Porlaka where they were to establish a beachhead of their own on the eastern shore of Lemondrol Creek.

At the same time as the 2nd Squadron was moving into Porlaka, the 1st Squadron advanced southward toward the base of Lemondrol; an Australian air commander arrived to coordinate bringing in Australian planes; General Swift came ashore and visited the front-line troops and toured the enlarging perimeter; B-17s continued to airdrop supplies and, for the first time since the invasion began, mail for the GIs. The first American plane landed on the airstrip, albeit it was an emergency landing.

March 7-8, 1944. Tuesday-Wednesday:
Hot
Rain
Poor visibility

The night of March 7-8 was the first night since February 29th that no U.S. soldier was killed on Los Negros; one GI was wounded. On March 8th, my father was deemed qualified in the military specialty of "Horse Cavalry Unit Commander."[18]

With the reinforcements of the 7th and 12th Cavalries in place, the airdrome, Salami Plantation, Porlaka,

---

who smiled at us and then committed Hara-kiri by banging hand grenades on their helmets and exploding them against their bellies."
18 Although the 1st Cavalry Division was no longer a mounted unit, designations such as this remained in use.

Jamandalai, and Lombortutu secured, and the rebuilding and extending of the airstrip now in full swing, it was time to begin the advance.

Near Momote (Associated Press)

Chapter Seven

The men of the 2nd Squadron had been in battle for more than a week: they had gone days without sleep and only rations to eat and the water in their canteens to drink; they had lived in foxholes, wondering if they would die in them as well; they had lost friends and fellow GIs, and they had won a hard fought series of battles during which they had killed over a thousand enemy soldiers. Although they trained long and hard in preparation for all of this, the men learned on the first night at Momote that no amount of training could have truly prepared them for the barbaric reality of war.

The fighting thus far had been largely defensive. Advancing through the jungle during an offensive was going to be a completely different experience. The men knew that, and the anxiety that had dissipated with their successes at the airstrip returned.

The following officially translated document, which was found on the bodies of a number of enemy soldiers on Los Negros, provides a frightening window into what American soldiers like my father faced when fighting in the Pacific:

Precautions To Each Unit Commanding Officer In Accomplishing Their Duty As Garrison Units. Issued By The Admiralty Garrison Unit Commanding Officer

In case provisions run short and come to a point of complete exhaustion, charge desperately into the enemy and by obtaining their provisions continue your fighting. When you suffer severe losses or become isolated and enveloped by the enemy, in any case you will not retreat unless ordered. No one will retreat on his own accord. Although to fight until the last man and commit suicide is familiar in form, they are entirely the opposite in spirit. The officers and men of the Garrison Unit must fight with the intention that each one will kill ten of the enemy. To become a prisoner is not only a great disgrace, but think of the great embarrassment it will bring upon your family and relatives. If you are about to fall into the enemy hands because of serious illness, etc., resolutely commit suicide.

Despite their rout at Momote, the Japanese garrison on Los Negros was intent on attacking the Americans again and again, regardless of the consequences. The only options the cavalrymen had against such a fanatical foe was to steadily and relentlessly pursue them, driving them further into a corner in the jungle, while at the same time wisely and aggressively defending their newly gained ground. It was going to be a marathon of kill or be killed and expect the unexpected from an enemy whose philosophy of war did not include the concept of honorable surrender.

While the bodies of more than eleven-hundred enemy soldiers were still being buried around Momote, at 11:30 A.M. on March 7th, amidst moderate rainfall and poor visibility, artillery and mortar barrages began hitting positions west of Lemondrol Creek.

At noon, a forty-man patrol from B Troop, voluntarily organized and led by the 5th Cavalry's intelligence officer, Captain William Cornelius, moved out from Porlaka in canvass and rubber boats to cross a six-foot deep section of Lemondrol to reconnoiter Papitalai Village. After reaching the western side, intense enemy machine gun and mortar fire opened up, forcing the patrol to withdraw back across the creek. The ambush left one enlisted man dead and four officers, including Captain Cornelius, wounded. The remaining men were relocated back to their positions at the airstrip: a platoon from F Troop was assigned as replacement.

Reinforcements and supporting units were brought forward from Momote and at 3:50 P.M., .50-caliber machine guns, 81mm mortars, and 37mm cannons began pounding the western side of the creek.

At 4:00 P.M., medics reported that Captain Cornelius' condition was improving as they administered a fourth pint of plasma.

By 4:20 P.M., the F Troop platoon had completed its crossing and had established a tenuous beachhead.

More soldiers from F Troop were shuttled across Lemondrol and reconnaissance patrols were sent out to determine the enemy presence in the area.

A supply line extending from Momote was established and rations, water, and ammunition were ferried across the creek as specially coated electrical wire to connect sound powered telephones was laid through the water.

The patrols advanced toward Papitalai Mission. But, after reaching about eight hundred yards into the jungle, they were pinned down by machine gun and mortar fire and forced to withdraw back to the beachhead.

At 5:30 P.M., Captain Cornelius died.

After consolidating and organizing the perimeter and setting up their FPL, the reinforced platoon dug in for the night behind barbered wire entanglements and a field of strategically placed antipersonnel mines.

As the sun began to set, the air of Papitalai filled with the roosting calls of the dozens of species of exotic birds unique to the isolated island; the constantly wet undergrowth twitched as tropical lizards darted about.

Just as it had occurred at the airstrip, the GIs were subjected to several attacks by small groups of suicidal Japanese overnight. All of the attacks were repulsed and artillery from 105mm Howitzers, called in from a forward observer, pounded the jungle to within fifty yards of the beachhead, keeping most of the enemy at bay, and the Americans on edge. One GI was wounded during the night.

Patrols sent out on the morning of March 8th attempted to reconnoiter the high ground south of Papitalai Mission. Again they met heavy resistance and were forced back. It was determined that a two hundred-foot high, heavily wooded hill, designated as Hill 260, was an enemy stronghold. A plan was drawn up to envelop the enemy forces on the hill involving elements of the 7th, 12th, and 5th Cavalry Regiments.

On the afternoon of March 8th, following air and artillery strikes on targets in Papitalai, a twenty-man platoon from the 12th Cavalry Regiment boarded landing craft just south of Salami Plantation and made an amphibious landing to the north of Papitalai Mission; elements of the 7th Cavalry Regiment boarded amphibious tractors and motored from Mokerang Peninsula across Seeadler Harbor and landed at Lombrum Point, west of Papitalai Mission.

The 5th Cavalry Regiment split into two directions. Elements from both squadrons crossed over Lemondrol and also along the eastern side of the creek toward the southeast point of the island. All of the advancing troops met small pockets of enemy resistance, which were silenced with machine gun fire, grenades, and mortar barrages. There were few American casualties. By nightfall, all the pieces were in place for the envelopment of Hill 260, which, if successful, would be followed by a coordinated advance across the length and breadth of Los Negros Island.

March 9th was the first clear day since the landing at Hyane. At 3:00 P.M., the 2nd Brigade of the 1st Cavalry Division—approximately four thousand troops—landed at Salami Beach and began mopping-up operations on Mokerang Peninsula. Once the area was declared secure, the Brigade would begin operations on Manus.

At 4:00 P.M., as Allied aircraft were landing at the now fully functioning airstrip, my father's platoon moved out from their position in Porlaka and crossed Lemondrol in canvas rafts to take up a position in the jungle about one hundred yards southwest of the beachhead. Their mission was to support the coming assault on Hill 260. After setting up a perimeter and establishing their FPL, they dug in for the night.

The rains returned.

The next morning, following a relatively quiet night in Papitalai, 5th Cavalry patrols were sent out to probe the corridor leading to Hill 260 and gather intelligence on enemy dispositions. When the patrols returned with negative reports, the decision was made to advance on the hill.

Advancing just about anywhere in Papitalai was a slow and very difficult exercise. Much of the area was hilly and covered with dense brush and triple-growth jungle. In the few lowland areas where there weren't swamps, the terrain was covered with tall cane fields and six-foot high kunai grass. Visibility was limited to five to ten yards. Virtually everything added up to conditions favoring the Japanese defenders who had established pillboxes and small dugouts throughout the area.

As the troops slowly advanced toward their objective, the Seabees worked doggedly to extend the supply lines, almost miraculously hewing roads and trails through the dense jungle.

Two tanks and bazooka and flamethrower squads were ordered into the area in preparation for the assault. The tanks quickly bogged down in the muddy terrain and became useless.

Bazookas and flamethrowers can be effective tools in the jungle. However, like all weapons, they are limited, and in certain conditions using a bazooka or a flamethrower does little more than disclose your position to the enemy. The only viable access to the top of Hill 260 was via a steep four-foot wide path that ran along a jungle-lined ridge or "hogback"—a very dangerous scenario for an advance and a questionable setting for a bazooka or a flamethrower squad.

By mid-afternoon my father's platoon, operating in concert with elements of F Troop, had reached the base of the hill and began ascending the narrow path toward an objective where they were to set up their guns in support of the advance. Their progress was quickly halted, however, by enemy machine gun fire and they were forced to withdraw back down the hill. The entire assault force was then ordered to pull back and an artillery concentration of more than two hundred rounds pounded the objective.

When the barrage was lifted, my father's platoon began ascending the hill a second time, but again they were forced to withdraw after meeting even stiffer resistance.

More artillery was called in and this time, some twelve hundred rounds hammered the hill. After a third attempt to advance met with the same results, a two-man flamethrower squad was sent up the path to clear out what was thought to be nothing more than an enemy machine gun nest.[19]

As the flamethrower squad advanced up the path, the roar of the weapon could be heard from the base of the hill, but the sound of machine gun fire soon followed, and then, only deathly silence: both men had been killed.

Now late in the day, the assault force withdrew back into Papitalai and dug in for the night, as additional artillery salvos slammed into the hill.

The only thing positive about March 10th was that it was the second day of clear weather.

Two more days and nights of artillery concentrations and several attempts to advance on the hill still failed to dislodge the enemy.

Hill 260 commanded a strategically important position overlooking Papitalai and in order for the 1st Cavalry Division to advance across the island, it could not be bypassed. A new plan was developed to envelop the hill involving the entire 5th and 12th Cavalry Regiments.

The 1st Squadron 5th Cavalry Regiment, which was now involved in patrol operations around Southeast Point, was chosen to make the major assault after moving back up to Porlaka and crossing over Lemondrol into Papitalai. The 2nd Squadron was relieved from its positions at Papitalai and Porlaka and ordered to move south along the eastern shore of Lemondrol Creek before heading west and then advancing northward toward Hill 260. The 12th Cavalry Regiment, which had established perimeters at Papitalai Mission to the north and Lombrum Point to the northwest, would converge on the hill from their positions. Allied aircraft which

---

19 After action reports state that the hill was actually being defended by about 200 enemy troops that were heavily dug in with snipers and machine gun squads positioned along the trail.

could now be launched from the airstrip at Momote and heavy artillery would bombard all of the area leading up to the crest before a four-stage final assault would be made by the 1st Squadron. The enemy would either be smashed in place on the hill or driven into the surrounding American positions and destroyed.

After crossing over Lemondrol and spending the remainder of March 13th patrolling the area around the hill, mapping enemy positions, and otherwise preparing for the attack, the 1st Squadron dug in for the night.

Meanwhile, the 2nd Squadron had successfully advanced around Lemondrol and past Porharmenemen Creek before digging in for the night just north of the swampy area around Ihon Lagoon.

To date, one hundred and forty-nine GIs had been killed, fifty had been wounded, forty were suffering from combat fatigue, and fourteen had fallen sick with malaria.

Chapter Eight

The final push for Hill 260 began on the morning of March 14th with heavy artillery concentrations. At 11:00 A.M., the artillery fire was lifted and elements of the 1st Squadron advanced to the first objective, encountering only light resistance. While the GIs held their position, a squadron of fighter-bombers from the Royal Australian Air Force attacked positions further up the hill. The bombing was scheduled to hit the first, second, and third objectives but after four bombs landed too close to the 1st Squadron's positions, the raid was called off.

As the rains returned, under a coordinated artillery barrage, using bazookas, machine guns, and rifles to knock out enemy pillboxes, the GIs successfully advanced to the second objective and dug in for the night.

Throughout the night, artillery and mortar barrages blasted the third objective every half hour. While the twice-hourly salvos were crashing in, the GIs were busy fending off small enemy counterattacks. The jungle terrain may have initially been to the enemy's defensive advantage, but as the American's advanced the tables turned and the well dug-in GIs easily repulsed the Japanese assaults.

Just after dawn the next day, encountering intermittent resistance, A and B Troops advanced to within sixty yards of the third objective. Following a thirty-minute artillery bombardment, patrols were sent out to reconnoiter the fourth objective about two hundred yards uphill—the crest of Hill 260.

The returning patrols reported having reached the objective and that there was little evidence of enemy activity there. However, after days of battling stiff resistance, no one was ready to take the information at face value. The enemy could very well be lying in wait in order to draw in the Americans, which was the strategy Colonel Ezaki had used to mislead Allied air reconnaissance into thinking Los Negros was abandoned; and it was also what he had tried at Momote on February 29th. The final assault on the crest of the hill was delayed another day so that additional ammunition and supplies could be brought to the forward units.

Because of the ongoing lack of non-combat troops, C Troop together with soldiers from the 82nd Field Artillery Battalion hand carried small amounts of rations, water, and ammunition up the one and a half-mile, steep and narrow trail—a five-hour round trip.

Meanwhile in the 2nd Squadron's sector, a reconnaissance platoon was dispatched to the southern side of Porharmenemen Creek to search for a large enemy weapons cache spotted there the previous day. The recon platoon found nothing. However, a platoon from E Troop that was advancing along the beach trail discovered numerous freshly dug foxholes in the brush and at the bases of large trees just north of the trail. It was estimated that a platoon and a half of enemy troops were in the area.

As the E Troop platoon advanced, they came under machine gun and rifle fire and were forced to withdraw and dig in for the night.

With the exception of having to shoot a dog[20] approaching its positions, the 2nd Squadron spent a relatively quiet night while the command worked at building up the supply line and strategized how to dislodge the enemy outpost causing the trouble.

On March 16th, while the 1st Squadron was holding its position on and around Hill 260, elements of the 2nd Squadron continued patrolling the swampy areas west of Ihon Lagoon, the jungle area of Puwas—about 3 miles west of Southeast Point—and the high ground of Palapi Hill to the north, as the rest of the Squadron slowly advanced from behind.

When the patrols reached the area around the base of Palapi Hill, they met heavy resistance, forcing the Squadron to hold their position at the Puwas Junction. In an attempt to bypass the trouble, E Troop moved further inland. But after crawling on their hands and knees through heavy undergrowth and vine-covered swamps where visibility was limited to seven feet, E Troop also got pinned down by heavy machine gun fire and was forced to retreat.

Due to the density of the jungle and a lack of heavy equipment, the supply line had not yet been sufficiently extended and the 2nd Squadron's forward elements, which had already lost five men that day, were forced to return to their earlier positions and dig in for the night.

The 1st Squadron spent most of the day of March 16th patrolling and consolidating its positions as the supply line was being strengthened and ammunition, water, and rations continued to be carried forward in preparation for the final assault on Hill 260. As one of

---

20 Natives reported that the Japanese had 11 dogs on the island that were trained to search the jungle and alert them to the presence of American troops.

the Squadron's patrols moved out, they came in contact with a four-man heavy machine gun squad, which they engaged and eliminated. Continuing westward, another patrol came across the bodies of eighteen enemy soldiers, apparently killed by American artillery, strewn alongside the jungle path. Before advancing past the position, the GIs fired into the bodies.

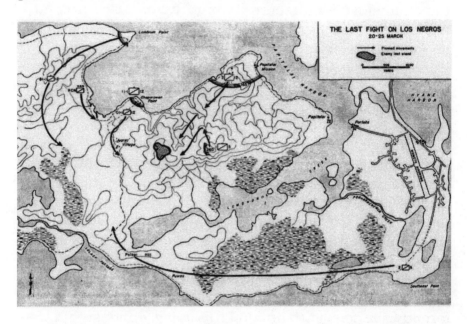

Back at Southeast Point, after a night of mortar and artillery concentrations that pounded enemy positions, at 8: A.M., under clear skies and good visibility, the 2nd Squadron once again attempted to advance.

E Troop, which was assigned to seize and hold the area of Puwas, advanced westward along the beach trail and then northward into the jungle. After overcoming small but organized resistance, the Troop continued to press on while one of its rifle platoons moved up on the right flank to protect the advance.

As the entire Squadron began to advance behind E Troop, they were immediately pinned down by heavy machine gun and rifle fire. The rifle platoon on the right flank attempted to envelope the resistance but was also met with machine gun as well as mortar fire, causing them to withdraw and rejoin the rest of the Troop.

The suspected reinforced enemy platoon was apparently concealed in tangled undergrowth so thick an enemy gunner "could not be seen firing from a distance as close as fifteen or twenty yards." The area also hosted ancient Moreton Bay Fig trees, whose gigantic aerial root systems provided natural enclosures where the enemy could establish pillboxes and aim their guns through imperceptibly small openings. The advancing GIs could literally walk right past these positions suspecting nothing, until it was too late.

After brief artillery and mortar barrages and a thorough hosing down of the area with machine gun fire, the Squadron resumed its advance toward Puwas, widening its front by moving units deeper into the jungle to the north.

As the Squadron moved stealthily forward through the jungle, a dog was seen feeding on the body of a dead Japanese soldier. A platoon was dispatched to investigate. As the GIs approached, the dog barked and the platoon immediately came under enemy fire, which was quickly silenced with an onslaught of grenades, machine gun and rifle fire. After the exchange, the Squadron advanced into Puwas.

The next objective for the 2nd Squadron was Palapi Hill, which would be followed by an advance further west into the Tauwi Hills. It was expected that both locations would be heavily defended since they were strategically important areas of high ground.

After advancing several hundred yards northwest through the jungle and skirting around Palapi Hill, my father's platoon moved into Tauwi on a mission to seize and hold a hill from which they would support an attack on Palapi.

After overcoming minor resistance and meeting the objective, the platoon set up their perimeter and established their FPL. As they were digging in for the night, Captain John Strong, commander of D Troop, and Major Frank Fordleigh, the Squadron's executive officer, accompanied by two enlisted men, approached my father's position from the rear. Strong began calling out, "Lieutenant Bennett! Lieutenant Bennett!" In addition to not using my father's code name, Strong was identifying an officer in the field, and by loudly doing so in the jungle, where the enemy can easily hide and where sound travels surprisingly well, he was violating basic rules of combat and thereby endangering the position. Crouched in his foxhole clutching his Thompson, my father, following both his training and orders, refused to answer.

Ignoring my father's non-response, Strong and Fordleigh walked to the crest of the hill to get a perspective on the terrain before nightfall. As the two officers stood there, silhouetted by the setting sun, the metallic rattle of a Japanese machine gun erupted. My father immediately ordered his men to open fire and told his radioman to call in coordinates for a mortar strike. He also requested additional ammunition and litter bearers. Captain Strong had been killed instantly; Major Fordleigh was taken away moaning: he died a short time later.

Shaken by the death of these two men, one of whom, Captain Strong, he had been with since his days at Fort Bliss, my father was also angry with them for getting killed. Rank protects no one in combat and mistakes result in dead soldiers. My father didn't need this incident to strengthen his own commitment to training. However, he used the tragedy as an object lesson for his men as to what can happen if they don't follow their training or if they fail to listen to orders. My father had been living constantly with killing for seventeen days and death had lost its normal shock value, as it had for most of the men. Within minutes of the event, the deaths of Captain Strong and Major Fordleigh became just another brutal moment in the ongoing nightmare of the war.

The rains resumed falling after midnight.

In the aftermath of the killings of Strong and Fordleigh, General Chase issued orders reminding all soldiers to meticulously follow their training and to use only the code names of officers when communicating in the field.

The enemy forces around my father's position were estimated to be at one hundred, half of whom were killed, the remainder fled into the jungle. In addition to Captain Strong and Major Fordleigh, a lieutenant and six enlisted men died that day in the 2nd Squadron's sector.

On the morning of March 17th, under clearing skies and good visibility, the 1st Squadron's final assault on Hill 260 began.

Following the usual fifteen-minute artillery preparation, at 8:45 A.M., B and C Troops advanced up the narrow ridge to within two hundred yards of the crest of the hill before getting pinned down by machine gun and rifle fire. After C Troop phoned in a request for more ammunition and litter bearers, B Troop, using C Troop as a pivot to maneuver, moved over the ridge and around the enemy's left flank. Slowly, the men hacked their way through the dense foliage in an effort to envelope the enemy. As the GIs advanced, they came across the pulverized remains of dozens of Japanese soldiers. When they finally reached the top of the hill, they found the area completely deserted. It was later determined that while the artillery and bombing had taken a horrific toll on the enemy, as evidenced by the bodies in the jungle, it had not altogether cleared them from the hill. However, the noise made by the men of B Troop hacking their way through the jungle spooked the Japanese defenders and they had retreated down the reverse slope and into the lines of the advancing 12th Cavalry Regiment, where they were killed.

By 1:10 P.M., after eight days of combat, Hill 260 had been seized and secured. The Squadron spent the rest of the day consolidating its positions, while supplies were hand carried up the hill and Seabees gradually extended the supply line.

Back in the 2nd Squadron's sector, supply dumps were established along the beach path and Seabees using bulldozers went to work clearing trails through the jungle. However, even with the heavy equipment only narrow swaths cut be cut through the dense growth, too narrow to get vehicles through.

The Squadron was ordered to maintain its perimeter and to use Halazone tablets to purify water from streams and pools until an adequate supply line could be established.

The night of March 17/18 was dry, and despite periodic enemy sniping and grenades thrown at their positions no GIs were killed in the 2nd Squadron's sector: four men were wounded.

On March 18th, the commander of the 6th Army, Lieutenant General Walter Krueger, arrived at the airstrip aboard a B-17. After meeting with General Chase and visiting the troops, Krueger re-boarded his plane and left the island.

As headway was finally being made in extending the supply line, at 2:00 P.M. the 2nd Squadron prepared to advance and a combat patrol was dispatched to reconnoiter the area northwest of Palapi Hill. The patrol ran into a hornet's nest of resistance and the Squadron itself was simultaneously ambushed, receiving fire from enemy machine guns, mortars, and snipers. In the ensuing battle twenty-two Japanese were killed; seven GIs lost their lives and twenty-five others were wounded.

On the morning of March 19th, the 2nd Squadron's forward elements were ordered to fall back from their positions in preparation for naval artillery and air strikes on Palapi Hill and the surrounding area. Allied warplanes strafed and bombed the hill, hitting it with more than a thousand rounds and dropping eleven 500-pound bombs; destroyers stationed four thousand yards south of Hyane Harbor launched fifteen hundred rounds of artillery, and 155mm Howitzers pounded the area from their positions at Momote. By the end of the day, Palapi Hill had been reduced to a defrocked, smoldering mound.

On Monday, March 20th, General Chase completed plans and issued verbal orders for the total occupation of Los Negros Island.

Living in the jungle, lack of sleep, and poor nutrition were taking a toll on the GIs. Diseases such as malaria and dysentery were becoming more prevalent. Several of my father's men were evacuated due to illness and replacements, if they were available, were sent in. One such case resulted in a tragic incident while my father's platoon was digging in for the night on March 20th.

One of the platoon's ammo bearers became seriously ill and had to be taken out; a buck private was sent in as his replacement. Because of the new man's inexperience in jungle combat, my father partnered him with his staff sergeant, OK Williams. Sergeant Williams instructed the man on his role should they be attacked as well as how the buddy system worked. As night descended, Williams volunteered to take the first watch. At the end of his shift he reached over with his rifle and nudged the new recruit. Startled and disoriented, the private came up shooting, killing Williams instantly.[21]

Unable to move during the night, Sergeant William's body remained where it had fallen. At daylight, emotionally wrecked by what he had done, the private was taken out of action and another replacement was sent in as litter bearers removed William's body.

With perhaps one exception, which is later discussed, more than any other combat-related incident during the war, including the killings of Captain Strong and Major Fordleigh, the tragic death of Ostle K. Williams, the young staff sergeant from California, the man my father could rely on in the heat of battle, and whom he sadly remembered sixty years later as "a helluva nice guy," symbolized the senselessness of war, where, as my father bitterly put it, *"Your life isn't worth a plug nickel."*

As the tropical rains resumed on the morning of March 21st, the 1st Brigade's coordinated advance began. At dawn, in the 2nd Squadron's sector, following an artillery concentration, G Troop began moving west and ran into heavy machine gun fire. My father's platoon, operating in support of F Troop, advanced westward all the way to Pitulu Lagoon without meeting resistance.

GIs operating near the beach path watched in disbelief as a Japanese submarine surfaced. Enemy soldiers emerged from the vessel and began swimming toward the shore. When the cavalrymen opened fire, the sub turned on a powerful searchlight, illuminating F Troop's position, and began firing three-inch guns. Two Allied PT boats patrolling about three hundred and fifty yards offshore opened fire on the enemy sub, which quickly

---

21 The 5th Cavalry's Operation Report states that Sergeant Williams was killed because he was, "moving around during the night." The report is erroneous. As he was an eyewitness to this event, my father's account, which is related in the narrative, is more reliable.

extinguished its searchlight and submerged. Two of the enemy soldiers managed to reach the shore, disappearing into the jungle north of F Troop's position.

While the 2nd Squadron's patrols continued to advance through the jungle, Seabees using bulldozers knocked down trees and cleared brush; demolition squads blew up tree stumps to prevent the enemy from using them as concealment; dump trucks hauled coral sand from the beach and filled in swampy areas to further develop the supply line, and ammo dumps were moved closer to the forward positions.

After his platoon advanced westward and took up a position on another hill, my father began feeling sick. Weak and breaking out with fever and chills, he feared he was suffering the initial symptoms of malaria.

Malaria is caused by parasites transmitted through the bloodsucking "bite" of the female Anopheles mosquito. The numerous streams and pools on islands like Los Negros made fertile breeding grounds for these insects. Consequently, the disease was rampant among men serving in the Southwest Pacific. To combat the epidemic soldiers were routinely provided with a drug called Atabrine.

Quinine, a medicine derived from the bark of the Cinchona tree native to the Andes Mountains of South America, had long been the drug of choice for preventing as well as for treating malaria. However, the Japanese had cut off the supply route of Quinine during the war. Atabrine, a synthetic alternative invented by a German researcher before the outbreak of hostilities, did not necessarily immunize against malaria in the dose that it was given to the troops; it primarily acted to suppress the symptoms.

Rumors, which some believe were started by the Japanese, that Atabrine caused sterility and other harmful side effects, persisted amongst the soldiers and many men would not take the drug.

Atabrine in fact did have a toxic effect on the liver, which caused the soldiers' skin to take on a sickly-yellow color. And there were other minor adverse reactions, such as, headaches, nausea, vomiting, and in a few cases temporary psychosis. My father had chosen not to take the drug.

In the midst of his sickness, in the hot and humid jungle, squatting in a foxhole with a pounding headache, fever and chills, my father chided himself for not following the army's instructions. Having yellow skin would be nothing compared to how he was feeling now. He swore to himself to never make the same mistake again.

After instructing his men to hold their positions, and temporarily assigning command of the platoon to one of his officers, my father headed back through the jungle to the Squadron's aid station where he was indeed diagnosed with a "mild case" of malaria. After being given medication, he was sent back to his platoon.

While the 2nd Squadron was advancing westward in the southern part of the island, in the 1st Squadron's sector, elements of the 12th Cavalry moved southwest under cover of mortar and artillery fire. Overcoming moderate resistance, the 12th Cavalry troops continued to press forward until dusk.

After settling in for the night in dense brush, the troopers silently watched as Japanese soldiers began filtering onto a nearby jungle trail, apparently organizing to infiltrate the American's positions. After waiting until they had assembled, the GIs opened fire, mowing down all of the enemy troops.

121

The 1st Squadron moved out from the area around Hill 260 and headed southwest, attempting to link up with advance elements of the 12th Cavalry. After coming under heavy machine gun fire, they retreated and called for an artillery concentration on the enemy positions. Trying again to advance and once more meeting heavy resistance, although only two hundred and fifty yards away from the 12th Cavalry, the Squadron was ordered to withdraw to their previous positions near Hill 260. Due to the Japanese having cut their supply line in several places the Squadron's advance from Papitalai was further delayed.

Artillery and mortar barrages resumed hitting suspected enemy positions.

March 21st was a busy day on Los Negros as activity grew to a fever pitch in preparation for the final push to occupy the island and complete converting it into an Allied air and naval base. While the 1st and 2nd Squadrons were pushing westward, P-38s scoured the island at treetop level attempting to draw enemy fire to disclose their positions; an anti tank unit moved into Porlaka to protect the 1st Squadron's supply line from enemy forces venturing down Lemondrol Creek, and native carriers shuttled rations and supplies to the men in the forward positions. At the now impossibly clogged Hyane Harbor, shiploads of equipment, ammunition, rations, and medical supplies were unloaded and transported all the way to the airstrip on conveyor rollers manned by a line of soldiers. Renovations and improvements at Momote were ongoing even as an increasing number of planes took off and landed.

Communications continued to be a challenge. The heavy equipment operating around the airstrip frequently cut telephone lines and the almost constant rainfall rendered many of the sound powered telephones useless.

On March 22nd, with clear skies prevailing, following periodic artillery strikes, the 2nd Squadron spent the day patrolling and after more artillery strikes, advanced west-northwest into the Tauwi Hills region.

At the same time, the 1st Squadron launched an attack westward across Papitalai. But despite laying down heavy artillery barrages the GIs ran into fierce resistance, which combined with the impenetrably dense cane fields made it impossible for them to advance and they had to pull back to their original positions.

A boat patrol was made of the southwestern end of Lemondrol Creek in search of enemy barges; none were spotted.

The forward units in both sectors were running low on food and resorted to sending up smoke columns so Allied planes could drop K-rations.

The Japanese fighters remaining on Los Negros had been pushed into the western center of the island by the advancing American troops. With the enemy now concentrated in an ever shrinking geographic area and becoming even more desperate—none had surrendered and only nine had been captured—advancing through the dense jungle became increasingly risky. And as the body count of enemy soldiers diminished so did critically important intelligence. In light of the situation, General Chase ordered more intense and sustained artillery concentrations to precede any advance and urged all of the men "...to be very thorough in searching the dead and to turn in those identifications." As an incentive, General Swift authorized cash awards[22] and a thirty-day leave in Sydney, Australia, to anyone who captured an enemy soldier.

---

22   The cash part of the awards was only authorized for enlisted men.

After the 2nd Squadron's seizure of the airstrip on February 29th, as an inspiration to the troops, Momote was renamed "Wainwright," in honor of General Jonathan Wainwright, the highest-ranking American officer captured during the war.[23] Now that Los Negros had been all but liberated, on March 23rd, General Chase ordered that the airstrip revert to its original name. Throughout the pacific war, General MacArthur took great pains to convey to indigenous populations that American forces were there to liberate, not to subjugate; by restoring the name 'Momote,' General Chase was following suit.

The same day, the 12th Cavalry finally made physical contact with the 1st Squadron of the 5th Cavalry at 11:30 A.M. Because their supply line had been severed, the 1st Squadron had gone without rations, medical supplies, and ammunition for two days; now they could be resupplied and their sick and wounded evacuated via the 12th Cavalry's supply line.

It was estimated that over two thousand Japanese soldiers had been killed thus far, and that the remaining enemy strength was over sixteen hundred. In addition, intelligence reports cautioned, "It is believed that the enemy can assemble four hundred to five hundred troops in the Loniu Village area and he can be expected to make a determined stand in that area." Loniu Village was located at the western end of Los Negros.

As my father's platoon was preparing their positions on the high ground in the Tauwi Hills in the early evening of March 23rd, what would be another all-night artillery barrage began. Not yet dark, my father was standing under a palm tree when suddenly a huge explosion rocked him. What he assumed to be an errant artillery shell had struck the top of the tree, spewing shrapnel in all directions, killing his radioman, and wounding several others. Fifty-five years later, in a halting and

---

23 In 1942, General Wainwright was captured at Corregidor where he had assumed command when General MacArthur relocated to Australia.

faintly quivering voice, my father struggled to recall the incident and the events that followed:

"I was standing in the cone of the explosion. I ran over there, picked up his...telephone...and...yelled into it 'Cease Fire! We've just had a short round.' The...next morning...after the...overnight barrage was lifted at about...seven-thirty-a-quarter-of-eight...we were ready to move out. I felt...itching in my...lower left ankle. I didn't pay much attention to it. We were covered with mud and...and had the clothes on for days. Anyway, we...started out...to advance and were pinned down by...heavy machine gun fire. So, we retreated back to our final protective line, set the gun...guns up again, and... then had an opportunity to...try to find a spot on my leg that...um...was itching. I just pulled my pant leg up and rolled down my sock and there was nothing there. So, I...lowered my pants, and sure enough...there was a festering wound in my upper left thigh. I went down to the...hospital unit in the rear, just a few hundred yards away, and...there was a piece of shrapnel in my...my leg...which...the...the...medical officer looked at...had me put on a table—somebody covered me with a sheet and I started to have a panic attack; that's when I first discovered that I was claustrophobic, anyway, four guys held me down, and...the officer...medical officer...pulled the shrapnel outta my leg, bandaged it up and sent me back up to the front. That was the end of that episode. I never felt anything...more in the way of pain or anything like that. So, the next morning, I figured...um...I mean contemplating moving out the next morning...tried to fig-ure out...uh...why the heavy artillery and mortar bar-rage was not...uh...killing the enemy forces up ahead of us. And...the conclusion I came to was that they...uh... were obviously wise to our tactics of lifting...uh...of fir-ing all night and then lifting the barrage at eight o'clock

in the morning. And I figured what they were doing is coming in close to our perimeter— in the night…to avoid the…artillery fire and then when the barrage is lifted… at…uh…say seven-thirty eight o'clock in the morning… uh…they would move back to their positions and man their guns. So…um…I ordered…um…a…uh…an extra round…an extra belt of ammunition for each gunner; that included the machine guns, the automatic rifles, and… everybody.[24] *I…told the troops that…um…when the artillery barrage…uh…lifted at eight o'clock the next morning, I would yell 'Commence Fire,' and…they were to open up and rake the entire front, including trees and anything in front and…then we would move out. Well, this proved to be very successful…and we advanced…about a thousand yards, which is almost impossible in the…in the jungle…and set up a final protective line. The final morning…we executed a plan…that had been thought out… and…the…riflemen would…advance, crawling on their bellies, and we, the machine gunners in my machine gun platoon, would cover them by firing over their heads as they advanced. When…it became…dangerous to continue the firing because of the possibility of hitting our own troops, I ordered the guns to cease firing and…there was deathly silence; there was…nothing. And…all-of-a-sudden, I heard some crying…over to my right…few yards. I went over there…and there was a tarp…which I flicked off with the…with the muzzle of my gun, and… the crying was obviously coming from there. There were enemy troops down in that hole. So, we were…I was not about to advance…leave that position and have…enemy troops behind our lines. So, I…threw a couple of…hand grenades into the hole, and…it didn't do any…they were still crying. So, I threw…two more concussion grenades into the hole, and…uh…kept yelling for them to come up and finally they came up. There were five of them. They*

---

24 The operational report states that 2,500 rounds were brought up to the position.

came up with their...arms...outstretched...up...up over their heads and we shook-'em down to make sure they didn't have...any hidden weapons on them. And...we... took 'em...I assigned...one prisoner to each of four of my men and took the other one for myself. The reason for this was that...due to the poor...poor intelligence...the...and the resistance that we were meeting in trying to move out, the Division commander had sent a memo around stating that...any prisoner that was caught, the person who... caught the prisoner...would receive thirty days leave in Sydney. So...in taking these people back the...rear echelon...I assigned...each of the four men a prisoner and took one for myself, and...we... were supposed to then wait for orders to go to Sydney on a thirty day leave. I got back to my platoon rather quickly...and...ordered them to...assume a formation and we would...advance forward in order to meet the troops that we had been covering as they advanced, which we did. We advanced practically unopposed."

Intelligence reports suggest that the artillery round that struck the tree was not from friendly fire; rather it was a 90mm enemy mortar. It appeared that the Japanese had calculated the location of my father's position based on where the American mortar fire was being laid. A spray of shrapnel had become embedded in his left leg and only the largest piece, about one-half inch long, had been removed at the aid station.

Intelligence reports also reveal that the enemy soldiers that my father captured were hiding in a tunnel dug off of a ten-foot deep shaft and accessed by a makeshift wooden ladder. The grenades that he had thrown "in that hole" had exploded harmlessly at the bottom of the shaft. However, the deafening noise from the concussion grenades was what finally flushed them out. The reports also state that the incident took place at 2:15

P.M. and that during interrogation, one of the prisoners reported that the remaining enemy troops on the island were in "high morale with plenty of food and ammunition" and were "prepared to fight until the last man." In response to being asked for his assessment of Americans as jungle fighters, the prisoner replied, "Japanese very good jungle fighter. Americans no jungle fighter... they move jungle, then fight."

It's uncertain what my father was referring to when he stated "the final morning." According to the operational reports, March 25th was not the final day of fighting on Los Negros nor was it so for my father. While the frequency of the skirmishes lessened, both squadrons continued to engage the enemy for about another week. And as they advanced westward, the supply lines became stretched so thin the forward units grew increasingly short on ammunition as well as rations.

On or about March 26th the Allies intercepted a communication stating that Colonel Ezaki, together with eight Chinese nationals,[25] was in the area between the 12th Cavalry's patrols and the 2nd Squadron's command post.

The 1st and 2nd Squadrons were converging on a narrow path called the Lolach Passage Trail, which began at a tributary of the Bismarck Sea near the southwestern end of the island and cut through the jungle all the way to Chaporowan Point on the northern coast. As they continued to advance, the GIs reported spotting "individual Japanese soldiers running naked through the jungle."

Once the squadrons converged, the entire Regiment began its final advance to Loniu Village.

On the late afternoon of March 26th, my father's platoon once again took up a high ground position and

---

25 Subsequent to their invasion of China, the Japanese used Chinese nationals as forced laborers throughout the Southwest Pacific.

began digging in for the night when a young gunner decided to do something remarkably foolish. Ignoring his training, the soldier stepped out in front of one of the heavy machine guns and began tapping the water jacket, attempting to sight the weapon. The gun discharged sending a .30 caliber bullet through his face, killing him instantly. Shortly after the litter bearers carried the body away, a messenger delivered a note from the new captain of D Troop (Captain Strong's replacement) instructing my father to write a letter to the young man's family:

"I wrote the letter and sent it back down the line. A short time later, a messenger brought the letter back with a notation from the captain, stating, 'Not flowery enough.' So I rewrote the letter and sent it back down the line again. The letter came back a second time with a notation stating, 'Still not flowery enough.' By the time I wrote the letter for the third time, the guy was eligible for the Congressional Medal of Honor!"

For the next two days, under clear skies, my father's platoon continued advancing and meeting minimal resistance until they encountered a group of Japanese soldiers holed up on the downslope of a hill, just under the ridge. The enemy's deeply entrenched position and the surrounding terrain made it impossible to hit them with gunfire or grenades. After requesting a demolition team, my father instructed his men to flank the enemy position and to fire on anything that moved.

The demolition team circled around the hill and then climbed to the crest, overlooking the enemy emplacement. Once they were in position, using Bangalore Torpedoes, a device originally designed to destroy barbed wire entanglements, the team threaded together several sections of the explosive-packed tubes and shoved the weapon over the downslope until it was just above the enemy position and then detonated it, sending a burst of shrapnel into the well concealed Japanese troops, killing all of them.

Before the 2nd Squadron made its advance into Loniu Village, the entire area was subjected to an intense artillery barrage, as well as aerial bombardment and strafing.

As advanced patrols moved along the shore of Lolach Passage, the bodies of about ten Japanese soldiers were seen floating in the water, apparent victims of the pre-advance preparation.

By the end of the day of March 28th, the entire 2nd Squadron was concentrated at Loniu Village, where they spent the night enduring little more than some harassing small-arms fire and a few flares fired at their positions.

Meanwhile, the 1st Squadron was still unable to advance due to the dense jungle and a shortage of ammunition. They could do little more than send out reconnaissance patrols.

During the night of the 29th, the 2nd Squadron sent out patrols into the area surrounding Loniu, which met no resistance and reported no indications of recent enemy activity. However, the patrols did report finding caves, one of which was large enough to conceal up to a hundred enemy troops. The only practicable way of clearing such large caves was with flamethrowers, but no flamethrowers were available in the 2nd Squadron sector so the caves were left guarded until the following day.

On March 31st, the 1st Squadron was finally able to make its advance into Loniu Village.

Over the next several days, small squads from both squadrons were sent out on mopping-up operations with special instructions to search for enemy documents. While the patrols were probing the area, for the first time since February 29th, the 2nd Squadron soldiers got clean uniforms and decent food. One of the returning patrols brought back a diary found on the body of an enemy soldier. The journal entries provided a far different assessment of the enemy's situation than that which was reported by one of the prisoners my father had captured:

"28 March. Last night's duty was rather quiet except for the occasional mortar and rifle fire that could be heard. According to the conference of the various unit leaders, it has been decided to abandon the present position and withdraw. The preparation for this has been made. However, it seems as though this has been cancelled and we will firmly hold this position. Ah! This is honorable defeat and I suppose we must be proud of the way we have handled ourselves. Only our names will remain, and this is something I don't altogether like. Yes, the lives of those remaining, 300 of us, are now limited to a few days.

"30 March. This is the eighth day since we began the withdrawal. We have been wondering around and around the mountain roads because of the enemy. We have not yet arrived at our destination but we have completely exhausted our rations. Our bodies are becoming weaker and weaker, and the hunger is getting unbearable.

"31 March. Although we are completely out of rations, the march continues. When will we reach Lorengau. As we go along, we throw away our equipment and weapons one by one.

"1 April. Arrived at native shack. According to communications, friendly troops in Lorengau cannot help but

withdraw. Hereafter there is no choice but to live as the natives do."

On April 1st, the 2nd Squadron marched from Loniu Village, down the Lolach Passage Trail and continued east via the beach trail until they reached the Momote Airstrip. It was a six-mile, three-hour march traversing an area that had taken more than a month of combat to conquer and that resulted in the killing of more than four thousand Japanese. That same day, my father was given a battlefield commission promoting him to 1st Lieutenant.

After getting settled in at Momote, a Seabee asked my father if he would take him to where one of the battles had occurred:

"We walked around the airstrip and entered into the jungle area. At some point, the guy became concerned as to how we would find our way out. I told him we'd just follow the phone wires. After reaching the location, I explained to him what had happened there, showed him where our troops were, where the enemy was, and some details of the battle. When it was time to head back, I looked around for a phone line, but there were lines running everywhere! So I said let's just head to the water. Well, when we finally emerged from the jungle we were a long way from the airstrip and there were no trails, so we swam back down to the harbor. It was a stupid thing to do; those were shark infested waters."

In fact, several soldiers died swimming in those waters, including Lieutenant Henshaw, the man to whom General MacArthur had awarded the Distinguished Service Cross for being the first soldier to hit the beach on February 29th.

Much has been said and written about the so-called "fog of war," where normative critical thinking is obscured and the value of human life is diminished. In his 1999 oral history, my father, his voice noticeably somber and somewhat tremulous, recalled an incident that happened at Momote, which, although it occurred after hostilities had ceased, must be viewed within the context of that often discussed phenomenon:

"One night, it was my turn to be Officer of the Guards, a function of just patrolling the perimeter of our encampment to make sure that the guards were on duty and paying attention. The tour ended at six o'clock in the morning and I came back in to the troop area. I was confronted by a couple of soldiers that had another soldier in tow, telling me that he had ransacked their tents during the night. I instructed these men to take the prisoner into the captain's tent to await his arrival for further disposition. I then walked into the tent, took off my gun belt, with my gun in the holster—just tossed it on the bed. The bed was just to the left of the opening as you walked in and the prisoner was placed on that bed—sitting. There was a U-shaped table facing the entrance. I was sitting at the top of the U facing the entrance, with other officers on my right and left. I was quickly attracted to the bed where I saw this prisoner raising a gun and point it in my direction. I just flew out the back of the tent and escaped... and heard the shot...came back into the tent and the 1st Sergeant, who had been standing in the opening, disarmed the prisoner, and then...then looked to my left and there was my fellow officer, Lieutenant Ben Reeser... ah...slumped over. I looked at him and apparently he was shot in the right shoulder, and, it being a .45-caliber, it penetrated his heart and he was killed."[26]

---

26 The 5th Cavalry casualty list states that Lieutenant Reeser, who also commanded a platoon of D Troop, was wounded on April 3, 1944. Since the fighting on Los Negros had ended before that date, it seems that this is referring to the same

Choking back emotion, my father stopped the tape. Sometime later, he bitterly concluded:

"The prisoner was taken to division headquarters, and we never did find out what they did with him. Probably transferred him to another outfit, or put him in a brig, or whatever."

On April 3rd, reconnaissance and weapons units were sent to Koruniat Island, a small atoll situated about six miles north of Mokerang Peninsula. Koruniat and another atoll had been cleared of enemy troops while the battle for Los Negros was taking place. Army engineers and Seabees began preparing a large area for a suitable campsite.

On the 8th of April, my father's unit was moved to Koruniat while he remained at Momote preparing to be flown out to Sydney for his thirty-day leave.

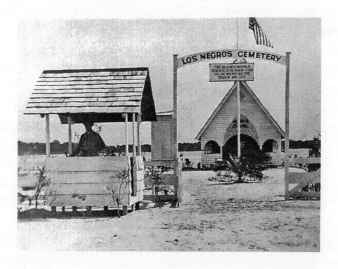

incident that my father spoke about. However, other records state that Lieutenant Reeser died on June 19th, which, if accurate, would mean that he initially survived the shooting. After the war, Lieutenant Ben F. Reeser's remains were disinterred from the temporary cemetery on Los Negros and reburied in the Manila American Cemetery at Fort Bonifacio, Manila, Philippines.

My father and a total of seven other men who had captured enemy soldiers, four of whom he had assigned prisoners, boarded a B-17 and took off from the airstrip that had been the place of so much bloodshed and misery. As the warplane flew out over the island and banked over the Pacific, my father, seated in the nose-gunner's seat, looked down at Los Negros and thought how beautiful an island it would be if not for the war.

For the next thirty days he tried to relax and have a good time in Sydney, but the tragic death of Lieutenant Reeser made that all but impossible.

Before returning to Los Negros, my father headed to the photo shop where he had had his portrait taken after his completion of Officer Candidate School. When he arrived, he saw the picture prominently displayed in the shop's window. Twenty pounds lighter and battle worn, he no longer looked like the robust, rosy-cheeked young man in the image. He arranged to have the photograph sent to Claire before he boarded another B-17 and headed back to Los Negros.

As the plane came in over the small island, my father gazed down and was amazed at the changes that had taken place in just thirty days: areas of dense jungle were now crisscrossed by a network of roads; there were two newly renovated and active airstrips[27] with elaborate dispersal areas; buildings and large Quonset huts occupied spaces where there had been only impenetrable brush and coconut groves; dozens of U.S. Navy ships were docked at the renovated Hyane and Seeadler Harbors, and a huge U.S. Navy battleship was raised out of the water within a floating drydock. Like his reaction to watching the building of the George Washington Bridge and crossing through the Panama Canal, my father was impressed by the accomplishments of man. And he was particularly awestruck by the power of the United States military.

---

27   Besides Momote, another airstrip had been built on Mokerang Peninsula.

After landing at Momote, my father was driven to Salami Beach where he boarded a tender that took him to Koruniat. While he was on leave in Sydney, the GI's had built an elaborate camp on the atoll, which compared to the conditions on Los Negros seemed like paradise. There were neatly arranged tents and mess halls, showers, and volleyball and basketball courts, a PX, Red Cross building, and a four hundred-seat chapel. There was even a boxing ring and a small theatre.

But the new camp was not going to be home for very long. Everyone knew that General MacArthur was heading back to the Philippines to retake what had been lost and to punish the enemy that had driven him out of what was in essence his home. There was most certainly a lot more fighting ahead, and that, of course, meant there would be more training, more exercises.

My father hated the war; he hated killing and he hated having to avoid getting killed, and to say the least he had no fondness for army living. Before being drafted in 1941, he had already spent thirteen years in institutionalized regimentation; he felt he deserved a better shake out of life.

But despite all of these justified feelings my father remained profoundly grateful to be an American and he harbored no doubt whatsoever of America's just cause in fighting the war. The Imperial Japanese had invaded China and mercilessly slaughtered and abused millions of that country's people. They had without provocation attacked the United States at Pearl Harbor. They were the monsters who had brutalized and murdered tens of thousands of GIs and Filipinos during the infamous Bataan Death March, and they were the forces of evil that together with the Nazis wanted to take over the entire world. This was the reality of the world that my father recognized and that realization is what strengthened him to put his personal life and his emotions on hold in order to, as he would say, *"Get the job done."* Feeling rested and inspired after his trip to Sydney, on an old army typewriter he hunt-n-pecked the following poem:

<u>The Yanks Are Coming</u>

I answered the call for a year ----- no more;
To help prepare my country for war.
But as the months slipped by, I could plainly see,
There'd be a helluva lot more than a year for me.

Poised way out west far beyond the sunset,
With dagger raised for the treacherous plunge;
The Mikado's band hopped up full of sake,
Hell bent for the Navy's harbor at Pearl.

They struck when the complacent Yank least expected
And never came back 'cause they thought they had wrecked it.
Wrecked it they did, as great fires attested,
And down at the bottom our proud navy rested.

So the Nips turned their efforts toward far off Australia;
To conquer the Aussies and get them in tow.
But they little expected, with ships resurrected,
The Yanks to deal them a mighty blow.

This we did, southeast of New Guinea, in the deep blue waters of the Coral Sea.
With a handful of airplanes and pilots with grit,
We slowed the advance of the onrushing Nip.

Then up from "Down Under," dispatched by MacArthur,
Came the first Yankee Doughboys to engage in the war.
They settled in Moresby, but it wasn't so long,

My Father

'Fore they were landed by plane on the north Guinea shore.
Who'll ever forget Buna, Sanananda or Finsch,
Where the Japs gave ground stubbornly, by the inch –
Where the trails running north are littered with dead
And the road to Tokyo lay straight ahead.

There, the ball started rolling; our team looked fine
The Marines struck at Gloucester and you could hear Tojo howl
When the mighty First Cavalry charged west of Rabaul.
The jig was up but the Nips little knew
That these were the tactics which would seal their doom.
We gathered momentum for the drive to the goal
As the folks back home delivered the coal.

The ships and planes were coming at last;
It won't be as tough as it was in the past.
We'll have all we asked for—power to spare,
To dig the miserable bastards out of their lair.

And when we make it too hot on hell's top shelf,
We'll singe his feet and expose the elf;
We'll grind him to dust in the jungle brush.

Drive on you Yankees, we must avenge the men who died on Bataan.
We said we would and our word is good -----
We're coming back as soon as we can.

By, Irving Bennett
1st. Lt. Cavalry

General Orders   Headquarters First Cavalry Division

No.   6   APO 201, 13 April 1944

Unit Citation
[The Presidential Unit Citation]

Under the provisions of Executive Order 9396 (Section I, Bulletin, 22 War Department, 1943), as amplified by Section IV, Circular 333, War Department, 22 December 1943, the 2nd Squadron, 5th Cavalry, is cited for extraordinary heroism in overcoming unusually difficult and hazardous conditions in battle.

On 29 February 1944, this unit landing on Los Negros Island, Admiralty group, New Guinea, which was held by a determined, entrenched enemy in greatly superior numerical strength, quickly destroyed the immediate enemy defense, established its beachhead, and occupied the enemy airstrip within a few hours. The forcefulness and aggressiveness of its assault overwhelmed the enemy initially, and the brave spirit of the personnel of the Squadron permitted the early seizure of a secure hold on the enemy territory. In subsequent operations for three days and three nights, the 2nd Squadron valiantly extended the controlled area by day and initiated the work prescribed in its mission under enemy fire, and by night stood by its defenses and repulsed determined and continuous infiltrating and harassing groups of the enemy, and on the second and third nights repulsed concerted counter-attacks in such force that annihilation of the Squadron might easily have resulted, except for the grim determination with which the Squadron maintained its defenses. (AG 201.22)

Innis P. Swift
Major General, U.S. Army
Commanding

The Admiralty Island campaign was officially closed on
May 18, 1944.

**2ⁿᵈ Lt. Bennett in Australia After Completion
of OCS. Oct. 1943**

**April 3, 1944. 1ˢᵗ Lt. Bennett at the Momote
Airstrip After a Month of Jungle Combat**

Chapter Nine

For the next six months the 5th Cavalry Regiment continued to train and conduct combat exercises on Koruniat and shore up defenses on Los Negros and Manus. It was also a period of time where a sense of normalcy, albeit military normalcy, returned to the men's lives. Instead of spending days fighting their way through the jungle and nights living in foxholes, they lived in tents and slept on cots; they had showers and ate hot meals and engaged in recreation, and for the first time since they left Australia there was regular mail delivery.

For my father, however, the time on Koruniat also meant suffering three relapses of malaria, for which he was treated and then, as he put it, "I was able to perform."

※ ※ ※

When General MacArthur was driven out of the Philippines in early 1942 and he famously vowed, *"I Shall Return,"* given the General's determination, his standing within the United States military, and his enormous popularity among the American people, not to mention his close relationship with and influence on President Roosevelt, there was little doubt in anyone's mind that MacArthur would deliver on his promise.

But retaking the Philippines meant far more than redeeming the famous commander's pledge or satisfying his infamous ego. His strategy of establishing air and naval bases to isolate and then destroy the enemy through attrition made control of the Philippine Archipelago essential. In so doing, MacArthur could choke-off the enemy's supply of vital war materials, cut his lines of communication, and put Allied naval, air, and ground forces to within striking distance of Japan itself.

Conversely, for Imperial Japan, control of the Philippines was critical to ensure its continuing supply of petroleum from the occupied Dutch East Indies.[28] Without a steady flow of oil, Japan's navy would have no means to fuel its warships; and without a viable naval force, Japan would likely lose the war in the pacific.

Consequently, Japanese warlords drew up aggressive and even desperate battle plans for the archipelago, reinforced their garrison in the Philippines, and installed their most legendary commander, Lieutenant General Tomoyuki Yamashita, the so-called "Tiger of Malaya,"[29] as the Commander-in-Chief of the Philippine Defenses.

During the first week of October 1944, the entire 1st Cavalry Division was moved from Koruniat Island to

---

28 Japan seized the area in late 1941 in order to exploit the region's oil fields and rubber plantations.

29 While commanding the Japanese 25th Army, in December 1941, Yamashita invaded Malaya and, using only 30,000 front-line troops, captured more than 100,000 British, Australian, and Indian troops. Yamashita's stunning military victory in Malaya marked "the single largest surrender of British-led forces in history," thus earning him the nom de guerre "The Tiger of Malaya."

Manus Island. From October 7th through October 10th, the Division engaged in amphibious warfare exercises and intelligence briefings in preparation for the invasion of Leyte Island.

Besides being the ideal strategic location to begin the battle for the Philippines, Leyte had special meaning to the GIs: the Japanese 16th Division, the outfit believed responsible for the notorious Bataan Death March, was garrisoned there.

On the morning of October 11th, the entire 1st Cavalry Division boarded troop transports of Admiral Kinkaid's 7th Fleet anchored in Seeadler Harbor. The 2nd Squadron of the 5th Cavalry Regiment, my father's unit, embarked on the naval attack transport the USS Herald. At 2:40 P.M., the convoy left Seeadler and steamed northward toward the Philippines.

Leyte is a 2,785 square-mile, irregularly shaped island located practically midpoint in the Philippine Archipelago. In 1944, the island's population, comprised mostly of rural farmers, fisherman, and their families, was about one million.

The island is essentially divided into two large valleys—Leyte Valley in the east and Ormoc Valley in the west—by a large, densely forested, north-south mountain range.

To the north of Leyte and separated by the narrow San Juanico Strait connecting the Sulu Sea with Leyte Gulf is the island of Samar. To the south and separated by the Surigao Strait, which joins the Bohol Sea with Leyte Gulf, is Mindanao Island.

Leyte had two main roads: Highway 1 and Highway 2. Contrary to the image their designation conjures, these thoroughfares were little more than dirt roads; wide in some places, narrow in others. Highway 1 was located about a mile inland and paralleled the island's eastern shore. Highway 2 intersected Highway 1 just south of the northeastern capital city of Tacloban and ran westward along the northern coast, through the northern base of the mountains, south through the Ormoc Valley, and then across the southern Leyte Valley and ending on the east coast. Combined, Highways 1 and 2 effectively encircled the island.

Besides the main mountain range, whose elevations reach up to four thousand feet, Leyte's topography consists of many smaller hills, large plains, and numerous swamps, ponds, creeks and several large rivers. The inland soil consists primarily of clay. Like Los Negros, Leyte's climate is typically tropical with an average rainfall of approximately one hundred and fifty inches per year.

From a military perspective, Leyte's deep harbors and sandy beaches made the island ideally suited for large naval vessels and amphibious assaults. In addition, its expansive plains provided ample space for establishing airstrips. Most importantly, perhaps, the island is situated approximately three hundred air miles from the Philippine capital of Manila, which is located on Luzon, the largest island in the Philippine chain and where General Yamashita had established his headquarters.

The Sixth Army was designated as the main combat force for the invasion of Leyte.

Still under the command of Lieutenant General Walter Krueger, the Sixth Army was comprised of two corps—X Corps and XXIV Corps, each consisting of two divisions. The 1st Cavalry Division was assigned to X Corps.

Shortly after departing Seeadler Harbor, the troop ships met up with another convoy carrying the soldiers of the 24th, 96th, and 7th Infantry Divisions, swelling the number of combat troops to over thirty thousand. The invasion of Leyte would commence with the largest amphibious landing of the war in the Pacific thus far.

The transport ships slipped through Leyte Gulf and into the dark waters of San Pedro Bay off Leyte's eastern shore in the predawn of October 20, 1944.

As the first rays of sunlight broke through the darkness, the GIs lining the decks of the transports looked out over the bay and were awestruck by what they saw—to the north, east, and south, as far as the eye could see there were warships—over seven hundred of them: To the west was the dark outline of Leyte Island.

As the men of the invasion force gazed in awe at the gargantuan gathering of naval power, a lone enemy bomber, the kind the GIs called a Betty, came in low from the north.

Despite an eruption of hundreds of naval guns discharging tons of ammunition, the Betty ran the miles-long gauntlet of warships and disappeared to the south, unscathed. After the surreal event, the warships turned their guns westward and began pounding the landing area and other pre-assigned targets inland.

The scene was a familiar one to the soldiers of the 5th Cavalry's 2nd Squadron, but the scale and intensity of the bombardment dwarfed that which preceded the landing on Los Negros.

In the dim light of morning, amidst the cacophony of war, once again the iconic figure of General MacArthur appeared at the railing of a navy cruiser. The Commander-in-Chief, ears plugged against the deafening roar of the naval guns and wearing the trademark hat he had worn on Bataan, intently stared through field glasses, watching the pounding of enemy positions and scanning the beach for the ideal spot to fulfill his sacred promise to return to the Philippines.

After a protracted three-hour bombardment and multiple waves of carrier-based fighter-bombers flying sorties over the landing area, the signal to deploy was given and the men of the 1st Cavalry Division, once again, steeled themselves for combat.

At the Los Negros invasion, which was initially planned as a reconnaissance mission, there was no fleet of vessels packed with supplies and armored vehicles, and the GI's were provided a minimum supply of ammunition and rations. At Leyte, accompanying the assault force were dozens of great cargo ships packed with equipment, weapons, supplies, and what amounted to several tons of ammunition per soldier.

As the men of the 5th Cavalry's 2nd Squadron climbed down the rope ladders of the USS Herald into the waiting Higgins boats, every GI was weighed down with a fully loaded pack that included a change of clothing, two days worth of three-meals-a-day rations, a gas mask, rain gear, and items of personal hygiene. In addition, each soldier carried three canteens of water, his personal weapon, grenades, and plenty of ammunition. The soldiers of the heavy machine gun platoons also had to shoulder their crew-manned weapons, tripods, and steel boxes filled with belts of .30 caliber ammunition.

Once fully loaded, amidst a growing and dense shroud of black and yellow smoke, like they had done at Los Negros the landing craft motored out to a line of departure from where they would make their final run to the beach.

San Pedro Bay. Oct. 20, 1944 (U.S. Signal Corps)

As the carrier-based planes attacked the island and the naval guns belched out violent billows of fire and smoke, my father stood once more in one of the small wooden craft waiting for the signal to head to shore on another military invasion of World War II. But this time as the shells screamed overhead, he and the other veterans of Los Negros weren't cheering: they knew what war looked, smelled, and felt like.

Like most of the men waiting to hit the beach, my father wondered, for just a moment, if this is where his luck would run out.

The mile-wide landing area where X Corps would storm ashore extended from Tacloban on the northeast coast to the mouth of the Palo River on the south. The 5th Cavalry Regiment was assigned to assault the northern flank of the landing zone, just south of Tacloban.

After arriving ashore, the entire Division would come under the authority of Major General Verne D. Mudge, as General Swift had been moved to another command.

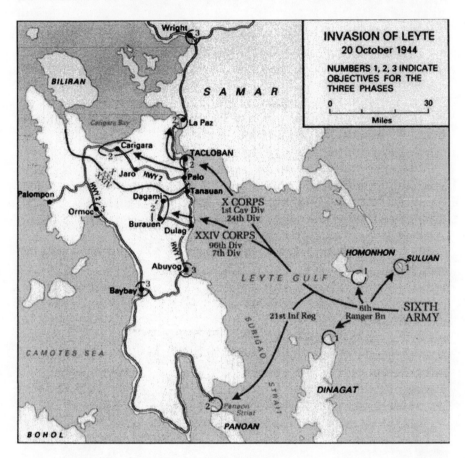

At 9:50 A.M., under continuing naval gunfire and airstrikes, the Higgins boats, escorted by LCIs[30] delivering murderous barrages of machine gun fire and rockets, left the line of departure and plowed through the dark, choppy waters toward the island.

About fifty yards shy of the beach, the Higgins boats stopped and the bow ramps were released.

---

30 Landing Craft Infantry. Ships specially designed for close-in fire support using machine guns and rockets during amphibious landings.

This time wading into four-foot deep water, the GIs slowly slogged forward. At 10:00 A.M., the first wave reached the beach. Succeeding waves came in at five-minute intervals. By 10:30 the entire Regiment was ashore and hugging the wet sand of the bomb-cratered embankment on Leyte's debris-strewn White Beach.

After establishing a beachhead, the 5th Cavalry Regiment began a one-mile advance straight inland to take up positions west of Highway 1, just south of the Highway 2 junction. Other 1st Cavalry units proceeded north to Tacloban, where they were to secure the critically important airdrome. The remainder of the Division moved northwesterly to seize and occupy the high ground overlooking San Jaunico Strait in order to secure the waterway and guard the northern flank of the beachhead.

In the southern zone of the landing area, soldiers of the 24th Infantry Division advanced westward toward the high ground that overlooked the beach and from where they had been receiving enemy machine gun and rifle fire.

Shortly after the 5th Cavalry began its push inland their advance slowed to a near stop when they hit a tallgrass-covered chest-deep swamp. The area had been mapped out in the pre-invasion planning, but a typhoon that hit the island two days before the landing had dramatically increased the size and depth of the bog.

After repeated trips across the swamp to move all of their equipment, and prying leeches off of their skin, the cavalrymen advanced to their objective about five yards past Highway 1.

My father's voice:

"...My platoon was dispatched to a certain area... where we would march a certain distance, I don't recall

just how much, and build a perimeter. On the way, we encountered a troop of Filipinos commanded by a colonel by the name of Hilario Moncado. This is a name to remember, for two reasons. One, he was unforgettable because he was over six feet tall, and that's most unusual for a Filipino; the other, you will come to learn as time goes by."

Hilario Camino Moncado was a native Filipino from the island of Cebu. The son of wealthy landowners, Moncado was a precocious and idealistic teenager who at fifteen years old decided to travel to Hawaii and join the ranks of Filipino migrant farm workers. Eventually moving to the mainland, as an adult, Moncado founded the Filipino Federation of America, before returning to the Philippines.

In 1934, Moncado managed to get himself elected to a minor position in the Philippine Commonwealth's Constitutional Convention. He founded the "Filipino Crusaders World Army" and, emulating General MacArthur— complete with replica uniform, crusher hat, aviator-style sunglasses, and corncob pipe—declared himself the "Supreme Commander-in-Chief" with the rank of "Five Star General."

When World War II broke out, Moncado formed one of the numerous small Filipino guerilla groups, many of which played pivotal roles in the eventual liberation of the Philippines. As my father alluded to, October 20, 1944, near Leyte's Highway 1 would not be the last time or place that he would cross paths with this charismatic character.

5th Cavalry combat patrols were dispatched to Hill 669 and Hill 1300, the next objectives.

The patrols made contact with the enemy about three-quarters of a mile south of the village of Caibaan.

In the ensuing firefight, one GI was killed and two others were wounded; ten of the enemy died.

Because of increasing enemy resistance and rough terrain, the Regiment stopped advancing some three hundred yards short of the objectives. At 9:35 P.M., the men dug in for the night.

While the assault force was advancing inland, activity at the beach was mounting. A continuous stream of naval vessels entered the already clogged harbor and thousands of soldiers and tons of equipment poured ashore.

General MacArthur, accompanied by the soon-to-be-installed Philippine president, Sergio Osmena,[31] and surrounded by a phalanx of officers and soldiers, waded ashore and proceeded to a hastily set-up radio system from where the General dramatically broadcast to the Filipino people his long awaited and historic return.

When the troops learned of his landing on Leyte, many of the GIs dismissed MacArthur's arrival and his dramatic speech as typical histrionics. Many believed the false rumors that he had abandoned the men on Bataan, and that his subsequent evacuation from Corregidor, which preceded the surrender of the troops there and General Wainwright's capture, were cowardly acts and they referred to him as "Dugout Doug." That attitude and the contemptuous moniker angered my father. MacArthur had moved his command from Manila to Corregidor after he had been driven off of Luzon; that was not abandonment; it was preserving the command so that he could continue to lead the troops. On Corregidor, the General had braved weeks of enemy air attacks while trying to organize defenses from a concrete bunker where he stayed together with his wife and child. He departed that besieged island only after multiple orders from President Roosevelt who wanted him to take command of the forces in the Southwest Pacific Area; that

---

31 Osmena was vice president under Manuel Quezon, who died in exile in 1944.

was not cowardice, it would have been insubordination not do so.

To my father, General MacArthur was the consummate military leader who sought victory while preserving the lives of his men and had amply demonstrated his courage under fire throughout his military career.

By the end of the first day of the campaign to liberate the Philippines forty-nine American servicemen had lost their lives, hundreds more had been wounded, and six were missing in action. For the 2nd Squadron of the 5th Cavalry Regiment it was a particularly bad day. While leading a reconnaissance patrol, the regimental commander, Colonel Royce Drake, and his men came under enemy fire and took cover in some underbrush. Unable to retreat and cut off from the rest of the Squadron, Drake was shot; he died about two hours later.

On October 21st at approximately 8:00 A.M., the Regiment was ordered to advance with both squadrons abreast—the 1st Squadron on the right flank, the 2nd Squadron on the left—to Hills 669 and 1300, northwest of the town of Caibaan.

As the Regiment entered Caibaan, they came under enemy sniper fire but were otherwise able to pass through without incident.

But when the cavalrymen approached the objectives, they ran into heavy resistance from enemy troops dug in near the base of Hill 669. The following is my father's description of what happened next:

"We had trapped about fifty of 'em. After signaling that they wanted to surrender, we ordered them to walk towards our position, their hands above their heads. The Japs didn't surrender and were tricky and known to conceal weapons, so when they got a certain distance from us, we ordered 'em to stop and strip. Suddenly, a guy in

the front falls on his hands and knees with a machine gun strapped to his back and two of the others manned the gun and began firing. From then on we changed our policy on taking prisoners."[32]

In the wake of the incident, the regimental command issued a stern warning that front-line units should call in artillery strikes before advancing on suspected enemy positions.

Later that day, the 2nd Squadron took up positions on Hill 669 and dug in for the night.

At sunrise the following morning, the Regiment, less elements of the 2nd Squadron, continued its northwesterly advance into the hills overlooking the villages of Caibaan and Pawing and the city of Tacloban.

As the day wore on, the already hot, muggy air got even steamier and it began to rain. By mid-morning the Regiment began losing men to exhaustion and dehydration. A request was made to allow the troops to descend into the cooler valley region. However, due to the nearby presence of enemy troops, the request was denied. After reaching their objectives, the exhausted GIs dug in for the night, as native carriers delivered desperately needed water, rations, and other supplies to their positions.

At 1:00 A.M. on October 23rd, an order was relayed to the 5th Cavalry's intelligence officer to prepare two buglers (without bugles), a platoon of thirty enlisted men and one officer armed with carbines, and five jeeps with drivers to report to Tacloban by 10:30 that morning. Further instructions were given that the men should be "clean shaven, wearing full field uniforms (minus pack),

---

32 The 5th Cavalry Historical Report states, "...the Japs waved a white flag as though to surrender. As our heavy machine guns were moving into position and the troops signaling the Japs to disrobe they unexpectedly opened fire wounding five of our men. Automatic weapons fire was placed on them killing thirteen, the remainder withdrawing over Hill 669 and contact was lost."

and cleaned up as good as possible."[33] At 7:35 A.M., the procession, led by Lieutenant John Gregory of Weapons Troop, left from the Caibaan/Pawing area to act as an honor guard for General MacArthur, who would conduct a brief ceremony installing Sergio Osmena as the President of the Philippine Commonwealth and designate Tacloban as the temporary capital of the Philippines.

While the ceremony was underway, the 5th Cavalry moved its regimental command post to Caibaan and relocated the 1st Squadron there. The 2nd Squadron remained on Hill 669 and three other hills, taking cover from occasional sniper fire and sending out reconnaissance patrols.

At 2:10 in the afternoon, one of the 2nd Squadron's hilltop outposts reported seeing four enemy tanks accompanied by infantry approximately two thousand yards from their position. The coordinates were reported to artillery units and the area was soon blanketed with shells.

The only diversion the 2nd Squadron had from the tough situation in the Caibaan Hills came from watching Allied planes and anti-aircraft batteries intercepting enemy fighters, which provided "...spectacular displays of aerial combat and AA fire."[34]

On October 27th, the first American P-38 fighter-bombers came roaring in over the island. That same day, the 5th Cavalry began preparations for an approximate thirty-mile westward push through the swamps, plains, and barrios of northern Leyte Valley.

---

33   5th Cavalry Regiment Historical Report.
34   5th Cavalry Regiment Historical Report.

Chapter Ten

General MacArthur's overall strategy to defeat the Japanese on Leyte was simple: stage a massive advance and herd the enemy into the Ormoc area on the western side of the island, and then annihilate them.

Although MacArthur's strategy was well thought out and perfectly planned, others in the Allied chain of command did not yet appreciate just how shrewd and fanatical the Japanese would be. After a week into the Leyte campaign, this naïveté proved to be almost disastrous.

As X Corps was preparing to advance westward, reports from Filipino guerilla units indicated that the enemy was in the process of building strong defensive positions at the northern port city of Carigara. In response, an attack was planned and the mission was assigned to the 1st Cavalry Division.

On October 29th, at 11:30 A.M., the entire 5th Cavalry Regiment was loaded onto trucks and transported nine miles east to the town of Alangalang. While the 1st Squadron remained there, the 2nd Squadron marched an additional three miles to Cavite, arriving at 5:00 P.M.

At 8:00 P.M. a typhoon struck.

After waiting out the storm, at 8:00 A.M. on the 31st, on orders of General Chase, the 2nd Squadron began a nine-mile westward march toward Carigara via the town of San Miguel. Their mission was to support the attack on the city.

After arriving at San Miguel at12:00 P.M., reconnaissance patrols were dispatched.

The patrols returned with reports of enemy troops in the area and that seven bridges spanning the Mainit River, which the Squadron would have to cross in order to advance on Carigara, had been burnt. D Troop, my father's unit, was dispatched to guard the remaining bridges.

While at San Miguel, the Squadron received reports from natives that small groups of Japanese in the area had been looting their shacks for food and in some instances beating and bayoneting villagers, before retreating toward the western hills. A combat patrol was dispatched which located and killed twenty enemy soldiers holding three Filipinos captive in a native shack.

On the morning of November 1st, following the usual artillery preparations, the 2nd Squadron advanced about five miles westward through a mix of swamps, marshes, and tall grass.

At 2:35 P.M., the Squadron arrived at the small village of Barugo where contact was made with the 7th Cavalry Regiment, the outfit that would be leading the attack on Carigara.

Natives again brought reports of groups of fifty to one hundred enemy soldiers in the area.

The next morning, following intense artillery barrages, the 7th Cavalry pushed into Carigara. However, when the GIs entered the city they found it deserted. The Japanese defensive preparations there, it turned out, had been a diversion.

After securing area, the 2nd Squadron returned to 5th Cavalry command and began mopping-up operations to clear Leyte Valley of enemy troops in preparation for the advance into the mountains that divided Leyte and Ormoc valleys.

My father's narrative continues:

"We engaged in combat activities, marching into the mountains toward the Ormoc corridor, where the Japanese were heavily entrenched. During that period, several days, there were…we were watching dogfights. We had P-38 airplanes, which were twin-boom planes, fighter planes; they were very, very fast. However, the Japanese Zeros were very maneuverable; they could out maneuver the P-38s because they could turn on a dime. So the air force devised a tactic to counteract that, which was sending two P-38s in tandem, one low to the left and one high to the right, and whichever way the Zero turned, one of the planes got 'em, and pretty soon there was no resistance.[35]

"In the ensuing days we came across a horse, a cavalry horse—American, which apparently had landed with a cavalry regiment. I forget the name of the regiment, but Richie Mark's brother, Hank, was in that outfit and they were on Bataan, in the Philippines, and he was in the Death March, and was killed. There's a sequel to this, which will come later."

While the 2nd Squadron was battling its way across northern Leyte Valley toward the ten-mile stretch of mountainous terrain known as the Ormoc corridor, the Imperial High Command had started the offensive to

---

35 In fact, Japanese air attacks increased in the ensuing days. Over the course of the campaign there were more than 450 air raids and hundreds of enemy planes were shot down. It may have been that in my father's area of operation there was little or no enemy air activity. More likely, however, this statement reflects a memory lapse since this was related 55 years after the events took place.

stop MacArthur's forces. My father wasn't aware of it at the time, but the deception at Carigara and the dog-fights between the Zeros and the P-38s that he referred to were part of the opening stages of the enemy's coun-terattack.

From October 25th through November 2nd more than one hundred and seventy-eight enemy vessels steamed into Ormoc Bay. A large percentage of these were barges and transports carrying tens of thousands of combat troops and thousands of tons of weapons, ammunition, and other supplies.

While Japanese reinforcements were arriving at Ormoc, the Imperial Air Force was preparing to launch hundreds of warplanes from their bases on Luzon. On the list of targets was General MacArthur's headquar-ters at Tacloban.

Concurrent to their ground and air offensive prepa-rations, the Japanese were also in the process of com-mitting practically the entire Imperial Fleet for an attack they hoped would destroy U.S. naval forces in Leyte Gulf. After the anticipated naval victory, General Yamashita planned to unleash his ground forces. Yamashita pub-licly boasted that just as in 1942 he had proposed "sur-render or annihilation" to the British commander in Singapore by demanding "Yes! Or No!" he would insist on the same from General MacArthur on Leyte.

As a result of radio intercepts, intelligence from reconnaissance missions, documents taken from enemy dead, and information provided by Filipino guerilla units, U.S. commanders learned of Yamashita's strat-egy and were struggling against moderate resistance and increasingly severe weather to step up operations. The soldiers on the battlefield knew nothing of the ene-my's plans. They only knew that they had been ordered to march into the four thousand-foot high, heavily for-ested mountains toward the Ormoc corridor because that was, as my father put it, *"...where the Japanese were heavily entrenched."*

To understand what the American ground troops faced on Leyte, and to better appreciate what men like my father went through and what the battle of Leyte meant to the outcome of the war in the Pacific, some discussion of the mammoth naval battle that took place in Leyte Gulf between October 24th and October 26th 1944 is important.

When it came to the importance of winning the battle of the Philippines there was no division within the Imperial High Command. However, there was bitter disagreement as to whether the final battle for the Philippines should take place on Leyte or on the main island of Luzon. General Yamashita, who had left Leyte several days before the American invasion there, strongly believed that the emphasis should be placed on defending Luzon, where he had established his command post and amassed the bulk of his forces, including more than a quarter of a million troops.

Imperial General Headquarters, on the other hand, thought that if MacArthur succeeded in taking Leyte, he would achieve a significant strategic advantage and have the time to construct airstrips and otherwise build up Allied offensive capabilities that could overwhelm their forces on Luzon.

Regardless of which strategy Japan would follow, all agreed that neutralizing the U.S. naval forces in Leyte Gulf was critical to halting MacArthur's advance in the Pacific.

To that end, on October 23rd, Japan began implementing a three-pronged plan to destroy the American armada in Leyte Gulf. The so-called SHO plan involved the following:

1. A contingent of aircraft carriers and other vessels that would act as decoy to draw away the Allied naval force in northern Leyte Gulf.
2. A group of warships, including the Yamato, the largest battleship ever built, would advance on Leyte Gulf from the north behind the diverted Allied forces via the San Bernardino Strait.
3. A 2nd fleet of Imperial warships would steam through the Surigao Strait and attack from the southern end of Leyte Gulf.

The plan also involved the most desperate and fanatical tactic of the war: the Kamikazes.

On October 24th Admiral William Halsey, commander of the U.S. Third Fleet stationed in northern Leyte Gulf, responding to sightings made by U.S. submarines and an erroneous report went in pursuit of the Japanese decoy fleet of escort carriers.

After learning of Halsey's pursuit of the enemy's carriers, Admiral Kinkaid broadcast a message to Halsey as to whether a task force had been ordered to protect the northern flank of the invasion forces. But Kinkaid's message did not reach Halsey for some three hours, allowing for the Japanese armada to pass through the San Bernardino Strait unimpeded.[36]

Through aggressive maneuvering and some creative tactics, such as a massive smoke screen to hide the actual size of his forces and making his ships more difficult to target, the commander of a nearby group of American escort carriers and destroyers (code-named Taffy 3), Rear Admiral Clifton Sprague, threw the oncoming enemy's command into a state of "tactical confusion."

---

36 Many have argued, including General MacArthur, the communication failure was caused by the lack of a unified Allied command.

While "in the midst of a maneuver and without forming a battle line," the commander of the Japanese force, Vice Admiral Takeo Kurita, who had established a pattern of knee-jerk reactions in battle, ordered "General Attack" on Taffy 3.

Mistaking the American escort group for something much larger, Kurita's forces began to panic and he lost "all tactical control." After receiving communiqués from Japanese intelligence on Luzon wrongly warning of additional American forces approaching from the north, Kurita feared that his only avenue of escape would be blocked and ordered his forces to retreat back through the San Bernardino Strait.

While all of this was going on in the northern area of the gulf, in the southern sector, Rear Admiral Jesse Oldendorf of Admiral Kinkaid's 7th Fleet had achieved a spectacular victory using a classic naval maneuver called "Crossing the T." By positioning his battleships, cruisers, PT boats, and destroyers in staggered formation across the Surigao Strait, Oldendorf locked the oncoming enemy's southern force into a column formation, severely restricting their targeting ability and leaving them exposed to "the full broadside guns of his warships."

When the smoke cleared over Leyte Gulf on October 26th, dozens of enemy vessels rested at the bottom of the Pacific and the remains of some fifteen thousand Japanese sailors and airmen lay scattered across the waters. Little more than a remnant of the once formidable Imperial Navy limped away from Leyte Gulf never to fight an organized battle again.

During the Battle of Leyte Gulf,[37] the U.S. lost six ships: some nineteen hundred American sailors and airmen perished; most of the casualties were from

---

37 The Battle of Leyte Gulf is often referred to as the largest naval battle in history. To date, it was the last battleship-against-battleship naval engagement.

explosions and fires caused by dozens of Kamikaze attacks.[38]

While the miraculous defeat of the Imperial Navy secured the beachheads and enabled the continuing resupply of American ground forces, it by no means meant that the battle of Leyte was over. The end of the Leyte campaign was still a month away, and the most arduous and bloodiest fighting lay ahead.

---

38   By the end of April 1945, the Japanese had launched more than 2500 Kamikaze attacks.

Chapter Eleven

Before ordering an advance into the mountains, General Krueger needed to protect against enemy reinforcements landing along the northwestern shoreline. X Corps was given the mission to secure the beaches from Carigara to the Capoocan-Pinamopoan area near the northwest tip of the island.

After carefully studying the disposition of Japanese troops, Kreuger developed a plan to block what was likely to be the enemy's strategy for a ground offensive—a drive from the Ormoc area northward and then eastward coupled with a flanking maneuver over the mountains and into Leyte Valley. At the same time Kreuger wanted to continue the advance in order to increase the pressure on the enemy forces, disrupt their attacks, and also herd them into a corner in Ormoc where they could be destroyed.

To accomplish both goals, Krueger ordered units of the Sixth Army to seize Highway 2 in the Capoocan-Pinamopoan area and then advance southward toward Ormoc, and other units in the southern Leyte Valley to advance westward all the way to the coast—destroying all enemy forces in the process—and then drive north-ward to Ormoc City. He also ordered a defensive screen established along the eastern foothills of the mountains in order to block the enemy from advancing over them into Leyte Valley. Upon orders, these blocking units would gradually advance into the mountains and then push southward and "seize all passes and practicable trails." The 24th Infantry Division was assigned the job of seizing Capoocan-Pinamopoan. The mission of set-ting up the defensive screen in the northern sector and then advancing into the mountains was assigned to the 1st Cavalry Division.

On November 3rd, the 1st Cavalry Division spent the day consolidating its forces near Carigara. The 2nd Squadron of the 5th Cavalry Regiment remained holding Barugo and the 1st Squadron did likewise at Cavite.

At 7:00 A.M. the following day, the 2nd Squadron was alerted to move from Barugo to Cavite to take up the 1st Squadron's positions while the 1st Squadron moved several miles southwest to the village of Tunga. The day took a gruesome turn when at about 3:00 P.M., a native brought the head of a Japanese soldier to the regimen-tal command post, stating that he had "killed the Jap" earlier in the day and that he was part of a group of about twenty-four unarmed enemy soldiers moving westward toward the mountains. Later that same day, a Japanese officer and his runner approached 5th Cav-alry positions in order to deliver a message to what they thought was the Japanese 41st Infantry Regiment. Real-izing their mistake a little too late, the two were killed as they tried to flee.

By November 5th, the 24th Infantry Division had com-pleted its mission of seizing Capoocan-Pinamopoan and began advancing southward. However, on the 6th, the

Japanese launched a counterattack and pushed the Americans all the way back to the northern coast. In so doing, the Japanese took control of an important and extremely rugged area of high ground named "Breakneck Ridge." After a weeklong, bitter, and bloody battle, the GIs retook the ridge, killing all of the enemy forces and securing the area.

Leyte Advance (Acme)

Also on November 6th, elements of the 1st Cavalry Division began their advance into the mountains. The 2nd Squadron of the 5th Regiment advanced westward on a mission to defend the town of Jaro, just east of the foothills, and to patrol the area between Jaro and Carigara Bay.

In response to reports that several hundred enemy soldiers, dressed as guerillas, civilians, and American GIs, were moving through the area, and other reports that the vicinity was "infested with Japs," heavy artillery concentrations were laid down to the front of the 2nd Squadron's positions.

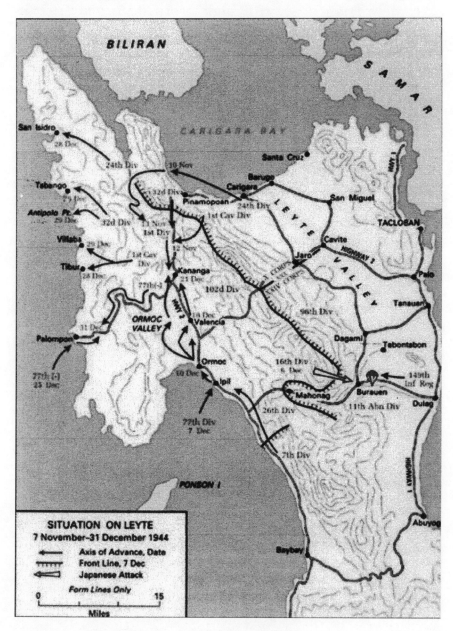

SITUATION ON LEYTE
7 November–31 December 1944

- ← Axis of Advance, Date
- ⊤⊤⊤⊤⊤ Front Line, 7 Dec
- ⇐ Japanese Attack

Form Lines Only

0   15

Miles

On November 7th, two enemy attacks were launched against the 2nd Squadron, killing fourteen GIs. On the same day, the island was hit with another typhoon.

Operations of the 5th Cavalry persisted over the next three days with the 2nd Squadron continuing to hold Jaro and securing the mountain passes along a two mile stretch from Mt. Pina on the north to Mt. Mamban on the south. Patrols were also sent out in preparation for the Squadron's advance into the mountains.

For the 2nd Squadron, moving into the mountains meant operating in terrain similar to what they had come to know and hate on Los Negros. However, the mountains of Leyte promised an even larger-scale and more punishing version of what the GIs endured on the jungle-covered hills of Los Negros.

Operating in the Ormoc corridor meant the men would often be hacking their way through dense jungle one yard at a time, grasping vines and bushes in order to climb or descend the steep, muddy mountainsides. It would also mean marching for days along treacherous mountain ridges that snaked through hundreds of square miles of enemy-infested territory.

The Japanese were experts at deception and after the American Invasion of Leyte had started, they were busy strategically lacing the mountains with camouflaged caves, bunkers, pillboxes, and booby traps.

The torrential rains of the typhoons had transformed the already soggy mountain passes and trails into ribbons of mud and normally peaceful mountain streams into raging torrents. And when, not if, another typhoon hit, seventy miles per hour gale-force winds would buffet the increasingly weary GIs. At night, a precipitous drop in temperature would chill them in their perpetually soaked and mud-caked fatigues. Despite preventative measures, diseases such as malaria, dengue fever, and jungle rot[39] would reach epidemic proportions and combined with combat casualties reduce their fighting strength to about fifty percent of the army's recommended number for this type of operation. The majority of these losses, about seventy-six percent, would occur in the infantry units.

Beginning with their advance into the mountains on November 11th, over the next three and a half weeks my father's platoon alternated between taking up defensive or screening positions and directly supporting an excruciatingly slow advance. During this period, as it was on Los Negros, sleep deprivation became the norm.

Every night on mountains that were often shrouded in dense fog, the men dug their muddy foxholes and established their perimeters and final protective lines. Due to the constant threat of enemy infiltration they ringed their perimeters with booby-trapped grenades.

As had occurred on Los Negros, enemy infiltrators often cut phone lines and much of the communications equipment that had survived the original landing became inoperable due to the practically incessant rain. Supplies could only be hand carried into the mountains by paid natives, or "Cargidores," who often became too fatigued to climb the mountain trails. Consequently, units frequently ran low on ammunition and had to subsist on one-third K-ration per day.

The following extract from an Associated Press report starkly illustrates the conditions and the fighting in the Ormoc corridor:

GENERAL MACARTHUR'S HEADQUARTERS, Philippines, Tuesday. Nov. 21 (AP)—Lashed by the third

---

39 "Jungle rot" is a severe bacterial, soft-tissue infection.

typhoon of the Leyte Island campaign, mud-begrimed American infantrymen fought off a new Japanese counter-attack and continuous armor-led pressure to close their grip around trapped enemy remnants in Northern Ormoc corridor, headquarters reported today.

Fierce winds and walls of rain hammered the fighting fronts, disrupted communications and challenged Leyte-based American airmen who, nevertheless, took to the air for offensive and defensive action...The Yanks repulsed another enemy counterattack west of Ormoc road, where a three-hour bloody battle was reported in Monday's communiqué...[40]

On November 29th, an enemy force consisting of about two companies (approximately two hundred soldiers) launched an attack against the 12th Cavalry on Mt. Cabungangan severing their supply line. My father's platoon and a platoon from A Troop were called in to support a counterattack to recover the position. Shortly before nightfall, the combined forces opened fire. However, enemy machine gun fire pinned them down and they were forced to remain in their positions throughout the night. At daybreak, with the assistance of additional reinforcements, the GIs launched a new and stronger counterattack. After a vicious all-day battle that included close-support from U.S' mortar teams, the Americans regained the position and secured the supply line. About half of the enemy forces had been killed, the remainder fled into the surrounding jungle.

In lieu of operable communications equipment in the corridor, squads were often sent out on two and three day extended patrols to make contact with various units to determine their locations, coordinate advances, gather intelligence, and assess the need for supplies.

40   Palm Beach Post Nov 21, 1944.

On December 4th, my father embarked on just such a patrol:[41]

"...I was then given an assignment to take a squad... patrol...to go a certain distance on a certain azimuth—an azimuth being a point on the compass—and to make contact with one of our own outfits that was to be found in that area to tell them where our unit was and to find out whatever we could; whether they had difficulty, whether they needed any further supplies, or whatever. This we did, and we found the outfit, and delivered the message. And then the following morning...we slept there that night...and the following morning we started out to go back to our outfit...so...umm...on the march at some point, I got very weary, and...umm...I was breaking out with chills and fever. The malaria had returned. And, so, we pulled off into the bush, off the trail, and the four soldiers with me took their shirts off and put their bodies up against mine, in a circle, so that they would keep me warm. During the night, we heard enemy troops marching just feet away from us. We kept very quiet and had our guns pointed in that direction in the event that we were spotted. However, we were not spotted, and the next morning we moved out and went to Tacloban where they took me to the aid station. I was examined, and then was sent aboard the ship...the hospital ship Mercy,[42] to be transported to Finschhafen, New Guinea, where the general hospital was. During the night there was a Kamikaze attack in the harbor. Of course the Mercy was lit up, which is par for the course, you know, hospital ships do not black out, and the international code of ethics in warfare (chuckling) is such that you don't shoot at a hospital ship. Anyway, all that night sailors were being brought

---

41 In the 5th Cavalry Unit Journal, at 1844 hours, entry number 28, this patrol is referenced as follows: ""D" Tr patrol at 1830 is 1 ½ miles on an azimuth of 210 degrees from hill 1234 bivouacing [sic] there for the night."
42 During the Leyte campaign, hospital ships evacuated only 848 GIs.

aboard the hospital ship Mercy with severe burns due to the Kamikaze attack on the ship in the harbor. So, we finally got to Finschhafen,[43] New Guinea, and they took me to the general hospital and they treated me and then... uh...we found out, in a couple of days, that the Mercy, deadheading back to Leyte, with five hundred doctors and nurses aboard, was torpedoed and all hands went down with the ship.[44]

Due to a shortage of litter bearers, my father, in fact, struggled for three days to hike out of the mountains and didn't make it to the hospital at Tacloban until December 9th. He was lucky: this time he was suffering a potentially fatal case of malaria. He had spent forty-six days in combat on Leyte.

The fighting on Leyte continued throughout December. The 5th Cavalry Regiment successfully advanced into the Ormoc Valley while continuously engaging enemy troops. Before the ground forces arrived at Ormoc Bay, sustained Allied air, artillery, and naval attacks had taken a devastating toll on Japanese ships and personnel. Although mopping-up operations continued into January, the Leyte campaign was officially declared closed on December 25, 1944.

In excess of three thousand American soldiers sacrificed their lives and tens of thousands of others were wounded or stricken by disease during the liberation of Leyte. Estimates as to the number of General Yamashita's forces killed range from forty-nine thousand to

---

43   He was actually taken to the hospital on Hollandia, New Guinea.
44   While the Japanese did indeed target hospital ships during the war, killing and wounding many, I have not found any report that the USNS Mercy was ever attacked. There was a kamikaze attack that hit the USNS Comfort in April of that year. My father's statement is likely the result of an erroneous rumor of the time.

fifty-six thousand. The Japanese 16th Division was completely wiped out.

Besides the massive and remarkably successful military operation, U.S. forces engaged in an impressive humanitarian effort on Leyte. Starting as early as mid-January and continuing throughout the military campaign, tens of thousands of tons of relief materials, including food, medicines, and clothing, were delivered to the island and distributed to tens of thousands of refugees. All of this was accomplished during a period of frequent enemy air attacks and when getting any supplies ashore posed enormous logistical problems due to the shortage of non-combat manpower. After the fighting ended, U.S. military commanders helped establish the island's new government, and army engineers supervised and assisted in the repair of buildings, the construction and labor for which was paid for by the U.S. Government. Hospitals and dispensaries were set up throughout the island, and some five hundred schools were started. My father was honored to have played a role in the military operation and grateful to have survived, but what made him most proud to be an American was the humanitarian effort conducted on behalf of the people of Leyte.

With the success of the Leyte campaign General MacArthur regained an important foothold in the Philippines. Nevertheless, the Japanese troops on Luzon numbered more than two hundred and fifty thousand and there were over one hundred airstrips on the island that were stocked with over a thousand warplanes. And in addition to the now swelling ranks of the Kamikazes, the Japanese, in their ever-increasing desperation and fanaticism, had established a large fleet of suicide boats and recruited thousands of young volunteers to ram these bomb-fitted vessels into Allied ships.

For Imperial Japan, the coming battle of Luzon meant their last stand before having to defend their homeland.

To my father, the pending battle meant that it likely wouldn't be long before he was taking part in another amphibious assault on another Pacific island.

Chapter Twelve

My father arrived at the 54th General Hospital in Hollandia, New Guinea, on December 13, 1944. When he left for the invasion of Los Negros in February, the Japanese still occupied a large portion of the enormous island, including Hollandia, and the thirty-five-hundred-bed hospital did not exist.

During the 3rd week of April 1944, while my father was on leave in Sydney, consequential to his capture of five Japanese soldiers, American forces executed an amphibious landing on the northeastern shore of New Guinea near the town of Hollandia. Once again, General MacArthur came ashore shortly after the initial waves of the invasion force landed. Within a few days, Hollandia and the surrounding area were securely in Allied hands.

As similar island campaigns were waged throughout the Southwest Pacific in preparation for the invasion of the Philippines, the need for medical facilities to treat injured and sick soldiers grew proportionately; the epidemic of malaria being the largest contributing factor: Over the course of the war, approximately half a million

174

men contracted the disease, more than sixty thousand of them died.

Since my father had been compliant with taking Atabrine after his experience on Los Negros, his subsequent bouts with malaria were probably the results of relapses. In any event, this time his disease could not simply be treated with a dose of Atabrine or Quinine and he had to be hospitalized.

Although he was temporarily out of action, my father was not intent on letting things stay that way. He wanted to get back to his unit and complete the retaking of the Philippines.

My father:

"...during my brief stay at the hospital[45]... one day Colonel Culp walked in...and saw me...came over to talk to me, asked me a lot of questions about what had happened. Obviously he had not come with us when we went to Australia; he stayed back at Fort Bliss. And when he heard my story, found out that I had been wounded and all that, he said to me, 'How would you like to join my outfit?' I said, 'What outfit is that?' He says, 'I'm with General MacArthur's Headquarters. I'm in charge of the..."

My father's voice faltered at this point and he suddenly stopped the tape for reasons that will soon become clear.

My father responded well to treatment and on January 12th he was discharged from the hospital and attached to the 21st Replacement Depot.

---

45 His personnel record states that he was hospitalized for 30 days.

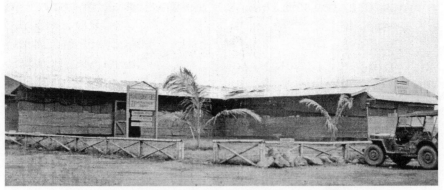

HQ 21ˢᵗ. Repl. Depot (courtesy Joe Rodimak)

Set up in Hollandia on a plot of cleared jungle just below the ridge where the 54ᵗʰ General Hospital was located, the 21ˢᵗ Replacement Depot was a bleak place. Its infrastructure consisted of a few dirt paths and its accommodations were tents. A large shack cobbled together from spare container wood and tin served as headquarters. The 21ˢᵗ functioned primarily as a processing center for soldiers awaiting assignment for various reasons; most predominantly combat related injuries or illness. Soldiers at the 21ˢᵗ who were in-between assignments were classified as "casuals."

Prior to his hospitalization, my father was what the army called a "line officer," 'line' being short for battle line. A high percentage of line officers wound up either dead or injured, for obvious reasons. And since my father was a living line officer and in possession of all of his limbs and mental faculties, and experienced line officers awaiting assignment was a highly prized species, he was likely going to be returned to combat.

Like most combat officers, my father was eager to rejoin his platoon. But the army's system made it unlikely that he would return to his men. When my father was taken out of combat for an indeterminate period of time, his platoon was assigned another commander. But there was another reason he would not return to his unit, and for a combat soldier, it was perhaps the most painful reason of all.

While my father was at the 54th General Hospital, the medical officer in-charge of his case decided based on his repeated bouts with malaria that if my father returned to combat, he would likely suffer more relapses of the disease. And a sick soldier, particularly an officer in-charge of a front-line combat unit, was a risk to himself and to his men. Therefore, the medical officer classified my father, "Permanent limited service," effectively ending his combat career.

From the day that the Japanese attacked Pearl Harbor my father wanted to be in a combat outfit. He had worked agonizingly hard for three years toward that goal and he had fought in the front lines of two brutal island campaigns commanding the same platoon. Men in combat develop a bond so close they are willing to die for each other. The medical officer's decision meant that bond had been forever severed and that was devastating. While recalling his encounter with Colonel Culp, my father began reliving that pain and disappointment. And because it had come about through what he believed was his own fault, i.e., for not taking the Atatbrine, he considered it a personal failure; he felt he had let his men down.

Nevertheless, Colonel Culp's offer to join General MacArthur's staff was an opportunity of a lifetime. If he could not be with his men, at least he could play an important role in the war effort by serving with the military leader he admired the most. While at the 21st. Replacement Depot awaiting disposition, my father wrote the following note:

New Guinea
Jan 16, 1945

Dear Major Wilwerding:

I wrote you about a week ago informing you of my temporary address for the next month or so. As you can see, there has been a change. The hospital facilities being overcrowded, we of the ambulatory class were transferred to the 21st Replacement Depot to await reassignment. Nobody seems to know how long a poor casual must wait to find a home but I am told unofficially that I may as well resign myself to an extended period of hibernation.

Hoping this finds you well and with best regards to Col. Culp.

I am
Respectfully Yours,
Irving Bennett

Colonel William Culp was a graduate of West Point and was the Executive Officer of the 1st Cavalry Division back at Fort Bliss. Now he was the Executive Officer of the Office of the Chief Regulating Officer (CREGO), a division of General Headquarters that was responsible for all troop movements by air, land, and sea in the Southwest Pacific Area. The Chief Regulating Officer (CRO) was Colonel Charles H. Unger.[46] Major Jerold Wilwerding, whom my father probably had known since his days at Fort Bliss, as well as when he was with the 7th Infantry Division, was the CREGO officer in-charge of personnel.

My father's note to Major Wilwerding reveals that despite all he had been through, he retained his sense of humor. But it is also telling insofar as his reference

---

46   Colonel Charles Herman Unger was killed in Korea on March 16, 1951.

to an earlier letter requesting transfer to GHQ coincides with the invasion of Luzon, which began on January 9th. My father was eager to get back into action.

On March 7th, after my father had indeed spent an "extended period of hibernation" at the 21st Replacement Depot, the adjutant general requested that he be assigned to "GHQ, APO 500"[47]—General MacArthur's Headquarters. On March 8th, Major Wilwerding sent an intra-office memorandum recommending my father for assignment "as soon as possible." Although still officially assigned to the 21st, my father left Hollandia that same day to return to Base K at Tacloban, Leyte, where he was attached to Headquarters Company as the Executive Officer.

After spending approximately two weeks at Tacloban, my father's situation was finally resolved with the following message from General MacArthur's headquarters:

COURIER SECRET   23 March/DMH

TO: CO REPLACEMENT COMMAND, USAFFE[48] APO 295.
FROM; HEADQUARTERS USAFFE APO 501 SGD
MacArthur
CITE TOR;   231925-1
IF AVAILABLE ISSUE ORDERS ASSIGNING 1ST LIEU-
TENANT
IRVING BENNETT, 02036580, CAV, PRESENTLY 21ST
REPLACEMENT
DEPOT DEPORT TO GHQ, APO 500, FOR DUTY WITH
GHQ
REGULATING SYSTEM. RADIO RTO TO EXPEDITE.
HIGHEST AIR

---

47   APO is an abbreviation for "Army Post Office". APO numbers 500 and 501 were assigned to General MacArthur's Headquarters.
48   United States Army Forces Far East.

PRIORITY AUTHORIZED FOR ACCUMULATION.
RADIO GHQ
ESTIMATED TIME OF DEPARTURE FOR NEW STA-
TION.

COPIES TO:
G-1, AG-PP, AG-O, USAFFE
GHQ, REG SYSTEM, AG GHQ,

DISTRIBUTION

ATTENTION   PERSONNEL

INFORMATION   AIR DIV
                   EXECUTIVEO
                   D/CRO

TOT; 232002-1

On April 3rd, my father was officially relieved of his duties at Headquarters Co. and assigned to General Headquarters Southwest Pacific Area, the office of the Chief Regulating Officer, to be transported by air to Manila by April 11th.

On April 7th, the following memo was disseminated:

R E S T R I C T E D

General Headquarters
Southwest Pacific Area

Special Orders)   APO 500
                                         7 April 1945

No.............97)   -E X T R A C T-

2. 1ˢᵗ Lt IRVING BENNETT 02036580 Cav having reported is asgd this hq for dy in the O of the Chief Regulating O.

By command of General MacArthur:

R. K. Sutherland,
Lieutenant General United States Army,
Chief of Staff

Official:

B.M. Fitch,
Brigadier General, U. S. Army,
Adjutant General.

DISTRIBUTION:

G-1	1	Hq Comdt	1
C Regulating O	4	Adv Ech GHQ	5
(Lt Bennett	3)	Rear Ech GHQ	5
AG	3	CG USAFFE	2

R E S T R I C T E D

Chapter Thirteen

Following the January 9th landing at Lingayen Gulf on the northwest coast of Luzon, U.S. forces began a 120-mile southward advance toward the capital city of Manila. General MacArthur, disappointed by not having seized Manila by the end of December,[49] began pushing his commanders to rapidly advance toward the city.

Despite major efforts by the Allies to make it appear as if the invasion of Luzon would commence from the south, and General MacArthur's propensity for the audacious, General Yamashita was not altogether fooled.[50] For the same reasons Imperial Japanese forces had chosen Lingayen to begin their invasion of the island in 1941,[51] Yamashita suspected MacArthur would launch an amphibious assault there as well,

---

49 The Japanese attacked the Philippines in December 1941, MacArthur's target date for the recapture of Manila, the end of December 1945, seems to have been influenced by this.

50 Yamashita positioned a significant contingent of troops to the south of Manila in response to an earlier feint by MacArthur on the southern island of Mindoro, which Yamashita could not altogether ignore.

51 Lingayen Gulf provided access to the central plains of Luzon, the only practicable route for heavy mechanized equipment, such as tanks and artillery.

and he also understood the former military governor's attachment to Manila.

Similar to his strategy on Leyte and Colonel Ezaki's tactics on Los Negros, Yamashita pulled his forces inland hoping to trap the Americans.

He relocated his headquarters to Camp John Hay in Baguio, about fifty miles northwest of Lingayen, along with one hundred and fifty thousand of his troops. He strategically placed tens of thousands more troops along the likely route of MacArthur's advance to Manila and ringed the capital city with tens of thousands more; another twenty thousand took up positions in the urban areas. By all accounts, advancing to Manila would be no cakewalk. Moreover, attempting to seize the city itself was likely to result in a bloodbath for the Americans as well as the civilians who would become trapped there.

However, General MacArthur understood General Yamashita better than Yamashita understood MacArthur. And, from a military perspective, no one knew the terrain of Luzon better than the former Field Marshal of the Philippine Army.

By landing his forces at the extremely hazardous southern end of the harbor at Lingayen Gulf, MacArthur established a beachhead beyond the range of Japanese artillery, and by ordering a rapid advance toward Manila, he effectively left Yamashita's one hundred fifty thousand-man Baguio-force sitting on its hands, to be dealt with by Admiral Kinkaid's eight hundred-ship armada (which included hundreds of carrier-based planes and long-range artillery units), Filipino guerillas, and, once the airfields were repaired and new ones established, American land-based airstrikes from heavy bombers.

By January 23rd, U.S. forces and Filipino guerillas had advanced through pockets of enemy resistance to Tarlac, about midway to Manila and just outside of

Clark Air Field.[52] Clark held special significance to the GIs and to General MacArthur in particular; the Japanese had used it to launch airstrikes against U.S. forces on Leyte, including the first Kamikaze attacks. The airfield also happened to lie at the entrance to the Bataan Peninsula, where MacArthur's forces surrendered to the Japanese in 1942. And when the tens of thousands of Allied prisoners were killed and tortured in the infamous Bataan Death March, the survivors passed by Clark's gates en route to the prison camps where they had been interned for the last three years. Bataan was an ever-present image in the General's mind and perhaps more than anything else it represented the defeat that he lived to avenge.

When the GIs began their advance to seize Clark Field, Yamashita's thirty-thousand-man-force, concealed in tunnels, caves, and camouflaged in the brush of the surrounding hills, opened fire. After a weeklong, intense, and bloody battle, which resulted in the death of thousands of enemy troops, Clark was again in American hands. But more important than the symbolism, the seizure of Clark Field was a strategic milestone in the campaign to recapture Luzon. As a large functioning air base, Clark would facilitate close air support to the advancing American troops, and because of its size, it could accommodate long-range bombers.

During the three-year occupation of Luzon, the Japanese established a number of prison camps throughout the forty thousand square mile island. Many thousands of Allied prisoners were being held in these facilities, including the survivors of the Bataan Death March. It

---

52 The Japanese attacked Clark Air Field on December 8, 1941, one day after attacking Pearl Harbor, Hawaii. MacArthur, who had learned of the events at Pearl Harbor by 5:00 A.M. on the 8th and who knew that the Japanese would likely attack the Philippines next, remains roundly criticized by military experts for his decision not to disperse the planes at Clark prior to the Japanese air raid that destroyed the Allied air forces stationed there.

has been claimed, but remains unsubstantiated, that in planning for the contingency of an Allied victory on Luzon, the Japanese issued orders to all of the prisons' commandants that if the capture of their camps was imminent, all prisoners should be liquidated. Regardless of the veracity of the claim, the Imperial Japanese had abundantly demonstrated their savagery throughout the war and General MacArthur rightfully expressed deep concern over the safety of Allied POWs. Subsequent to the capture of Clark Field, he issued a directive to form special units called "Flying Columns" that were to rapidly advance into enemy held territory and liberate the prison camps.

On January 31st, a group of Alamo Scouts and Filipino guerillas staged a daring rescue of hundreds of POWs being kept at a stockade near Cabanatuan, some twenty-five miles behind enemy lines. On the morning of February 4th, a Flying Column comprised of elements of the 1st Cavalry[53] and the 37th Infantry Divisions entered Manila and liberated two of the largest POW camps,[54] freeing some four thousand prisoners.

Later that same day, the 2nd Squadron of the 5th Cavalry Regiment attempted to seize Quezon Bridge, the only bridge left standing that crossed the Pasig River dividing east and west Manila. Heavy enemy resistance forced the Squadron to withdraw and the Japanese subsequently dynamited the bridge. After army engineers and Seabees constructed a pontoon bridge, the U.S. forces crossed over the Pasig and encircled the city.

Because of the risk to the civilian population, General MacArthur initially issued orders severely limiting the use of artillery and airstrikes on Manila. However, when the increasingly besieged enemy began destroy-

---

53 The landing on Luzon took place only 9 days after the end of the Leyte campaign. Because of the severe losses to the Division at Leyte and the immediate commencement of the Luzon campaign, the 1st Cavalry was held back from the landing until this date.

54 The camps were located at Santo Tomas University and Bilibid Prison.

ing the city and engaging in the wholesale slaughter of non-combatants,[55] MacArthur lifted his order and enemy emplacements were pounded wherever they were located.

As the fighting in Manila reached a crescendo toward the end of February, remaining elements of Japanese forces retreated into the walled city of Intramuros,[56] holding approximately four thousand civilians hostage. They also took up positions in various government buildings, including Manila City Hall and General MacArthur's former residence atop the Manila Hotel; the later still contained many of the General's personal effects.

Over the entire course of the advance to Manila, as well as within the city itself, General MacArthur moved along the front lines. In downtown Manila, he accompanied the soldiers fighting their way from floor to floor inside the Manila Hotel and, later on, established his headquarters in the ruins of Manila City Hall.

By April, Manila was securely in Allied hands with only small pockets of enemy resistance remaining to be mopped-up.

But the cost of taking the city was enormous. The overwhelming majority of the once densely populated metropolis had been reduced to smoldering rubble with tens of thousands of bodies strewn amidst the ruins. With the sole exception of Warsaw, Poland, the destruction of Manila was greater than that of any other city during all of World War II.

---

55 The atrocities committed by the Japanese troops in Manila were without limit: women were violated; entire families were slaughtered; hospitalized patients were strapped to their beds and the facilities set on fire; infants were mutilated, etc. It is estimated that during the U.S. siege of Manila, Japanese troops killed in excess of 100,000 Filipinos and others.

56 Built by the Spanish in the 1500s, Intramuros is a city within a city that is surrounded by a forty-foot thick stone wall.

❖ ❖ ❖

On April 12, 1945 my father boarded a plane at Tacloban headed for Manila:

"...on the trip to Manila, the captain of the plane came over the intercom and told us that President Roosevelt had died. Of course, we were all very sad about that. But we continued on. Arriving in Manila, I reported to General Headquarters and was assigned to a station at Lingayen Gulf, where I would be attached to the 49th Fighter Group. I would be billeted with them and my duties were to issue the priorities of travel in and out of that area. The 49th Fighter Group consisted of a bunch of young guys that were crazy. They were flying milk runs over Baguio, which is the capital of Luzon, oh, about fifty miles north of Lingayen. They would drop their bombs, and do whatever they had to do, and fly back into the base at Lingayen Gulf, and they would... I'd be lying on the beach, and these crazy guys would fly upside down, buzzing us on the beach. They were that nuts. And then they would swoop...turn and swoop over the bay, or the gulf, and make passes at each other—they'd play Chicken! Ya' know; see which one would flinch first. And sure enough, two of them went in head-on, and exploded, and that was the end of that exercise.

"The 5th Cavalry had made an advance from Lingayen Gulf to Manila and the object was to attack the Santo Tomas University, which is a big compound surrounded by a very thick wall, where they held prisoners, most of them Americans, and they were to disarm the guards and free the prisoners. It was called a Flying Column—the 5th. I went along with 'em and we knocked out the guards that were on the walls. There was no big problem 'cause we out-manned 'em so heavily, and we freed the prisoners. The prisoners came out, they looked like they came from Auschwitz, they were emaciated, and we sent them

down to the rear echelon where they were taken care of. That was the end of that, we never saw them again."

My father's narrative detailing his locations and assignments during this period are supported by the documents in his personnel file with one exception: the liberation of Santo Tomas University. As related above, according to my father's service record he left Tacloban for Luzon on April 12th, which coincides with the date of President Roosevelt's death, an event that he would likely have remembered where he was at the time. However, the liberation of Santo Tomas took place on February 4th, some two months earlier. In addition, my father's description of Santo Tomas sounds convincingly like Intramuros. The evacuation of all of the prisoners at Santo Tomas took months and he may have been confused as to what he had actually witnessed in April of that year. However, this theory does not fit with the detail in his description, e.g., "We knocked out the guards that were on the walls." It is also possible that he was embellishing. However, this seems farfetched since self-aggrandizement was never a trait that I noticed in my father and he was, in fact, meticulously honest. The more likely explanation for the discrepancies perhaps can be found with the passage of so many years and an operation similar to that which took place at Santo Tomas. On April 27th, American and Filipino forces liberated a group of Allied prisoners that had been held for approximately three years at Camp John Hay[57] in Baguio. Documents contained in my father's personnel file indicating that he was in the Baguio area at the time of the liberation of Camp John Hay suggests that this was the operation that he took part in.

---

57 During the Japanese occupation of the Philippines, General Yamashita used Camp John Hay as his headquarters. On September 3, 1945, Yamashita emerged from the mountains of Baguio and surrendered to General Jonathan Wainwright, who had been freed, at Camp John Hay. Following a lengthy trial for war crimes, on December 23, 1948, General Tomoyuki Yamashita was found guilty and executed by hanging at Camp John Hay.

My father continues:

"Colonel Culp then ordered me to report to his headquarters,[58] *which was located in the City Hall in Manila. Shortly thereafter...uh...we visited a place called..."*

The tape runs out here and continues on the other side:

"...a holy city within a city consisting of cathedrals, churches, that sort of thing. The Japanese had retreated into that area and our troops bombed the area and destroyed a lot of the churches and took all the Japanese prisoners that were left."

Here, my father is clearly describing Intramuros.

Colonel Unger issued the orders for my father to report to GHQ in Manila on May 7th. On May 8th, the following message was sent from the commanding officer at the airstrip at Lingayen Gulf to Colonel Unger:

GHQ REGULATING STATION
ROLIG[59]

APO 70
8 May 1945

Col. C. H. Unger,
Chief Regulating Officer
General Headquarters, SWPA,
APO 500

---

58   Colonel Culp only requested the order, stating, "ORDERS BEING REQUESTED HERE ASSIGNING LIEUTENANT BENNETT FOR STATION AND DUTY CREGO PD ORDERS FOLLOW VIA COURIER UPON RECEIPT OF ORDERS DESIRE HE PROCEDE CREGO WITHOUT DELAY PD
NOTIFY CREGO DEPARTURE."
The same day, Colonel Unger issued the actual order, which states, "Request orders be issued directing 1st Lt Irving Bennett, 0203680, CAV. Now at APO 70 [Dagupan], to proceed by air on or about 8 May 1945 to APO 500 for station and duty in the Office of the Chief Regulating Officer.
59   ROLIG is an acronym for "Regulation Office Lingayen Gulf."

Dear Colonel Unger:

Since the arrival of Lt. Bennett at ROLIG, I have kept in close touch with his activities. He has learned that the Field Regulating Officer functions as a coordinator and his work is entirely different than that of a line officer; that tact is needed to get the operators of transportation to use all of their facilities; and an air officer cannot sit in his office and expect passengers to get loaded.

Major Wren speaks highly of Lt. Bennett and my personal observation is that he is on the job. He is interested in his work and aggressive. I believe hc will be a creditable CREGO representative at any air field. Lt. Bennett will leave as soon as his orders arrive.

In reference to the improvement of Luna strip, nothing new has developed. The ATC officer did not inspect the strip; at least I cannot find anyone in the base who has seen him and he did not call ROLIG. I will keep you advised.

The news from Europe is certainly great.[60] Perhaps it will not be too long until you and I will be celebrating with Rex to the enticing music of tinkling mint julep glasses.

With best personal regards, I am,

Sincerely Yours,
W.C. Crocker
Lt. Col., F.A.
Regulating Officer

---

60   Following the piecemeal surrender of Nazi forces throughout Europe, on May 8, 1945, the same day that Lt. Col. Crocker wrote his message, British Prime Minister Winston Churchill announced that, "Hostilities will end officially at one minute past midnight tonight..."

Over the next several months GHQ was primarily occupied with the planning of and preparation for Operation Downfall, the invasion of Japan. With the war in Europe over and more than thirty divisions of soldiers and marines headed toward SWPA, CREGO had its hands full coordinating the movements of more than one million ground troops alone.

Operation Downfall consisted of two stages: The first phase, called Operation Olympic, involved landing more than three quarters of a million troops on the island of Kyushu on November 1st. The second phase, code named Operation Coronet, was scheduled for March 1st and would involve hundreds of thousands of additional troops that were to invade the island of Honshu; General MacArthur himself planned to lead this phase.

While my father was with GHQ and not on assignment shuttling to locations around Luzon, such as Batangas in the south and Dagupan in the north, he spent his days in an office in the bombed out and bullet-riddled shell of the Manila City Hall, where, on occasion, he would watch General MacArthur pensively pacing on the balcony of his office.

As it is in the corporate world, officers in the military are afforded certain privileges, one of which is entrée to the officers' club. During World War II such installations were often times housed in tents or abandoned structures. Officers retreated to these clubs to relax, socialize, listen to music, play cards or ping-pong, and perhaps drink a beer or the local intoxicating beverage. While in Manila, my father had two memorable experiences at the local officers' club:

On one occasion, while relaxing with a beer, he overheard two 2nd lieutenants at a nearby table talking about General MacArthur in increasingly unflattering terms. When one of the men used the phrase "Dugout Doug," my father decided he had heard enough. Angrily approaching the two junior officers, he pointedly asked them, "Excuse me, have either of you ever met General MacArthur?" When the two men sheepishly replied in the negative, my father, despite never having personally met the General himself, sternly responded "Then keep your mouths shut because neither of you have any idea what the hell you're talking about." The incident concluded with the two chastised lieutenants respectfully replying "Yes, sir."

The other incident was much more serious. But first, a little background:

Unfortunately, consistent with America's prevailing attitude of the time, the U.S. Army was segregated during World War II. Blacks had their own units, slept in separate quarters, and traveled apart from other soldiers. My father despised bigotry of any sort. He had felt the pain of discrimination as an orphan *and* as a Jew and he viewed segregation as nothing less than officially sanctioned bigotry.

Although not religiously observant, my father was proud of his Jewish identity. However, wishing to avoid the anti-Semitism that he knew would be prevalent in the army, when being processed for induction in 1941 he marked the field designated for religious preference as "None." Because black soldiers had no such convenience my father empathized with them all the more so.

Back to the 2nd incident at the officers' club:

My father was watching a heated ping-pong match between two officers, one of whom was black. The black officer hit a particularly good return and my father felt moved to say, "Good shot, brother." The term 'brother' in 1945 had no racial implications, it was simply an expression of camaraderie and my father was merely expressing his support for the man. For some reason, the black officer didn't take the comment as a compliment and instead retorted, "I ain't no brother to no goddamn Jew!"

It was the wrong response to the wrong guy.

The officer's hateful statement ignited my father's rage. Launching himself at the man who had made the vile remark, he proceeded to deliver a lesson in what *not* to say to someone who had grown up in a Jewish orphanage in New York City. After leaning over the bleeding and moaning man and firing a final burst of verbal instruction, my father brusquely left the club.

In the wake of the incident, he found himself facing the threat of a court-martial for "Conduct Unbecoming an Officer and a Gentleman."

The system of military justice prior to World War II dated back to the British Articles of War of 1774 and it bore little resemblance to the criminal justice system of today. It was designed primarily to enforce discipline within the ranks of what were relatively small armies. Impromptu courts-martial were often carried out in the field of battle by a panel of unqualified "judges" with little consideration for defendants' rights or due process. Those convicted of the most serious offenses, e.g., murder, rape, plunder, and desertion, were summarily executed—usually by firing squad. After World War I ended, the military draft stopped and the country reverted to a small standing army. Between World War I and World War II the system of military justice underwent little change.

During World War II, more than sixteen million men and women served in the armed forces and there was little, if any, investigation into the character or criminal background of draftees. Those conditions placed an enormous burden on the military justice system and fueled its too often arbitrary and capricious nature. Consequently, soldiers feared the system regardless of the circumstances that may bring them before a military tribunal. Over the course of World War II, there were about two million courts-martial resulting in an average of more than sixty general courts-martial convictions per day.

After investigating the incident and reviewing my father's service record, the military tribunal decided not to mete out the harshest penalty and issued my father a reprimand, as well as briefly suspending his commission.

The horrifying images of the Nazi Holocaust were just coming out of Europe at the time and the fact that the senior officer on the panel was Jewish may have contributed to the tribunal's leniency toward my father for an incident that could have easily resulted in a court marshal conviction. And, sadly, the fact that his antagonist was black probably also played a role in the tribunal's soft decision.

In recounting the confrontation decades later, my father expressed no regret for his violent response. In fact, he seemed to still be angry; angry at being called a goddamn Jew, and angry that a man, to whom he was showing support, who of all people should have understood the sting of bigotry had made such a loathsome remark.

I have no doubt that despite his having been entirely justified in his reaction to the bigot my father made no excuses before the tribunal and took full responsibility for his actions: such was his way.

Not long after the unfortunate episode, and possibly because of it, my father put in a request for temporary leave to the United States, arguing that he had not had a leave for the past fourteen months. However, before the request was fully processed, for unexplained reasons he rescinded it.

During the months of June and July, Manila began to regain a semblance of normalcy. Traffic jams developed in the main thoroughfares, and small businesses, such as restaurants and nightclubs, reopened. For many of the American servicemen stationed there at the time the restoration of civilian life in Manila meant a reprieve from the stress and, of course, the dangers of combat. Nevertheless, the trauma, psychological as well as physical, wrought by the war remained ever-present.

My father:

"...walking down the street one day, who do I run into but Richie Mark, who was on his way to Bataan to...uh... claim the remains of his brother's body and to bring it back to the states."

Once again, my father's voice begins to break and he stops the tape.

Throughout the Pacific war, the Japanese had proven themselves an intractable enemy that simply did not surrender.[61] Consequently, despite Air Force Major General Curtis LeMay's fleet of B-29s firebombing Japanese cities with devastating results since early March 1945,[62] in August of 1945 few believed that the war was nearing a conclusion.

My father, continuing some time later:

---

61   It has been widely chronicled that although during the course of World War II individual Japanese soldiers surrendered to Allied troops, not a single Japanese unit did so despite the death of some three million of their people. Even after Imperial Japan signed the instrument of surrender, consequential to the dropping of the atomic bombs, tens of thousands of individual Japanese soldiers continued to fight on throughout the pacific, some of them for many years, a few held out for decades.
62   Official U.S. Government estimates state that LeMay's strategic bombing campaign had destroyed approximately forty-percent of more than sixty Japanese cities.

"*There was a custom at General Headquarters that any communications into or out of the headquarters was disseminated and distributed to each officer on MacArthur's staff, of which there was a thousand. One night, I and a couple of other officers...uh...went to a nightclub... uh...in Manila, and on the way we stopped at a government store and bought a...all they had left was gin... bought a quart of gin. Upon entering the nightclub, the maitre'd took the bottle of gin from us and assigned us to a table and in a few minutes he brought out set-ups so that we could have drinks out of our bottle. When the bottle was drained, and the music stopped, we started out, and the last thing I remember was getting my hat from the hatcheck girl and getting into the car. The next thing I knew, I was on my hands and knees climbing up the steps of the hut that had been assigned to us right opposite the Manila Hotel. Obviously I had been poisoned, the maitre'd had pulled a switch on the gin, the government gin was good, but...of course, they had rotgut and they pulled a switch. The next morning, I had a terrible hangover, and one of the guys came in and said, 'They just dropped the atom bomb on Hiroshima.'[63] And I said, 'yeah, they dropped it on my head.' I didn't know what he was talking about. Anyway, I soon found out. And back at the desk at the City Hall we received a copy of a communiqué that was sent by the Japanese...to paraphrase it; they were suing for surrender with certain exceptions. And the exception was that...uh...the... [Emperor] Hirohito...was to be left in place and not put in harm's way or relieved of his responsibilities. MacArthur then wired the Japanese a response and he said, 'we will accept unconditional surrender only,' and there was no reply. So, three days later we dropped the bomb on Nagasaki,[64] and immediately a*

---

63 August 6, 1945.
64 August 9, 1945.

*communiqué came back to headquarters, 'we accept your
unconditional terms...'*[65]

My father wasn't the only one at GHQ who didn't
know about the atomic bomb: While General MacArthur
was aware of the Manhattan Project, he, like many others, was doubtful that scientists would be successful in
building a working device. It wasn't until the day before
the first bomb was dropped on Hiroshima that MacArthur was informed of the plan via a special courier dispatched from Washington.

In the days following Japan's acceptance of the terms
of surrender, officials in Washington and at MacArthur's headquarters in Manila were busy preparing for
the occupation,[66] meeting with Allies, and finalizing the
details of the surrender ceremony.

On August 6th, just hours before the atomic bomb
was dropped on Hiroshima, President Truman had
appointed General MacArthur the Supreme Commander of Allied Forces in the Pacific (SCAP). According to the Potsdam Declaration, that designation meant
MacArthur would govern the occupation of Japan. Truman also had assigned to the General the authority to
conduct the surrender proceedings.

On Sunday, August 19, 1945, in response to General
MacArthur's demands, sixteen representatives of Imperial
Japan boarded two specially marked Bettys and began
their journey to Manila to discuss details of the pending
occupation and the surrender ceremony with GHQ officials.
The defeated enemy's unarmed bombers were escorted by
eighteen P-38s from the 8th and 49th Fighter Groups.

---

65   In their 2nd communiqué, the Japanese accepted the terms of the July 26, 1945
Potsdam Declaration, which contains no specific mention of the emperor. However, their response also stated that they would not accept any agreement that
would "prejudice the prerogatives" of the emperor as "a Sovereign Ruler." The Allied
response, which was accepted by Japan on August 15th, reiterated that the Emperor
would have to submit to the Supreme Commander of Allied Forces.

66   GHQ was not involved in the negotiations of the surrender itself, but MacArthur
had already drawn up plans for the occupation long before the Japanese surrender.

On August 20th, as the Japanese envoys arrived at Rosario Manor,[67] just down the street from the Manila Hotel, to meet with General MacArthur's Chief of Staff, Lieutenant General Richard K. Sutherland, and other GHQ representatives, MacArthur looked on from a second-story balcony of his headquarters. Standing beneath him on the street below, a group of about forty GIs and Filipinos gathered to watch, among them was my father.

Subsequent to the Japanese capitulation, my father, it appears, was being prepared for duty in Japan. On August 27th, a request was submitted to the CRO, based on his eligibility of his last four months serving with CREGO, for qualification of Military Occupational Specialty (MOS) as a Troop Movements Officer. Two days later, Colonel Unger granted the request. But the assignment never came about as my father requested a furlough to the states.

My father:

"MacArthur had been planning the invasion of Tokyo, and of course it never came about, because of the surrender. We were expecting to lose a million men. It was a difficult job. Anyway, it was now time to go home. There was a point system; for the time that we spent in the theatre, so many points; for the time that we spent in combat so many points, and so on. And according to the point system, if you qualified to go home, you were issued a priority of travel. I was on the first ship home. I had all the necessary points."

According to the military's point system of the time a soldier needed 85 points to qualify for furlough. The overwhelming majority of soldiers, including officers, never qualified for such. My father earned a total of 98 points:

---

67   Rosario Manor was a two-story apartment complex, located on Adriatico Street, which had survived the Japanese demolition teams and U.S. artillery. The building was being used at the time as the American Embassy.

1. For the number of months in the army since 16 September 1940 a soldier received 1 point: my father had 50 such points.

2. For the number of months served overseas since 16 September 1940 a soldier received 1 point: my father had 23 such points.

3. For the number of decorations and bronze service stars awarded for service since 16 September 1940 a soldier received 1 point: my father received 25 such points.

On September 2, 1945 the Japanese formally surrendered to the Allies aboard the Battleship Missouri in Tokyo Bay. That same day my father embarked a troop ship headed for home.

Following the remarkably brief ceremony that officially ended the war in the Pacific, General MacArthur broadcast a masterfully crafted speech to the American people in which he poignantly set the standard for the country's attitude towards its fighting men:

"And so my fellow countrymen, today I report to you that your sons and daughters have served you well and faithfully with the calm, deliberate, determined fighting spirit of the American soldier and sailor, based upon a tradition of historical truth as against a fanaticism of an enemy supported only by mythological fiction. Their spiritual strength has brought us through to victory. They are homeward bound—take care of them."

My father:

"I arrived in Vancouver Barracks then took the train to Santa Barbara where Claire met me and we drove home. That's the end of the war."

**GHQ CRO Staff in the Courtyard of the Manila City Hall
(Lt. Bennett inset) Aerial View (Associated Press)**

Chapter Fourteen

With the announcement of the end of the war, America erupted in jubilant celebration. In every major city, confetti streamed from offices and streets filled with people celebrating the nation's victory over the evil empire of Japan and the diabolical Nazi supremacists. And every soldier, seaman, and airman was a hero. It was the happiest of times in America.

When my father arrived at Vancouver Barracks, there were no cheering crowds or flag waving throngs. With the exception of some cameramen and reporters, the first ship of returning troops arrived in relative anonymity on a breaking dawn of the first week in October 1945.

But my father wasn't interested in celebrations. He was grateful to have survived the war, proud that his country had prevailed, and he was eager to move on. He had endured enough of military life and jungle combat. All he wanted was to see his family and live the life of his dreams he had thus far been denied.

After being relieved from active duty on October 8th at Fort MacArthur, my father boarded a Southern Pacific rail car headed south to Santa Barbara. About six hours later, he stepped down from the train into a crowd of hundreds of well-wishers waving small American flags. Smiling at the welcome, his eyes eagerly searched for Claire. Shouldering his duffle bag, he waded through the gathering as strangers patted him on the back and yelled congratulatory phrases and expressions of gratitude. The celebratory scene faded into the background when he spotted his beaming sister.

Claire hadn't changed. She looked as elegant and robust as ever, and her vivacious smile, which always managed to brighten a room, seemed to light up the whole world. After a long, strong embrace, my father and his sister, wiping away her tears of joy, walked from the train station to the parking lot, got into Bud's car, and headed south to Los Angeles.

As they cruised down the coast, in the midst of their non-stop dialogue, when my father asked about Bud and Wayne, Claire began to cry. Responding to her brother's gentle prodding, she hesitantly opened up: Bud had left her. Well, sort of. After Bud had been drafted, one day in 1942, Claire answered a knock on the door and found a young woman standing there who proceeded to tell her that she was madly in love with her husband. When Bud returned home on leave, Claire confronted him about the affair and kicked him out. Bud requested a transfer to Europe. At first he was stationed in France, but after VE Day he decided to stay on with the army and was moved to Germany, where he was now heading a vehicle repair operation. Claire had been home alone with Wayne since the revelation of Bud's infidelity. Wayne was now almost eight years old.

But the painful events involving Bud and her separation from him weren't all that was upsetting Claire. Since he had left for overseas, my father had been sending her his military pay, which she was supposed to be depositing in his bank account. But having had little or no support from Bud for some time, Claire had spent it all. It was everything that he had.

My father was naturally troubled by the revelation, but his sister meant the world to him and no amount of money could disrupt that relationship. Even if it had been someone not so close to him, my father would have felt the same compassion he now felt for his sister in her time of need. He told her not to worry about the money. He was glad that she used it to support herself and Wayne and assured her that everything would somehow work out.

My father was disgusted and angered by what Bud had done. Betrayal of any kind was a cardinal sin to him. Nevertheless he refrained from expressing any bitterness to his sister. Bud had also gone through a lot in his life, and he had been an integral part of their little family from the early days.

When he arrived back in L.A., my father moved in with Claire and Wayne in their one-room unit in the dingy Tranmore Apartments on North Lucile Avenue. He got his old job back at Century Distributing and continued working there for the next several years. Eventually, the store expanded its sales' inventory from carpets and linoleum to include radios and Emerson televisions. There were no programs yet, but the salesmen, intrigued with the new device, would stand around watching test patterns.

As a child, Wayne didn't feel close to his father, who was seldom around, and when he was, Bud's role was primarily that of a disciplinarian. Although he craved a better relationship, part of Wayne felt a sense of relief that his father was no longer in his life.

Wayne's connection with his uncle, on the other hand, was very close. He recently recalled his reaction when my father came home from the war:

"He was like a father to me. I was overjoyed to see him again after all those missing war years and saw him as a war hero."

After his young lifetime of hard experiences and on the heels of almost five years of military living, training, and combat, my father was well prepared to mentor his nephew and he was a solid and competent teacher. He helped Wayne with his homework and coached him in sports, and also taught him such mundane things as how to knot his tie and shine his shoes. And when the need arose, he trained him in the one lesson he was most experienced—how to deal with bullies.

My father noticed that Wayne had been coming home from school and acting unusually quiet. Concerned, he sat down with his young nephew and asked what was bothering him. It turned out that Wayne had been suffering a school bully for some time. "Every bully is a coward," my father told him. For the next several weeks he engaged Wayne in daily exercise and self-defense lessons. Wayne recently recalled his uncle saying, "Keep your guard up, jab with your left hand and when you see an opening deliver a solid right hand. If you are knocked down, get up and keep on fighting."

When he felt that Wayne was ready to confront the bully, he told him to "Get to work."

When Wayne arrived home from school that day, as my father remembered it, he came running up to him overflowing with triumphant excitement, yelling "Unc! Unc! It worked!!!" Here's how Wayne recalled the incident:

"At Lockwood grammar school, a Mexican kid started to bully me. Your father gave me lessons in self-defense that I used to challenge the bully in the coatroom at school. My fighting back stopped the bullying cold... I used his teachings again in junior high school and fought the school bully after school at an event that was attended by many people."

Wayne also remembered his uncle's personal habits:

"He always dressed well, showered a lot and bought multiple bottles of Witch Hazel and other products that he used and liked."

Wayne saw my father suffer relapses of malaria and other things that brought the shadow of the war too close to home:

"I was scared and worried about his illness, his skin would turn yellow. He would sweat and wake up screaming. He was reliving the war and the fighting in the jungle."

And for years after the war, wherever he walked in public, my father felt an irrepressible desire to look behind him.

While my father was living with Claire, the subject of their relationship with Harry was avoided, as the conversation inevitably would degrade into expressions of anger and resentment. However, the topic of their father's estate was on the front burner.

When Harry died, he left a will that bequeathed to his three children about one hundred thousand dollars and several pieces of real estate. Apparently having second thoughts about disinheriting his oldest son after seeing him go off to war, he wrote my father back into his will.

After Harry's death, a relative of Rose's contested the will, claiming the property and the money belonged to Rose. Claire and Phil were not fighters by nature and, perhaps feeling guilty over how their father had made his money, or just plain resentful of him, they were going to let it go. My father, on the other hand, was a fighter and would not stand for it. Legally, it was Harry's property, and as far as he was concerned, Harry owed his children...big time. My father got a good lawyer and successfully defended Harry's Will.

In 1949, Bud returned from Germany. He and Claire reconciled and the family, including my father, moved into a larger apartment on Orange Grove Avenue in the Fairfax area.

Later that year, Claire gave birth to her and Bud's second child, Dennis, and my father decided it was time to move out. He initially moved into a cabin on a boat docked at Marina Del Rey that was owned by his friend, Swede Larson. Larson was an actor, and for some time my father had been considering getting into the business.

But his friend's lifestyle of parties and heavy drinking was not to my father's liking and after six months on Larson's love boat, he got his own place.

After Harry's estate was settled and with access to the benefits of the newly enacted G.I. bill, my father was in the best financial position he had ever been in. He bought one of the new Studebaker automobiles and, early in 1951, quit his job at Century and began to pursue a career in acting. Using part of his government benefits, he enrolled in a two-year program at the Geller Theatre and School of Dramatic Arts.

After World War II, the American economy was undergoing a remarkable renaissance: gasoline and food rationing had ended; consumer spending skyrocketed; innovations in aviation, cars, electronics and communications were transforming lifestyles, and affordable mortgages sparked a housing boom to keep pace with the baby boom. From 1940 to 1960 America's Gross National Product grew three-fold. And the entertainment industry, which had fared well through both the Depression and the war years, was running at full tilt. Movie stars and the two-dimensional glamour of Hollywood were captivating the nation, and much of the world, more than ever.

Enrolling in dramatic school was a strange decision for someone who wanted a career in medicine or law so desperately he was willing to sue his own father for college tuition, but time and the war (and money) had changed my father. And physically, he had blossomed into a stunningly handsome man. He had, as they say, movie-star looks. Claire supported her brother's decision; she too was enchanted by the glamour of Hollywood.

The Geller Theatre and School of Dramatic Arts was located in Los Angeles near the corner of Wilshire Boulevard and Fairfax Avenue. It was a well-known and well-respected acting school where many of Hollywood's greats had learned their craft. When my father began there, the school was under the leadership of a highly respected acting instructor named Michael Chekhov, whose list of students having achieved success is both long and illustrious.

Chekhov was a no-nonsense professional who demanded hard work from his students. My father wasn't interested in someone babysitting him through acting school. He was serious about learning the craft and determined to be the best he could be at it. Chekhov's style fit him perfectly.

Over the next two years, my father delved deeply into all facets of acting and worked diligently at his chosen profession. He learned how to walk and talk all over again, how to use visualization to affect his emotions, and how to say lines naturally. He used to say a good actor could appear to be yelling without ever raising his voice. He practiced his diction almost pathologically, often times biting down on a cork and repeating sounds that forced him to enunciate clearly.

During his frequent visits to Claire's apartment, my father engaged Wayne in aspects of what he was learning and encouraged him to get involved with acting, as well as sports. Wayne remembered my father from those days as being "young, athletic, handsome, always well-dressed, well-groomed and a favorite of the ladies." He saw his uncle as having "Executive Authority," meaning the character to instruct and lead others, something that Wayne felt contributed to my father's success in the army. And he frequently reminded Wayne of the same principle he applied to himself, "No matter what you do, be the best at it."

My father performed in numerous plays at Geller's and other theatres around town, such as The Call Board Theatre, or The Pasadena Playhouse, and was receiving glowing reviews from well-known Hollywood critics like Wylie Williams, Paul V. Coates, and Katherine Von Blon. He signed on with agent Virginia Doak and started getting advertising jobs and small parts in feature films starring top-shelf names. As early as 1952, my father's career in Hollywood seemed promising.

He hated his given name, Irving, and had been using the name 'Mark' professionally for the past year. On November 2, 1952, in Los Angeles Superior Court, my father's petition to legally change his name to 'Mark' was granted. Having already achieved a degree of early notoriety, his name change was highlighted in a prominent, but brief, Los Angeles Times article the next day.

**My father and an unidentified actress during a live
performance at Geller's circa 1951**

As part of his new image, he traded in his Studebaker for a red Thunderbird convertible.

Then, as it is now, Hollywood was rife with infidelity, scandal, and alcohol and drug abuse, to name only
a few of the town's sordid qualities. It just wasn't pub-
licized or spoken about as openly as it is now. With
the exception of taking up smoking again, practically
everyone in Hollywood smoked in those days, my father
never descended into the cesspool of Hollywood culture.
He even soon quit smoking when he suffered a bout of
laryngitis before a particular performance. As he told it,
"I threw a full pack in the garbage and never picked up
another cigarette again."

With Bud's return to the family fold in 1949, he and
my father reestablished their relationship as if nothing
had happened and the two became tennis partners. But
after suffering renewed symptoms of malaria, which
he attributed to overexertion in the California sun, my
father switched his pastime to golf and began taking
lessons at the Fox Hills Golf Course in Los Angeles. He

grew to love the game and in fairly short order became a respectable player, scoring in the 80s.

Looking for a game at Fox Hills one day, my father was paired with a tall Filipino fellow that he thought he recognized. It turned out to be Hilario Moncado, the self-styled "Five-star General" whom he had met just west of Leyte's Highway 1 in October 1945.

Moncado told my father that after the war he had become a contender for the Philippine presidency. However, Moncado said, the United States had other ideas about who should lead the commonwealth and paid him one dollar for every guerilla under his command, of which he said there were a million, and hustled him off to the states.

In reality, Moncado was charged with collaborating with the Japanese during the occupation and imprisoned by the post war government. He was eventually acquitted[68] of all charges and moved to Los Angeles where he had become a sort of cult leader among the local Filipinos, many of whom considered him to be the reincarnation of the Christian messiah—a belief that Moncado himself seems to have fostered.

When he wasn't walking on water or claiming to have single-handedly won the war against the Japanese, Moncado was on the golf course, and he had become an admirable player who could hit a drive as far as anyone. He even authored a book on the game, which he titled "The 360 Degree Power Swing."

After the two became regular golfing partners at Fox Hills, Moncado asked my father if he would write his memoirs. Flattered by the request, he probably would have obliged the "General" had it not been for the pursuit of his acting career.

---

68 After the liberation, many Filipinos were accused of collaboration and imprisoned; most of them were acquitted after General MacArthur intervened. MacArthur felt that few Filipinos who had cooperated with the Japanese should be branded as collaborators since they were simply doing whatever they could "in the interest of their people during a brutal occupation."

My father eventually lost touch with Moncado, who died at a relatively young age in 1956. Nevertheless, Hilario Camino Moncado is still the official President of the Filipino Federation of America, although no one has seen him at a meeting in more than fifty years.

After his graduation from Geller, a friend of my father, Morris Stromberg, who was a singer, told him about auditions being held at the Las Palmas Theatre in Beverly Hills for a play being produced by an ex-vaude-villian named Will Morrissey.

My father was a hustler. By that I don't mean that he hustled people in the scheming sense of the term, he was anything but that. He was a doer, someone who didn't sit around waiting for opportunity to knock. As he had done many times since he began moving from acting school to seeking professional roles, he signed up to audition for a part in Morrissey's new play. The tryout would be the genesis of a close relationship between my father and a man who in many respects embodied the Broadway theatre.

My Father circa 1953

Chapter Fifteen

*"Every country gets the circus it deserves.
Spain gets bullfights. Italy gets the
Catholic Church. America gets Hollywood."*
— **Erica Jong**

The son of a civil engineer who made his living securing city contracts and a mother whose prohibitionist passion motivated her to toss axes through saloon and liquor store windows, Will Morrissey was a hard-drinking, hard-fighting, multi-talented, and charismatic Irishman who grew up in New York City at the turn of the 20th Century—the heyday of Broadway musical theatre.

Morrissey got introduced to theatre arts as a young man while managing one of his father's construction projects at a local theatre. When the director of a play complained that Morrissey's ten riveters were destroying his rehearsals, Morrissey "promoted" a nice fee out of the frustrated man and leveraged himself into a non-speaking part in the production. For seven dollars a week, Morrissey laid in a bed on stage and "died," as an overly dramatic actress begged him not to.

No matter the anonymity of the part, the experience of being on stage in front of a live audience was enough to ignite Morrissey's passion and so began his theatrical career.

Subsequent to his nightly demise, Morrissey became an assistant stage manager and then began playing minor roles in small productions. His involvement with the theatrical world grew when he started performing in Shakespearian plays and tried his hand at singing and songwriting, for which he clearly had an aptitude. While performing his own piano compositions—stopping in-between lines to crack jokes—in a theatre in Harlem, Morrissey was discovered by George M. Cohan. Cohan liked the Irishman's wit and thought he had enough talent and personality that, with a little coaching, he could go places.

Cohan got Morrissey to join the Vaudeville Comedy Club[69] and made him one of his "pals," as Cohan referred to his troupe. As a result of Cohan's mentorship and influence, Morrissey's career diversified and he evolved into a prolific playwright, lyricist, composer, and a producer and promoter of musicals. He became a colleague of show business icons like Flo Ziegfeld, Earl Carroll, Marcus Loew, Richard Rodgers and Oscar Hammerstein, Lee and J.J. Shubert, to name but a few.

During the 1920s, 30s, and 40s, Will Morrissey traveled the country putting on shows, hanging out in clubs, which he referred to as "upholstered sewers," hobnobbing and partying with show business folks, and generally gallivanting with his "gang" of young thespians, who affectionately called him "Uncle Willy." His shoestring productions were usually flops, and he typically skedaddled out of town before his creditors or the unions could catch up with him. Morrissey often found

69 A fraternal organization of entertainers formed in 1906.

his inspiration, and his relief, in just about anything that came in a corked bottle and exceeded twenty-five percent alcohol content.

Tales of Morrissey's exploits during those years are both legion and tawdry. For example, there was the time he was at a housewarming party for a fellow vaudevillian who had just completed building a large estate in California overlooking the ocean. Drink was flowing and, as usual, Morrissey was getting his fair share of what he called "giggle water." During an intoxicated exchange with silent film cowboy star Tom Mix, Morrissey's penchant for satirical insults and wry humor got him in hot water. It was the dawn of the talking picture era and speculation was rife in Hollywood as to who would and who wouldn't make the transition to the new medium. Morrissey had recently produced a play that included a drugstore cowboy character who, in mocking reference to Mix, he named 'Tom Dix." Mix took offense at the mordant jab and made his sentiments known to Morrissey. It was in that context that Morrissey is purported to have said to Mix, "Your horse Tony has a great future in the talkies. The horse can at least snort. But what can you do?" That's when the housewarming turned into a drunken brawl.

According to Morrissey, Mix threw the first punch, which missed its mark and landed on the mouth of Midgie Miller, Morrissey's then wife. The Irishman countered with a solid left hook to the cowboy's jaw, knocking him to the floor. When Mix got to his feet Morrissey landed another roundhouse that sent the silver screen legend down for a second time. The next time Mix staggered to the vertical, Morrissey launched an overhand right that hit air, causing him to cartwheel onto the floor, at which point Mix jumped on Morrissey's back and, in expert cowboy form, repeatedly squeezed his knees together hard enough to break six of Morrissey's ribs. After more battling, which included the use of some handy props, such as a piano that was dropped onto Mix's ankle, both pugilists wound up bruised and bandaged and in the Venice Police Station. The fracas garnered front page headlines the next day and a subsequent lawsuit in which Mix requested a jury trial. Morrissey wound up getting arrested again for throwing a punch at Mix in the courtroom.

Eventually everyone was exonerated and Mix and Morrissey made up over drinks in a local club.

It wasn't the only time that Morrissey tangled with the law or otherwise sullied the civil justice system. One time, Morrissey found himself being called as a material witness against some mob figures. To avoid testifying, he arrived at the court staggeringly drunk, prompting the judge to wave his testimony. In a similar scenario, when he was summoned to appear in Los Angeles Superior Court pursuant to a warrant issued out of New York, Morrissey showed up loaded again. This time upon entering the courtroom, Morrissey staggered over to the jury box, reached over to one of the female jurors, and while pinching the cheek of the plump woman said, "Baby, you look like one of my old chorus girls." He spent the next five days in the slammer for contempt of court.

Chronically short on cash, Morrissey often found himself in embarrassing and sometimes outright dangerous situations. During the 1920s, he shoestringed together an elaborate production called "Music Hall Revue" and took it on the road. More than once Morrissey bounced his cast members' paychecks or was unable to pay lodging bills or train fare, leaving the whole troupe stranded. On one occasion, while Revue was playing the California circuit, Morrissey stopped the show in the middle and announced to the audience that the curtain would have to come down because one of his backers, or "angels" as they were called in show business, had reneged. A successful agent, later turned successful producer, named Edward Small was in the audience and loudly offered to take up the financial slack. The show went on.

On another occasion, Morrissey "promoted" funding from rival Chinese factions for an off-the-wall project in L.A.'s Chinatown district. When the contending Oriental gangs discovered what each other was doing, a Tong[70] war erupted, sparking, among other things, a shootout in the streets of L.A. Morrissey escaped into the Hollywood Hills where he hid out until the feud settled down.

During prohibition years Morrissey got backing from bootleggers and other racketeers, a common practice among showman of the day. After the opening night of a production he had put on with ten thousand dollars in mob money, Morrissey was confronted with a .45 stuck in his back and a voice in his ear demanding the cash: Apparently, the backer's boss hadn't approved the investment. The backer's body was later found in a graveyard in Brooklyn.

Due to the "kindness" of the mobsters, the show finished its engagement and Morrissey got away with his life, and a profit of five dollars.

In-between promoting, producing, performing, songwriting, drinking, scheming, and fighting, Morrissey got married, often, five times according to him.

Outside of his bad habits and despite his predilection for producing theatrical turkeys, Will Morrissey was a savvy showman who was respected by his colleagues and a valued mentor to young entertainers. By recognizing their talent and giving them a break, Morrissey became the footstool to success for many young artists who went on to become top names in the entertainment field. His list of discoveries includes legendary figures

---

70　"Tong" is the name given to secret Chinese societies.

such as Bing Crosby, Gracie Allen, Milton Berle, and numerous others who as Morrissey would say, "GOT UP THERE."

With his white mane and showman's allure, Morrissey looked like a sophisticated W.C. Fields or perhaps a smoother rendering of the conning wizard from the *Wizard of Oz*. When word got out that Uncle Willy was coming out of retirement to produce a play, which he fittingly titled *On a Shoestring*, up and coming actors like my father flocked to the auditions.

After my father's tryout, Morrissey approached him saying he liked what he had seen. The two went out afterward for drinks and spent hours chatting. When my father picked up the tab, Morrissey exclaimed, "What is this, an actor with money?" He offered him the lead.

Although he was nothing like Will Morrissey, neither in terms of character nor in lifestyle, nevertheless, the two became close and Morrissey came to see his new discovery as his "alter ego." Perhaps my father represented things that Morrissey wished he had been, rather than the things that he really was.

My father respected Morrissey's experience and knowledge of the theatre. He considered his relationship with the Broadway impresario as an opportunity to learn, further hone his skills as an actor, and to network in the entertainment industry. But I suspect that his attraction to Morrissey involved something else as well. Just as Morrissey may have been mistaking that which he saw in my father as himself, perhaps he viewed Will Morrissey in a similarly wishful way. Morrissey was a showman who lived a colorful life and stood on a stage while people applauded him. Recognition! It was the opposite of an institutionalized orphan among a thousand others.

As far as Morrissey's benign debauchery was concerned, my father never participated in any of it. Although he found tales of Morrissey's exploits amusing.

Since his retirement, Morrissey had been living in Santa Barbara at the California Hotel, where he played the piano bar in exchange for room and board.

In getting older Will Morrissey wanted a finale—a show that would immortalize his life's work as a shoestring producer.

When the casting for *On a Shoestring* was complete, rehearsals began and Morrissey's new "gang" worked from morning to night. When he was away, which was usually to do some promoting or secure his job at the California Hotel, Morrissey turned over the production to my father.

After three weeks of rehearsals, the show was getting tightened up to the point where it was ready to open. But Morrissey still needed funding. He snagged two potential "angels" who wanted to see a full performance before writing any checks. Morrissey arranged for it, and prepared an audience of two hundred shills to impress the backers.

However, at rehearsal the night before the performance, the leading lady and another actress got into an argument over the leading man (my father), whom both had fallen in love with. To settle themselves down, the two women went out drinking. But they got so sauced they couldn't make the performance the next day. When the show didn't go on, the backers bailed. Morrissey ran out of money and the rehearsals stopped. *On a Shoestring* never opened. Will Morrissey's dream of theatrical immortality vanished.

After the play's downfall, Morrissey turned his attention to his memoirs, which, like Hilario Moncado, he asked my father to write. While he would remain friendly with Uncle Willy, he felt that it was time to move on if he was to build his own career and turned down the offer.

For much of his life, my father remained enamored with Will Morrissey and cherished the time he spent with him. He even committed to memory a nostalgic ditty that Morrissey had written and that he planned to publish one day if Morrissey had not been able to do so:

There Must Be A Heaven For Clowns

What happens when the funny man can't make us
laugh anymore
Where do they go at the end of the show
When they pass through that exit door.
Is there some place then for the women and men
Who've made us laugh on earth
Some little nook in that Holy Book
For those dear old dispensers of mirth

There's a place for the good, a place for the bad
A haven for weary, a home for the sad
The Redman believes in the happy hunting grounds
So there must be a heaven for Clowns
We've got to have someone to laugh at our jokes
We need straight men to help us with pokes
Just listen at night to those funny, funny sounds
Up there in Heaven with clowns
The stars all look like circus faces
We've seen in other places
A lot of rainbow chasers
Chasing the merry go-rounds.
Who puts the big-top in place every night
Who makes the moon laugh, the Milky Way white,

If Barnum and Bailey's up there
There must Be a Heaven For Clowns
—Will Morrissey[71]

After his association with Will Morrissey, my father resumed auditioning for parts. He scored a few hits, including a day's work on a Lana Turner film, which was being shot on location in Kanab, Utah. But like almost all young actors, he spent most of his time looking for work.

Harry had a cousin living in L.A. by the name of Rose Merman. Rose was fond of my father and didn't like how Harry had treated him. Rose's husband, Doc Merman, whose real name was Louis Immerman, was a production manager at one of the major movie studios. Wanting to help my father, Rose suggested that he visit Doc and interview for a part in an upcoming musical. Doc was friendly enough at the meeting and my father thought it went well, but he didn't get the part.

Rose also liked to play matchmaker, and she knew someone she thought would be just right for my father.

The girl's name was Maxine Fromkess. She was a beautiful twenty-three-year-old who had moved to California from New York when she was nine years old. Maxine's father, Leon Fromkess, was a well-known Hollywood producer; and he would become my father's father-in-law.

---

71 Shortly before his death in 1956, Will Morrissey wrote his memoir, titled *On a Shoestring (Wildon paul, ltd. Publishers)*, in which this poem appears.

Chapter Sixteen

The third of four brothers, Leon Fromkess was born on November 23, 1901. His father, Hugo, was a part owner in a family liquor business, his mother, Emma, worked at a fabric store.

In 1919, Leon graduated high school from the all boys Dewitt Clinton School in New York City. He had a strong interest in business and dreams of one day entering the corporate world. That fall, he enrolled in a class in Corporation Finance at Columbia University. But when Hugo's business closed due to Prohibition, and then he unexpectedly died, Leon had to quit school and go to work.

After getting a job with an importer and distributor of commercial tableware, Leon became a travelling salesman, crisscrossing the country by train while lugging trunks filled with samples of various lines of foreign and domestic made dishes. Within a few short years, he established a significant client base of restaurants, hotels, and department stores, as well as a smattering of mom-and-pop outfits. His most lucrative accounts were in California, where in Los Angeles he kept a car in storage in order to service his clients who were spread throughout the length and breadth of the state.

By 1926, during his thrice yearly, ten-week-long sales' trips, Leon was racking up orders of between $85,000 and $95,000 per trip. Working on a ten percent commission, he was making about $30,000 a year, plus additional sums from a cadre of jobbers. In 2010 dollars, Leon was raking in the equivalent of more than $300,000 a year, selling dishes.

In 1926, Leon was introduced to a stately young lady by the name of Rita Minton.

Born Rivka Minzesheimer on September 8, 1902, Rita was the only child of Fred and Bertie Minzesheimer, whose American roots went back to before the civil war. When Leon met her, she was living by herself in a bran-new landmark building called the Chalfonte Hotel located at 200 West 70th Street on Manhattan's fashionable Upper West Side. She was an aspiring opera singer, and purportedly a former Ziegfeld Girl.

Leon and Rita fell deeply in love and became engaged in June of 1927.

A month later, Leon embarked on one of his cross-country sales trips, which he planned to cut down to six weeks to get back sooner to New York and marry Rita. In order to see all 150-200 of his regular customers in more than a dozen states and almost two-dozen cities, Leon had to hustle even more than usual. In fact, he was moving so fast his firm, in phone calls and telegrams, was urging him to slow down.

But Leon was driven; Rita was constantly on his mind. He phoned her regularly and sent her on average two letters and a telegram each day. Before he met Rita, Leon looked forward to the road trips. He enjoyed the challenge of selling, seeing his good friends and colleagues on the road, and painting more than a few towns red. All of that had now become impediments keeping him from being with the love of his life. He became so lonesome and lovesick, before he was halfway through his trip he felt like smashing his samples and getting on the next train back to New York.

Once he reached California, Leon decided that this would be his last road trip. He and Rita would be married and he'd use his substantial savings to find another way to make a living without having to "leave New York ever again."

On Wednesday, November 2, 1927, at six o'clock in the evening, Leon and Rita were married at the Park Royal Hotel at 23 West Seventy-Third Street in New York City.

Within a year Leon had quit his job and started working as a stock salesman for the New York Curb Market.[72] Rita gave up her aspirations for the theatre. Instead, she devoted herself to her husband and his career.

As he had done selling dishes, Leon quickly built up a strong clientele, eventually earning a reputation as a top-notch broker. Among his clients was a cousin of Rita's by the name of Joe Brandt. Brandt was a founding partner in a company originally called the CBC Film Sales Corporation, which made money primarily by leasing silent films to movie houses through a nationwide distribution network known as the States Rights System. Although CBC was a successful player in the film industry, it was disparagingly referred to as "Corned Beef and Cabbage" by the major film concerns of the time. To improve their image, Brandt and his two partners, Harry and Jack Cohn, changed the company's name in 1925 to Columbia Pictures Corporation.

With the advent of the first talking motion picture in 1929,[73] Brandt and the Cohn brothers saw an opportunity

---

72 The New York Curb Market got its name from where much of the stock trading took place—on curbs. In 1921, the Market got its own building on Greenwich Street in Manhattan. Eight years later, it became the New York Curb Exchange, and finally, in 1953, the American Stock Exchange.

73 *The Jazz Singer* starring Al Jolson.

to expand their operation, but they needed capital. Hence, Brandt approached his cousin's husband, Leon Fromkess, who suggested that they take the company public and sell stock to raise the money. Brandt and the Cohns liked the idea and engaged Leon to put it together.

Leon secured the investors, drew up and submitted the offering of approximately 400,000 shares of stock. The deal generated about $1.25 million for Columbia. Leon settled for a modest commission plus company stock.

Brandt brought Edward Small, the agent that had bailed out Will Morrissey and who was now a producer, into the operation.

When the stock market crashed later that year, Fromkess segued into the motion picture business, becoming Columbia's financial expert.

In 1930, Rita gave birth to the couple's only child, whom they named Maxine Elyse.

During the next six years, Leon worked hard at building Columbia into an international operation through the development of franchises.

Most motion picture concerns, particularly the major studios, had lost big in the crash of '29, but with the proceeds of the public stock offering Columbia flourished and began moving its operation to newly built facilities on the west coast. Harry Cohn, becoming increasingly paranoid and obnoxious as Columbia's success grew, began bullying everyone out of the company with the exception of his brother Jack, whom he pushed into corporate isolation. Unwilling to suffer Cohn's abuse any longer, Fromkess and Brandt left the company and joined with another relative of Rita's, a film salesman by the name of Arthur Sachson, to restart a motion picture operation that had gone into crisis when its two principle owners split up. The company was called Monogram Pictures. Once again, Fromkess took the company public, and after raising a similar amount of capital as for the Columbia deal, he became Monogram's treasurer and executive producer.

In 1938, after the reorganization, Monogram began producing low-budget films using child actors who had outgrown their stereotypes and series films based on urban themes, such as *The East Side Kids* and *The Bowery Boys*.[74] The studio also put out widely popular western series, starring such names as John Wayne, Bob Steel, Ray "Crash" Corrigan, and Tom Mix, Will Morrissey's one time sparring partner and bareback rider.

In 1933, Rita's uncle, Max Minzesheimer, married the widow of motion picture and theatre magnate Marcus Loew, a union that could only benefit Leon's career.

While Leon was working with Monogram, a man whom he had met during his days as a stockbroker named Robert Young approached him for advice on how to run a movie operation. The meeting would mark a turning point in Leon's career and that would eventually bring him out to Hollywood.

Robert Ralph Young was a young Texan with a childhood fixation on trains that never waned. He was a college dropout who had worked his way up from an unskilled laborer through the corporate world and eventually into important positions with DuPont and General Motors. Later, he became a financial manager for General Motors and DuPont financial expert, and chairman of the Democratic National Committee, John J. Raskob.[75]

Young and Raskob are reported to have parted ways when the two disagreed over the future of the stock market—Raskob was bullish on the market, while Young was predicting its collapse. Young, obviously, turned out to be prescient.

---

74 The Bowery Boys became the longest running feature film series in motion picture history.
75 Ironically, Raskob was a registered Republican.

By selling short on his investments before the Stock Market crash and then buying up failed businesses and selling them at a profit, Young made a fortune. In 1931 he bought a seat on the New York Stock Exchange.

During his days on Wall Street, Young became increasingly angry at the control the banking industry was exerting on the railroads and how it was adversely affecting consumers. Using his own growing wealth and shoestringing other investors into his business schemes, Young gobbled up as much railroad stock as he could, eventually becoming one of the most powerful railroad magnates in the country.

In the late 1930s, Young became embroiled in a bitter legal fight with DuPont over control of the Chesapeake and Ohio Railroad. Young had the controlling block of common stock in the C&O and DuPont had the preferred stock. If Young defaulted on paying investor dividends, a growing possibility at the time, DuPont could wind up getting control of the railroad. Seeking a way to fend off the threat, Young found his leverage in a failing California film processing company called Pathé Laboratories. Pathé owned a huge block of DuPont stock. Young bought the company, thereby acquiring the stock. In order to exert pressure on DuPont, Young threatened the company with a minority lawsuit. The dispute was finally settled with Young selling the DuPont stock back to the company and DuPont allowing Young to gain control of the C&O.

While he had achieved his goal insofar as the railroad was concerned, Young, however, found himself in a different predicament—he now owned a failing company, Pathé, which, if not made profitable, could drain his resources and threaten the continued growth of his railroad empire.

To solve the problem, Young was advised to form a motion picture company that could provide Pathé with enough business to make the company profitable. It just so happened that along with the Pathé acquisition came a lien on a failing movie operation in California called Progressive Pictures, and Progressive happened to own a small studio located at 7324 Santa Monica Boulevard, near the corner of N. Poinsettia Place in Hollywood. Thus, Young approached Leon Fromkess, who had by then gained a reputation as a successful financial expert, reorganizer, and producer in the motion picture industry.

On Fromkess' advice, Young created a new corporate entity using some of Progressive's existing organization and renamed it Producers Releasing Corporation (PRC).[76] He appointed his brother Kenneth as chairman of the board. Fromkess, remaining in New York, was brought in as vice president and general manager in-charge of sales and foreign distribution.

Not long after PRC got underway, the studio's president, a man by the name of O'Henry Briggs, wound up in a dispute with the Youngs. As Leon Kaplan, who was PRC's legal counsel, recalled, Briggs purchased the rights to a story about unwed mothers, a controversial topic at the time. Robert Young took exception to Briggs' purchase, and the story was shelved. More importantly however, remembered Kaplan, the company was failing to produce films fast enough to rescue Pathé. At Young's request, Fromkess moved to California and soon replaced Briggs as President of PRC. He brought with him his wife, Rita, and nine-year-old daughter, Maxine.

What made PRC unique even among B-studios of the time was the meager budget that Fromkess allocated to producing films and how fast they were completed. Most

---

76   For a brief period between the Progressive and PRC designation, the operation was called Producers Distributing Corporation.

PRC films cost about eighty thousand dollars each, or about one-fifth the cost of the average feature film, and they were pumped out at a rate of about one per week.

By snagging talented actors whose careers were just getting off the ground and others whose were in decline, and spending little money on equipment, such as scenery, Fromkess was able to make marketable films at costs that almost guaranteed profits. In less than a year after he took over the operation, PRC became arguably the most successful of the B-studios.

Amusingly, Fromkess' list of players under contract included some of Hollywood's oddest characters, such as a man who went by the name of Parkyarkarkus (a play on the slang phrase "park your carcass"), and "Prince" Michael Romanoff of Russia, who became well known for his upscale Beverly Hills restaurant, which he naturally named Romanoff''s. This self-proclaimed "direct descendant of the Czar" was in reality Harry Gerguson, a former ward of the Hebrew Orphan Asylum, and purportedly the only child on record to have been expelled from that institution.

Fromkess' work ethic, polished appearance, gentlemanly ways, smooth demeanor, and business acumen—the same traits that made him a successful dish salesman and stockbroker—inspired loyalty among the employees and helped propel PRC ahead of other so-called "Poverty Row" studios, despite the poor quality of most of its films.

Robert Young may have organized PRC solely as an adjunct to Pathé, but by 1945, the studio, under Leon Fromkess, had become a moneymaking operation with a library of some three hundred films.

During World War II, with the exception of propaganda pieces, American made films did not get shipped overseas. When the war ended a mad dash ensued for the European film market. Fromkess, on behalf of PRC, scored the biggest foreign mogul of them all: British entertainment magnate J.Arthur Rank.

But Rank didn't just want to act as a distributor of PRC films; he wanted a foothold in Hollywood to expand *his* empire, which, among other things, meant upgrading PRC's product.

At the time, Robert Young was vigorously pursuing control of the New York Central railroad and more income from his motion picture operation would help facilitate that. Influenced by Rank, Robert and Kenneth Young wanted to change PRC's image from that of a cheap, B-studio and began pressing Fromkess to produce bigger budget films.

Fromkess disagreed with the direction the Youngs were taking PRC and he tried to persuade them that attempting to compete with the major studios would result in financial disaster.

But the Youngs remained adamant in their position and began looking to replace the PRC executive staff with names not associated with B-films.

On August 27, 1945, Leon Fromkess, together with almost the entire executive staff of the studio in tow, resigned from PRC. Word of the resignations hit the papers the next day.

The Youngs forged ahead with the Rank deal. Within two years, PRC, which was renamed Eagle Lion Pictures, went deeply in debt and wound up being taken over by New York lawyers Robert Benjamin and Arthur Krim, who installed Warner Brothers' producer Bryan Foy to run the studio's overall production. To head production of crime stories, Foy brought in mobster Johnny Roselli, who together with his associates had slithered their way into Hollywood by loaning money to studio heads, such as Harry Cohn, and controlling the unions.

Eagle Lion went defunct after a few years. Pursuant to a lawsuit, the entire PRC film library wound up in the hands of a New York film salesman and distributor named Armand Schneck. The studio was eventually torn down and the property now hosts a strip mall and parking lot. The only reminder of the lot's filmmaking history is an eight-foot tall, sheet metal sculpture of an old movie camera. The actual street address of PRC is now ingloriously displayed above the door of a Chinese takeout.

Robert Young became stuck in what some have called an unjustified morass of legal difficulties and an unearned public relations black eye over his control of the railroads. On the morning of January 26, 1958, while in the midst of a significant court challenge that didn't look as though it was going in his favor, Young ate breakfast, read the paper, and then retreated to an upstairs room in his Palm Beach, Florida estate, where he closed the door and put a double-barreled shotgun in his mouth and pulled both triggers.[77] Ironically, Young's lawyers prevailed in the lawsuit after his death.

At the time of the PRC turmoil, Samuel Goldwyn Studios, located across the street from PRC, were in financial as well as production crisis.

A pioneer of Hollywood, Sam Goldwyn had long established himself as a successful producer of quality films, but the war had changed everything and his studios were now floundering. According to his son, Sam Jr., Goldwyn had people advising him to make bigger budget pictures while others were saying he needed to cut costs. Goldwyn was an intuitive filmmaker and he was good at it, but he was not a sophisticated businessman. With Leon Fromkess's track record of success in making film operations profitable, Goldwyn saw him as someone who could be instrumental in lifting the stu-

---

77   There was never an official investigation into Young's death, and while he was having difficulties with keeping control of the railroads for a variety of reasons, at the time of his suicide Young's wealth remained secure.

dio out of its doldrums and he offered him the position of Vice President in-charge of Production. Fromkess, it turned out, was the right person at the right time.

His five-year, sixteen-page, exclusive contract with Goldwyn was finalized on April 15, 1946. The agreement was worth about two and a half million dollars in 2010 dollars.

Fromkess went right to work at his new post at Goldwyn. The day he arrived, the studio began filming *The Best Years of Our Lives*, an impressively woven together series of dramatic stories about the lives of returning World War II veterans. Next to *Gone With The Wind*, the film became the biggest moneymaker in Hollywood history, raking in ten million dollars in the first year alone, and winning seven Academy Awards.

Over the next five years, Fromkess headed production on a number of very successful films, including big-budget productions such as *The Bishop's Wife, The Secret Life of Walter Mitty*, and other Hollywood cinema classics.

As vice president in-charge of production of Goldwyn, he was involved in virtually every aspect of production as well as marketing and distribution. His vast experience with low-budget filmmaking made him an expert at saving the studio money, as well as generating profit.

Working under Goldwyn was often a very unpleasant experience for Fromkess. Sam was demanding, egocentric, often given to angry outbursts, and he insisted on unflagging loyalty from everyone on his payroll. Leon had become an expert at making people think he was agreeing with them, "You're absolutely right," he would say, and then do as he pleased. But with Goldwyn, who exerted authoritarian control, Fromkess did not have that freedom. In a 1998 interview with this author, Sam Goldwyn Jr. recalled how on one occasion while at the studio he ran into an exasperated looking Leon who vented, "Sometimes I don't understand your father. Sometimes, no matter how I try to explain something to him, he just doesn't hear me. He just doesn't operate on logic..."

In 1947 Leon underwent an operation at Cedars of Lebanon Hospital for bleeding ulcers.

In 1950, Fromkess wound up in a confrontation with Goldwyn over an issue involving Sam's wife. Frances Goldwyn, a devout, albeit anguished, Catholic, became captivated with a story about a young Catholic man who goes off the deep end after his mother dies and winds up killing a priest using a crucifix as a weapon. Fromkess later claimed that he objected to the story. In a 1970s interview with author Carol Easton, he recalled the confrontation with Goldwyn that ensued:

"Frances brought the galleys to my office, all excited. It would make a great picture she said—I must drop everything and read it. The next day, we had a meeting in Goldwyn's office. Frances was all aglow and aglitter about it. She was one of the most ambitious women you would ever meet; she asserted herself more and more, but never in front of her husband. I told Goldwyn I'd never make it as a picture, that I thought it was sacrilegious even *trying* to make it! He jumped up from his chair—typical—and said, 'Goldwyn makes the pictures!'"[78]

According to his son, Sam Goldwyn was "crazy about Leon." But if Sam's Catholic wife didn't think the story was too controversial, who was Leon Fromkess, a man who had made B-pictures, and his underling, to decide otherwise?

The film, *The Edge of Doom*, wound up getting made and was released in 1950. The picture bombed, and its title aptly projected the future of Goldwyn Studios.

---

78 Carol Easton "The Search For Sam Goldwyn" William Morrow & Co 1976 PP 270-271.

By 1950, the motion picture industry was under a four-pronged attack: The United States Supreme Court had ruled that the studios were in violation of antitrust laws and must divest themselves of the ownership of movie theatres; the House Un-American Activities Committee was targeting the industry, particularly independent producers, such as Goldwyn, for promoting communist ideology and/or employing communists and communist sympathizers; a company that started out as a talent agency, owned and operated by a former ophthalmologist, Dr. Jules Stein, and his right-hand man, Lew Wasserman, a former theatre usher, was destroying the so-called "studio system" by paying residuals to actors, and the television industry was emerging.

On March 19, 1951, after five years of successful filmmaking at Goldwyn, less than a month before his contract was to expire, Fromkess tendered his resignation in a terse, three-line letter:

"I hereby submit my resignation as Vice President of Samuel Goldwyn Productions Inc., effective at your pleasure.
"Very truly yours,
Leon Fromkess"

With his strong reputation as an executive producer who could make successful movies at a price, major studios, such as Paramount, began courting Fromkess to head their overall production. But after the gut-wrenching experience with Goldwyn and with the changes taking place in Hollywood, Leon turned down the studios' offers.

But Fromkess was not thinking retirement.

As he had demonstrated since his days as a salesman and his associations with Columbia, Monogram, PRC, and Goldwyn, Fromkess had a knack for forward thinking and he saw television as the future of American entertainment. Many movie people, including Sam Goldwyn, whom Leon had unsuccessfully tried to convince to get into television, saw the medium as cheap entertainment (i.e., B-movies) that was beneath their dignity. Leon perceived things differently: he loved the business he was in but he wasn't a purist in the movie making sense; he was first and foremost a businessman and he saw television as a consumer friendly form of entertainment with vast potential. It was unique thinking at a time when test patterns were the most common television broadcasts.

In 1951, Fromkess accepted an offer to head production at Jules Stein and Lew Wasserman's Music Corporation of America's new television division. He relocated to the old PRC lot and put together MCA's Television Revue and produced the new entity's first product, the Gruen Guild Theatre.[79]

But MCA's foray into television hit a snag when the Screen Actors Guild (SAG) cried foul. According to SAG, MCA was in violation of union rules by representing players as well as producing shows, a clear conflict of interest.[80]

In 1952, Fromkess decided to go on his own. He left MCA and on February 8th, with backing from oil magnate and real estate investor Harry Rothschild and his brother Victor, formed a new motion picture and television production company, which he named Arrow Productions. Leon brought in Arthur Sachson as vice president in-charge of sales.[81]

---

79 *Gruen Guild Theatre*, alternately known as *Stars Over Hollywood, Chevron Theatre*, and *Gruen Guild Playhouse*, was a series of half hour melodramas.
80 SAG ultimately granted MCA a waiver and the company went on to successfully produce television shows using Fromkess' assembly-line formula. Many have speculated that Ronald Reagan, who was under contract at MCA as an actor and was the president of SAG at the same time, had a role in the unprecedented exemption.
81 Sachson, who had worked with Fromkess at Monogram and also at Goldwyn handling the company's East Coast sales and distribution, seemed to shadow Leon for most of his career.

Fromkess got wind of an intriguing story about a white medical doctor and his adventures in deepest, darkest Africa and purchased the property. *Ramar of the Jungle* became Arrow's first production.[82]

With his office at KTTV Studios in Hollywood and using Griffith Park as the location for shooting jungle scenes, Fromkess began producing half hour episodes of *Ramar* and selling them to the new television networks. The show became an instant success and Arrow entered into agreements with various companies for the manufacture and marketing of spinoff products, such as toys and comic books. Fromkess also combined episodes of *Ramar* to produce three feature-length films. With the income generated by *Ramar*, Arrow purchased more properties and began enlarging its operation.

The company was growing at breakneck speed and needed larger facilities than KTTV could provide. Consequently, Fromkess relocated yet again to the former PRC lot. After the move, Arrow geared up to begin production on a series of half-hour television shows titled *King Arthur and the Knights of the Round Table*, budgeting twenty-five thousand dollars for each episode, a sizeable amount for a TV show in the early 1950s.

Production of the *Ramar* series was stepping up as well and the show was going to be syndicated to several markets across the country through Arrow's newly established distribution subsidiary.

Edward Small was a shrewd businessman who had built up a sizable personal fortune. Since his days as an agent, when he had bailed out Will Morrissey, and his involvement with Fromkess at Monogram, Small had established his own production company and, like Fromkess, had become a ubiquitous figure in motion

---

82 It is uncertain as to whether Fromkess purchased *Ramar* before or after he formed Arrow Productions. There is some speculation that Fromkess saw the potential of *Ramar* and that it was Ramar that inspired him to start Arrow.

picture production. When word spread that Fromkess was gaining momentum with Arrow, Small approached him with an offer to buy out Rothschild.

During the week of May 16, 1953, a deal was consummated in which Small bought out Rothschild for six hundred thousand dollars and became a fifty-percent owner in Arrow. Under the agreement, Fromkess would continue producing *Ramar*, as well as some of Small's theatrical films, and make Arrow's funds available to other independent producers to finance their projects and distribute them under the Arrow name. In essence, the deal increased the company's properties, stoked production, and made Arrow a distribution center for independent producers.

Again needing bigger facilities, Fromkess relocated his office to Goldwyn Studios. Despite his differences with Sam, the two were still on good terms and Leon remained respected and well thought of at the studios.

From 1951 through 1953 a plethora of television-related businesses popped up and buyouts and take-overs were common. While Edward Small was buying his way into Fromkess' Arrow operation, he was also partnering with a wealthy entrepreneur by the name of Milton Gordon in a company they called Television Programs of America (TPA).

Milton Gordon was a Chicago lawyer who made a lot of money manufacturing and selling military uniforms at the start of World War II. Gordon's company had received funding from a well-known New York financier by the name of Walter E. Heller. Heller's company was one of the largest factoring[83] companies in the country.

In 1945, Leon Fromkess engineered a business deal between a New York textile financier by the name of Abe

---

83 Factoring is basically buying a company's accounts receivable at a discount. It is not the same as a loan and it usually involves small to mid size companies that cannot obtain bank loans. Heller's company was listed on the NYSE.

Hirsch, Walter Heller, and Milton Gordon. Leon convinced Hirsch to start financing motion pictures, one picture at a time. Heller, hearing of Hirsch's subsequent success, decided to venture the same. But soon after realizing that he didn't know anything about motion pictures, Heller called Hirsch who called Fromkess who in turn called Leon Kaplan (Robert Young and PRC's former attorney). The three went to Chicago to meet with Heller and a deal was struck whereby Heller would finance pictures and Hirsch's company would supervise everything for a ten-percent interest without any investment or responsibility for the loans. Under the terms of the agreement, Heller financed several films that were produced by United Artists and which were significantly successful. About two years later, Heller's company bought out Hirsch's position and began making motion picture loans on its own. Milton Gordon went to work for Heller, eventually becoming vice president of the company. In that capacity, Gordon engineered the takeover of United Artists and its eighteen-acre studio lot, which was owned by Mary Pickford, Charlie Chaplin, Douglas Fairbanks, and D.W. Griffith, and then later taken over by Sam Goldwyn.

With Small now a partner in Arrow, TPA was in a position to leverage out Fromkess. Small had already apparently wooed away Arthur Sachson who, by 1953, was heading sales for Small's production company. By mid-September 1953, Small and Gordon's TPA had virtually bought out Arrow Productions. Fromkess was retained as executive in-charge of all production.

Leon left the Goldwyn facility and relocated his office back to KTTV Studios.

Over the next year and a half, TPA acquired dozens of properties, established distributors across the country, marketed a bevy of products related to their shows, established a subsidiary in Canada (Normandie

Productions),[84] and produced more than a dozen popular television series, including four of the most beloved shows of early television, *Lassie*, *The Lone Ranger*, *Fury*, and *Ramar of the Jungle*, the latter becoming the most widely syndicated television series in existence, capturing virtually every market in the country.

By 1954, the year that my father met Maxine Fromkess, TPA was one of the largest and most successful producer/distributor of television shows in the world.

---

84 Sigmund and Sam Neufeld, two brothers that had worked for Leon at PRC pumping out mostly cheap westerns and sci-fi, were heading the Normandie operation. In 1954, popular actor John Ireland sued Leon Fromkess and Normandie Productions for $1.7M for slander and breach of contract. Ireland, who was contracted to play the lead in a new TPA series, *New York Confidential*, alleged that Fromkess had fired him amidst accusations that he was a communist sympathizer, a charge that Ireland vehemently denied. The suit was settled for an undisclosed amount.

Chapter Seventeen

Maxine Elyse Fromkess was born on September 6, 1930 in the borough of Manhattan and spent much of her early childhood under the care of a nanny. She attended the Robert Louis Stevenson Elementary School until age nine, when her family moved to California because of her father's business.

In California, Maxine attended the exclusive Hollywood Professional School, which catered to child actors and the children of show business people. She began high school at the even smaller but equally exclusive Mar-Ken School. While at Mar-Ken, Maxie, as her classmates called her, developed a desire to become an actress and she began performing in school plays. In July of 1945, she started taking dramatic lessons at the Bliss-Hayden School of Acting, a respected dramatic school and small theatre located on Robertson Boulevard in Beverly Hills. At Bliss-Hayden, Lelia Bliss, co-owner of the school together with her husband, Harry Hayden, personally coached Maxine.

Maxine's classmates at Mar-Ken were apparently impressed with her thespian skills, writing in the 1945 school journal, "Maxine Fromkess's future as a dramatic actress on the New York stage is pretty certain." And Maxine's hands, with her long, elegant fingers, were chosen to constitute part of what her classmates fantasized as "The Ideal Freshman Girl."

For unknown reasons, Maxine left Mar-Ken before the school year ended and transferred to Beverly Hills High School. However, she soon checked out of Beverly and returned to Hollywood Professional, from where she would graduate in 1948.

Maxine's daily routine largely consisted of going to school half days (Hollywood Professional School ended at 12:20 in the afternoon), coming home for lunch, heading to Bliss-Hayden for a drama lesson, visiting her parents at PRC, occasionally stopping at a store to shop for a dress, a pair of shoes, or the like, and then coming home to meet her tutor for a lesson.

Maxine and her parents rarely ate dinner at home, preferring instead to dine at a variety of high-end Beverly Hills' restaurants, such as Romanoff's, the Brown Derby, Scandia, the Beverly Wilshire Hotel, and Chasen's. When the family was at their home in the Rossmore Arms apartments in Los Angeles, they often had guests, most of whom were older family members or movie-industry friends and associates.

As a teenager, Maxine's life was filled with activities. Besides her daily routine of school, dramatic lessons, and tutoring, she had swimming lessons, sewing lessons, dance lessons, singing lessons, and shorthand lessons.

Being the only child of a successful producer in Hollywood had other advantages as well: Maxine had her hair done at Westmore's, Hollywood's first family of make-up; she often lunched and otherwise hobnobbed with celebrities or other industry people; she shopped at exclusive stores almost with impunity; when her father went out of town on business, which was usually to New York, Maxine, as well as her mother, Rita, traveled with him, and she frequently vacationed with her parents at Arrowhead Springs, Las Vegas, and Palm Springs.

When they first arrived in California, the Fromkess family joined the Wilshire Boulevard Temple, Los Angeles' oldest Reform Jewish congregation and the epicenter of Reform Judaism in Hollywood.

Built with money largely provided by the movie moguls, the Wilshire Boulevard Temple was an imposing, gothic structure capped by a huge byzantine dome. The Temple's tiered and sloped sanctuary had a seating capacity of several thousands and its more than football field-length walls were decorated with elaborate, biblically-themed murals that were painted by artists commissioned by Warner Brothers Studios, the same organization that had built the Hebrew Orphan Asylum's Warner gymnasium. The congregation's leader was a jowly, cigar-chomping, burly man with a deep, gravelly voice by the name of Rabbi Edgar F. Magnin.

A native Californian who at one time wanted to be a writer, Rabbi Magnin was a beloved, fatherly figure to many Jews in Hollywood. That being said, it's difficult to refer to the rabbi as a "spiritual leader," as his connection to religion was at best unconvincing. While he celebrated the Jewish holidays, albeit in a non-traditional way, and was somewhat versed in a variety of Jewish subjects, Magnin could often be seen together with the entertainment industry's elite at the Hillcrest Country Club—Hollywood's Jewish answer to the "restricted" country clubs of the time—where he engaged in card games, drinking, and other such non-rabbinical activities. In fact, Rabbi Magnin distained traditional Judaism and often besmirched those who were faithful to the Torah's tenets, which he believed to be antiquated and in some respects divisive. For example,

241

he would not permit anyone to wear a yarmulke inside his temple, although he allowed church services to be held there on Sundays.

Among the Jews of Los Angeles, Magnin was often referred to as "Father Magnin" and to outsiders as "the rabbi to the stars."

While the Fromkesses were active in the Wilshire Boulevard Temple and maintained a close relationship with Rabbi Magnin, their religious experiences were diverse: they were also members of the Christian Science Church; a popular contradiction among Hollywood's confused Jews of the times.

On April 22, 1946, about a month after he went to work for Goldwyn, Maxine's father purchased a modest house on Elm Drive in Beverly Hills, just around the corner from the Magnin's residence on Maple Drive. It was the family's first privately owned dwelling and along with it came a new beaver coat for Maxine, a maid, and a new dog.

With her father's move to Goldwyn, Maxine's life outside of school became even more privileged and glamorous. Instead of hanging around the relatively small and dreary PRC facility, she had the run of an eighteen-acre movie lot that included sound stages, office complexes, workshops, props, costume and make-up departments, stars dressing rooms, and a large commissary, to name just a few of the studios' amenities. In March 1947, Maxine accompanied her parents to the Shrine Civic Auditorium for the 19th Academy Awards where, at fifteen years old, she sat amongst Hollywood's most notables and watched as *The Best Years of Our Lives* won seven times. Later that spring, Cary Grant, the heartthrob of millions of women in America, escorted Maxine to the Ice Capades.

As she got older, Maxine developed an active night-life. Several times a week she went out on dates that included dinner and dancing at famous Sunset Strip hot spots, such as the Mocambo, Ciro's, and the Trocadero, or movies, prizefights, bingo games, concerts, plays, and baseball and basketball games.

On her way to or from the Goldwyn lot, she still occasionally stopped to visit some of her old friends at PRC.

Maxine was proud of her father and loved him dearly. He was her hero and the most precious thing in the world to her, a sentiment that her father shared and which was recently echoed by Sam Goldwyn Jr., "When you asked Leon about Maxine, you could see his eyes light up. She was obviously the apple of his eye."

On October 26th, 1948, following three days on location in Senora, California with her father for the filming of *Roseanna McCoy*, Maxine checked into Cedars of Lebanon Hospital for a thyroid operation. She was hospitalized for twelve days.

In February of 1949, Maxine's father unexpectedly sold the house on Elm Drive and the family moved to an apartment on Holloway Drive in West Hollywood.

Maxine Fromkess lived a charmed and privileged life. The only glitch seemed to be that she was frequently sick, albeit with vaguely diagnosed maladies.

Chapter Eighteen

With backgrounds so radically different and a fifteen-year age disparity, one would think that my father and Maxine Fromkess would have found little in common, or that Maxine's parents would view my father as unsuitable for their daughter. But neither Maxine nor her parents seemed to have any reservations. My father had some money, thanks to Harry's estate and his efforts to defend the will, besides he was so stunningly handsome and his personality so appealing, that his social status and age made little difference to the many women that yearned to date him.

To my father, everything about Maxine, especially her warmth and enthusiasm for fun, was like an antidote to what he had suffered through for much of his life. And Leon and Rita represented what he longed for most in his life: a loving and supportive mother and father.

Although she was fun loving, Maxine seemed mature beyond her twenty-three years and could be unusually serious minded. Physically, she had blossomed from a plain-Jane child with elegant hands into a strikingly beautiful woman. In keeping with the times, she, like her classmate at Bliss-Hayden, Marilyn Monroe, had her sandy-brown hair bleached blond, and favored deep red lipstick and fingernail polish

Maxine's father's status in the motion picture and television industries was a potential benefit to my father's career, which may have played a role in his attraction to her. But if it did, it wasn't a leading role. My father would never put money before principle and dating a woman for such reasons was anathema to everything he stood for. In fact, it was one of the things he found contemptuous about Harry's marriage to Rose.

Although he dressed meticulously in finely tailored suits and high-end shoes, wore a heavy gold-linked watch, matching star sapphire ring, and drove a shiny, black Cadillac, Leon Fromkess wasn't pretentious or arrogant, and he lived in a sparse but handsomely furnished apartment. When you engaged him in conversation Leon's deep, rich voice, tinged with a modest measure of New York, and his refined, conservative demeanor, reminiscent of an English gentleman, projected the aura of an important personality.

Leon was a gold mine of Hollywood history and anecdotes about the industry and my father would talk with him for hours on end, eagerly listening to everything he had to say. My father recalled having asked him what accomplishment in his movie-making career he was most proud of. Without hesitation, Leon said *"The Best Years of Our Lives."* He came to respect Leon not just as a filmmaker, but also as the venerable patriarch of a close-knit family.

Maxine's mother, Rita, was quite the contrast to her husband. She dressed well and her black hair, with a streak of silver running from her widow's peak, was always nicely coiffed and dramatically accentuated her deep-red, full lips. Even without her three-inch spike-heel shoes, Rita was taller than her husband and heavier framed. And as much as Leon was genteel and even-tempered, Rita was outspoken and aggressive. She also had a peculiar, nervous habit of moving her scalp back and forth, as though she was wearing a loose-fitting wig, and a boorish tendency to chew food with her mouth open.

Despite her idiosyncrasies, my father appreciated Rita as a take-charge kind of person, a caring mother, and a strong, supportive wife.

Claire was fond of Maxine, finding her to be an elegant yet down to earth young woman. But though she could not put her finger on anything specific, Claire's instincts told her that something wasn't quite right with Maxine, and she did not trust Leon and Rita. Furthermore, she felt her brother was ignoring these intangible warning signs because of Leon's notoriety in Hollywood.

Following an incident involving her brother at a local restaurant, Claire's concerns intensified.

My father had gone out to dinner with Leon, Rita and Maxine. While waiting for their orders to arrive, a patron in the next booth, who was being loud and obnoxious, made a snide comment about Rita. My father admonished the man for disrespecting a lady. When the guy continued to mouth off, he angrily suggested that he either "find another place to sit, or keep your damn mouth shut." Things quickly escalated and the two men stood up and faced off. My father took the first swing. But, as had happened to Uncle Willy with Tom Mix, his haymaker missed its mark. A full-fledged brawl ensued. When the dust settled, other than a broken pair of reading glasses, he, together with the Fromkesses, exited the restaurant unharmed, but leaving the loud mouth reeling, and the restaurant in turmoil.

My father wasn't proud of what he had done, but neither was he ashamed. In his zeal, he had simply wanted to defend the honor of a lady and he felt his sister was being overprotective, and that her suspicions were unwarranted.

After the atomic bombs were dropped on Japan, uranium became a sought-after commodity. In 1954, two uranium deposits were discovered in Kern County, California, just north of Bakersfield. Upon learning of the find, Bud persuaded his brother-in-law to join him on a dig. After buying a small Geiger counter, a shovel, pickaxe, and new boots, the two travelled to the Sierra Nevada Mountains in search of buried, radioactive treasure.

On December 16th, while searching off of a dirt path called Piute Road, their Geiger counter alarmed. After mapping the area, my father and Bud drove back to L.A., where my father went to the local Western Union office and telegrammed Uncle Willy: "Meet Me Bakersfield Tomorrow Found Uranium Bring Gang To Dig Hole," he facetiously wrote. Remarkably, Morrissey showed up the next day and the three intrepid prospectors staked a claim, which my father named "Red Piute IV." However, the project was scrapped when no investors could be found and my father and Maxine Fromkess got engaged.

On March 6, 1955, in a simple ceremony attended by family members and a few select friends, my father married Maxine Fromkess at the Beverly Hills home of Rabbi Edgar Magnin, followed by a reception at the Beverly Hills Hotel.

The reception was an elegant but modest affair attended by about a hundred guests. Entertainment was provided by big band musician Les Baxter and a few select members of his orchestra.

When the music stopped, my father and Maxine exited the hotel to a shower of rice thrown by the few remaining guests, including Uncle Willy, who had shown up in an old tuxedo and managed to remain sober the entire night. They were going to spend their honeymoon at the California Hotel in Santa Barbara and conveniently Uncle Willy needed a ride back there as well. On cue, Morrissey walked down to the end of the hotel driveway where my father picked him up and the three headed north to Santa Barbara.

After the honeymoon, the couple returned to Los Angeles to their newly rented apartment at 8569 Burton Way, not far from where Leon and Rita lived.

My father continued with his acting career and his new father-in-law helped him score a few gigs, including leading roles in episodes of several TV series, such as *Death Valley Days,* and some TPA productions.

But Leon Fromkess didn't particularly like actors and understood the uncertainty of the profession as well as anyone. He wanted his son-in-law to move into production alongside him. It was a sensible suggestion from a credible source and my father prudently agreed to make the switch. He was put on the TPA payroll at thirteen thousand dollars per year as production coordinator of the popular western series *Fury. Fury,* starring Peter Graves, was the story of a widowed rancher, a wild horse (Fury), and an orphan boy, the only one that could ride him.

As he worked alongside his father-in-law, my father became impressed with how well Leon ran things: his uncanny ability with numbers, and the calm, creative manner in which he handled problems that would have driven most executive producers into fits of anger. An amusing anecdote that my father related, colorfully demonstrates the point; it involved an Internal Revenue Service audit.

When the IRS agent, a tall, lanky, bureaucrat-type named Bruce Biggs, walked into Leon's office, he probably thought he was going to snag a big fish. In reality, although Biggs didn't know it, he was already standing in the trap.

Leon first overwhelmed the government man with paperwork. Biggs wasn't surprised; he'd seen the same stunt many times before. However, the sheer volume of what was dumped in front of him this time was shocking. It would take weeks to scrutinize the boxes of intentionally jumbled paperwork. But that was just the stick; the carrot came next: "Has anyone ever told you that you'd be perfect for westerns?" Leon dangled.

Biggs wouldn't have ordinarily fallen for such an obvious con job, but coming from TPA's executive producer was overwhelmingly seductive and he took the bait, Hollywood-hook, line, and sinker.

Biggs was escorted to the make-up and costume departments, where he was prepared for his screen test. No one but my father and Leon knew what was really going on.

The cameraman and director could hardly contain themselves when the gangly and hopelessly untalented IRS man, looking ridiculous in pancake makeup and stereotypical western getup, including a ten-gallon hat, catatonically read his lines.

Biggs acting career predictably ended there. However, he quit the IRS and became Leon's personal accountant. The audit resulted in no deficiencies, of course.

On December 28th, 1955, Maxine gave birth to a baby boy who was named Leon Fromkess Bennett. Leon Jr., as he would come to be called, was to be the standard-bearer of his grandfather's legacy.

Twenty-one months after Leon Jr. was born, on September 18, 1957, Maxine gave birth to the couple's second son, whom they named Michael Mark Bennett.

Chapter Nineteen

M y family moved into a three-bedroom duplex on Alfred Street in the Pico-Robertson area of Los Angeles. A middle-aged black woman from the south named Bertha Mae Rhoden, whom everyone simply called Mae, came to work for us. My father continued working on the *Fury* series.

After the TPA buyout of Arrow, *Fury* was the new company's first production and it remained one of TPA's top products. But as is often the case with child actors, Bobby Diamond, who played the orphan boy Joey in the series, was outgrowing his original role. To fill the void and give greater depth to the story, my father suggested adding a younger character to the show. Auditions were held and out of two hundred and twelve potential candidates, my father zeroed in on an eight-year-old, bright-eyed kid with a cleft chin and a pompadour hairstyle named Roger Mobley. Ray Nazarro, the *Fury* series' director, wanted another prospect, a mischievous-looking youngster with a blond cowlick by the name of Jay North.[85] Mobley got the part.

Roger Mobley and two of his siblings performed a musical act at county fairs and similar venues around Texas. After the trio appeared on the popular TV show *Ted Mack's Original Amateur Hour*, the children's father, Lance Mobley, got a phone call from Hollywood agent Lola Moore. Moore thought Roger was a natural and convinced the senior Mobley to bring his young son out to California to audition for the new *Fury* series character, Homer "Packey" Lambert.

After the audition, a panel that included my father and director Nazarro interviewed Roger. It turned out that Mobley had no acting experience whatsoever. But that made no difference to my father. Like agent Moore, he saw Roger's natural talent and felt he could mentor the boy in any way needed.

When my father learned that Roger's mother, Charlene, had been snookered into a contract giving forty-percent of his earnings to a Texas based manager, he took Roger and his parents over to the Beverly Hills law office of Richie Mark, whom my father met in Manila in 1945 when Richie had gone there to claim the body of his brother who was killed in the Bataan Death March. After the war, Richie had used his G.I. Bill benefits to pay for law school. While their personalities were different, Richie being more reserved than my father, the two men shared similar values and character and continued their friendship after the war. Richie was able to get Roger's abusive contract nullified and my father signed him up with a legitimate agent for a normal fee.

On Roger's first day on the set, Ralph Black, the assistant director, introduced the eight-year-old to his horse, Stove Legs, and told him to "just ride around and

---

85 Jay North went on to become famous for the lead role in the television series *Dennis The Menace*.

get used to it." It was the moment of truth for Roger: during the interview he had lied about knowing how to ride.

After observing the obviously inexperience boy atop the horse, director Nazarro called Roger off to the side. Nazarro, whom Roger recently recalled as being a short, mustachioed man with dark eyes and a prominent nose whom everyone called "Little Caesar," fumed at the petrified child, telling him, "I didn't want you in the first place!"

In addition to having no acting experience and unable to ride a horse, Roger had another problem: a pronounced southern drawl, which none of the other actors shared and would therefore seem out of place in the story.

With his reputation on the line and a miffed Nazarro sniffing for Roger's blood, my father went to work teaching young Mobley how to neutralize his drawl. Roger's mother started bringing him to our house on Alfred Street and, as he had done with Wayne, my father taught him proper diction, having him endlessly repeating sounds—*"dee, dee-dee-dee, dee-dee dah dah dah, on the tip of the tongue, on the tip of the tongue"*—while biting down on a cork or a pencil with his front teeth. Wayne, who became a professor of speech, recently explained the exercise:

"The cork was an impediment used to make you work harder to be understood. Demosthenes, the great Geek orator, had a speech defect in his youth. To overcome it, he went down to the seashore, put pebbles in his mouth, and then tried to speak loudly and clearly over the waves. He learned to overcome his speech impediment by exercising the muscles of his lips, tongue, and mouth.

"In the case of Roger Mobley, the cork may have been used to move him away from his drawl. However, he must also have had to learn proper placement of tongue and lips in General American pronunciation and proper accenting of words—things your father knew about. All of these things together were necessary to help remove a Southern draaaaaawwlllllll that might have been very pleasant to the ear but politically incorrect at that time..."

Director Nazarro kept a chip on his shoulder when it came to Roger, seizing any opportunity he could find, or manufacture, to come down hard on the kid. But having my father in his corner meant that Mobley had a strong advocate and his mere presence on the set was usually enough to keep the tyrannical director in check.

Just as things were getting better for Roger in terms of freedom to play his part without having to worry about Nazzaro bashing him, he experienced a setback.

After completing outdoor filming at Iverson's Movie Ranch located in the hills just north of Chatsworth, the cast and crew of *Fury* relocated back to the KTTV studios in Hollywood to shoot interior scenes. At the conclusion of the first day's shoot, Roger's mother took him to a little league ballgame where he wound up getting hit in the face with a baseball bat. At six o'clock the following morning, Roger, accompanied by his mom, showed up for work with a broken nose, two black eyes, and a swollen face.

Preempting any potential abuse by Nazarro, my father, who was always the first one to arrive on the set, pointedly told the director to "shoot around the kid until his face heals."

Nazarro was an experienced and accomplished director and my father respected him for that, even though he disagreed with him over who should get the part of Packey. But to my father, the director's menacing and otherwise cruel treatment of Roger was nothing less than bullying, which meant that Nazzaro was picking a fight he was going to lose.

Besides mentoring him in diction and running interference for him, my father often took Roger aside and told him in fatherly tones about how he was "a better man" than the director, and that he "shouldn't be afraid of Nazzaro." The coaching settled Roger down and he grew more confident in his role. Until, that is, he suffered another crisis.

During the filming of a scene in which Roger was to jump on the back of the bad guy, everything was going according to script until the actor threw Roger to a group of men waiting off camera to catch him. As the burly character manhandled Roger, the butt of his rifle accidentally slammed into the child's mouth. Watching the scene replayed at the daily rushes, my father cringed and his heart bled as he saw the violent blow and Roger lying on the ground crying, "Mamma, mamma, mamma."

Later, in a similar scene, Roger wound up getting more seriously injured. This time when he was being tossed aside, the hammer and firing pin of the rifle caught him in the crook of his elbow, ripping open a gaping wound, severing a vein and exposing the tendons. When the rushes of the episode were viewed, Roger's blood could be seen spurting into camera range.

After his arm was hastily bandaged, Roger was rushed to a hospital in Chatsworth, where doctors used eighty-seven stitches to close the gash.

Despite the seriousness of his injury, Roger didn't miss a day's work, even that of the accident itself.

Roger's parents, whom my father remembered as "some of the nicest people you'd ever want to meet," were good, hardworking people, and enormously proud of their young son. They were also very grateful to my father for taking Roger under his wing.

Roger Mobley's experiences as an actor, of which his relationship with my father was pivotal, are a welcomed contrast to the tragic fate of many of Hollywood's child stars. His recent reminiscences of his days working at TPA are both instructive and inspiring:

"Other than being afraid of Ray Nazarro, it was absolutely wonderful being on the *Fury* set. I would wake up in a different world every day. I spent my summers being surrounded by horses and very interesting people. My favorites were the horse wranglers and the stuntmen. I had nothing but fun. My experience was fantastic. But I still managed to live a normal childhood. My dad drove a truck, my mom carried me to the studio, I played little league ball, I went to public school and had a pack of non-actor friends, and I lived in Whittier, which is like thirty-five miles from Hollywood, which back then might as well have been a hundred thirty-five miles."

Ray Nazarro wound up getting canned from *Fury*. Roger played the part of Packey for three years under a new and kinder director. He also went on to act in more than seventy-five prime time television shows and star in several Disney feature films, before being drafted into the United States Army.

During his military service, Roger became a Green Beret serving with the 46th Special Forces Co. operating in Thailand, Laos, Cambodia, and Vietnam.

Now in his sixties, a proud father and grandfather, Roger Mobley still feels guilty at having lied about his horseback riding experience. And to this day he remembers my father with fondness and respect as someone who was "the epitome of a gentleman," in an industry where there were few gentlemen, and as "just a tremendously handsome guy."

Shortly after my parents' marriage, my mother began having vaguely diagnosed health problems, which became more frequent and incapacitating, and, eventually, day nurses had to be called in. Consequently, from practically the time of my birth, Mae handled basically everything regarding the care of my brother and me.

Also, shortly after my brother was born, Rita grew ever more domineering, and she increasingly rubbed my father the wrong way. Of particular annoyance was her insistence on feeding my brother as though she was stoking a locomotive, as well as her demonstrative favoritism towards him after I was born. When she showed up at the house one day with an entire crate of California oranges "for little Leon," my father had had enough. He took the crate from her, walked to the front door, and threw the whole thing onto the sidewalk. Then, in his intensely inimical way, he turned to Rita and said, "The next time you bring anything over to this house, you better bring something for both of these children *or I'll throw you out!*" Once again, someone doing something hurtful to a child was cause for my father to mount an angry and vigorous defense.

The confrontations would increase in frequency as well as intensity.

Chapter Twenty

Texas oil baron Jack Wrather got into the picture business after World War II. In the 1950s, he started buying up television stations and soon founded his own broadcasting corporation. In 1957, Wrather bought the *Lassie* and *Lone Ranger* series from TPA, although they continued being produced at TPA's rented facilities using the company's employees.[86]

The following year, Wrather partnered with the owners of the London Palladium, Lew and Leslie Grade, to form a company called the International Television Corporation (ITC). Later that year, ITC began negotiations with Edward Small and Milton Gordon over the purchase of the rest of TPA's products. In early 1959, ITC completed the acquisition of TPA for a whopping eleven million three hundred and fifty thousand dollars.[87] As my father remembered, my grandfather received about three hundred thousand for his contribution to the

---

86 The same year, when Walt Disney had stretched himself to the limit in building up his theme park in Anaheim, California, Wrather financed the building of the Disneyland Hotel, eventually becoming the owner.
87 It was the equivalent of approximately one hundred million in 2011 dollars.

company and may have retained an interest in some of the original TPA properties.

With the sale of TPA, Pop, as my brother and I called him, decided that after thirty years in the business it was time to retire.

My father, on the other hand, was facing unemployment with a family to support, including a frequently ill wife. Going back to acting was not an option. Despite difficulties with Rita, his relationship with Leon remained solid. The two often lunched together and closely followed the stock market, an interest my grandfather had retained since his days as a broker and one my father had become intrigued by. When the negotiations for the sale of TPA started looking like the deal would go through, Pop suggested he enter the brokerage business. Once he'd obtained his license and secured a job, my grandfather would channel his industry colleagues and others to him. By having his son-in-law as his personal broker, Pop would have an inside track on hot stocks and someone who would give his portfolio top priority. My father liked the idea. He would be starting with a leg up in a profession with greater potential than his job at TPA.

In 1959, after passing the licensing exam on his first try, my father landed a job as a broker with the Beverly Hills office of the major securities firm Hayden Stone. Soon afterwards, in agreement with his father-in-law, he held a cocktail party to drum up business. Many Hollywood notables and some of California's big business and political movers and shakers attended, including California Governor Goodwin Night, Los Angeles District Attorney Ernie Roll, and gambling-syndicate boss Bob Gans. Although my father didn't know it, Gans, together with a former corrupt Los Angeles police officer named Guy McAfee, reportedly controlled gambling and prostitution operations on the Sunset Strip and other locations around L.A. Gans slot machine empire alone was reputed to be in excess of twenty thousand machines. While the party was underway, Gans approached my father:

"Bob Gans asked me for five business cards. Monday morning I received more orders than I could handle. The house manager said that they never had anyone open as many accounts as I did."

My father had become vaguely aware of Bob Gans reputation from an earlier, unrelated incident: Supporting hospitals and old-age homes were the popular charities among the television and movie industry people of the day. My mother and grandparents had been featured in the society pages for years for their involvement in such activities. As part of his social networking in Hollywood, after his marriage to my mother, my father joined the Mt. Sinai Hospital Men's Club, whose primary function was to raise funds for the building of a new hospital.[88] Planning a major fundraiser for the new facility, my parents paid a visit to local radio and television celebrity and conservative political commentator George Putnam.[89] They intended to ask Putnam to be the toastmaster of the event. Bob Gans, a large benefactor of the hospital, was being honored at the affair as "Man of the Year." Decades later, my father recalled the meeting, and also offered some revelations:

"Everything went fine and then, I don't know some short time later [Putnam] called us and asked us to come down to see him. So we went down to the studio and we saw him and he was quite irate that we didn't

---

88 The new hospital involved a merger between Cedars of Lebanon and Mt. Sinai hospitals and was named Cedars Sinai.

89 Putnam, at the time, hosted the highest rated newscast in Los Angeles. Over the course of his more than 70-year career, Putnam served as the anchor for every major Los Angeles area television and radio news station.

tell him about Bob Gans background. He had some nefarious history that we didn't really know about [at the time]...Putnam had a television program, the early days of television, and he kept commenting on Ernie Roll's crooked activities, and he used to have a chair sitting right next to him and inviting Ernie Roll to come up and to be interviewed on television. And he never did. He refused. We used to go to the racetrack—your grandfather loved the races—and it was there that I found out, from your grandfather, that Ernie Roll was taking his payoff at the track...from various sources, ya know, and also, Sam Katzman, who was a producer—cheap westerns, he used to take his payoff from everyone he hired, made 'em kick back money, see, and he would go to the racetrack and he would launder the money at the racetrack..."

The fundraiser took place at the Ambassador Hotel and went off without a hitch, with George Putnam as the master of ceremonies. Spontaneous laughs were provided when in a response to a call for donations, a well-known wealthy businessman with an Eastern European Jewish accent pledged "Fy towzen dahllas... anonymous!"

It was at yet another hospital fundraiser, the Children's Aid Society of Mt. Sinai Hospital, where my father ran into a demon from his past, Lionel J. Simmons.

Although somewhat nonplused at seeing the former orphanage superintendant,[90] my father was congenial and made some small talk with Simmonds. But after the brief encounter, he walked away in disgust at the

---

90 Prior to World War II, the Hebrew Orphan Asylum shut down operations due to the movement toward smaller, home-like facilities. During the war, the facility was used as a barracks of sorts for the army. After the war, all but the Warner Gymnasium was demolished and the property reverted to the city of New York. It is now a park with a small section of the Warner Gym remaining as the only reminder of the HOA's existence.

memory of abuse he had suffered in the HOA under the Colonel's administration.

In 1961, my father put a down payment on a large ranch house in a new and exclusive enclave of the San Fernando Valley south of Ventura Boulevard and just east of Sepulveda Boulevard. Besides its four bed-rooms, three baths, sunken living room, screened-in porch, and modern eat-in kitchen, the house at 3901 Woodfield Drive featured a semi-circular driveway, a two-car garage, and a large backyard complete with a full-size, in-ground swimming pool including a diving board. He traded in his Thunderbird convertible for a Lincoln Continental. He also purchased season tickets to the Los Angeles Dodgers baseball games—box seats along the third base line, just a few rows from the field at the newly built Dodger Stadium.

My cousin Dennis recalls that period:

"I remember the days when your father worked at Hayden Stone on Wilshire and Beverly Drive, my mother and I would regularly go there as the market was closing, to have lunch with him (probably dur-ing the summer time for me, as I would have been in school otherwise). Leon [Fromkess] was often there, and I remember him going to lunch with us along with a man who was an actor, whose name escapes me at the moment. Your father did not go to coffee shops for lunch; he took us all to the Tail O' The Cock, which was an upscale restaurant on La Cienega Blvd. They had linen table cloths, cocktails were ordered, etc. One ate a steak sandwich there, I recall, not a burger! Your dad was a big spender and lived well. He drove us in his cream-colored Lincoln Continental."

The only thing that seemed to be missing from my father's new lifestyle was membership in a country club. That vacuum was filled after he met with an entrepreneurial Texan by the name of Bob Dedman. Dedman had recently started a company called Country Clubs Incorporated[91] and he was in California finalizing plans and signing up new members for his venture's second project—a private club that would include three golf courses, two swimming pools, tennis courts, and a large clubhouse. Dedman's philosophy was that by building clubs with diverse activities that could support a larger than average membership, he could create private clubs that were affordable to the middle class.

After spending the day with Dedman, which included flying in a small Cessna over the planned site of the new facility in the northern foothills of the Santa Monica Mountains, my father put a six-hundred dollar deposit down on a thirteen-hundred dollar lifetime family membership in the soon to be completed Deauville Country Club.

My father, it appeared, had finally made it. He was no longer looking through the candy store window.

His background notwithstanding, or perhaps because of it, when my father married my mother he pretty much dove head first into all aspects of her family's lifestyle, including their association with the Christian Science Church. Among other things, Christian Scientists generally don't believe in traditional medicine as a first option when treating illnesses. Consequently, when he experienced symptoms of what could have been a heart attack, my father did not seek medical care.

While Claire had remained suspicious of my mother's family and felt that her brother was increasingly

---

91 Bob Dedman eventually became known as "the richest man in golf" and Country Clubs Incorporated, now called "ClubCorp," is currently the largest operator of private clubs and resorts in the world.

living beyond his means, she generally kept her feelings to herself. But when the incident of his suspected heart attack and refusal to seek medical care took place, Claire became alarmed, and she made her feelings known in passionate terms.

My father reacted by dismissing his sister's concerns in his typically adamant way and the two personalities came to loggerheads over the issue, resulting in their not speaking to each other for about a year.

Cousin Dennis:

"One trait that your dad and my mom shared was stubbornness and a tendency to stick to principle, right or wrong. I think this was the main reason why their falling-outs lasted so long: neither would bend nor budge regardless of the hurt they caused on each other and themselves. Their relationship was so close and so intense that they could either be very close or completely separated. I know my mom tended to see things as either black or white, so it could be one or the other with her and Mark."

My father eventually went to see famed Beverly Hills cardiologist Dr. Eliot Corday, who found no evidence of a heart attack. He and Claire eventually mended their differences, or as Dennis put it, "they ended their Cold War," and my father brought Claire, Bud, Wayne and Dennis with us on vacation to Palm Springs, where we all stayed in private bungalows at the recently built Ocotillo Lodge, the latest vacation hot spot of the Hollywood elite, and where I was content to spend the days sitting in the kiddie pool.

Back at our house on Woodfield, my father started teaching me how to swim. It took a while to get me over my terror of the water, but my father's past as a competitive swimmer, which was readily apparent from his proficiency in the pool, and his fatherly love, strength, and patience won out. I went from being an edge-clinger or hanging on to his strong, athletic arms, to a fearless and agile swimmer. He taught me how to use my legs to propel myself through the water, how to turn my head and breathe while swimming, and how to do the Australian crawl and Butterfly styles of swimming. Once I became good at holding my breath under water, my father would chip golf balls into the pool and my brother and I would dive in and race to the bottom to retrieve them. I was small and skinny, Leon was big and husky, I usually came up with the ball first and was rewarded with the only prize I ever wanted—my father's loving, proud smile.

It was on Woodfield that opportunity arose for my father to teach my brother his famous lesson on how to deal with a bully.

Leon was on his way home from school one day when a local punk pounced on him. With the tormenter in hot pursuit, Leon ran home and fearfully told our father what was going on. After taking him outside to confront the bully, who, remarkably, was waiting in the front yard, my father turned to my brother and instructed, "You don't run from bullies, you punch them in the face. Now go get him!" After a few minutes of the two boys tussling on the ground, my brother clearly gaining the upper hand, my father stepped in and pulled Leon off the beaten kid and told the little coward, *"Now, get outta here!"* I stood to the side watching the whole scene and feeling awestruck by my father's strength and determination. I was proud of my big brother too; he had stood up to a bully.

My brother and I frequently enjoyed playing in the grass-covered backyard of that house. My father had two golf clubs cut down to as he would say "midget size" and he taught us how to play.

Leon and I were typical siblings and from time to time we'd horse around or get into tiffs. When that happened, Mae disciplined us by breaking off a thin branch from one of the large Magnolia trees on the property and used it as a switch across our legs. After employing the technique only a couple of times, all Mae had to do to get our attention was threaten that she was "gonna getta switch and whup you boys."

On one occasion when I was about four or five years old, I vividly remember getting myself into hot water with Mae completely by reflex. I was sitting on a stool at the kitchen counter having a conversation with Mae when I said the word 'damn.' I don't recall what prompted me to use that word, or where I picked it up at such a tender age. But in response to my inappropriate language, Mae yanked me over to the kitchen sink, picked up a bar of soap and proceeded to pry my mouth open and force it inside, grinding the bar against my struggling-to-be-clenched teeth. Despite the rough treatment, deep inside I sensed that Mae was doing what she felt was needed to teach me a lesson. In other words, she was acting out of her love and concern for me, not her own anger.

When my father learned of what had happened, his reaction was one of concern over what I had said, a twang of sympathetic pain for what I had endured, and solemn resolve that I needed to learn an important lesson. Although I wouldn't use the procedure on my own children or recommend it to others, to this day when I think back about the incident, I still respect Mae for what she had done and how she had done it. Most of all, I smile inside about my father's perfectly balanced, fatherly reaction, but I can still taste the soap.

The only memory I have from those days of having tested my father's patience to the breaking point occurred one night at dinner. We were all seated around the kitchen table and Mae began serving split pea soup, which I abhorred. Momentarily forgetting about my aversion, she placed a bowl of the slimy looking stuff in front of me. In a bad mood to begin with, I angrily shoved the bowl away, directly towards my father, causing the green gunk to slosh into his lap. I was instantly mortified. As my father rapidly rose in anger, wiping the hot goo from his shirt and pants, I made a beeline for my room and hid underneath the covers of my bed, cowering in mortal fear. My father entered the room and, seeing how frightened I was, simply said, "You're going to bed without dinner," turned off the light and closed the door. I went to sleep feeling sad but lucky at having dodged a bullet.

It was in that house that I first saw any hint of my father's experiences during the war.

Leon and I shared a bedroom just across the narrow hallway from our parents' room. The master bathroom had two doors, one of which opened to the narrow hallway facing our room. While standing in the doorway of our bedroom one evening, I saw my father through the open bathroom door. He was wearing an undershirt and boxers and had his left foot perched atop the commode and was softly grunting while doing something to his leg. Curious, and a little worried by the strained sounds my father was making, I walked up next to him and silently watched as he pushed his thumbs down and inward from either side of a spot on the top of his thigh. As he squeezed and quietly grunted, a small, dark object began to approach the surface. As he continued to squeeze, the entity, irregularly shaped and a little larger than a pea, slowly began to emerge. Grasping the object between his fingers, my father pulled it out of his leg. After looking at it for a moment, he dropped it into the water where it sank to the bottom without resistance. "What was that, Dad," I asked. He said something vague and meaningless about "the war." I didn't ask any more questions. Much later in life, I learned that what my father had squeezed out of his leg was shrapnel from the Japanese mortar that had exploded in the palm tree on that jungle hill on Los Negros in March of 1944: the mortar that killed his radioman and wounded several of his other men.

While my father was steadily building his brokerage clientele, he also invested in a fledgling business with an African American friend, Pat Moore, who developed a hair straightening gel. I remember Pat as a kind, gentle, and very handsome man. My father had been using the gel to straighten his hair since he became a stockbroker.

Not yet three years into retirement, in July of 1962, Pop partnered with a wealthy businessman by the name of Sam Firks to produce several feature films. Their new partnership was called F&F Productions.

My father on Sam Firks:

"Gambling was legal in Los Angeles when I came in 1933. Bob Gans was friendly with Mayor George Shaw, and Sam Firks worked for Bob Gans, handling his overseas slot machines in the Orient. And when Fletcher Bowron defeated George Shaw for mayor,[92] he outlawed gambling, and that brought Sam Firks back here and by that time the war was over and Bob Gans helped Sam get into the building business, where he made his fortune."

As the business relationship between my grandfather and Sam Firks progressed, my parents became socially friendly with Sam and his wife, Gerri.

---

92   Shaw was actually recalled before Bowron was elected.

From the deep recesses of his memory, Dennis, Claire's youngest son, recently recalled when, at twelve years old, he went to dinner with my parents and Sam and Gerri Firks:

"The dinner at Trader Vic's was, I suppose, simply a social event with my parents, yours, and the Firks... My recollection of Sam is that he was very outgoing, friendly and sociable...I was much more interested in Gerri, who was very sweet and friendly to me. She seemed to be pals with your mother; they were both much younger than their husbands, pretty, blond, and glamorous. I was seated next to Gerri, and she doted on me, ordered me a Virgin Mai Tai, which came in a pineapple like all the adults received. The waitress was not sure which one was for me, and everyone thought it was great fun that I might have gotten a real Mai Tai. It was a lively and fun evening."

1962 was a good year for my father. He had two sons, a beautiful wife, and a good job with a promising future in a field he had come to enjoy immensely, as well as a large house and membership in a country club.

But all was not harmonious on Woodfield Drive.

Chapter Twenty-One

"Look out kid, they keep it all hid."
— Bob Dylan

After we moved to the house on Woodfield, despite her affiliation with Christian Science, my mother continued seeing doctors on an abnormally regular basis; and she began spending more time with her parents.

Adding to her troubling activities, she had been frivolously spending money at an increasing rate and running up large bills at local department stores. Warnings from my father that they were living beyond their means went completely ignored.

With my brother in school and my father working all day, Mae was practically my only company and sole caretaker.

When my mother started running a prolonged fever in the spring of 1964, she was hospitalized at Cedars of Lebanon for observation. Several days after her admission, a doctor at the hospital called my father to discuss her condition. He said that they were unable to find any signs of disease and asked if she was taking any medication. The question rang an alarm bell; it was a bell warning of an approaching train wreck that my father had been more or less pushing aside for years.

My father became concerned about my mother's frequent health problems and her continuous doctor's appointments shortly after their marriage, but because these issues and activities were ever-present, they evolved into the proverbial elephant in the room that nobody notices.

In November of 1960, when my brother and I were four and three years old, respectively, while we were living on Alfred Street, Mae had been having trouble sleeping and doctors at the City of Hope Medical Center[93] gave her some sleeping pills. When one day she returned to the house after running an errand, she found my mother sprawled out on her bed and the day nurse trying to figure out what had happened. When she went to her room that night to get ready for bed, Mae discovered that the sleeping pills, which she had kept in her purse, were gone. My father was not told about the incident.

On another occasion, the wife of Beverly Hills developer Paul Trousdale—the couple were family friends—had been visiting when my mother asked her to stay with the kids while she ran out for something. Mrs. Trousdale later reported to my father that she had seen "Maxine driving all over the street."

And on a third occasion during the four years that we were living on Alfred Street, family friends, Alfred and Rhoda Hyman, approached my father, telling him that my mother, while visiting their apartment, had taken pills[94] from their medicine cabinet. After my

---

93 The City of Hope was established by Jewish charities in 1913 primarily to isolate and treat victims of tuberculosis, which was epidemic at the time. In the 1950s, the medical center served poor and indigent patients from the predominantly African American and Hispanic areas of Los Angeles.
94 These were likely Phenobarbitals, as reported by Rhoda Hyman to the author in 2011.

father confronted her about the accusation in the presence of Mae, my mother admitted to having stolen the pills.

In the winter of 1963, after we had moved to the house on Woodfield, Mae had just returned to work from a two-week vacation when the neighbor's maid, Annie, related to her incidents of my mother's bizarre behavior, saying, "Max had been acting up." Mae subsequently found a stash of pills in a brown paper bag in a locked cedar closet in the house. She left the bag in place and told no one. When she went to retrieve something from the same closet days later, the bag had disappeared. It later turned up inside the obviously bulging pocket of a robe in my mother's bedroom closet.

When my mother developed a rash on her face and pus-filled sores under her fingernails, my father, suspecting that pills were behind the symptoms, went to Mae's room in search of the drugs, deducing that my mother might have hidden them there thinking it was a safe hiding place. When he found the pills in Mae's drawer, he summoned my mother to the room. With the three of them assembled, my father asked Mae about the pills. In response, Mae, angry and dismayed, accusingly looked at my mother, who conspiratorially winked at her. My father caught the exchange and instantly knew what was going on. After he confronted her, my mother admitted that the pills were hers and agreed to throw them out.

When the doctor asked him about whether his wife was taking any medications, my father said that he suspected she might be taking pills and would find out and call him back.

Mae was dedicated to her job and especially to caring for my brother and me. She loved us as though we were her own children. She had said nothing to my father about my mother's use of pills and erratic behavior because she felt it wasn't her place to get involved, and she may have feared that if my father knew everything, it would lead to the breakup of the family. However, Mae would never lie to my father, and when he asked her about my mother's drug use she told him the truth. When he asked if she knew where my mother kept the pills, she led him to my mother's closet and pointed to a brown, alligator-leather bag that contained a stash of pills. They included prescription narcotics as well as over-the-counter cold remedies containing powerful ingredients, such as codeine, which were uncontrolled substances in those days.

Faced with the now undeniable reality that his wife had a serious drug problem, my father knew that the next decision was going to be a tough one: whether or not to have her institutionalized. It was a question that he agonized over for more reasons than will be revealed now. But suffice it to say, his family and all that he had finally achieved after a lifetime of hardships and disappointments was in danger of exploding from within, and the safety and welfare of his children were at stake.

His next move was to discuss the situation with his wife's parents.

At first, Leon and Rita seemed disbelieving that their daughter was addicted to drugs. But after a long discussion, they acknowledge the problem and agreed that she needed to be hospitalized, and against her will if necessary. They also intimated that my father should be the one to make the decision, which made sense, since he was after all her husband. However, my father sensed that there was something else at work in my grandparents' suggestion; something he would soon come to realize.

When the doctors at Cedars declared my mother to be medically stable, she was transferred to a private facility in Los Angeles that dealt with drug addiction.

After only a day in the facility, she phoned my father begging, crying, and pleading with him to take her out. According to my father, my mother sounded "pathetic." "I didn't have the heart to keep her there," he remembered decades later. He told her that he would take her out on condition that she would stop taking pills and seek help while at home. She agreed and he picked her up the next day.

Back on Woodfield, a day nurse was hired to care for my mother and the wife of the custodian of the Christian Science Church kept watch over her during the nights. She was not allowed to travel out of the house alone.

On the morning of November 25, 1963, my father came into my brother and my bedroom. Standing by my bedside, with his hand lightly stroking my head, he said, "There's no school today, you can sleep late." Groggy and struggling to open my eyes, I asked "Why?" "President Kennedy was killed," he said sadly. The president had been gunned down in Texas the preceding Friday. That Monday, a national day of mourning was declared and all public institutions, including schools, were closed. As my father left the room, I remained in my bed feeling the sense of doom, but also reassured by my father's strength. It was the strength of his character that came through in his voice and his strong but gentle touch. It was the strength of a man who had struggled all of his life, and who knew violent death as only a combat soldier could know it.

As the weeks after her brief hospitalization went by and she regained more freedom, my mother's erratic behavior resumed.

When she got behind the wheel again, her driving was nothing short of outright dangerous. She would weave all over the road, drive off curbs, and fall asleep at traffic signals. Mae reported this to my father, saying, "Maxine doesn't have full control because of the pills." My brother and I, who frequently rode with her in the car, also expressed our fear of getting hurt to our father.

In addition to her physical symptoms, erratic driving, and antisocial manifestations, my mother exhibited other disconcerting signs; during the daytime, she rarely wore anything other than a nightgown, merely throwing on a robe when she needed to go out somewhere, and she slept much of the day.

Then things turned intensely bizarre.

My mother started walking the halls of the house all night, turning lights on and off, going in and out of Mae's room, going in and out of the house at all hours and for no particular reason, and repeatedly starting and stopping the washing machine. At six o'clock on one particular morning, my mother came into the house after wondering who-knows-where for who-knows-how-long and proceeded to Mae's room where she woke her up to tell her that my father had "made the daughter of a member of my church committee pregnant." It was only for the sake of the children that Mae did not quit her job right then and there.

For some time my father had been confiding his growing distress over his wife's drug problem to a number of friends and relatives. Everyone it seemed was aware of her strange behavior to one degree or another. Some, it turned out, had known of her drug abuse and hypochondria for many years. One couple told him that my mother had been "taking pills since she was seventeen years old" and that even as a teenager she had a reputation of going through people's medicine cabinets. My father began to realize he had been duped; Leon and Rita's surprise at learning of their daughter's drug problem was an act.

On the night of August 17, 1964, to all intents and purposes my parents' marriage came to an end after the most frighteningly bizarre incident of all.

While my father was showering, my mother, dressed in her nightgown and slippers, woke my brother and me and told us to come with her. We dutifully followed her out of the house and slowly walked down Woodfield Drive in our pajamas, as she stared vacantly into the night saying something about "going to see the father." We reached about a block away from the house when she inexplicably turned around and led us back home. When we entered the house, my father, who had become alerted when he couldn't find his wife and children anywhere, immediately herded Leon and me back to our room and put us to bed. Unable to sleep because of the unsettling experience and the increasingly loud voices of our parents, we got out of our beds and stood in the open doorway of our room and watched a scene that neither of us have ever forgotten.

My father was standing a few feet away from my mother, who was sitting on the floor, crying and grasping a telephone. Enraged, my father lunged forward and grabbed the phone, violently ripping the cord out of the wall. Imitating a scene I must have witnessed on television, I held my clenched fist to my mouth like a microphone and said in my best boxing announcer's voice, "Lay-dees and gen-tle-men, welcome to the fight of the week!" My brother elbowed me. "Shhh, it's not funny," he whispered. I must have learned to use humor to deal with discomforting situations by then.

In the midst of the turmoil someone had called my grandfather as well as the police; both showed up.

Around 10:00 P.M., my mother gathered Leon and me into the master bedroom and made us lie down under the covers on her side of the queen-size bed; she placed a dark-blue vinyl satchel under my pillow. Minutes later, a Los Angeles police officer came to the doorway of the room. My mother, standing at the foot of the bed, acting angry and agitated, yelled, "GET OUT OF THIS ROOM, MY CHILDREN ARE SLEEPING!" My brother and I lay silently on our backs watching the drama, understanding nothing.

The officer looked at us, and then retreated out of respect.

While the turmoil continued to rage, my father's concern turned to his children: he had to shelter them from additional trauma.

When the car arrived in the driveway at about midnight, my father bundled up Leon and me and shepherded us out the front door and into the back seat, where he instructed us to lie down on the floor, before Uncle Bud drove off to his house in Bel Air.

Chapter Twenty-Two

My father spent the day after the insane and chaotic night scrambling to deal with the situation with my mother and strategizing how to protect his children and care for them, not to mention meeting his obligations at work.

While he had his hands full trying to contain the fire, my mother and her parents were making sure it consumed him: they were huddling in the Beverly Hills law offices of Herbert G. Baerwitz where a Complaint for Divorce was completed and signed that same day.

The complaint named my father, Hayden Stone (his employer), Security-First National Bank and the United California Bank (the banks he did business with), Claire, Bud, Phil, and any other unnamed persons that my father may have had a shared interest with. My mother was petitioning the court to place a lien "forthwith" on everything and anything he owned, including the properties from Harry's estate.

In addition to alimony and child support, she was asking the court to require my father to pay for her *lawyers'* fees; Baerwitz was only one of five.

The complaint included a questionnaire in which my mother itemized her "necessary monthly expenses." She was demanding $1290 per month (about $9,000 in 2010 dollars), not including child support and attorney's fees, from a man whom she simultaneously was claiming had a monthly income of $1500. Her demand included $180 per month for "a Christian Science Practitioner."

In addition to her economic assault, my mother was demanding the court issue an order of protection to prevent my father from having any contact whatsoever with my brother and me, claiming that my father "since the marriage has treated plaintiff with extreme cruelty and has wrongfully inflicted upon her grievous mental suffering."

The document was so comprehensive and detailed it suggests that it had been prepared, at least in part, in advance of the night of August 17th.

Through their lawyers, my mother and her parents were attempting what amounted to the total economic and personal destruction of my father. He wasn't in combat in the jungles of the southwest Pacific anymore, but he was in the fight of his life facing the delusions of my mother and the viciousness of my grandmother supported by the wealth, power, and influence of my grandfather.

My father turned to Richie Mark.

Richie Mark was a tall, hulking, and mild mannered man—a stereotypical gentle giant. He was also a smart and legitimate lawyer, as opposed to the type of lawyer that would file the kind of lie-filled petition seeking someone's utter destruction such as what my mother's lawyers had filed.

When Richie read the complaint, he was disgusted but not surprised: he knew the law firm.

On August 19th, my father brought my brother and me back to the house on Woodfield and into the care of Mae. Although my mother was still living there, she was physically and mentally incapable of caring for us and spent much of the day in bed or with her parents. After he was served with the divorce documents, my father, knowing that Mae was a capable guardian and would make sure no harm would come to the children, took the initiative and moved out rather than subject my brother and me to loud arguments. He rented a room and garage space in a house at 169 North La Peer Drive in Beverly Hills.

On October 2nd, Richie Mark filed an answer to my mother's complaint denying each and every allegation. My father agreed to cover her "reasonable attorney's fees," however, he added, he would not and should not be made to pay for her multiple lawyers. He pledged support for his children regardless of the outcome of the custody trial and that he would continue to pay the mortgage and utilities until court-ordered disposition of the house was completed.

In petitioning the court for custody, my father appropriately stated that his wife was "incompetent to care for our children" because of her drug use and mental state.

Subsequent to Richie's filing the answers, my father received what is referred to in legal jargon as 'Interrogatories,' or a formal list of questions. He honestly and thoroughly answered each question, which included a year-by-year breakdown of his income and assets as well as his liabilities.

When he met my mother, my father's net worth was approximately $125,000, the bulk of which was from Harry's estate. At the time that my mother filed for divorce, his liabilities, which were largely bills my mother had accumulated, practically doubled that of his assets. In addition, he had also taken out a $5,000 loan to purchase stock on behalf of his father-in-law, which my grandfather was now claiming my father owed him. There was little, if any, equity in the house on Woodfield.

As far as the properties from Harry's estate were concerned, my father had already cashed out of those for $25,000, which, together with an additional loan from Claire and Phil, he had used to support the family.

Richie drew up his own interrogatories and served them on my mother. Her answers contained more outlandish allegations and lies as well as a disturbing revelation: By the time my father had met my mother, when she was not yet twenty-four years old, she had already been married and divorced twice. The first marriage lasted from 1949-1951. The second took place in 1953 and ended in a quickie-cheap Las Vegas divorce in 1954, just before my father met her. Both previous husbands were decades older than she was.

After reading his wife's answers to the interrogatories, my father's realization that he had been deceived intensified. The mature-beyond-her-years, beautiful, young woman with the loving and supportive family that he was so excited to join and on whom he had spent his inheritance amidst promises of success as an actor-cum-producer-cum-stockbroker, turned out to be a group of charlatans. It was hard to dislike his father-in-law, but the respect that he once had for him gave way to contempt, contempt for allowing his daughter to run amok in a host of ways, and contempt for allowing his loud and obnoxious wife to ply her trade of meddling and manipulation with impunity. Leon and Rita had deceived him in order to divest themselves of their troubled daughter and now they were trying to destroy him. He should have heeded his sister's warnings.

But more than provoking his anger, the interrogatories ignited within my father his determination to fight. He had to get his children to safe harbor as quickly as legally possible, and he would spend his last penny to do so if he must.

Chapter Twenty-Three

The hearing began with my mother being wheeled into the courtroom by a white-uniformed nurse. The ploy was not only intended to substantiate her claims of abuse, but also to inflame the passion of the judge against my father.

A number of my grandfather's industry cronies testified in support of my mother's claims that her husband was cruel and abusive, although none could cite a single such incident. One witness, a director who had long worked under my grandfather in motion pictures as well as in television, exemplified the pathetic collusion. In the midst of the director's bogus testimony, the judge interrupted him: "Excuse me, sir, are you reading your testimony?" After the director sheepishly stated he was merely "referring to my notes," the judge harshly admonished him, saying, "Put your notes away, and if I catch you reading again, sir, I will find you in contempt of court."

My father was called to the stand and after denying each and every allegation, he testified in detail about his wife's drug abuse and mental state. He also testified that the children should in the interim be placed in foster care with relatives, as opposed to general foster care, to reduce the traumatic consequences of the breakup of the family. Since my mother had no relatives capable of caring for small children, my father requested that temporary guardianship be given to Claire, who had a wholesome family and lived directly across the street from a public elementary school. Richie Mark had already filed a motion to that effect.

The court ruled in favor of the motion for guardianship and also found that none of the accusations against my father were true. The divorce was granted with a stipulation that it would not become final until the conclusion of the custody trial.

My father was ordered to pay my mother six hundred dollars per month alimony (about half of her claimed living expenses) plus child support, despite the fact that my brother and I would not be living with her. With the exception of his car, all of my father's assets, including his partnership in the hair-straightening business and the Deauville membership, were declared community property. He was given the option to buy out my mother's share of the club membership for three hundred dollars, which he subsequently did. The claims that my mother had made against Claire and Phil were dismissed, as their share in Harry's estate was properly declared not community property. The house was ordered sold to the highest bidder.

For my father, who had little besides his work income, which had dropped to a five hundred dollar per month draw against his commission, it was a severe economic blow.

Subsequent to the events of the night of August 17th, my grandmother, as my father told it, during a confrontation with my father, threateningly sneered, "I will break you down to your underwear," and as he recalled decades later, "She did."

The court's monetary ruling was not unexpected, the trend in divorce cases had for a long time been heavily tilted towards the wife. But the gender bias created an even greater concern for my father: custody of minor children was invariably granted to the mother. My father was fighting for the sanity and the souls of his children and that was all he really cared about. He remembered the trauma of his own youth and how he felt abandoned by his father. By having his children temporarily living with Claire, they were being protected for the time being, but the big fight was yet to come.

For the next year, my brother and I lived with Bud, Claire, Wayne, and Dennis at their house in a portion of the Santa Monica Mountains often mistakenly referred to as the Hollywood Hills. We attended the Roscomare Road Elementary School, and, when the weather permitted, we spent a lot of time swimming in their large backyard pool overlooking the Stone Canyon Reservoir. Uncle Bud was always kind, but ever the mischief-maker. He enjoyed scaring us with tales of the large sea monster he said lived in the reservoir and that if we watched carefully, we could see the beast surface on rare occasion. I believed him and searched in vain for a glimpse of the scary creature. Aunt Claire made certain that we were looked after and clothed and fed properly.

Leon and I fared well in our new environment, although we had become afraid of the dark and needed to have the closet light on when we went to sleep at night. I had recurring dreams of being chased by a snake and unable to run due to feet of lead, which may explain why I eventually became a very fast runner.

On Sundays our mother would pick us up for visitation. It was on one of those days that I wound up losing a couple of teeth.

I sat in the back seat of my mother's powder-blue De Soto, pulled over to the curb, as she was having a conversation with someone standing outside of the car. I was sticking my head out of the window looking around when, getting ready to pull away, she closed the electrically powered window, trapping my head between the glass and the doorframe. The vice caught me at just the right angle to push my lower jaw upward and forward, forcing two of my front teeth out at a ninety-degree angle. With my mouth clamped shut, I could not scream.

Responding to my brother's yelling, my mother, who had been oblivious to what she was doing, lowered the window in a panic. Visibly shaken, she drove straight to a dentist's office where my teeth were extracted. The incident naturally angered my father, who blamed it on my mother's drug abuse.

While he was busy getting his affairs in order and putting in long hours at Hayden Stone, my father eagerly assisted Richie in preparing for the custody trial. He came up to Claire's house to visit my brother and me regularly. It was during one of those visits that I had *my* first experience with a bully:

Although Roscomare Road Elementary School was directly across the street from the house, it was at the crest of the winding, narrow road, making it too dangerous for kids our age to cross alone. In the mornings, Aunt Claire would usually accompany us across the street and in the afternoon, when I was dismissed earlier than my brother, I would wait at the curb for someone to come out and escort me back to the house. While I was innocently waiting to be crossed after dismissal one day, an older boy, perhaps twice my size, without provocation suddenly knocked me to the sidewalk, sat on top of me, and proceeded to repeatedly punch me about the head. My cousin Dennis, peering through a window, witnessed the event and alerted my father who happened to be there at the time. He bolted from the house, flew across the street, and grabbed the bully by his shirt, tossing him backwards into a hedge like a piece of refuse. My father stood me up and, as I sobbed uncontrollably, brought me back into the house, where Aunt Claire provided a piece of sucking candy to calm me down.

The bully's parents subsequently filed a complaint against my father for "Manhandling," thereby providing good insight as to why their kid was the way he was.

As I stood beside my father at the hearing, the judge read the complaint and asked for an explanation. My father described what had prompted his action and told the judge that he accepted responsibility for what he'd done and apologized, saying, "It won't happen again, your honor." Walking out of the courthouse bewildered and disappointed, I asked, "Why did you apologize, Dad?" Looking strong, although I could see he was swallowing his pride, he said, "Sometimes it's better to just get it over with even if you know you're right, Mickey." It was not what I expected of my father; he was an athlete and a fighter; he was the guy on the white horse who always won against the forces of evil; he was my hero, *and he had done the right thing.*

What I didn't understand was that he was also in the midst of a fight for his children and it was best to get this matter off the radar before his ex-wife and her parents found out and exploited it for all it was worth.

Not long after the interlocutory divorce was granted, my father began dating Louise, a pretty divorcee from Tennessee with big hair, a hoarse smoker's-voice, and two daughters roughly the same age as my brother and me. My brother and I reacted to Louise predictably. We were little kids who were saddened and confused by what had happened with our parents and our home and Louise's coming on the scene just seemed to confound both of us even more.

Unfortunately for Louise, she became a target of my mother and grandparents, who found out about her through a private detective they hired to gather evidence against my father for the custody trial. They were now accusing him of adultery. Louise was summoned to court for a hearing on the matter. Dennis, who was about fifteen years old at the time, came along for support:

"I accompanied your dad and my mom and Louise to the hearing. As we all walked together toward the door to the courtroom, we had to pass the Fromkesses and your mom, who were seated outside the courtroom. As Louise passed in front of Rita, Rita leaned her head back and made the throaty sound one makes before expectorating. I don't think she actually spat at Louise, but it was clearly intended for her."

When the custody trial got underway, my father took the witness stand and was subjected to a blistering cross-examination by, as my father remembered it, Herb Baerwitz. Baerwitz accused him of abandoning his wife and children for an adulterous relationship and asked him what kind of father would victimize his wife and then deny his children their mother's love?

Baerwitz was distorting my father into the villain instead of the one who had been deceived and had spent nine years committed to a sick woman who was incapable of caring for her children. It was pure legalized evil.

But it was also very shrewd lawyering, and Baerwitz was obviously an expert at it.

My father knew exactly what Baerwitz was trying to do and he remained strong throughout the questioning with one exception: When the accusations, regardless of how devious and fallacious they were, reminded my father of the pain that he had endured as a child because of his father's irresponsible actions, it was like a knife in his heart and he began to cry. He was crying for his children, and perhaps something else, something that was buried deep in his psyche that I would uncover forty years later.

Without missing a beat, Baerwitz sought to neutralize any effect my father's emotions might have on the court: "You're an actor aren't you?" he said in a mocking tone. When my father answered affirmatively, Baerwitz thundered at him "AND AS AN ACTOR YOU CAN CRY ON A MOMENTS NOTICE, ISN'T THAT TRUE MR. BENNETT?" My father, after wiping his eyes with his ever-pocketed, clean, white handkerchief, locked his steely blue eyes on the double-chinned, gravely-voiced Hollywood lawyer, and with a powerful dose of honesty drilled a hole in Baerwitz oversized head by manly admitting that he could not. My father was a good actor, but not that good.

Toward the end of the custody trial, in a very unusual move, my brother and I were summoned to testify in open court. We had been named as witnesses by one of my mother's attorneys who was intending to elicit testimony suggesting that we were being manipulated by our father, who was "poisoning" us against our mother. The trauma that such an encounter might cause to two young children meant nothing to this man and, sadly, his client, or rather her handlers. Why not request an in-camera interview or a meeting with a social worker or court appointed expert? Nothing like that was suggested because this man wanted us on a witnesses stand so he could intimidate us into saying something against our father. There was nothing sacred to these people, not the truth, not justice, and not even the welfare of the children.

Although I was only eight years old at the time, I still remember the experience:

Wearing a suit and clip-on tie, I was escorted to the witness stand and asked by the clerk to place my right hand on a bible. After the clerk read the oath, I simply stood there looking at him, having no idea what I was supposed to do. When he told me to say, "I do," I looked up at him and said meekly, "Yes," after which he opened a small swinging door leading into the witness box and asked me to climb up and take a seat.

The witness box seemed cavernous, and although it was only a couple of feet above the main floor of the courtroom, it felt as though I was sitting in a tower.

I might have been intimidated in those circumstances, but as I looked out over the room I saw the silver-haired, princely figure of my father sitting in front of me, *and I felt no fear.*

After a warm smile and fatherly greeting from the judge, one of my mother's attorneys, a contentious, fast-talking, little man (he appeared little from my elevated perch) began asking me questions. When I started to answer, the judge instructed me to speak into the microphone. I struggled to lean forward to reach the device, and after clearing my throat, which elicited muffled laughs from around the courtroom and a loving smile from my father, I answered some meaningless question as best as I could. The attorney began peppering me with questions as though I was a criminal defendant in a murder trial. I didn't understand anything he was saying. I turned to the side and, looking up at the judge, politely said, "He's talking too fast." The judge instructed the attorney to slow down.

I was asked a series of questions about an earlier encounter where I had seen my mother but did not run to greet her. When asked why, I simply said, "I don't know."

But I did know, I just didn't know how to express it, or was too afraid to say so. It's hard for a kid to feel close to someone who has for your entire existence functioned in a drug-induced stupor. I loved my mother, but I didn't feel close to her. Had I seen Mae, I would have stopped at nothing to run to her and grab her, holding on for dear life. Just as Baerwitz had tried to do, this new lawyer was trying to take the truth, which was that my mother was a drug addict and that her parents were enablers and more, and mangle it so as to make my father the scoundrel.

After a few minutes of testimony, I was excused and stepped down from the witness box.

In addition to being a high-powered Hollywood attorney who was intimately tied to my grandfather and his friends and associates, the lawyer who questioned me was the California State Athletic Commissioner—the government official in-charge of the State's notoriously corrupted professional boxing and wrestling industries. This was the man whom my mother and grandparents had hired to attack my brother and me. The depravity of it was not lost on my father.

After my brother finished testifying, both of us were brought into the judge's chambers.

No longer wearing his black robe, the judge invited us to sit down, as he casually took a seat a little off to the side and facing us.

A quiet, yet warm and friendly man as I remember him, Judge Stevens Fargo engaged my brother and me in some small talk, noting at one point that I looked like

I could use a few pounds that Leon could donate. With my brother being husky and straight haired, and me curly-headed and scrawny, we resembled miniaturized versions of Laurel and Hardy; the judge seemed to get a kick out of us.

After the chitchat, Judge Fargo posed the question that was the reason for bringing us to his chambers: "Whom do you want to live with?" he asked me first, presumably because I was younger and more likely to be influenced by my older brother's response. "My dad," I replied without hesitation. Leon answered exactly the same, "My dad."

On February 4, 1966, as my parents and their lawyers stood before Judge Fargo, the final judgment for child custody in the case of Bennett v. Bennett was rendered in California Superior Court. After a rambling introduction, Fargo addressed the critical point: "...it is for the best interest of the children that the custody be in the defendant."

My mother gasped, and then wept. She was given rights of visitation on weekends with strict instructions on when we were to be returned to our father and that we could not be removed from the jurisdiction of the State of California. Both parties were admonished to not refer to the other party disparagingly in the presence of the children.

Approximately eighteen months after the events of the night of August 17, 1964, my father was granted custody of my brother and me. It was a remarkably unusual decision for the times. What swayed the judge, my father later opined, was the testimony by one of the day nurses about my mother's drug abuse and similar testimony by Mae.

My father had lost his dream and his property and he was practically broke, but he had won the most important victory of all.

For my mother and grandparents the decision was devastating. Despite all the corruption and dysfunction that marked their lives, they were still a mother and grandparents.

Chapter Twenty-Four

The judgment gave my mother visitation rights during the school year on every Sunday with expanded visitations during the summer months, including two full weeks provided that my father was given ten days prior notice. My brother and I would spend alternating secular holidays with either parent and the Jewish Holy Days of Rosh Hashanah, Yom Kippur, and Passover with our father.

My father would have to continue paying six hundred dollars per month alimony for the balance of the year, after which the amount would be reduced to three hundred per month until further order of the court.

After the judgment was rendered, my father rented a three-bedroom apartment on Corning Street in the Pico-Robertson area of L.A. My mother moved into her parents' new apartment on Coldwater Canyon in the San Fernando Valley neighborhood of North Hollywood.

⚜ ⚜ ⚜

Leon and I were certainly glad that we would be living with our father, but the events of the last year and a half had left us shaken, confused, and insecure. Regardless of how dysfunctional our mother was and the turmoil that had become pervasive in the house on Woodfield, it was still our family unit and now that was permanently gone.

During the year that my brother and I were living at Aunt Claire's, even though we were in a wholesome environment with nurturing relatives, we felt like fish out of water; now we would be three bachelors, a somewhat unsettling scenario for two children eight and ten years old.

Never having forgotten the feelings that he suffered as an orphan and his displacement after Harry's broken promises, my father understood our trauma. And although he could hardly afford paying her salary and the extra food and utility expenses it would entail, he brought Mae back to live with us, which was why he rented a three-bedroom apartment instead of a more affordable two-bedroom unit.

My father also had to sell his Lincoln and leased a two-door Mustang coupe.

My brother and I were enrolled in the Carthay Center Elementary School, about a mile from our new apartment.

Just as he we all had settled into our new routine, my father was dealt another blow when one of his biggest clients came to his office requesting a questionable stock transaction. My father refused to process the order, but his client kept pressing him on it. After he sent the insistent investor to the house manager for the final word, the manager called him on his desk phone telling him to go ahead with the deal.

Several weeks later, the Securities and Exchange Commission (SEC) sent the firm a letter stating the transaction was picked up during a routine audit and that it was indeed a violation of SEC rules and ordered remedial action. The manager told my father he had to reimburse the house five thousand dollars in order to bring everything into compliance with SEC regulations. My father angrily refused and reminded the manager of the sequence of events and his phone call giving him the go-ahead. The manager went on to lie to the SEC, telling them that the broker had acted without approval and was refusing to correct the problem. My father's brokerage license was subsequently revoked. He was now without income with two children to care for, living expenses, a housekeeper, and alimony to pay my mother. And without a broker's license, there was no prospect for employment for the foreseeable future. Yet again in his life, my father was suffering from someone else's misdeed and their refusal to take responsibility, instead laying the blame on him.

Once again he would have to fight.

My father immediately filed an appeal with the SEC detailing the true facts of the case and stating that as a broker, under house rules and procedures, it was virtually impossible for him to process the order without the manager's approval.

In the interim, while the SEC was reviewing his appeal, my father was offered a job by the sympathetic manager of another, smaller brokerage firm, Robert Scott. However, he could only work under a licensed broker, and even that would be on probation until the SEC ruled on his appeal. He was back in business, at least temporarily. Then again, he had lost all but a few of his clients.

When Wayne found out about his uncle's financial troubles through Claire, he unexpectedly showed up one day with a check for a thousand dollars. I had never seen my father cry and couldn't imagine him ever doing so. But this time, when he told me about what Wayne had done, I could see him choke up a little, thinking about his nephew's love and generosity.

Despite his financial straits, my father remained a generous person, providing my brother and me with our every need. We never felt impoverished or cheated. As an example of his charity to others even in the midst of his own monetary woes, I remember leaving our apartment one day and driving down Corning when my father spotted what looked to me like an ordinary bum walking down the street. He grimaced and let go a pained puff of breath and said, "Hold on a second, Mick." After stopping the car in the middle of the street, he stepped out, approached the bum, handed him something, and quickly returned to the car. Curious, and a little concerned, I asked, "Who was that, Dad?" "He was a broker I used to work with. He's having a tough time. I gave him twenty dollars." He cynically added, "He's probably heading straight to the liquor store." I was young, but I understood what I had just witnessed and I felt proud of my father and loved him even more for what he had done.

The appeal to the SEC took about a year. The ruling was in favor of my father and he got his broker's license back. His integrity was restored and he could hopefully get back on his feet again.

But my father barely had time to catch his breath when he was notified that my mother had filed an appeal of the judgment for custody.

My brother and I were getting a little older and more independent by this time. Leon got a job selling newspapers at a local newsstand. I was getting into some childhood mischief, like stopping by the La Brea Tar Pits on my way back from school and coming home smelly and smeared with tar. My father started spending more time with Louise. I became ever closer to Mae.

Leon and I continued our visitations with our mother and grandparents without complaint. We often went out to eat and I recall on one occasion riding in the back seat of the famous funnyman Morey Amsterdam's car. Morey, whom I remember as a kind gentleman with a great sense of humor, and the iconic comedian Milton Berle, whom I did not particularly like and found not at all funny, were among my grandfather's closest friends.

We often spent time visiting Pop at Goldwyn Studios where he maintained an office while making films financed by Sam Firks. We wandered the lot and occasionally visited sound stages, where we noisily tortured directors who would stop filming and angrily ask, *"Who are those kids?"* We particularly enjoyed hanging out with Iron Eyes Cody. Cody, who was Hollywood's "house Indian" in those days, was working in two westerns Pop was making at the time. He rarely spoke, but walking around with a genuine Indian dressed in full regalia was captivating for us two kids. I got a particular thrill out of eating in the studio's commissary where the sound-effects men, while taking their lunch breaks, would eagerly entertain us with their remarkable talents of imitation, such as barking like a dog, screaming like a monkey, or whinnying like a horse, all with amazing exactitude.

On one of the family visitations, my brother and I were treated to being part of the audience of the new Bozo the Clown television series at KTTV Studios. At the end of every show, Bozo would pick a kid from the audience to play some game for a chance to win the Treasure Chest of Toys. I hated clowns, and when the terrifying-looking, giant mutant with the overgrown, red, bulbous nose, enormous, floppy, red shoes, and screaming-orange wings of hair pointed to me with his glove-covered targeting finger, I rapidly shook my head in a panicked "No, no, no!" Bozo the monster instantly shifted his aim to my brother. An extrovert, as compared to his little brother's shyness, Leon eagerly jumped from his seat into the center ring of "Bozo's Big Top" and proceeded to win the contest and the Treasure Chest of Toys. A few days later, deliverymen came to our Corning Street apartment with the Bozo booty, which included two bran-new Shwinn bicycles—the latest Sting Ray model with chopper-style handlebars and a sissy bar.

During that first summer, with our father's permission, Mom, Pop, and Barr, which is what we called our grandmother for some mysterious reason, took us to Las Vegas for a vacation. I still remember the long drive through the desert and how my grandfather would periodically reach over to the glove compartment, remove an amber-colored bottle of MAALOX, and take a swig of the milky liquid. I knew it was medicine, but there was something about the way my grandfather drank the stuff and the white residue he licked off of his lips that made it look delicious. Apparently, he still suffered from the ulcers he had developed while working under Sam Goldwyn.

While in Las Vegas we stayed at Pop's favorite hotel, the Riviera. My brother and I spent most of the time hanging around the pool—Leon jumping off of the high-dive, and me, frightened of heights, staying as far away from the diving area as possible. Children were not allowed in the casino and besides swimming and meals, there was little else for us to do.

On the way back to L.A., we stopped at the Denny's restaurant in Barstow. As I watched my grandfather eat, there was something about his demeanor that worried me, something manic.

Back on Corning, my brother and I found friends our age in the area and spent our share of time riding our new bikes around the neighborhood and playing on the sidewalk. Our fun became interrupted, however, when a neighborhood hag started appearing in an upper floor window of the adjacent apartment building and yelling at us for making too much noise. We could never actually see the woman, but we were routinely subjected to her intimidating shriek of *"You children get out of here!"* and the like. When my brother and I told our father about the problem, he knew exactly what to do. "Let's go," he said, and escorted us outside. With our father lagging behind so that our tormentor wouldn't see him, my brother and I made our way down the sidewalk. As if on cue, the witchy voice screeched *"I told you kids to get away from here!"* In a perfectly timed ambush, my father stepped into view and, looking up at the window, yelled back in a commanding voice "What's the matter with you, weren't you ever a child?" We never heard another word from the miserable one after that. My father had once again confirmed his hero status.

Those days on Corning as well as some of the days from before the family upheaval provided Leon and me with our only fond childhood memories. The visitations also gave us a feeling of family togetherness, although it did seem a little strange having a two-part family. It was a routine and a semblance of normalcy that my father felt reasonably secure about. That is until the day my brother bolted into the apartment from his newsstand job heaving with sobs of terror.

While Leon was going through his routine selling newspapers at the northeast corner of the intersection of Pico Boulevard and Robertson Boulevard, he noticed a man on the southeast corner taking pictures of him. Becoming alarmed, he gave the vendor his supplies, hopped on his bike and pedaled as fast as he could for home. Terrified by the thought of the stranger following him, he could barely hold back his tears. Arriving home, he dropped his bike on the sidewalk and ran upstairs into our apartment, where his emotions caught up with him.

My father immediately knew what was going on: my mother and grandparents had hired a private detective to find dirt that could be used in the appeal of the judgement for custody.

My father was furious. Not because he was the target of the so-called investigation, but because of the trauma that the desperate move had inflicted on his son.

He wound up writing a letter to Judge Fargo informing him of what had happened and how it had traumatized his son. There were no further incidents after that.

Leon and I were largely unaware of the tribulations and the pressure that our father was under in those days. He was not a complainer and never involved us in his domestic battles or financial difficulties. But my father was not a stoic either; I could sense his troubles and felt sad for him, and, strangely perhaps, that made him and me closer.

After the investigator incident, life on Corning was cruising along for my father until his youngest son managed to get hit in the mouth with a baseball bat while at school recess, despite the fact that I was playing left field at the time.

The inning had just ended. As I was absentmindedly walking in from the field, a kid taking hard and fast practice swings at home plate accidentally let go of the bat, sending the club cartwheeling through the air and directly into my upper lip, splitting it wide open all the way up to my nose. It was lights out for me. I could only later remember hearing a female classmate scream, "MICHAEL WHAT HAPPENED?"

The principal came running out to the playground and carried me into the nurse's office, where I was laid on a cot and the school nurse applied towel after towel to my mouth in an effort to stop the profuse bleeding.

My father was called. As Providence would have it, he was not out to lunch that day.

When he walked into the nurse's office and saw me lying there, my lip distorted into a bloody blossom of exposed tissue and a three-foot high mound of blood-soaked towels piled to one side, my father's heart sank. He had seen plenty of blood and gore during the war, but this was different, this was his young son.

But just like I imagine he had performed during the war, my father did not become paralyzed with emotion. Remaining calm and thinking clearly, without hesitation he carried me to his car and drove off to a hospital where there would likely be a plastic surgeon.

My father waited for several hours while two doctors worked to put my lower face back together again. He could only hope that the surgery would not leave me with a lip too badly disfigured.

The procedure was successful. In fact, it was so successful, before-and-after pictures of my mouth were eventually published in a physicians' reference book on plastic surgery techniques.

Thanks to my father and two great surgeons, I was left with little more than a faint scar.

Chapter Twenty-Five

My mother's appeal of the custody judgment was denied and my father's business started on the upswing again. He traded in the leased Mustang for a Volvo and the four of us moved into a three-bedroom apartment on Densmore Avenue in the Encino area of the San Fernando Valley. Leon and I were enrolled in the Hesby Street Elementary School. In response to our pleading, my father brought home a new puppy, which Mae named Patsy.

My father was still working at Robert Scott, and when he wasn't at the office or seeing Louise, he played golf. He loved the game and he loved being outdoors. Deauville, which had changed its name to Braemar Country Club, was located in a picturesque setting. The club's three, lush, green golf courses—two championship 18-hole courses and a 9-hole pitch-n-putt course—wound peacefully through the rolling foothills of the Santa Monica Mountains. Going to "the Club" became my father's one and only getaway and he occasionally brought my brother and me there, taking us up to the pitch-n-putt course or leaving us to swim in the

Olympic-size pool. Because his membership was for life and didn't require dues, the Club was the only vestige of my father's few successful years.

But my father continued to be stalked by trouble. This time it came in the form of an Internal Revenue Service audit. His business related entertainment expenses, which had sparked the audit, were substantial, but they were not eye-popping, and they were almost solely the result of taking his biggest client to lunch.

Henry Sassoon was a Jew who had fled Abdul Nasser's Egypt after the dictator ordered his army to attack the newly recognized state of Israel in 1948. Sassoon came to America with practically nothing and had made it big as a builder. His rags-to-riches story symbolized the American Dream and he became an inspirational figure to many in the Sephardic Jewish community of Los Angeles. Sassoon loved the stock market, and he was loyal to my father as his broker.

In the days before the Internet and cable television, practically the only way an avid stock enthusiast could get real-time information was by watching the "Big Board" or the ticker tape machines at a brokerage house, which is why my grandfather after the sale of TPA spent hours sitting beside my father at Hayden Stone. During 1966, Sassoon came to my father's office daily, watching, analyzing, and trading. When the New York market closed, which was at 1:00 P.M. on the West Coast, my father would take him to lunch. For a client like Henry Sassoon, only the finest restaurants would do.

My father explained his relationship with Sassoon to the IRS and he was able to justify his expenses with thorough and precise documentation, unlike my grandfather who managed to weasel out of an IRS audit by seducing the auditor. As he had learned to do in the HOA and further refined as an officer in the army, my father kept meticulous records. When the audit was concluded, the only problem the IRS found was that he had erroneously filed his 1964 return as a "Head of Household," rather than as "Married." Insofar as the IRS was concerned, an interlocutory divorce was not the same as a final decree. The error actually entitled my father to more deductions than he had originally claimed and he wound up with a more than four thousand dollar tax credit.

Although he had prevailed with gaining custody of his children, the SEC revocation of his broker's license, and now the IRS audit, it didn't mean that my father's troubles were over. In fact, another upheaval was just around the corner.

During that first summer on Densmore, our mother had just dropped off my brother and me following a weekend visitation. Mae was away on vacation and our father, anticipating that he might not be home when we returned, had given us a key to the apartment. When Leon and I walked in the door, we immediately went looking for Patsy, but the dog was nowhere to be found. We called our father at Louise's house. He told us that because there was no one to care for the dog while we were on visitation and Mae was on vacation, he had given her away. My brother and I were crushed, and we felt betrayed by the way in which the deed was done. We called our mother to tell her what had happened:

"Come live with us and we'll get you a dog," my mother said. She wasn't simply exploiting the situation, she honestly felt her children's pain; I could hear it in her voice.

Leon and I had for some time been feeling that our father was increasingly switching his priorities from us to Louise, and we instinctively believed that that was somehow behind his taking away Patsy. The divorce and all that surrounded it had left us emotionally dependent on our father. We were hungering for love, normalcy, and consistency, and the dog filled some of the void and eased a little of our pain. We replied to our mother's compassionate and heartfelt plea with "Yes," we wanted to live with her.

Pop, who had been listening in on the dramatic conversation, dictated a letter to Leon, which, in essence, simply said that we no longer wanted to live with our father but with our mother. He then instructed both of us to sign the letter and for Leon to run down to the corner and put it in the mailbox. While Leon was out, I became frightened and overwhelmed with guilt about what I had done. I called my father at Louise's and was telling him what was going on when my brother returned home and overheard me. He panicked and ran out of the house.

At hearing my brother bolt from the apartment and the door slam shut, a sickening feeling came over me; I felt as though I had caused a catastrophe. I had first betrayed my father by signing the letter, and now, because of my phone call, I had betrayed my brother as well. I became paralyzed with worry and fear, as I stood in that apartment completely alone.

My father immediately concluded that my mother and her parents were solely responsible for the crisis. He was wrong.

That night, Wayne and my father went to retrieve Leon. When my mother answered the door and saw Wayne standing there, she turned to her father, who was sitting in the adjoining living room, in fear and wanting to know what to do. "IF HE COMES IN HERE, I'LL KILL HIM!" my grandfather shouted. With that, my mother slammed the door.

My father wasn't willing to take the confrontation any further and he and Wayne left.

My brother, meanwhile, hearing what was going on and fearing that he would be physically forced to face an angry father, had climbed into the bathroom window, intending to jump out and run away if he had to.

The next day, my father called Richie Mark who notified the court of the violation of custody.

After a brief hearing in which my brother testified that he wanted to live with his mother, Leon was taken by a U.S. marshal to MacLaren Hall, a notorious juvenile detention facility and residence of homeless and abused children. He had effectively been arrested.

My father was clearly within his legal rights and he was tough when it came to fighting a battle. But he had not anticipated the repercussion of his tenacity on my brother, and it was too reminiscent of what had been done to him as a child. He relinquished custody. Leon was released from MacLaren after a couple of hours.

My father was never interested in having his children live with him for purely selfish reasons, or at any cost to my brother and me. He would not have pursued custody if he felt it better for his children to reside with their mother. In 1968, when the above events transpired, my brother was twelve years old. He was certainly not an adult, but he was old enough to make the decision that he made; and with his assertive personality, he was better equipped to survive the rough waters he was likely to face than I would have been. More than anything, my father did not want his son to have to endure any more distress.

My father and I shared a unique bond. As the youngest, weakest, and most vulnerable child, his great sense of compassion for children was keenly focused on me. He knew how attached I was to him, but he also knew how sensitive I was and he sensed how I grieved inside at being separated from my brother and he wanted to take up the slack somehow. Somehow, he thought, he would make it up to me.

I continued to make scheduled visitations to my mother, grandparents, and now my brother. But things were not the same and I began to feel like an outsider. That sense of alienation intensified when my mother and grandparents held a birthday party for my brother.

The event was attended by a group of my brother's friends and featured the usual cake, ice cream, and opening of presents. A raffle was held and when the winning number was called, I held up my slip of paper and calmly said, "I have the number." Without hesitation, my grandfather, who was sitting in his favorite chair on the opposite side of the living room, angrily shook his head. He told my brother to pull another number out of the jar. I was confused and saddened: Why was I not allowed winning and why was my grandfather angry? My mother felt my pain and began to plead with her father. But my grandfather was adamant, and his word was law.

I never liked parties, not even my own, and I had no yearning to win anything, but this was something of a completely different nature. I sat there enveloped in hurt, but showing or telling no one.

On a later occasion, while riding in Pop's car as he drove down Coldwater Canyon with my brother beside me and my mother and Barr in the back seat, I made one of my usual wisecracks in the context of some insignificant conversation. In response, Barr reached forward and bopped me over the head with a rolled up magazine. I probably deserved it. But in the context of being singled out like some sort of stepchild, it was the straw that broke the camel's back and the tears began to flow. Pop rebuked Barr with an annoyed *"Reeter"* (New Yorkese for Rita), who coldly called me a crybaby. My grandmother had long established herself as some-one who, for unexplained reasons, didn't like me. She responded to practically everything I did with antipathy even before the divorce. As I sat there with tears stream-ing down my cheeks, I could feel her anger. My grand-mother had managed to break my already cracked, glass heart. I just wanted to go home to my father.

When I got back to the apartment, I told my father about both incidents and said that I didn't want to go there anymore. Disgusted and pained at the hurt his son had had been caused, my father solemnly said, "You won't have to go there any more, Mickey." It would be five years before I would see my brother, mother and grandparents again.

For my father, his once robust family had now whit-tled down to just himself and his ten-year-old son...and Louise. As for me, I had my father, and I had Mae.

Chapter Twenty-Six

"People let me tell you 'bout my best friend
He's a warm hearted person who'll
love me till the end..."

—"Best Friend," by Harry Nielson, from
"The Courtship of Eddie's Father."

My father had long been accustomed to dealing with his pain. His challenge now would be trying to ease his youngest son's angst and provide him with a normal childhood, a difficult task for any single parent; perhaps even more difficult for someone who had grown up in an orphanage.

I started playing little league baseball in the summer and Pop Warner football in the winter.

My father was seeing Louise almost nightly, but he made time to watch my weekend baseball and football games. He was proud that his little guy had become one of the best pitchers in the league, and he could hardly wipe the smile off his face when while playing shortstop, I made an unassisted triple play. It didn't matter to him that, admittedly, I had no idea what happened; he beamed with pride anyway.

When the football season started, because I was a fast runner, I alternated playing halfback on offense and safety on defense. One of the other teams had an offensive runner who was virtually unstoppable. Not only was the guy fast, he was big, and when he came barreling through the line no one was willing to confront him; they just stepped out of his way, fruitlessly trying to grab him from the side. I complained to my father that every time that kid got the ball it was a guaranteed touchdown and that wasn't fair. My father dismissed my complaint, saying, "That's ridiculous. If you guys would stop acting like a bunch of sissies and hit the guy straight on, below the knees, put your shoulder into it, like this, see, *he'll go down, guaranteed!*"

My father watched from the sidelines as I took my position on defense. The ball was snapped and the quarterback made the hand-off. Sure enough, the guy came running through the line and, as usual, easily breaking every attempt to stop him. I sped forward and did exactly as my father had said—I went low, put my shoulder into it, and hit him right below the knees. The guy went down, just as my father promised.

As I lay on the ground feeling like a train had hit me, the sense of shock by the kids on both teams was palpable; someone had stopped the unstoppable. I sat out the rest of the quarter in pain and feeling little consolation. But I'd shown my father that I believed in him, and the other players that it could be done, which permanently changed the dynamics of the game. That childhood incident proved to be an important life lesson; sometimes you have to grab the bull by the horns, take the pain, and get it done. It was only one of the many such lessons that my father taught me. And on that day, he also taught it to every kid on the field.

My father also started taking me out to play golf more often. Unlike football and baseball, golf was a sport that we could play together and the game, for me, became synonymous with my father.

Our father-son activities didn't just involve sports, however. "C'mon Mick, let's go get a Tasty Freeze," or "How 'bout a 31 Flavors?" he'd often say, and off we'd go, me getting chocolate or chocolate mint, and my father getting whatever sugar-free flavor they had. He had been diagnosed with diabetes a couple of years before and was resolute about not cheating. I felt sorry for my father having to eat the bland stuff and always offered him a lick of mine, which he rarely accepted. But when he did, *I* felt better.

The highlight of that period was the time my father took me for a two-day trip to San Francisco.

I'd never been in a plane before and was a little apprehensive. I had always been frightened of heights and high speed; once making the operator of a kiddie rollercoaster stop the ride so I could get off. But my father had a unique kind of confidence that bred courage and I wound up enjoying the flight.

We stayed in the St. Francis Hotel. When I asked him how he knew about the place, without elaboration he said, "I stayed here when I first came to California." At the time, I knew nothing about Harry, or practically anything else in my father's background. The day after we arrived, he took me on a helicopter ride and a New York Giants' doubleheader at Candlestick Park. The trip turned out to be a memorable father-son experience.

When I wanted to go fishing, my father took me to a local lake where we rented tackle and a rowboat. When my arms grew tired from rowing, which didn't take long, he took over and rowed the rest of the way—at double my speed.

I had an older friend in the Boy Scouts, and although I was too young to join, my father knew the adult troop leader and arranged for an exception to be made. When an overnight field trip was scheduled, because I was underage my father had to accompany me. After arriving at the campground, he was shown his accommodations: "I haven't slept in a tent since the war," he said, his consternation quickly turning to resolve.

Indeed, after Leon had left my father tried everything he knew to make me happy. And I still had Mae. He had managed to create a pretty good scenario for me with the few resources that he had.

But as the year after Leon's leaving wore on, my father's presence, and companionship, became scarce again. He was spending more and more time with Louise. And he also seemed to be getting short tempered. Mae noticed it too.

Besides being my guardian and caretaker and the closest thing I ever had to a true mother, Mae was also my friend. We went shopping to the Piggly Wiggly together, and talked about school, friends, and life in general. I told Mae whatever was on my mind, often times while sitting in her room while she ironed and folded clothes, as some insipid soap opera played on the small black and white television perched on her dresser. It was in that setting that in response to my complaining about what was happening with my father that Mae dolefully said, "Your father done already lost your brother. He keep it up, he gonna lose you too."

I didn't know it at the time, but something besides Louise was affecting my relationship with my father; the stock market had been on a downward slide for some time and the situation was getting worse. He had been through similar episodes before, but this time the bear market was gaining momentum and that posed another, more acute threat to him.

As his business improved, he had been trying to leverage his gains through buying stocks on margin, which basically meant he was borrowing money from the brokerage house to finance large stock purchases. When buying on margin, if the value of the stock increases you can cash out, quickly pay off the loan, and significantly increase your gain. But, if the stock goes down a certain percentage the brokerage house will issue a margin call, requiring you to make up the difference. Investors dread margin calls; my father started getting them.

The situation went from bad to worse with margin calls coming in one after another while interest on the loans continued to accrue. Before long my father was unable to pay anymore margin calls and have enough money left over to meet our living expenses. He was deeply in debt and rapidly heading towards bankruptcy. He started scrambling to try and buy time by cutting expenses. But the market kept plunging.

When my father told me that he had to let Mae go, my head spun and my heart began to break. I begged and pleaded with him not to, but the look of resolve in his eyes told me that nothing could alter his decision. In my heart I blamed Louise. After all, my father had time and money to take her out to dinner and presumably to buy her gifts. Why not cut those things out? Why not just cut out Louise altogether? Why take away Mae?

When it was time for her to leave, Mae stood in front of me in the living room, put down her bags, and hugged me to say goodbye:

I cried in anguish from the very depths of my soul and would not let go of her, begging her not to go. Struggling to overcome her welling emotions, trying to convey strength, Mae said, "It's time for you to be a big boy, Michael. You'll be all right. I'll come visit and I'll call you." I wouldn't let go and only cried harder, "No, no, don't go, Mae, please don't go!" Trying even harder not to break down, Mae stiffened, "C'mon now, Michael, don't make Mae cry, boy," but the tears streaked her brown cheeks. There was nothing more to say, nothing more I could do; nothing Mae could do; nothing anyone could do. My father stood and watched the heartrending scene, bearing his own pain.

For a few months after she left, Mae would call me. And for a couple of years, every September 18th an envelope would arrive addressed to "Master Michael Bennett," inside was a birthday card from Mae; but I never saw Mae again.

Discharging his debts through bankruptcy was my father's only way out of the mess he had put himself in. It was a painful decision; not just because of what it would do to his credit, but because not paying his debts even through a legitimate mechanism was against his core principles. My father blamed only himself for his troubles; he had been reckless in trying to rebuild his financial status. But there was no choice so he filed for relief under Chapter 7 of the Federal Bankruptcy Code and applied for food stamps.

We started eating out at cheap, fast food restaurants and he put me on a five-dollar-a-week allowance, three dollars of which he made me put in a bank account so that I would "learn the value of money." He also started taking me to Louise's house more often, which I secretly dreaded.

While heading out to Louise's for dinner one evening, as we approached the bank of mailboxes near the entrance gate to the apartment building, my father handed me his key and asked me to get the mail from our box. As I retrieved the letters, I noticed that one was addressed to me; it was my bank statement. My father asked to see it.

Fearing what I knew the document would reveal and my father's reaction, I tried to keep it from him. "It's just my bank statement," I said, struggling to hide my anxiety.

Since Mae left, I had been spending more time with the kids in the apartment building, which meant I was getting into mischief. One of my friends had the bright idea to have a card game in which we would play for money. I had never gambled before and although I wasn't comfortable with the idea, I wanted to be a part of the gang; so I played, and lost seven dollars. Fearful of losing honor among my friends, I went to the bank and forged my father's signature, which was required on a minor's account, and withdrew the money.

My father, suspecting I was hiding something, angrily grabbed the envelope out of my hand and opened it. As he was reading the statement, he came across the incriminating evidence. "What is this?" he asked accusingly.

Before I could respond he smacked me on the back of the head, shoved me a hundred and eighty degrees around and growled, "Get back upstairs!" As I started to walk toward our apartment he kicked me, hard, in the rear. While fighting to contain my tears for fear that my friends might see, I quickly marched past the apartment house pool, up the stairs to the second floor, and down the railing-lined walkway towards our apartment, my father menacingly striding behind me the entire way.

Once inside the apartment I headed straight for my room. But before I got there he spun me around again, grabbed me by my shirt, and lifting me into the air pinned me against the wall. "What are you, in cahoots with your mother?" he scowled as I hung there in abject terror.

I failed to understand the connection; what I had done had nothing to do with my mother; what had I done that provoked such blind rage in my father? In an instant, my already shrunken world had become enveloped in darkness. I wanted to curl into a ball and die.

While my father's reaction was inexcusable and abusive, it was the only time during my life that I can recall him striking me. Although I remained deeply pained by what he had done, I came to view it in the context of the great stress that he was under at the time. It was out of character for him, just like it was out of character when he gave away the dog. However, the wrath he displayed that day was reminiscent of the intense anger that I saw in him as he stood over my sobbing and frightened mother on that August night in 1964. It was the anger he had developed at being bullied as a child, and it was the anger he felt for his father. It was something else too, something even more deeply hidden.

In the ensuing days neither my father nor I said anything about the incident and our relationship mended for the most part. In fact, as his financial situation became more desperate, and I became aware of it, I offered him the balance of my bank account. My father felt terrible about taking the money but he needed it, to care for me as much as anything. He expressed his sorrow and his pain at having to take his son's savings and said that he would make it up to me one day. He told me how much he loved me for wanting to help him. He meant it, and I knew it. But I also perceived his shame, and my heart ached for him.

We still played golf together, still went out for the occasional ice cream cone, and still ate out at fast food joints. One of our favorites was a place called The Nordic Inn, which we jokingly referred to as "The Vomit Inn" because they always served the same mediocre variety of meatballs, rice, soggy vegetables, and rice pudding with cherry sauce at the all-you-can-eat buffet.

There was a popular television series of the time about a widower, his only son, and the Oriental house keeper who became the boy's surrogate mother. *The Courtship of Eddie's Father* was a poignant tale of the ups and downs of those relationships and the distress that Eddie experienced at his father's pursuit of female companionship. It was my favorite program; it was very much my life. I watched it in my room religiously, on the little black and white TV that used to be in Mae's room.

My father's Jewish identity came exclusively from his experiences at the Hebrew Orphan Asylum, which didn't amount to much of anything positive or meaning-ful. Consequently, while he had a proud sense of being a Jew, he had no real definition of what that meant and therefore never practiced anything in the way of Jewish "ritual" or tradition and was unable to pass anything on to me.

But having friends who were Jewish and more con-nected, at least superficially, to some extent had an influence on me. As I was approaching my thirteenth birthday I asked my father if I could get Bar Mitzvah les-sons, even though I had no idea what that really meant. Although he couldn't afford to pay for them, my father said yes and I contacted the man who was teaching a friend of mine.

Twice a week, this disheveled looking fifty-ish-year-old man in a cheap, wrinkled, and ill-fitting suit showed up at our Densmore apartment and taught me a Hebrew blessing without explanation or commentary. After a few such sessions, all of which ended with me giving the teacher the cash my father had left for him and him asking for a swig of my father's bottle of JB Scotch, I lost interest. The schlub lost a watering hole.

Chapter Twenty-Seven

Just as I was entering the insecure and confused state of adolescence and had finished my first year in junior high school, my father and I moved into a one-bedroom apartment on the third floor of a typically Los Angeles, stucco-iced apartment cube on Coldwater Canyon about a mile north of Ventura Boulevard. We continued to live on his meager income and food stamps.

But despite our impoverished status, outside of our relatives and a few close friends, no one could tell that my father had fallen on hard times...again. He still dressed impeccably and had exchanged the leased, boxy, cream-colored Volvo for a sleek, black Chevrolet Monte Carlo. He was as handsome as ever and still walked, talked, and held himself in that unpretentiously suave manner that made me proud to introduce him to my friends, and sometimes embarrassed when their mothers swooned over him.

But I looked up to him for reasons well beyond his appearance. Perhaps the best way to convey this is through an anecdote: He and I were having dinner at Louise's one evening when, in the midst of their adult conversation, one of them used the word "class," as in high class. Louise turned to me and condescendingly asked, "Do you know what 'class' means, Michael?" Without having to even ponder the question, I replied, "Yes, it means looking like you have money when you don't," and then turning to my father I added, "Like you, Dad." Louise's eyes widened and her jaw dropped; she had no idea what I thought of my father or how I looked up to him until that moment. My father smiled, and for an instant, I thought I saw him get a little misty eyed.

After we moved into the new apartment we stopped going out to eat.

Instead, my father taught me how to cook; nothing elaborate, just stuff like eggs and hamburgers. He also showed me how to do the laundry using the building's coin-operated machines and how to iron. Oh, how I hated to iron!

The bedroom was small and we positioned our beds diagonally across from each other. It took a little getting used to for me to be sleeping in the same room as my father, but he didn't seem to mind. We both went to sleep at the same time, and although he got up before I did, without fail every morning at six o'clock, he'd let me sleep while he shaved and readied for work. At seven o'clock sharp he would come into the bedroom and start singing to the tune of Reveille, *"Ya gotta-get-up, Ya gotta-get-up, Ya gotta-get-up in the morning…"* The song irritated me like nothing else, which is why it worked getting me out of bed.

The new apartment was even closer to Louise's house and her demands on my father's time were increasing, which was getting on his nerves. One day while he was on the phone with her, I heard him angrily say, "Look, I've had enough. I've got a young kid here I've gotta take care of!" and he hung up the phone. Surprised by what

I'd heard, I said nothing, but I admit I felt pretty good, like when the sun comes out on a rainy day.

But Independence Day was barely two weeks old when the phone rang and it was Louise. In a deeply depressed voice she asked, "Can I speak with your father?" I handed him the phone; she was back! Years later my father told me that Louise had threatened to commit suicide.

On the morning of February 9, 1971, I was sleeping soundly when the bed began to shake violently, waking me. It was just after six o'clock and my father was getting ready for work. As the shuddering intensified, with eyes half open, I asked him what was happening: "It's an earthquake. It'll stop in a second," he answered from the bathroom. But the shaking got worse, and I could hear things crashing to the floor in the kitchen. "Maybe you better get under the bed," he calmly instructed. "No, I'm coming in there with you." I stood in the bathroom doorway under my father's arm as the building rattled and shook.

After what seemed like an hour, but was in reality only a couple of minutes, the shaking stopped and there was eerie silence. My father, his face partially covered in shaving cream, and I instinctively walked down the short hallway to the kitchen where the crashing noises had come from; all of the cabinet doors were swung wide open and the floor was littered with broken dishes. It looked as though the room had been ransacked. A magnitude 6.6 earthquake had hit the area. The epicenter was near the San Fernando Valley community of Sylmar and had ruptured a more than ten-mile long section of the San Fernando Fault Zone.

My father, obviously concerned but calm and collected, told me to retrieve the broom from the nearby closet. As we worked together to clean the mess the aftershocks started. The jolts, although not as strong or sustained as the initial quake, were significant, as high as 5.5 on the Richter scale—a device that became part of Californians' lexicon from that day forward.

Not knowing if the danger had passed, he decided that we should leave the building. And since the schools were certain to be closed what better way to spend an earthquake than on a golf course? We went to the Club.

Opting to stay away from the elevated concrete slabs of the freeway system, which turned out to be a smart move as some twelve sections of overpasses had collapsed, my father drove south on Coldwater before turning west on Ventura Boulevard for the approximate ten-mile drive to Braemar. As he made the turn onto Ventura, he directed my attention toward the sidewalks, which were littered with broken glass and mannequins that had tumbled out of shattered storefront windows. I had never seen anything like it. To my father, it reminded him of the war; perhaps a very small taste of what he had seen in Manila in 1945. I could see him set his jaw and steel his resolve. I was glad to be with him. Despite the feeling of doom enveloping the entire city that day, my father's confident, take-charge attitude made it feel like an adventure.

We drove the rest of the way listening to the radio news reports: A new hospital in Sylmar, a building that had been constructed utilizing the latest so-called "earthquake proof" methods and materials, had collapsed, and the nearby Van Norman Dam was in danger of bursting, prompting the evacuation of some forty thousand people from the surrounding area. The 1971 Sylmar Earthquake as it came to be called resulted in the death of sixty-five people and caused about a half a billion dollars in property damage.

A few days after the quake, my father returned to work, I returned to school, and Los Angeles returned to its pre-quake homogenized hedonism.

In 1972 we were still living in the Coldwater Canyon apartment and I was in my last year of junior high school. My father continued working for Robert Scott but his business was stagnant, and the bankruptcy continued to haunt him; he couldn't even get approved for a credit card. He began writing a theatrical play, a musical comedy about the stock market. He sat for hours at our small dining room table intensely two-finger typing on an old, manual machine. He bought a used reel-to-reel tape recorder and started dictating into that as well.

My father eventually completed the play and even had a musical score written and produced. He also dreamed up a new television game show. It was the hey-day of those testaments to greed that enticed people to make fools out of themselves in front of the world. His idea was to have contestants putt their way around a series of miniature golf holes for cash and other prizes. He named the show, *Putt Your Way to Fame and Fortune.*

I thought both schemes were pretty bad and that they would go nowhere, which both eventually did, but I never had the heart to tell my father and instead lied about how I thought they were "great ideas" whenever he'd ask my opinion.

My father ultimately abandoned the game show idea. But from time to time and for the rest of his life the moribund play would re-emerge, like some featherless phoenix in a cornfield.

My father's time spent with Louise eventually reached past critical mass and our father-son activities all but ended. I kept up the golf routine, although alone and with even more intensity, probably as a vicarious way of staying close to my father. Around the same time, I became gripped with the recently released film *Patton,* starring George C. Scott. Scott played the gruff, swaggering, famed World War II U.S. Army General George Patton. Although Scott's portrayal of the General's personality appeared nothing like my father's, the loner/hero pathos and of the character reminded me of him. I saw the movie three times in the span of a few weeks, each time by myself.

It was during this period that I had a reunion of sorts. My father had dropped me off at the local driving range when I accidently bumped into an older kid. We both excused ourselves and started to move on when for some unexplainable reason we stopped and looked at each other. "Mike," the tall, husky teenager with the deep voice said. I looked in his eyes and although I didn't completely recognize him, I said "Lee?" It had been five years since my brother and I had seen each other. Adolescence had physically changed us to the point of almost non-recognition.

Chapter Twenty-Eight

When I anxiously told my father about the meeting and that I was going to visit Leon, my mother and grandparents, he was happily surprised: "Absolutely, I think you should. I never tried to keep you from seeing anybody," he remarked.

Although I wasn't aware of it, my brother, mother, and grandparents had moved into an apartment on Coldwater less than a mile from where my father and I had been living the entire time.

I walked down the street to the reunion not knowing what to expect. Would I be welcomed with open arms, or would I be greeted with disdain cloaked in a veil of pleasantries? Or, maybe I would be rejected altogether?

My mother became teary eyed at the sight of her youngest child. My grandfather was warm, but reserved. As for my grandmother, she was civil, and cold. I kissed each of them on the cheek. They all appeared older than I remembered them. Barr had aged the most and was markedly round-shouldered; her scalp still moved.

We spoke for a while and had a bite to eat before I returned to the empty apartment. When my father came home, he asked how the meeting went and I basically told him that it went fine without much elaboration. He didn't push the subject and expressed no displeasure at my visit.

The get-togethers continued for a while, but the old feelings of alienation were still there and I eventually faded away again.

While I was in high school, it became my turn to be schooled in my father's method of how to deal with a bully. Every day at Phys. Ed., this guy would find me and shove me, trying to provoke a fight. I told my father what was going on: "What's his name?" he asked. "Seltzer and he's big," I told him. "The bigger they are, the *harder* they fall. The next time he comes up to you, I want you to count three buttons down on his shirt, focus on that spot, then, I want ya' to say 'Seltzer, *fizz!*' and pop 'em, right there, like this, see, put your shoulder into it. He'll never bother you again, guaranteed. Remember, *every bully is a coward!*"

The next day at P.E., sure enough, Seltzer strutted over, intent on trouble. I did exactly as my father taught me, even down to the "Seltzer, *fizz!*" and that put an end to the bullying, "guaranteed." Seltzer and I eventually became friends. Like Wayne, I even had the opportunity to put my father's lesson successfully to use again when another school bully tried to push me around.

A 1970s California teenager's social life largely consisted of cruising Van Nuys Boulevard on Wednesday nights and weekend parties at the homes of kids whose parents were away. When my father told me that he had to go out of town with Louise one weekend, a light bulb went off.

I told my closest friend, Andy Zuckerman, about my father's plans and we both thought that it would be a good opportunity to throw one of the notorious California weekend soirées. I started having second thoughts, however, when the following day it seemed that every kid in school knew about the party. I began envisioning throngs of rowdies descending on the little one-bedroom apartment, followed by a squad of L.A. Police cruisers responding to the 911 calls of irate neighbors. I thought about hanging a "Party Cancelled" sign on the door and hiding out at Andy's house, but that would have made me a pariah at school the following Monday. So, I decided to go through with the party and hope for the best.

The "guests" started arriving soon after dark. Within a couple of hours, the tiny apartment was packed with longhaired-types, a smattering of jocks, a collection of loud, airheaded teenage girls, and a contingent of tattooed, leather-clad bikers who parked their choppers on the front path of the property. Before long, beer was being delivered by the case and the apartment was enveloped in a fog of cigarette smoke. The noise level was deafening. I wondered if I'd survive the night.

When my father returned from his weekend with Louise, he confronted me: "I heard about what you did, the building manager told me." I waited for him to lower the boom. But instead of getting angry, all he said was, "I shouldn't have left." I was impressed, and also ashamed.

By 1973, my father had spent fourteen years as a stockbroker, the last seven trying to recover with only periodic success. Now the country was being hit with the Arab oil embargo and my father finally threw in the towel and went into real estate. He obtained his license and in June of 1974, started working for Forest E. Olson Realtors.

But California real estate was depressed during that recessionary period; he was getting nowhere and needed income. Through the good graces and helping hand of a friend of his, he started training as an insurance adjuster for automobile claims. For a couple of months he tagged alongside a seasoned adjuster learning the business. The head of the company took note of how rapidly the new recruit caught on, his determination and work ethic, and offered him a job. It may not have been Hollywood, and it wasn't Wall Street; it was back alley body shops and the curbs of policy owners' homes where they parked their damaged vehicles waiting for the adjuster to write an inflated report. But it was a job and my father was grateful to have one. As always, he would make the best of it.

In February of 1975, my father informed me that my grandmother had died and suggested that I pay my respects, which I immediately did.

The sadness that had descended on my grandfather and my mother after Barr's death seemed to dissolve any antipathy they may have had for me and I began visiting them regularly. I was always greeted with a hug and a kiss from my mother and a warm "How are ya', mah' boy?" and a sloppy grandfather-kiss on the cheek from Pop. By then, my grandfather had officially retired from moviemaking, although people continued to send him screenplays and he remained on the lookout for a story that might spark his interest. He still followed the stock market and would often ask me to pick up the latest edition of the Wall Street Journal or Baron's from the nearest newspaper box.

That summer, my father and Louise got married in the rabbi's office of a local reform synagogue. Louise had been pushing marriage for some time, but my father had put it off until just before I went away to college. Louise's father, Bernie, who had owned a successful clothing business in Tennessee, had put a down payment on a house in North Hollywood. After his wife died, Bernie moved out to California and was now living in the house together with his daughter. My father moved in with them after I left for the fall semester of my freshman year at the University of Houston. U of H had the best golf team in the country at the time, which was why I chose to go there, and thanks to government loans and grants the tuition was covered. However, I would still need pocket money. Over the previous couple of years I had worked at several jobs, such as caddying at local country clubs for the rich and frequently flatulent whose divots often traveled further down the fairway than their golf balls, but who thought owning the heaviest leather golf bag in existence lowered their handicaps. I also served as a valet parking attendant at Chasen's restaurant in Beverly Hills, where a parade of Hollywood notables arrived nightly in their Bentleys, Ferraris, and Lamborghinis, but whose generous tips were compulsively snatched away by the concession's owner. However, my savings were hardly enough to get me through the school year and my father pledged to send me a hundred dollars a month to help.

Chapter Twenty-Nine

While I was getting established at Houston, my father settled in at his new home and his new life with Louise. He continued to hone his skills as an adjuster and develop contacts with body shops and mechanics throughout the Los Angeles area. I called him regularly. He always sounded glad to hear from me and usually made a point of encouraging me to apply myself to my studies; and he never failed to send me a hundred dollar monthly check.

I was also keeping in touch with my mother and grandfather. However, my grandfather wasn't happy about my calls. In the days before calling cards and cell phones the only practical way for a student to make a long distance call was from a pay phone, collect. If I wanted him to continue accepting my calls, he insisted, I would have to reimburse him. I did that for a while, sending a few checks, but my calling frequency dropped down because I couldn't afford it. Then my mother stepped in and told me to call collect and often.

In addition to keeping up with a full load of classes, I participated in a work-study program on campus and moonlighted as a waiter at the Houston Country Club. The job at the club, however, ended after I spilled an entire tray of mint juleps down the back of one of the guests on Kentucky Derby Day. But I had saved enough money to buy an old, two-door Mustang.

When the school year ended I drove back to L.A. for the summer and moved into Louise's house. Well, sort of. I was provided with a bed in the corner of the top floor office; despite the fact that there was an unoccupied bedroom down the hall, which Louise said she was preserving for her youngest daughter...who had moved out more than a year earlier.

I went to college for three reasons: golf, peer pressure, and my father's expectations. In other words, I had no idea what I was doing in college or whether I even wanted to be there. That summer, I decided my first year at Houston would also be my last.

When I told my father that I wasn't going back to college, he was instantly disappointed, and we eventually locked horns over the issue. Louise was also disturbed by my decision, but not for the same reasons as my father; she just wanted me out of her house; better yet, out of the state.

I wound up renting my own apartment, which my father subsidized, but the relationship between us kept going downhill and finally hit rock bottom when I tried to hash out our differences one day. The conversation went from bad to worse when my father said, "I've given you everything," to which I said something like, "Yes, but there's always been a string attached." I didn't mean to say that, it wasn't true. I meant to say that giving or not giving me things had nothing to do with my complaint; that material things were no replacement for the longing that I had for a father-son relationship that once existed but was unnecessarily traded away. And I wanted to tell him that labeling me as some sort of looser at nineteen years old because I didn't want to go to college was cruel.

My father looked as though he had been punched in the gut by what I said. Louise sat there with that "I told you he was no good" look on her face. With cold anger in his steel-blue eyes, my father said, "From now on you get nothing from me." I didn't speak with him again for a year and a half after that. However, I did hear from Louise: she called me at the gas station where I was working to rank me out.

That same summer, the summer of 76', my mother called me in a panic saying that my grandfather had suffered a heart attack. I went straight to the hospital.

After he returned home, I came by daily to take him out for short walks around the neighborhood, during which I asked him a lot of questions about his work in the early days of Hollywood, "We made a lot of pictures in those days," I recall him saying on one occasion. When I would ask if he knew some of my favorite actors, it turned out he knew all of them.

With my father no longer providing any assistance and one of my jobs (I had two) eliminated due to budget cuts, I moved into a cheaper apartment. The place consisted of a small room, a bathroom so tiny I had to do contortions to close the door from the inside, and a miniature refrigerator and hot plate.

Although there was no incident that precipitated it, I started fading away from my mother and grandfather again; I suppose I was just engrossed in my own troubles and wanted to be alone.

My reclusiveness ended when my phone rang on March 11, 1977: "Michael, this is Bethel Smith, your grandfather has passed away, it's time for you to be a man and take care of your mother."

I had met Bethel Smith a couple of times while at my mother and grandfather's apartment, but I had no idea who she was. As it turned out, Smith was the Commissioner of Los Angeles County, an appointee of Los Angeles County Supervisor Kenneth Hahn, and she was heading an initiative that my mother was involved with called "Woman at Work," whose mission was to rehabilitate women with substance abuse problems and get them into the workforce.

I felt miffed over Smith's implication that I had somehow been shirking my responsibility toward my mother. At the same time I was plunging into sadness at the news of my grandfather's death. "Of course, I'll be right over," I said, before driving to my mother's apartment.

Two days later I found myself in the small chapel of the Home of Peace cemetery sitting in a pew next to my mother, my brother on her other side. A group of perhaps thirty friends, relatives, and associates of my grandfather and mother were also present. Rabbi Edgar Magnin delivered the eulogy.

When Magnin finished, my brother and I held on to our mother as we passed by the open casket containing our grandfather's body. Beneath a pane of glass was what looked like a wax dummy; I knew it wasn't a dummy, but my grandfather was no longer inside the body I was looking at; that was just a shell.

The casket was wheeled through the mausoleum's marble corridor and down an isle to the crypt. As my brother and I sat on chairs flanking our mother, the casket was raised on a mechanical lift about twelve feet in the air, and then inserted into a curtain-covered void in the wall. I erupted into sobs; Pop was gone, and so was the vague hope that I had held in my heart since I was a small child that somehow my family would become one again. I hadn't cried since the day that Mae left. My mother seemed surprised at my sudden emotion.

I suppose my father found out about my grandfather's death from reading about it in the newspaper, but I had no way of knowing it. He didn't know that I had moved into my mother's apartment.

Chapter Thirty

My mother functioned well; she was congenial, well spoken, and dressed impeccably in custom tailored suits. Her hair was always professionally coiffed and her makeup perfectly, albeit liberally, applied. Only those who knew her well or were looking for it could detect her unnaturally stiff posture and the slight lack of coordination in her movements. When she was at home, however, and wearing a housecoat and slippers and without makeup, what I saw was disturbing. Her face was pockmarked, her hairline receding, and while she had always been thin her arms were as skinny as rails; she appeared decades older than her forty-six years.

From time to time while I was growing up my father made remarks about my mother's drug use. However, although the memories were obviously bitter to him, rarely, if ever, did he disparage her out of vindictiveness; he viewed her as sick, not evil, and his comments were always in response to my queries. Nevertheless, his few references to pills meshed with my own memories from the night of August 17, 1964, and the image of my mother as a drug addict was always in my mind. I started to snoop around. The typical places—medicine chests, nightstands, and dresser drawers—turned up nothing. When I opened the door to my mother's large walk-in closet, I was awestruck; there were literally hundreds of pieces of clothing hanging perfectly on two tiers of racks lining the walls; shoeboxes were stacked three rows high on the shelving above, and dozens more on the floor.

My mother was a neat freak. She couldn't even stand for a garbage can to have anything in it, let alone for something to be out of place. It was that obsession which gave away the hiding place of her drugs. My attention was drawn to a large shoebox slightly askew on the floor. When I opened it, inside I found a virtual pharmacy of amber-colored bottles of prescription drugs. There were multiple containers of Valium, Tuinal, Seconal, and Talwin, among others. The labels indicated that they had been prescribed one to three days apart and were filled at different pharmacies. All of the labels bore the name of the same doctor, Dr. Federico Oucest.[95]

I had met Dr. Oucest at least a couple of times over the past month or so when I drove my mother to appointments at his Beverly Hills office. A diminutive, gray-haired, mustachioed man with a gruff voice and impatient manner, Dr. Oucest controlled people through intimidation. His undersized and sparsely-furnished waiting room, which was separated from his inner sanctum by what appeared to be bulletproof glass, gave me the creeps. After I found my mother's stash of drugs, I called him:

"Dr. Oucest?"
"Yes."

---

95 Judy Garland and Marilyn Monroe—both of whom were addicted to prescription drugs and died from overdoses—were among his patients. Oucest (a pseudonym) was a well-known Hollywood "script" doctor.

"This is Michael Bennett, Maxine Fromkess' son."

"Yes."

"My mother has been acting strange lately, as though she's been taking too much medication. I found a box filled with bottles of pills."

Oucest's coarse voice became somewhat strident: "I want you to flush them all down the toilet…"

"I did that."

"Get rid of everything, the bottles, the labels, everything," he continued, trying to sound matter-of-fact.

"I did that," I repeated.

The stridency in his voice came back with a vengeance: "Good. Now, I don't want you or anyone in your family to ever call me again." Click!

I sat there holding the receiver and looking at the collection of drugs on the table in front of me. I may have been nineteen years old, but I wasn't *that* naïve.

I dumped the contents of the shoebox into a brown paper bag and returned the empty box to its place in my mother's closet. I then drove over to a friend's house and, after explaining what was going on to him and his mother, hid the drugs in their garage before driving back to the apartment. When my mother returned, I confronted her.

She reacted to what I had done with instant anger and agitation; I violated her privacy. I wasn't buying it. I had uncovered her lifelong "secret" and I sensed she was trying to muscle her way out of it. I told her that I wanted my mother, my real mother, not a doped-up version, and that I was going to get her off of the drugs. I gave her a choice: she could go through detox at a facility, of which I knew of none, or at home.

After some argument, my mother began to submit. She wanted to live and she was summoning whatever strength she could.

As we sat there discussing what to do, my mother said that she knew of a place where she could go to get off the drugs. I was perplexed. At that point, I knew little about her past and nothing about her previous, one-night institutionalization.

With my mother directing, I drove to a large concrete building somewhere in L.A. After parking the car, she and I walked through the oversized and reinforced front doors of the structure. The lobby, if that's what it was, seemed cavernous, cold, and deserted. There was what appeared to be a heavy, locked door, and some sort of reception window, but there was no one behind it. As we slowly paced around the empty, institutional-gray room, my mother suddenly stopped, and with tears welling up in her eyes she said, "Baby doll, I can't do it, I'll go through this at home." With her head on my neck, she sobbed, *"Why did Pop have to leave?"* As I imagine my father felt when she called him from perhaps the same facility thirteen years before, at that moment, in the beginning of the summer of 1977, my heart broke for my mother; she was so sick and so alone.

My grandfather had made a wise decision many years before in securing for his daughter what is now referred to as "Cadillac" insurance policy. It provided one hundred percent coverage for everything, including round-the-clock nursing, and unfortunately all the drugs she could ever want, so long as a doctor prescribed them.

About forty-eight hours after her drugs were taken away, my mother began to exhibit signs of withdrawal: she became agitated, her skin started to get clammy, and she was increasingly confused. But she had the presence of mind to call in a full-time nurse.

By the next day, the symptoms had severely intensified.

As I parked my car in the small lot behind the building after returning from work, I noticed my grandfather's brother, Saul, walking down the alley. We embraced and I asked him what was happening with my mother. All he could do was shake his head and mutter something about "she's saying things" and "seeing things."

Uncle Saully was a no-nonsense personality who constantly chewed on an unlit cigar and walked like his head was perpetually against the wind. Family legend had it that he fled New York after throwing a furrier who tried to cheat him down a flight of stairs. My grandfather always called him by his nickname, 'Bull.' Upon my reunion with the family, he was at first suspicious of me, but we eventually established a strong and loving bond.

As Uncle Saully shuffled away down the alley, I ran upstairs to the apartment. When I entered, I could hear my mother's loud ranting coming from her bedroom.

The nurse reported that during the day, my mother ran out of the apartment, naked, and into the courtyard, where she was corralled while talking to a tree. Back inside the apartment, she tried to climb into the oven.

The withdrawal symptoms reached a peak that night.

I had taken up residency in my grandfather's room, sleeping in his bed. At about 3:00 A.M., for no apparent reason, I suddenly awoke. My eyes immediately focused through the open door and into my mother's room where I saw the nurse escorting her from the bathroom. Suddenly, her legs gave way. Struggling to hold her up, the nurse cried out "Michael!" I shot out of the room and grabbed my mother's collapsing body, lowering her to the bed; she began to convulse. I draped myself on top of her and reached over with one hand and took hold of her tongue. I had never witnessed a convulsion before, but I had heard about the danger of people swallowing their tongue during seizures.

The episode probably lasted less than a minute, although, like during the 1971 earthquake, time slowed to a crawl and it seemed much longer.

When she came out of it, my mother had no idea what had happened and was confused by the position she was in. She was soaking wet with perspiration.

After helping the nurse get her back into bed, she began to loudly and incoherently rant. I grabbed the Los Angeles Yellow Pages phone book and dialed the number of the first listing under 'Doctors.' Amazingly, the doctor himself, whose name I cannot recall, answered. I related what I knew about my mother's history of drug abuse and what was happening:

"I can hear the commotion," the doctor said, in a kind and compassionate voice.

"You say you have a nurse there with you?

"Yes."

"I'm going to call in a prescription to an all night pharmacy. It's on Lankershim (a major street about 3 miles away)."

"Ok."

"It's going to be an injection; the nurse will be able to administer it."

"Ok."

"It will settle your mother down, but you will need to get her to the hospital afterwards."

"I understand. Thank you, doctor."

After filling in the nurse, I put my clothes on over my pajamas, ran down to my car, and drove through the dark and deserted streets to the pharmacy.

When I returned to the apartment, I rushed to my mother's room where the frightened nurse was sitting on the bed lightly restraining her. I took over as the nurse prepared the syringe.

"I WILL NOT ACCEPT YOUR HYPODERMIC! I WILL NOT ACCEPT YOUR HYPODERMIC!" my mother repeatedly yelled in a distorted voice. I held her cold, clammy, skinny arms down and leaned over her as she continued to yell while the nurse administered the injection of Thorazine.

Within seconds, my mother became docile. Minutes later, she was unconscious and her body began to 'thump' as though she was being jolted by a defibrillator. I called 911.

When the paramedics arrived, they strapped my mother, still unconscious, and her body still thumping, onto a gurney and took her to Cedars Sinai Hospital, where she would spend the next six months.

This was the kind of gut-wrenching hell that my father had lived with for nine years; and it was his wife, not his mother.

Chapter Thirty-One

Knowing my father, during the time that he and I weren't speaking he probably carried on as he always had: with determination and resolve to make the best of his life. I imagine that Louise sensed the pain he felt, but didn't show, at the severing of our relationship. Louise was empathetic that way and she was devoted to my father. But I'm sure she was also glad that I was finally out of the picture. Neither of them knew what was happening with my mother.

My mother's hospital room soon filled with flowers. In addition to the regular hospital staff, private-duty nurses tended to her needs around the clock. I visited her almost daily.

Getting control of her withdrawal symptoms was accomplished quickly, but she was still a very sick woman. Her doctor took me to the side one day and after gazing down at the ten-inch-thick medical chart on the cabinet next to him, looked up at me and shook his head. He said that my mother had taken so many drugs and for such a great length of time that her body had metabolized them, meaning that numerous systems had changed due to the constant presence of the chemicals. One of the consequences was the destruction of her intestinal mucosa, causing her body to no longer normally absorb the nutrients in food. As a result, although my mother ate well, including her beloved, twice-daily portions of ice cream, she was malnourished; she weighed eighty pounds.

The malabsorbtion syndrome was irreversible, and it was her most pressing medical problem. It would take radical surgery to prevent her from essentially starving to death. Two-thirds of her stomach would have to be removed.

It was obvious that the kind, young doctor at Cedars was concerned for my mother and that he had much sympathy for her condition despite its self-inflicted nature. But when he reported to me that she had had a double mastectomy, although there was no indication that she ever had breast cancer; a hysterectomy, again, with a lack of evidence of medical necessity; surgery for thyroid cancer, and that all of her teeth had been removed, he seemed both angry and disgusted.

With the drugs in her system now at a controlled level, my mother's personality started coming back. She became assertive with her nurses and, even with being as sick and physically weak as she was, she conducted her affairs over the phone, which, as far as I could gather, mostly consisted of matters relating to her father's estate. In some ways it appeared as though she was more productive and engaged at the hospital than at home. When she made a point of telling me that Groucho Marx was dying in the room across the hall, there seemed little sadness in her voice. Instead, she sounded as someone comfortable in their element.

I had an uneasy feeling about my mother returning home. Although she was stronger physically as well as emotionally, she was also easily agitated. And the big question was would she revert to her addiction? Sure enough, not long after her release from the hospital, the symptoms of drug abuse reappeared.

I could not go through another cycle of insanity. I packed my meager belongings and left. My father had lasted much longer in the crucible than I had.

❖ ❖ ❖

My first place of refuge was with my brother. Leon was attending UCLA at the time and was living in one of the fraternity houses just off campus. He had an under-sized sofa in his small room where I slept for a few days until my cousin, Wayne, and his wife, Yvone, offered me a room at their house in Bel Air. I was working as a salesman at a shoe store in the Topanga Plaza Mall at the time.

My stay with Wayne and Yvone ended and the "reunion" with my father occurred when I came down with a severe case of mononucleosis.

After a couple of weeks of being unable to get out of bed and barely having an appetite, Wayne became concerned that since he and Yvone were working full time and there was no one around during the day, I wouldn't get the care I needed to get better. He decided to call my father, who one day appeared in my sick room. "C'mon, I'm taking you with me," he said plainly, still looking angry. I didn't want to go, but I was in no condition or position to argue. Neither of us spoke to each other during the drive to Louise's house.

Because I was so sick I was given special consideration and allowed to crawl into bed in the room perpetually reserved for Louise's non-resident daughter.

During my long bedridden recuperation, Louise made compassionate gestures to provide me with food and drink. My father made a point of coming into the room when he returned from work, taking my temperature, and asking if I needed anything—soup, tea, crackers, and the like. Despite our estrangement, I was still his son and he was still my father.

But the days at Louise's soon took on an insane atmosphere.

Louise's father, Bernie, was still living in the house. His bedroom, where he spent almost all of his time with the exception of meals or watching a sporting event on television, was next door to mine. Louise began stomping up the stairs and berating her elderly father: "You ruined my life! You destroyed me!! I hope you're happy now!!!" were some of the invectives she'd blast at him before stomping down the stairs, only to return a few minutes later to spew forth a thing or two she'd just remembered. Louise repeated her cruel drill several times a day, day-after-day. Poor Bernie, he just lay there, flat on his back in bed, staring at the ceiling and puffing air past his lower lip as though he was short of breath. Fortunately he wore two hearing aids that he could just turn off.

When she wasn't unloading on her poor father or complaining about some psychosomatic ailment, Louise was usually reclining in the same corner of her den sofa, thumbing through retail catalogues and chain smoking; the house and everything in it reeked of stale cigarettes.

Being in Louise's place was like going from one den of madness to another. I couldn't wait to get out of there. I couldn't fathom why my father would have opted for a life with this woman. Having once tried to speak my mind and meeting with disastrous results, I kept my mouth shut.

After several weeks locked in Louise's asylum, I was feeling strong enough to get around a little. My closest friend, Benny Mizrachi, and his mother recommended that I go to Israel and volunteer on a kibbutz. They knew I was in a pathetic situation and wanted to see me get away from it.

The idea of going to Israel appealed to me and I made arrangements through the Israeli Consulate. Before I traveled, however, my father, who didn't object to my plans, but still felt disappointed that I wasn't going to college, wanted me to go to the doctor first to make sure that I was fit enough to travel. I was given the medical all clear, obtained my passport and international driver's license, sold my car, and purchased an open, one-year round-trip ticket to Israel.

During the days leading up to my scheduled departure, Louise saw fit to try every tactic she could conjure up to get under my skin. She of course made a special effort to once again turn my father against me through her persistent brainwashing sessions. Unfortunately, my father allowed himself to be provoked by Louise and once again we exchanged words of some sort.

This time it was my turn to determine my fate.

I stuffed everything I had into a duffle bag I had purchased at a local army/navy surplus store and relocated to my brother's dorm room again until my flight left for Israel. But before leaving Louise's, I wrote a note, which simply stated, "I didn't ask to come here." At that moment I hated my father and I didn't care if I ever saw him again; I hated Louise even more.

Chapter Thirty-Two

"V'heishiv Leiv Avos al Banim,
V'leiv Bonim al Avosam…"

"And I will return the heart of the fathers to the children,
and the heart of the children to their fathers…"

— The final words of the prophet Malachi

Getting off of an El Al plane in Tel Aviv and loading onto a bus filled with Hebrew speaking soldiers carrying assault weapons was a culture shock for a kid from California. Getting off at the wrong bus stop in the middle of who-knows-where and where nobody spoke English, hitching a ride in a farmer's jalopy, trudging through sand dunes toward an unknown destination (pointed out by the farmer) while schlepping my sixty-pound duffle bag made me wonder what I had done. Finally making it to the kibbutz office only to find a sign posted on the door saying "Go Away. No New Volunteers," and then being questioned by soldiers in a jeep with a .50 caliber machine gun mounted on it asking why I left my bag unattended was like being stranded inside of a nightmare.

On the advice of the heavily armed welcoming committee, I took a bus to the city of Hadera, where I hoped to transfer to another bus to Jerusalem. Benny's uncle lived in Jerusalem, and he was the only contact I had in that part of the world.

While waiting on a bench at the Hadera bus station, a young soldier sitting next to me asked about the camera hanging on my shoulder. Relieved that somebody spoke English, I hesitantly handed my Canon 35-millimeter SLR to the red-bearded young man in green fatigues with an M-16 casually propped between his knees.

After a brief discussion about the camera, the soldier asked what I was doing in Israel. When I told him my kibbutz story and that I was now on my way to Jerusalem, the soldier looked dismayed: "You won't get to Jerusalem, the busses will stop running because of Shabbat," he said. I had no idea what he was talking about and just sat there looking puzzled. "My name is Ra'anan," he said extending his hand. "Mike," I replied. "Why don't you come with me? You can stay with my family. We'll help you get settled on kibbutz on Sunday. I can tell you for sure you won't get to Jerusalem today." There was something very genuine and kind about the soldier and I agreed to go with him. What choice did I have anyway?

With camera slung over my shoulder, duffle bag somewhere, rifle barrels and butts pressed up against me from all sides, I stood, swayed, and almost fell onto the seated passengers aside me several times as the rickety sounding bus swerved and barreled to I didn't know where. Welcome to Israel!

Ra'anan Dunovitch lived with his parents and younger brother, Donny, in a clean and comfortable apartment in the city of Bat Yam, about an hour's drive north of Tel Aviv. Ra'anan's parents were Holocaust survivors.

Donny was about to begin compulsory military service and was hoping to get into naval commando unit.

The Dunovitch's treated me, a total stranger, like a member of their family. That Friday night I experienced my first Sabbath meal, which was followed by a trip to a local movie theatre, where I fell asleep as the show started and didn't wake up until Ra'anan nudged me saying it was time to go. I never did find out what the movie was about.

On Sunday Ra'anan made some phone calls and then drove me to the entrance of Kibbutz Palmachim. I never saw Ra'anan or his wonderful family again, but I am forever grateful to them.

Kibbutz Palmachim was so named because it was established by a group of soldier-farmers called the Palmach, who had fought heroically during Israel's struggle for independence. It is located on the Mediterranean coast not far from Bat Yam.

My job on the kibbutz alternated between guiding crane cables around giant concrete blocks and maintaining irrigation lines in cotton fields. On occasion, I went skinny-dipping inside a water tower; I shared a shack with a nice but reclusive Dane and ate a lot of vegetables, bread, and cheese in the collective's dining hall. After about three months of this excitement, I decided I had enough, so I left.

For the next two weeks I traveled by bus and lorry through the Sinai Desert, reaching as far south as the tip of the peninsula before turning around. When I finally made it to Jerusalem, I ventured through the narrow streets and alleyways of the old city until I reached the so-called Wailing Wall. While standing before the enormous stone barrier and wondering what the attraction was all about, I was approached by a tall, skinny man who spoke English with an American accent:

"Where ya from?" he asked.

"California," I answered.

"What are you doing in Israel?"

"Traveling," I responded simply.

"How'd ya like to meet a wise man?"

(No self-respecting Californian would turn down such an offer.)

"Ok," I said, taking the bait.

After following the skinny American across town by foot, I met the wise man that changed my life forever. He turned out to be a linebacker-sized white-bearded rabbi from New York whose students endearingly called Reb Noah.

Rabbi Noah Weinberg grew up in New York City. He was the youngest son of a dynastic Hassidic rabbi who died when Noah was fifteen years old. Through his travels to Jewish communities across America as a textile salesman, the rabbi became deeply disturbed at the abysmal lack of self-knowledge among American Jews. A deep thinker and a sensitive soul, Rabbi Weinberg soon developed a yearning to stem the tide of Jewish assimilation in America. By reaching out to secular Jews and introducing them to their heritage in a language they could understand, hc hoped to start a Jewish renaissance, à la Moses Mendelssohn only without the contaminants.

Over the course of the next nine months, I studied Jewish philosophy with Reb Noah, to whom I asked every question that was on my mind, and attended classes given by various rabbis affiliated with his yeshiva, Aish HaTorah. I learned everything from the Hebrew alphabet to the history of the Jewish people to rudimentary aspects of Jewish law and more.

Reb Noah not only possessed enormous wisdom and insight, he was an expert listener who heard where people were coming from and felt their pain. He was no "guru," and certainly no charlatan; he was a down-to-earth man who through years of dedicated study and personal struggles had acquired much wisdom and refined his character. He had a profound and genuine love for his people, indeed for all humanity, and he strove to see the meaning in everything. He became my mentor and my spiritual father.

Through Reb Noah's influence and teachings, as well as that of other Aish HaTorah rabbis, I came to appreciate who I was as a Jew and began a lifelong bond with the incomparable beauty and wisdom contained in Judaism's voluminous, sacred texts.

In essence, through his outreach, Rabbi Noah Weinberg was returning a heritage that the Maskilim two centuries earlier had stolen from generations of Jews; a heritage that had taught the world all of its great principles, but that had sadly been replaced with various and sundry "isms," and the vapid identity of such things as owning Cadillac automobiles, eating bagels and chopped liver sandwiches, throwing ostentatious Bar Mitzvah parties...and Hollywood.

Among the principles that I grew to appreciate was the tenet to honor one's father and mother, and that that honor transcended any disagreements one might have with his or her parents. Contrary to common perception, it's a commandment that serves the interest of the child more so than that of the parent. It is a deeply profound concept that deserves elaboration. But suffice it to say for now that it was the basis of why I wrote letters of reconciliation to my father as well as my mother.

I followed up the letter to my mother with a phone call. I feared what her condition might be and I didn't want to wait until it reached her before letting her know how I felt. It turned out that she had already received it. Our brief conversation was warm and loving. She cried at the sound of my voice, and followed up with her own letter:

"Michael dear, I could not begin to tell you how much your letter and phone call meant to me. It gave my life a new inspiration...I too always was your mother, and always will be your mother, and I too want you to know that you will always have a home to come to, and I too will always be at your side. I love you with all my heart.

"I am very proud of what you are doing and how hard you are studying..."

"...I want you to know that all of our friends, including Rabbi Magnin, were overwhelmed with joy, when I told them that you have written and called me...

"...Call me anytime, collect.

"Your Mom Always"

My father, in turn, sent me a letter in which he expressed appreciation for my writing him and that it was apparent that I was under the tutelage of someone of "good character." He also admonished me for sending the letter to his business address rather than his home, stating, "Louise is my wife and I won't have you excluding her from our relationship." That demand caused me to hold my emotion in check.

My experience in Israel took a strange detour when I heard about a demonstration being planned that would take place at the Western Wall.[96]

---

96 The Western Wall, aka the Wailing Wall, is a remnant of the structure that surrounded the mountain on which both the Temple of Solomon and the Second Temple once stood.

Earlier that year, the Ayatollah Khomeini had returned from his exile in France to lead the Islamic Revolution in Iran. The chief Islamic clergyman in Israel, the Grand Mufti of Jerusalem, cabled Khomeini congratulating him on his success and promising a similar revolution in "Palestine." The Mufti's message was leaked to the press and a group led by the militant rabbi, Rabbi Meir Kahane, had planned a demonstration at the Western Wall decrying the Mufti's sedition and calling for his arrest.

Never having seen a demonstration but hearing about many of them while growing up during the 60s, I was intrigued. I decided to head down to the Wall with two fellow students from the yeshiva. En route, we met up with a group of Rabbi Kahane's followers who invited us to join them. Long story short, I wound up barricaded inside the Waqf—the office of the Muslim High Council—as a riot of angry Arabs developed outside.

The police and army eventually arrived, put down the riot, and unceremoniously dragged my friends and me into armored vans and deposited us at a local prison.

Now occupying a large concrete and stone cell, with a perpetually burning light bulb dangling from the twenty-foot high ceiling and a hole in the floor for bodily necessities, in an ancient poky called the Russian Compound, I settled in with my eleven cohorts; Rabbi Kahane and his lieutenant were arrested on conspiracy charges the following day.

As if the whole experience wasn't strange enough, while I was enjoying my incarceration, a middle-aged American man with whom I shared a connection was brought in to the prison.

I had already learned some things about proper prison etiquette at that point: you never talk to the interrogators; you always hide contraband; you let the guards know that this is *your* home and that they are

merely visitors, and the first thing you ask any new prisoner is "Whatta-ya-in-for?" Well, this poor fellow made
some lame excuse about being in Israel to make a film
and he had somehow innocently—everyone in prison is
innocent—been arrested:

"My family was in the picture business," I said.
"What's your family name?"
"Well, it's not my name, it's my grandfather's name;
it's Fromkess."
"Leon Fromkess? Your grandmother is Rita and your
mother is Maxine; I know your family."
"What's your name?" I asked.
"Lasky, Bill Lasky."

Together with Sam Goldwyn[97] and Cecil B. DeMille,
Jesse Lasky was one of the founders of Hollywood filmmaking. Bill was Jesse's youngest son. Although Jewish
by birth, he had converted to Christianity and was in
Israel trying to make a religious-themed film.

While I was spending my days and nights in Jerusalem's Russian Compound prison, and occasionally being interrogated by agents who did not realize I
didn't understand Hebrew because I remained silent,
my mother was growing concerned about why I had not
contacted her and she began making calls to the yeshiva
office. Knowing where I was but not wanting to alarm
my mother, the secretary kept putting her off by saying
I was on a field trip and would be back in a few days.

But as the days kept adding up my mother became
suspicious, and *very* worried. Finally she was told what
had happened and where I was.

Back at the prison, I was completely unaware of the
events involving my mother when a guard called me to
the cell door, unlocked it, and escorted me to a holding

---

97   Sam Goldwyn was at one time married to Jesse Lasky's sister.

cell, where a finely-dressed African American man was waiting for me. He introduced himself as a representative from the U.S. embassy:

"Do you want me to help you get out of here?" the man asked congenially.

"No, not really" I politely answered.

"Why not?" he asked, sounding surprised at my refusal.

"Because I'd rather not get the U.S. Government involved. This is a problem that I have with the government here. I'd rather let it play out through the local system," I explained.

The man said respectfully that he understood and before leaving handed me his business card, saying, "If you change your mind."

While I was being taken back to my cell, I wondered why the consulate representative had selected only me when ten of the other guys were also Americans.

A few days after the visit from the U.S. Embassy representative, guards came to our cell and rounded up our group. We were handcuffed, manacled, and chained together, before being loaded into vans and driven to court for a hearing.

As all twelve of us were hobbling through the courthouse reception area in one long line, a woman called out something in Hebrew to one of the guards escorting us. The guard unlocked the chain linking me to the others and ushered me to a wall phone, handing me the receiver. My mother was on the line. I could tell from the quiver in her voice that she was frightened and worried. "I'm fine, Mom, don't worry, it's just a regular thing over here, a misunderstanding, something everybody deals with. I'll be back at the yeshiva soon and I'll call you." I handed the receiver back to the guard and continued my hobble-walk to a courtroom where the rest of the chain gang was already seated on benches waiting for the hearing to begin.

The proceeding lasted about an hour and concluded in a plea bargain and with the judge admonishing us for what we had done, saying in Hebrew, "These types of activities increase the tension with the Arabs." We were all given suspended sentences and released on one-year probation, provided we stayed out of trouble.

After being transported back to the Russian Compound, we gathered our belongings from the cell and were released. I had been there for twenty-three days.

Last seen, Bill Lasky had been moved to a cell located around the prison's yard and was housed with a group of Arabs, for whom he was making tinfoil crosses.

I later learned that it was my mother behind my U.S. Embassy visitor. I was told that through some political connections in California, she was able to get a message to then Vice President Walter Mondale, who facilitated the consular's visit as well as her phone call to me at the courthouse.

My father knew nothing about what had happened.

Chapter Thirty-Three

My mother had moved into a tenth floor apartment on Fuller Avenue in the La Brea Towers, behind CBS Studios in the Fairfax area of Los Angeles. She was working as a deputy commissioner on the Alcoholism Advisory Board under Los Angeles County Supervisor Kenneth Hahn. The job provided her with an official ID, badge, and a business card, all bearing the seal of the County of Los Angeles. With her history of addiction, I found it at least a little odd that she was on a substance abuse advisory board. While I was in Israel, she told me that I could stay with her when I returned. Instead, she had made arrangements for me to stay in a room in the garden apartment of the development's handyman, a wiry little guy named Harvey.

I contacted my father as soon as I returned to the states. Since I didn't have personal transportation, we met at a kosher eatery in the Fairfax area. I briefed him about my year in Israel and he told me about how he had started his own appraisal business. The meeting was congenial, albeit somewhat subdued. We spent about an hour together and made plans to play a round of golf at the Club. I initiated an embrace and we parted.

Over the next year and a half, although I had grown past my obsession with golf, I frequently joined my father for a round just to spend time with him.

Louise, who at first denigrated my religious convictions, started showing an interest in my growing but still immature knowledge of Judaism, often engaging me in philosophical and theological conversations.

All in all, the relationship between my father and me was on the mend. The special bond that we shared had never been truly severed. And we still shared a common heart.

About a month after I moved in with Harvey the handyman, he informed me that staying with him much longer was going to be a problem. For some time, he had been dating a Filipino woman who was working for my mother as an aid of sorts and they were planning to get married. But Harvey's romance wasn't the only reason for his wanting me out: my mother, he said, had not paid him the rent. Until Harvey said that, I had no idea of any such arrangement. Harvey kindly offered to let me stay until I found other accommodations.

When I informed my mother of my pending homelessness, she merely said that she'd take care of it somehow and made no suggestion of my moving in with her. At that point I realized what was going on: she had been keeping me at arm's length to prevent my intervening with her drug habit again.

The old symptoms of slurred speech, the stilted walk, and the unnatural stare were back. My grandfather's Cadillac was so dinged and dented it looked a wreck; numerous cigarette burns beside the driver's seat marred the gold damask upholstery.

And, worst of all, Dr. Oucest was back on the scene.

In addition to the signs and symptoms of her ongoing drug abuse, my mother was flashing her deputy commissioner's badge and claiming to be with the health department to avoid paying restaurant bills, and she was going to pawn shops. While alone in her apartment one day, I answered a call from a representative of American Express who asked to speak to "Leon Fromkess." When I told the man that my grandfather had died more than two years prior, he said that someone had been regularly using his credit card, and that the account was deeply in arrears. I felt compelled to tell the AMEX rep that I believed my mother was broke and that a stop should be placed on the card.

Being a drug addict is bad; being a desperate drug addict is even worse. This time I knew my mother would have to be institutionalized if she was going to survive: I thought of a plan.

"I understand that you feel you have to do this Michael and I admire you for it. I just don't want you to get hurt in the process," my father said when I told him of what I was about to do.

My brother, who was in his first year of law school in Sacramento, was in complete agreement and very supportive of the plan. While growing up, Leon had suffered through much more than I had with our mother. He was trying to build a life away from the craziness that had surrounded him since he was twelve years old.

This time I didn't bother looking through drawers and cabinets, I went straight to my mother's new walk-in closet and quickly located her deadly treasure trove—same box, same drugs, same doctor, different pharmacies. I emptied the box, but left two pills on her dresser.

After she returned home and changed into her housecoat, I noticed the pills on her dresser were gone. I waited for them to take effect. In less than an hour she was dozing off on the living room sofa, a lit cigarette burning yet another hole in the seat cushion.

"Mom, wake up," I gently nudged her. "I must've fallen asleep," she slurred, awkwardly trying to brush away the still smoldering hole. "Let's go for a ride," I said nonchalantly. Always willing to "take a ride," my mother gathered her purse and we left the apartment. The ride I had planned was to the University of Southern California Hospital Psychiatric Emergency Room.

As expected, and to my relief, my mother fell asleep en route, holding yet another burning cigarette, which I gingerly slid out of her fingers and snuffed out in the ashtray.

When I stopped in front of the ER entrance, she awoke from her drug-induced slumber: "Where are we?" she said, struggling to focus. Saying nothing, I got out of the car, walked around to the front passenger door and grabbed her, lifting her out and carrying her toward the entrance. "We're at the hospital, Mom. You need help and this is the only way I know how." Confused and agitated, my mother angrily told me to let go, but I carried her through the doors and into the waiting room where I put her down and rang the call bell.

While I stood holding on to her arm, two young doctors entered the waiting room. After taking one look at the strung-out woman standing in front of them, the doctors probably already knew what they were dealing with.

With my mother starting to shiver with fear and struggling to appear sober and defiant, I gave the doctors a brief history of her drug addiction and said that she needed help. Flashing her deputy commissioner's badge, my mother began threatening the two physicians. One of the doctors craned his neck to read the ID in the leather wallet held up in her trembling hand.

"That doesn't mean anything to me," the doctor said matter-of-factly. My mother began to plead; but she wasn't making any impact.

We were asked to remain there for a few minutes and the two doctors exited back through the locked door leading to the hospital area. "I have to make a phone call," my mother announced, and then walked over to the wall phone. She fished some change out of her purse and with her now uncontrollably shaking hand managed to dial the phone number of Supervisor Kenneth Hahn.

After a brief, desperate attempt to convince whomever was on the line that her son was wrongly trying to have her admitted to a psychiatric hospital, followed by a few minutes of silence, and then another brief exchange, my mother handed me the phone. The male voice on the other end identified himself as Supervisor Hahn's deputy and asked for my version of what was going on. After going through the same brief speech I had given the two doctors, the deputy responded, "I've already spoken with Supervisor Hahn and he is aware of what's happening. He's concerned about what type of place your mother will be in." "It's the USC Medical Center," I told him with conviction. The deputy said he understood and asked to keep him informed. I hung up and turned to my defiantly poised mother and said, "He said to keep him informed." She looked like a trapped and frightened doe.

When the doctors returned to the waiting room to escort my mother inside for evaluation, she collapsed in my arms. I carried her to a chair in the examination room and returned to the waiting area.

Half an hour later one of the doctors emerged to tell me that they were going to admit my mother against her will. He said that it was explained to her that she had the right to file a Writ of Habeas Corpus, which he expected she would do, and that would result in a hearing before a judge within seventy-two hours.

The doctor escorted me to the room where my mother was. She was sitting in a chair next to an examination table, clutching her purse, agitated and angry beyond the point of tears. "I'm going to file for a court hearing. I will not forget would you have done, Michael," she threatened. I tried to explain to her that I was not her adversary and that I wanted her to get help. Refusing to look at me, she turned her head in defiance. I stayed with her for a few minutes and then left.

I had seventy-two hours to prepare for the hearing that would decide whether my mother would get the help she had long needed or whether she would be released back onto the slippery slope, at the bottom of which was her grave. I needed to call my brother and my father.

Chapter Thirty-Four

"You should call Richie Mark. Maybe he can write a letter to the judge about your mother's drug abuse going back to the divorce. It might help. I admire what you're doing, Mickey. Let me know if you need anything. Good luck," my father sympathetically said when I called him from Harvey's apartment. In every conversation that I would have with him about my mother's condition and my efforts to intervene, my father never once tried to discourage me, he only offered support. Nor did he express any anger toward her, only pity.

I phoned my brother in Sacramento to let him know how things had transpired and about the upcoming hearing. I also told him that the doctors at USC wanted to meet with both of us the next day and he would have to leave for Los Angeles right away.

My father had given me Richie Mark's home number and I called him next. Richie said he would do whatever he could and asked me to get the name of the judge. As soon as I hung up from Richie, the phone rang:

"This is Herb Baerwitz."

I recognized the gravelly voice instantly.

"I wanna know what you're doing to your mother?" he demanded.

"I'm trying to save her life, Mr. Baerwitz. My mother is a drug addict and she's killing herself," I said with conviction.

"I don't know anything about this," he replied, sounding less confrontational.

"It's been going on for a very long time, Mr. Baerwitz," I accusingly retorted.

"Well, keep me informed," Baerwitz said, actually sounding a little compassionate.

My mother had obviously made her second call from the hospital, but she was running out of options; or at least I thought so.

I told my father about Dr. Oucest and that I wanted to sue him. "Call Dr. Breckler, your old little league coach, he's a malpractice attorney now," he advised. I did.

"Forget it. You'll never touch him, he's been up before the boards before, the doctors wrote the laws in California," said Dr. Al Breckler, whose voice I hadn't heard since I was ten years old.

My brother had driven through the night from Sacramento to make the appointment at USC. The young female doctor behind the desk was friendly and professional, just like the two physicians who had done the original intake. She asked Leon and me some questions about our family history and what we knew about our mother's drug abuse. The doctor seemed incredulous over her condition and commented as to how Leon and I were so "normal." The remark was meant as a compliment, and we took it that way; but it also saddened us as it brought home the reality of how sick our mother had been for virtually all of our lives.

The doctor went on to explain that California law provided for free legal representation for relatives of people in our mother's situation if we wanted it, which we did. The entire meeting lasted about half an hour.

We met with the lawyer representing us the day before the hearing. The short, middle-aged woman, with obvious experience in these types of cases, and a bundle of energy, expressed her sympathy for the tragic situation and promised to help to her utmost. She explained that for a court to order an involuntary commitment, we would have to prove to the judge's satisfaction that our mother's condition met the legal standard, which, she explained, was that the person was "a danger to themselves or others." After some further discussion, it was determined that in addition to the doctor from USC I would take the stand and testify in open court against my mother.

After the meeting, I called Richie with the judge's name and then drove my grandfather's once shiny Cadillac to his house in Beverly Hills.

Richie appeared just as I had remembered him: a large, soft-spoken man with a gentle demeanor. After a brief conversation, during which he asked about my father, Richie handed me an unsealed envelope addressed to the judge, whom it turned out he knew. As my father had done, Richie expressed his respect for what I was trying to do but was doubtful that it would be successful.

Except for the elevated judge's bench and witness box, the hearing room didn't look like a typical court; there were no dark, paneled walls, no carpeting, and no jury box. The rows of florescent lighting fixtures, portable tables, and folding chairs made the outsized space seem more suitable for an institutional dining hall than for a courtroom.

The attorney representing us called my brother and me to one side of the room. As she was instructing us as to how the hearing would be conducted, two male attendants escorted our mother into the room and to a table facing the judge's bench. She was wearing the same housecoat and shoes she had on when I brought her to the hospital three days prior.

After the clerk called the court to order, our attorney presented the case for having our mother committed to the custody of the state for the purpose of psychiatric treatment because she was both a danger to herself as well as others. She called the first witnesses: the psychiatrist from USC.

The doctor testified as to our mother's clinical symptoms that were present at the time of her admission and went on to explain how she exhibited the signs and symptoms of long-term narcotic and barbiturate abuse. She also summarized the information garnered from her interview with Leon and me.

"Your Honor, the Plaintiffs call their next witness: Michael Bennett."

As I sat in the witness box, I looked out on my mother sitting at the defense table about twenty feet ahead and flanked on either side by her two attendants. After three days without makeup or a visit to the beauty parlor, and on just enough medication to forestall withdrawals, she looked strung out and unkempt, as well as angry and scared.

Responding to the lawyer's questions, I related my personal experiences with my mother's drug abuse: her delusions, hallucinations, slurred speech, car accidents, falling asleep at the wheel and at home while holding lit cigarettes, and so forth. When I described the incidents leading up to her six-month hospitalization at Cedars two years before— running outside naked, talking to trees, and trying to climb into the oven—other defendants who were waiting for their cases to be heard erupted in laughter. Pounding his gavel, the judge thundered "WE WILL HAVE QUIET IN THIS COURT-ROOM!" The room fell silent. I was angry; my mother appeared humiliated. The judge instructed me to continue.

As I went on to describe other aspects of her self-destructive and otherwise dangerous behavior, she, now appearing strangely confident, glared at me.

I concluded my testimony by telling the judge that my mother's drug abuse was an issue in the divorce trial of my parents and for that reason, custody of my brother and me was given to our father, "and I have a letter from my father's attorney explaining that," I said, as I handed the judge the envelope from Richie. At that, my mother's confidence and defiance faded. She appeared frightened and anxious and looked around as though searching for some unseen advocate.

Without expression, the judge silently read the letter, placed it back in the envelope, and handed it back to me before announcing his ruling:

"It is obvious that your mother is a very sick person. Under California State Law, a person can only be held against his or her will if they pose a danger to themselves or others. Under the circumstances and the current way in which the law is interpreted, I cannot conclude that your mother meets those criteria."

I felt as if darkness had descended. I knew it was the end of my relationship with my mother; and I couldn't help but feel the judge's decision was in effect her death sentence. How could the judge find her so obviously sick and yet release her? What was needed to *"meet those criteria,"* a body?

I drove my mother home from the hearing. The ride was, needless to say, uncomfortable. "I can forgive you for what you've done, Michael," my mother flatly intoned. I didn't feel I had done anything to require forgiveness, and I sensed that she was manipulating me; she didn't want to lose me. But it didn't matter. I had already made up my mind. By staying around my mother, all I would be doing is watching her destroy herself, and getting destroyed in the process. "I can't help you any more, Mom," I said glumly.

When we arrived at her apartment on Fuller, I called my closest friend, Benny, and asked if he could pick me up and give me a ride to the yeshiva in the valley where I had been studying since my return from Israel. Benny and I had been friends since junior high school and he was privy to everything that was happening in my family. He sensed the seriousness in my voice and there was no hesitation in his response. I gathered the few belongings that I had, and, as my mother stood in a defiant posture, but with tears welling up in her eyes, I left her standing in the foyer of her apartment.

I called my father with the news: "You did your best, Michael, more than your mother deserved. You have nothing to regret. It's sad. She'll probably wind up killing herself."

Those last words of his may sound cruel, but they weren't meant to be. They came from deep sadness and the strength that my father had developed after dealing with a lifetime of challenges the likes of which would have destroyed most people. He said what he said to impart his strength in me, not merely to express his cynicism.

I spent a few days living at the yeshiva while looking for a job and a place to live. I found both through a local Jewish employment service.

For the next year and a half I worked for the Jewish burial society known as the Chevra Kadisha, which also owned a mortuary. During the day, I handled the final arrangements for people that had passed away, many of whom were indigent and alone. At night, I slept on a convertible sofa in the office...next to a display rack of caskets.

In the weeks and months that followed the hearing, my brother had several phone conversations with our mother during which he told her that he loved her but that he didn't want to have anything to do with her until she got help.

"Why do you have to be the one to do it?" my father asked after reading the article in the morning paper about my arrest. "That's what every parent would say, Dad," I respectfully said. He didn't respond.

Since my stint in the Russian Compound for the Mufti caper, I had become something of a militant. When I learned that a local "synagogue" was really a headquarters for Christian missionaries who were targeting young Jews for conversion, I decided it was my obligation to liberate the Torah scroll they had.

I had become close friends with Irv Rubin, the West Coast Director of Rabbi Kahane's Jewish Defense League. One of Irv's longtime members, whose Yiddish name was Label, and I had become something of a duo of vigilantes dispensing Jewish justice whenever and wherever *we* decided it was needed. We responded to reports of anti-Semitism or Israel bashing, be it by Jew or Gentile, by confronting the perpetrators and, if necessary, not turning the other cheek. On the evening of

371

April 27, 1980, Label and I decided to case the missionary center, a large facility that boldly sported on its façade the name "Ahavat Zion Synagogue,"[98] to plan the liberation of the Torah scroll. When I saw that the group's members were engaged in a meeting, I convinced Label we had to act right away. I would block the door leading to the meeting room while he grabbed the Torah from the synagogue's ark.

Label was a short, stocky guy with fire in his eyes and a vicious one-two punch that could easily take down a person twice his size; Irv called him "the fighting-eating-machine."

But while Label's proficiency as a warrior overcame any height disadvantage he may have had in a fight, it wasn't enough to compensate for carrying a three-foot tall Torah scroll crowned with silver bells that tinkled at the slightest movement. As he carried the huge scroll outside through the wrong door (we had parked our getaway vehicle on a different side of the building), I abandoned my position and went out after him. Seeing my short, stocky friend wobbling away with that huge scroll with the bells clanging away made me laugh so hard I almost doubled over.

Running through a nearby wooded area, we came across what looked like an unused playground. I took the Torah from Label and gingerly placed it in an empty metal trough, planning to retrieve it when the heat died down. We then exited through the woods and onto the Ventura Freeway.

After walking down an entrance ramp and onto a main street, we started looking for the nearest phone booth to call for backup. Police cars were speeding in all directions through the area.

We spotted a gas station. As Label and I casually walked past the gas pumps headed toward the pub-

---

98   Ahavat Zion is Hebrew for "The Lovers of Zion."

lic phone booth, a squad car waiting to turn away in the nearby intersection suddenly U-turned and raced straight for us. When the patrol car hit the upslope of the driveway at high speed, the front wheels leaped off the ground.

"Freeze!" shouted the voice over the loudspeaker as two LAPD officers jumped out and leveled their service revolvers on us. Standing with our hands above our heads and illuminated by the police car's high beams, Label and I were frisked, handcuffed, and I.D'd by one of the cult's leaders who had seen us. We were loaded into the police cruiser and taken to the Van Nuys lockup.

Label's handcuffs were removed due to his having a bad shoulder and he was placed in a holding cell. I was chained by one hand to a bench seated next to a Hispanic guy, who was chained by both hands. I was a smoker in those days and lit up while I sat there waiting to be processed. The Hispanic prisoner asked for a cigarette, which I obliged with my free hand and lit for him. "What did they arrest you for, man?" my Spanish friend asked. Thinking this guy wouldn't know what I was talking about if I told him I had stolen a Torah from a missionary group, I conjured up a tale he could relate to, and that would earn me some respect if I wound up sharing a cell with him. "They say we killed a couple of Nazis," I indifferently stated, nonchalantly drawing on my cigarette. "*They oughtta let-chu guys go!*" my new Chicano admirer said.

Label and I were strip searched (during which Label taunted the cops with a snide remark, which almost got him beaten), fingerprinted, and booked on a charge of "Grand Theft." Our yarmulkes were confiscated as evidence and at my insistence we were provided with makeshift ones cut from a towel. As I was being brought in for questioning, one of the cops looking at my tzitzis— the four-cornered garment with knotted strings that a religious Jew wears—asked, "What's that?" I thought I might have some fun. Pretending I didn't know what he was talking about, I said, "What?" "That string," the cop demanded. "What string?" I feigned. "That string hanging from under your shirt," "Oh, that's a ripcord, one tug and the whole station goes up!" I said in my best serious voice. The cop jumped back, before his buddy admonished him for being so gullible.

Label and I were released several hours later after a JDL representative arranged to post bail through a local bondsman.

I returned to my job at the Chevra Kadisha.

Uncle Phil called me the following morning right after my father had. A onetime radical activist himself, he seemed tickled at the report he saw on the morning news about his nephew's arrest. Concerned about the legal trouble I might be facing, he offered his support.

The next phone call I answered was from my mother: "I can help you, Michael," she said, her voice syrupy from the effects of drugs. Sadly, I hung up without saying anything.

The following day, with charges pending and the local news hyping the incident, I sat with my father at his dining room table and discussed what had happened. Once he realized that I would not be deterred from my idealism, he took out a piece of paper and a pencil and proceeded to draw a map of how the mission *should* have been executed. Despite his son's foolish behavior and decades since his days in combat, he was still a leader of men, a commander. At that moment, I felt especially proud to be his son.

After some mysterious person uncovered the cult's source of funding and threatened to release the information to the press, the charges against Label and me were dropped. The press obtained the information anyway and reported on it. The so-called "synagogue" was eventually demolished.

My father didn't support my militant activities, but he didn't oppose them either. Those were the days long before the attacks of 9/11 and worldwide terrorism. In the wake of the Holocaust, Jews had an undeserved reputation of not fighting back. Consequently, when young people like Label and me were arrested for militant Jewish activities, the police and the courts were often lenient. Nevertheless, my father was troubled by both the danger I was inviting and the legal problems I was incurring. However, he found it hard to argue against the principles behind my actions.

Surprisingly, Louise was more supportive of my militancy than my father, even telling me on one occasion to "Bring me a Nazi, I want one of those."

I discovered that despite the complaints I had against her, Louise was a proud Jew and was willing to speak out. In fact, she had been a political activist of sorts, although in a far less radical fashion. Strangely perhaps, my activities as a Jewish militant served to bring my father, Louise, and me closer together.

By the fall of 1980 I had saved enough money to keep afloat in Israel for the next year or so and I purchased a one-way ticket to Tel Aviv. I intended to continue my studies and hopefully make a life there. Before I left, my father sadly informed me that Richie Mark had suffered a massive stroke. As it turned out, Richie's brain hemorrhage occurred while he was in court during a trial. I found out what hospital he was in and went there. Standing in the doorway to his cubicle in the ICU, I gazed at the felled gentle giant and read several chapters from a small book of Psalms. I asked G-d to have mercy on Richie Mark's soul; and to remember him for the good deeds he had done for my father and for me.

Richie passed away a few days later.

I soon returned to Israel.

My father continued working to build up Bennett Appraisal Services and to seek refuge on the weekends playing golf at the Club.

Chapter Thirty-Five

In Jerusalem I met a girl from Delaware with a vivacious smile and an irrepressible zest for life named Sharon Spiegel.

In 1971, when she was fifteen years old, Sharon's father, Fred, a former World War II sailor and longtime employee of the DuPont Corporation, passed away. Her mother, Ruth, had kept the family going ever since.

Thanks to a government scholarship, Sharon was able to attend Temple University in Philadelphia, from where she graduated in 1977 with a degree in Occupational Therapy. After completing her affiliation, she accepted a job offer at Nyack Hospital in scenic upstate New York.

After her first year at Nyack, Sharon took a three-week vacation to Israel and fell in love with the country. When she returned to America, she made up her mind that Israel was where she wanted to live.

In the winter of 1980, Sharon officially immigrated to Israel and attended a four-month ulpan, or Hebrew language program, on a kibbutz. After completing the course, she got a job as a therapist at Jerusalem's

Shaare Tzedek Hospital. When I met her, Sharon was sharing an apartment with two roommates in the Jerusalem neighborhood of Kiryat Moshe. I was studying in a yeshiva just a few blocks away.

After five weeks of dating, while we were riding on the Number 1 bus en route to the Western Wall, I proposed and Sharon said, "Yes." It was January of 1981.

"That's terrific, Mike. I'm sure she's a fantastic girl, I can't wait to meet her," my father said when I phoned him with the news. I knew that he would fall in love with Sharon and was excited for him to meet her. The wedding date was set for August 16, 1981.

Sharon left Israel for Wilmington in June to prepare for the wedding. I followed a week later and stayed in a small yeshiva in Queens, where I continued my studies and simultaneously looked for an apartment and a job. We planned to live in New York until we could save up enough to move back to Israel.

Things were progressing nicely until the late afternoon of July 7th, when I was called to the yeshiva's public phone:

"Mickey," my brother's voice was solemn in a way I had never heard before.

"Lee, what's wrong?"

"Mom's dead."

After a brief conversation, the next phone call I received was from a detective with the Los Angeles Police Department:

"I'm sorry about your mother, Michael," the detective compassionately said.

"I have to ask you a couple of questions," he added.

"I understand," I sorrowfully responded.

"Do you think there was any foul play?"

"No, my mother had a drug problem for a long time. She was very sick, detective."

"I don't think so either. The housekeeper was hysterical. Your mother left a note. It just said, 'I want to be with my Mommy and Daddy.' Do you want it?"

"No," I said softly. I did not want a keepsake of my mother's last tragic act of insanity.

"I understand. Take my phone number down and if you need to, call me for any reason," the hardened cop empathetically offered.

With her parents gone, her sons and friends alienated; her health in perpetual decline because of drugs, and broke, my mother was at the dead end of a street she'd been on for most of her life. When the nurse's aide that was with her heard the unusually loud blare of sirens coming from the side of the building where my mother's room was located, she went to investigate. When her repeated knocking on the door went unanswered, she opened it; my mother was nowhere to be seen. Drawn to the open window by a dreadful curiosity, the woman crossed the room and looked out. On the sidewalk, ten stories below lay the crumpled figure of my mother, clothed in her familiar housecoat. She was forty-nine years old.

I was back in L.A. in less than a day standing in the room at the Chevra Kadisha where I had lived and worked and was now making arrangements to bury my mother, whose shattered body lay in a room just a few feet away.

In Judaism, among the laws governing death and mourning is the prohibition against embalming and the requirement that the body be buried in the earth. My mother had made arrangements for a mausoleum crypt next to her parents. Regardless of her wishes, I could not violate Jewish law.

If Edgar Maginin was the rabbi to the stars, Alvin Malinow was their mortician. My mother had a signed, albeit unpaid, contract with Malinow and he did not want to bury my mother according to Jewish law. A fight over my mother's funeral was brewing. It was a fight I was not going to lose, no matter what. But before taking drastic action I called the State Board of Funeral Directors:

"Under the circumstances, Mr. Malinow is required by state law to follow your wishes," the woman at the State Board of Funeral Directors said.

"What if he refuses?" I asked.

"Then you tell Mr. Malinow that his refusal will be another thing in the hearing against him!"

I made an appointment to see Alvin Malinow that same day:

"I will not bury your mother according to Jewish law!" Malinow adamantly stated as I sat before him in his office.

"Then that will be another thing in the hearing against you that's going to be held by the State Board of Funeral Directors," I calmly retorted.

Malinow, a diminutive man, hit the roof; he was practically foaming at the mouth. I sat there unmoved.

"Tell me what you want?" he begrudgingly asked after his rage subsided.

"I want my mother buried according to Jewish law, Mr. Malinow, nothing more, nothing less."

"Fine, but Rabbi Magnin will conduct the service," Malinow relented.

Although I strongly disagreed with him on philosophical and theological grounds, I had nothing against Rabbi Magnin personally. And I saw it as appropriate that he deliver the eulogy since he had known my mother from the time she was a little girl and she thought of him as her rabbi.

The following day, my brother and I together with about twenty friends and associates of my mother gathered in the chapel of the Malinow and Silverman Mortuary. Rabbi Magnin delivered a kind eulogy during which he reminisced about my grandfather and his career as a producer, my grandmother, and of course my mother, whom he recalled as having suffered from being sick for as long as he could remember.

When he was finished speaking, the stocky, jowly rabbi, whom I had only known from a distance for much of my life, wearing his black robe walked down the aisle directly toward me. Stopping just feet away, Rabbi Magnin offered the ancient Hebrew words of comfort spoken to a mourner: "Ha Makom Yenachem Eschem B'Soch Sha'ar Aveillei Tzion V'Yerushalayim"—May G-d comfort you among the remnants of the mourners of Zion and Jerusalem. I was taken aback by Magnin's knowing the original Hebrew, and touched by his use of it.

With that, music began to play over the chapel's sound system. Music is prohibited at Jewish funerals. Label, my partner in Jewish militant mayhem, immediately went to the control panel and switched off the recording. Alvin Malinow came rushing into the room and reached for the switch to turn it back on; Label physically stopped him. Malinow stormed out of the room, but came back a minute later with a rather large employee. Pointing at Label, he seethed, "I want him thrown out of here!" Stepping between Malinow's goon and Label, I glared at both men, "You'll have to throw me out too." The music remained off.

Together with my brother and a couple of friends, Label and I carried my mother's casket outside to the waiting Chevra Kadisha hearse and drove to the Home of Peace Cemetery.

At the graveside service, Rabbi Yehuda Lebovics, who was associated with the yeshiva I was learning at in L.A., performed the service, which he concluded thusly: "We ask you to forgive us if we did not do enough to help you." The rabbi's words spoke volumes about a man who had never met my mother; and they were a remarkable contrast to those uttered by Edgar Magnin who had known her since she was nine years old. Choking on emotion, I struggled to recite the Mourners Kaddish— the ancient Aramaic memorial prayer for the dead, a version of which I would recite three times a day for the next eleven months.

I returned to New York the next day to sit shiva. I cried over my mother's utterly sad life.

My father's response to what happened was sensitive and appropriate. He, like just about everyone who knew my mother, was not surprised by her death. But he was nevertheless saddened, saddened by her tragic life, and saddened for my brother and me.

But he also conveyed the strength of character that so embodied him; that grit your teeth and let's-get-it-done attitude. In so many words my father told me to be strong and carry on with my life; that I had done all that I could and now it was time for me to move on. Such was his attitude about dealing with his own life's difficulties, and such was his comfort and instruction to his son.

Sharon and I were married in her hometown of Wilmington, Delaware. My brother and my friends Benny and Label flew in for the wedding, so did Rabbi Tzvi Block, the head of the Aish Hatorah branch in L.A., who conducted the service together with Sharon's rabbi. My father did not come. He said it was because of his business obligations and that he would rather Sharon and I have the money an expensive trip would cost and that he and Louise would have a party for us when we came out to L.A. It was an excuse, and I was deeply disappointed. I knew of Louise's fear of flying, and just about everything else: dogs, germs, neighbors, cars, elevators...you name it Louise feared it, but I hoped that my father would have taken a stand and ignored his wife's neurosis for this of all things. I sensed my father's regret and perhaps his shame when he told me over the phone that he couldn't make the wedding. But I wanted no part of his check or of any party. I wanted my father at my wedding.

I had no doubt that Louise had prevailed upon my father not to come by making him feel guilty if he left her. Even if she had a legitimate phobia, why not push your husband to attend his son's wedding? Why hold him back from such a momentous occasion and from a son who had just lost his mother in the most tragic of ways? And why would my father of all people not have the strength to do the right thing? It was the same old pattern of behavior that had driven a wedge between the two of us when I was a kid. Nothing had changed and I could not understand it. Despite my feelings, I told my father it was ok.

After the wedding, Sharon and I settled into a one-bedroom apartment in Queens.

Chapter Thirty-Six

Sharon found a job at Jacobi Hospital in the Bronx. The institution was named after Dr. Abraham Jacobi who played such a pivotal role in protecting the health of the children at the Hebrew Orphan Asylum. I started my own house painting business.

Our daughter, Meira, was born on February 28, 1983.

Later that year, Sharon and I and the baby traveled to L.A. to visit my father. I knew he would not come to New York for the same reasons that he did not come to the wedding, but I wanted to give him the pleasure of seeing and holding his first grandchild.

The new baby brought a smile to his face the likes of which were beyond compare. I could see both the solace and joy he felt as he held his granddaughter in his arms and lovingly gazed at her. Perhaps my father felt at that moment that the years of struggle and turmoil were worth it.

Louise was gracious and accommodating, as well as animated to the point of rejuvenation at the sight, sounds, and feel of the new baby. She became like a typical grandparent, wallowing in the right to spoil her

grandchild with frilly outfits and colorful toys. Ev
nie came to life: He rose early in the mornings, shaved,
slathered in cheap cologne, and dressed like I imagined
he did in the days before he lost his wife.

Since my mother's death, my brother and father
had rekindled their relationship. Leon had graduated
from law school but failed to pass the notoriously difficult California Bar Exam on his first try. Feeling discouraged, he wanted to quit law and go to work in my
father's appraisal business. My father wouldn't hear
of it and prevailed upon Leon to study harder and try
again, "Don't be a quitter," he always said. He let Leon
work for him to earn some extra money in the interim
and told him that once he passed the bar, he would help
him get started in business.

Leon passed the bar exam on his second try and true
to his word, my father helped him set up his first practice in family law.

In the ensuing years, Sharon and I had two more
children, Yair and Yehuda, and we moved to a larger
apartment in Brooklyn. Every year I took at least one of
the children for a ten-day visit to L.A. to see my father.
During each trip, I would pay my respects at the graves
of my mother and grandparents, as well that of Harry
Bennett, who is buried in the same cemetery, next to
Rose, in the Kalisher family plot.

From the time that my father married Louise, I had
not seen or heard anything about Aunt Claire. On occasion I'd ask my father about her and he'd set his jaw
and say something about Aunt Claire and Louise "not
getting along," or Claire not wanting him to have a relationship with anyone but her. According to my cousin
Dennis, Claire's youngest son, the division between his
mother and my father was sparked when Louise sent
Claire a new purse for her birthday.

Claire and Louise had an off-and-on but generally decent, albeit unbalanced, relationship over the years. Louise never hesitated to call on Claire when she had something on her mind or just to chat. Claire was patient with her, listening, empathizing, and offering her best advice. She became sort of a friend/therapist/confident to Louise. But inside, Claire viewed the relationship as burdensome. When Louise arranged to have the birthday present sent via the mail directly from the store, rather than personally presenting it to her, she took offense and made her feelings known to her brother. My father probably told his sister that she was being petty and making something out of nothing. But such expressions would only have served to aggravate Claire further and cause her to dig her heels in even deeper. As my father attempted to mediate the crisis, the two stubborn women forced him into making a choice, a choice between his wife and his sister: he chose his wife.

Cousin Dennis' analysis:

"Your dad was right about Claire. She was very possessive about Mark, undoubtedly stemming from their years together in the orphanage. They were the only loved ones they knew from a very young age and had a deep bond and a co-dependence. Claire was in many ways a mother substitute for Mark. As a mother, Claire required complete devotion and loyalty. Marriage by any of her boys (including Mark and Phil) was seen as some sort of disloyalty, a betrayal. My relationship with my mother became quite difficult immediately after I married (actually from the minute I told her I was getting married)...It's not a coincidence that Claire broke off with Mark each time he married—it was disloyalty, and no amount of friendliness on the side of his wife could make it ok (not that there weren't valid issues as well).

"I don't blame Claire—she had to be the strong one when she and Mark were abandoned, since she was older (also it was her nature). But it meant she didn't have someone to take care of her. She was always very needy that way, though simultaneously very big-hearted and generous. But her need would outweigh her generosity when the boys got married, as she no longer had a monopoly on their affections. And rather than accept and embrace the wives, she fought them to try to maintain control, which only alienated the boys (I speak for myself and your dad here, not Wayne). So she ended up losing a lot, but could not help it because the behavioral pattern was ingrained from those terrible, endless, lonely early years. It's a tragedy, and the blame goes to Grandpa Harry, in my opinion."

Dennis concludes:

"...Uncle Phil worked out a way to handle Claire (who was none too fond of Paulie either). He would visit her a few times a week by himself. Our family rarely socialized with his family other than the major holidays. Phil must have realized that he had to give Claire the attention she needed in order to stay connected, but he essentially kept Paulie in the background more or less. I don't think Claire ever called Paulie just to chat, in the way she and Louise would chat. I don't think she probably ever did with your mom either. Mark was a much deeper connection to her than Phil, though she was possessive about Phil in many ways."

When Sharon and I visited my father and Louise after our daughter was born, he told me that Claire had been diagnosed with pancreatic cancer, a one hundred percent terminal diagnoses at the time. He wanted us to visit her, which the four of us did. Although she was very sick, and I had not seen Aunt Claire in more than five years, the cancer had not yet ravaged her and she appeared as I had remembered her: robust, gracious, and still with a smile that lit up the room. It turned out to be the last time that I would see her.

Dennis recalls the brief, sad, and dramatic reunion between my father and his sister:

"Your dad and Louise came to the hospital a day before Claire passed away. She always had lots of friends there in the evening gathered around her bed. When your dad and Louise walked into the room there was an audible gasp—everyone knew about the split and how close they used to be. I remember Claire saying "Oh, Mark!" when they came in. She was very weak and not talking much by then. Everyone got up and went outside to give them some private time. I think Louise stayed in the room part of the time, and then came out alone. Mark and Claire were alone for quite some time. Neither of them said to me what they talked about, but one can imagine it was a tearful time.

"Interestingly the doctor had told us a day or two earlier that she was hanging-on, did not want to let go, and that we needed to let her go. I think actually she was waiting for Mark to come before she could leave. Both Claire and Mark had a stubborn kind of pride, and obviously Claire had decided she was not going to make the first move, and so she waited stubbornly, holding back death, for him to show up. Uncle Phil had called Mark that day (they were not on good terms at that time either) and told Mark "If you ever want to see your sister alive again you better get down to the hospital tonight."

Claire, the sister with the smile that lit up my father's world, passed away the next day, February 17, 1985.

In the late fall of 1986 about six weeks following the birth of our third baby, Yehuda, my father came out for a two-week visit. He had not been back to New York since he left the orphanage in 1933. Given his history with Louise it was a remarkable breakthrough.

Sharon was on maternity leave and while I was working during the day, she, my father, and the kids had a ball. They went shopping on the crowded nearby Kings Highway, took the kids to the playground, and even spent a day at the Bronx Zoo, where Sharon got a lesson in how to deal with a stubborn child:

Our two-year-old, Yair, had been suffering a serious case of the terrible-two's; offer him a cup of apple juice and BOOM, he'd be on the floor kicking and screaming; if we put him down when he wanted to be held, BOOM, on the floor again, and so on. We never knew what might set him off and Sharon was at her wits' end. Well, when they got to the zoo, Yair wanted to be pushed in the stroller, but the privilege had to go to the new baby and Yair worked his magic right there on the long, winding entrance path of the zoo. Sharon was about to relent and pick up the hysterical child when my father intervened: "Don't pick him up. Leave him right there and just keep on walking," he instructed Sharon, who stood paralyzed with indecision. She was afraid to buck her father-in-law but her heart was bleeding for her son.

"Don't worry, honey, you're doing the right thing. He'll be fine. I'll stand behind him. You just keep on walking, he'll come," my father reassured. Sharon kept walking, Yair screamed and kicked, my father stood guard, and eventually everybody had a nice day at the Bronx Zoo.

When I heard about the incident and my father's taking control of the situation, I smiled and thought back to so many similar instances where he exerted what Wayne called "Executive Authority" when I was growing up. Instead of resenting him as some may have reacted, Sharon felt the love with which the fatherly lesson was delivered and her respect for him grew even more. My dad was being a father to my wife, who had lost her own father when she was so young. And the scene had taken place in the city where my father had grown up. The next day he took Sharon out to buy a double stroller.

During his visit, my father asked me to drive him to where he used to live. At the time I knew practically nothing about his childhood, or any other period of his life from before my birth for that matter. Like any son, I had always wanted to know about his past, but something undefined said it was a taboo subject. When he made the request, I became excited that I would finally learn something.

With my father giving me directions (remarkably, he still knew how to get around), we drove to the Grand Concourse in the Bronx: "My gosh! Look at this place! This was brand new when I lived here," he bitterly remarked while looking at what had become an inner-city war zone.

When we reached the building whose address he remembered from fifty-three years before, my father craned his neck to look past me and out of the driver-side window. Staring at the graffiti-covered edifice and the derelicts and drug addicts hanging around the once elegant building, he said, "Pshhh, I've seen enough.

Let's get outta here." He remained largely silent the rest of the way home.

When it was time to return to California, I drove him to JFK Airport, parked the car and, carrying his suitcase, walked beside him to the terminal. After he checked his bag, we walked to the "Passengers Only" area. I kissed my father goodbye and stood there watching as he walked to the gate to board his flight:

His elegant walk, the straight posture of his still robust physique, and his handsome white mane; there goes my dad...my dad...my beautiful dad.

He was still my hero. I missed him already.

In 1987 Bernie died. Louise was finally free from his intrusion into her life. But she now suffered from a new malady, one that couldn't be cured by the Valium she was addicted to and that she could not blame on anyone but herself: Louise was now saddled with guilt over how she had treated her own father. No one can know for certain what drove Bernie to swallow the pills that ended his life, but his daughter's unrelenting psychological blows and verbal abuses certainly didn't make his "Golden Years" very lustrous.

Chapter Thirty-Seven

Sharon's mother married a rabbi from Baltimore the year after we were married. Baltimore is only about two hundred miles from New York and we had made numerous trips there over the years. We liked the community, the schools were good, and real estate was more affordable than in New York, making owning a home a future possibility for us. In the fall of 1990, six weeks after the birth of our fourth child, Amitai, Sharon and I packed up the family and drove to our new apartment in Baltimore. Sharon was offered a job at a nearby hospital and I restarted my house painting business.

The move turned out to be a good one. We were living in a clean and well-kept apartment complex in a nice neighborhood; the children were attending excellent schools and had plenty of friends and places to play. My father was relieved that we had made the move.

In May of 1993, he called me and I knew from the instant I heard his voice that something was wrong. As my father was telling me the sad news that Uncle Phil had died, for a split second his voice broke with emotion: "I don't know what the hell's the matter with me," he said, quickly regaining his composure. "It's your brother, Dad. It's normal," I responded, awkwardly trying to comfort him in a respectful way.

My father and his brother became estranged during the difficult years following the divorce. From what I could gather, he had asked Phil for a loan and Phil refused. Feeling jilted, as he was the one responsible for having secured Harry's estate, my father told Phil he never wanted to speak with him again for as long as he lived. Phil was devastated by the breakup. With the exception of a brief reunion that I managed to arrange, my father and his brother never saw each other again.

I knew that Uncle Phil had a heart attack a number of years back. When my father told me that he died, I assumed it was due to a cardiac issue. I found out the truth about what happened more than a decade later.

After Phil underwent cardiac bypass surgery in 1980, he began to exhibit some odd physiological symptoms. His doctor suspected something and ordered tests on the blood used to transfuse him during the procedure. It turned out that one of the units was contaminated with HIV: Uncle Phil, the socially conscious sibling, had died of AIDS.

❖ ❖ ❖

When my father turned 80, on June 11, 1995, he was ready to retire. It wasn't that he didn't have the strength or the stamina to continue working or that he had enough money to retire on, he just didn't feel like driving around the city and traipsing through automotive repair shops anymore. He wanted to relax a little. He didn't have much savings, as he had always been generous to others. But with his monthly Social Security check, and some supplemental income from smartly managing Bernie's estate money, he and Louise would have enough income to get by.

On September 2, 1995, Sharon gave birth to our fifth child, a boy we named Yoni.

After retirement, my father spent much of his days following the stock market, playing golf, joining my brother for lunch, watching Leon's son participate in team sports, and otherwise taking it easy. However, his relationship with Louise was hitting rough waters.

In later years, during my annual visits to California, I noticed my father's increasing lack of patience with Louise and his growing irritation with her almost endless complaints and criticisms of everything and anybody. Since his retirement he didn't have the distractions he once had and Louise's issues had now come into close focus. He couldn't so easily turn a blind eye any more. Nevertheless, I felt sorry for him.

With my father's generous help, in 1996 Sharon and I bought an old house in a quiet neighborhood in Baltimore. I was in the process of fixing up the place when things between my father and Louise started getting worse.

When speaking with him over the phone, often I could hear frustration and growing anger in his voice. Although he didn't want to discuss it, it was obvious that the source of what was bothering him was Louise. I thought it might be a good idea for him to get away for a little while. I was also cognizant of his age and wanted him to spend some time with his grandchildren. Once again he headed east for a ten-day visit, alone.

In 1999, responding to pressure from Louise, my father asked me if I would come out to L.A. to paint their house. I had done just that a number of years earlier, but the Southern California sun and L.A. smog had taken a toll and the exterior was due for a repaint. I flew out to L.A. with my one employee, Dennis, to do the job. My father covered the travel expenses.

In-between climbing up and down ladders, scraping, caulking, and painting, I could tell that the tension between my father and Louise had increased and was now at a worrisome level. Despite knowing that he had to some degree brought this situation on himself by tolerating Louise's neurotic behavior for so long, I still felt sorry for him. It wasn't what I wanted for him, especially not at this stage of his life. But there was little that I could do except try to be a good son.

Not long after I returned to Baltimore, he informed me that Louise had been diagnosed with lung cancer. I flew back out to L.A. for the surgery.

As I waited with Louise in the pre-surgical prep area of the UCLA thoracic surgery unit, I was struck by one question that it seemed every patient was asked: "Are you still smoking?" The place was an assembly line for smokers with lung cancer.

When it was time for her to be taken to the operating room, I went upstairs to the lobby, where I huddled with my father and Louise's two daughters, Janet and Darla. After some discussion about how long the surgery would take, one of the daughters announced that she was hungry. More conversation ensued about where to go for lunch; but first, shopping for new clothes.

I had been sitting in the lobby for several hours reciting Psalms when my father and Louise's daughters returned. Shortly thereafter, the surgeon came into the waiting area, reported that the operation was successful, and that Louise was in recovery. When the doctor left, Janet, Louise's younger daughter, became emotional and said, "I thought mom would croak." First the lunch and shopping excursion while their mother was in life-threatening surgery and now this base remark, made me ashamed and angry that my father had allowed himself to be part of such a crude and selfish family.

The day after the surgery, I went with my father to visit Louise at the hospital before returning to Baltimore. As we sat in chairs across the room from Louise, who was being tended to by a nurse, she began complaining about something and started abusively insulting the young woman. "Stop it will you, she's trying to help you," my father scolded his wife. He could not stand abuse, regardless of the circumstances. "Dad," I whispered, as I reached over and gently took hold of his arm, "she's in pain."

Later that year, the situation between my father and Louise was reaching the crisis stage. "You don't sound too good, Dad. What's going on?" I asked during one phone call. "Nothin," he responded unconvincingly. "There's something, I can hear it in your voice. Is it Louise?" "Yeah," he curtly answered. "What can I do?" I offered. "Nothin, I have to deal with it," he concluded.

I started calling my father more frequently, engaging him in conversation, telling him what the kids had done that day, and so on. I also tried getting him to voice some of what was bothering him, hoping to talk him through it, get him to loosen up, take it easy. I was afraid for his health at least as much as I was pained by his emotional distress.

I also started discussing the situation with Louise, who initiated the first dialogue with me about what was happening. Our conversations rapidly became more frequent and long-winded, at times taking place three to five times a day.

Louise told me that she tried to get my father to go with her to a marriage counselor but he stubbornly refused. "I'm not saying that I'm guiltless, Michael, but I just can't deal with your father's anger; he's the last angry man; I didn't fight in World War II; I suppose if I was a television set, we'd get along just fine; your father wants to be entertained. The problem is I'm not a clown or a juggler that can entertain your father," she disdainfully ranted during one conversation, and then added, "Please don't tell your brother about what's happening with your father and me. If Karen finds out about it, I'll just die!" Karen is my brother's wife. Louise didn't like her either.

While I wasn't quite sure of what Louise was talking about with her references to the war and jugglers, I did understand her mention of my father's anger; although I would certainly not characterize it as something chronic or even unwarranted. I agreed with her that they should get counseling and convinced my father to give it a try.

But the therapy lasted only one session before my father pulled the plug. "I never heard anything more ridiculous in my life," he reported to me about what had taken place in the therapist's office.

Louise's oldest daughter, Darla, called me to discuss the crisis. I was surprised. Other than seeing her at the time of her mother's surgery, we had not had a conversation in decades.

Darla suggested that her mother and my father should move into a retirement facility. I saw several problems with the idea: first, my father was completely independent and vibrant, and he would view such a place as little more than an old-age home; second, while Louise did little more than occupy a corner of the sofa, she was secure in her environment; third, although she was abusive to her father, Louise remained attached to the house that he had bought for her and had lived in. My father had been trying to convince her to sell it for several years when the local real estate prices had reached record levels, but Louise steadfastly refused to budge and there was nothing indicating her position had changed. Finally, I sensed there was something behind Darla's suggestion, something that bothered me most of all.

For as long as I could remember, Darla and her mother didn't get along. Their relationship, from what I perceived, consisted almost exclusively of contentious phone conversations. Why was Darla suddenly so concerned for her mother's welfare that she would call *me*? And how would her mother and my father moving out of the house solve their relationship problems? It occurred to me that Darla merely wanted to warehouse them so that she would not have to deal with her mother. Darla was trying to use me to facilitate her plan in order to avoid being stuck with her mother if the relationship were to end.

Toward the end of the conversation, Darla unexpectedly asked, "Do you feel like you want to rescue your father, Michael?" The question caught me off guard; it didn't make sense in the context of our conversation. "Yeah, I do," I replied honestly.

I became very concerned about my father. He was living in misery and at his age, the daily stress could be deadly. And if I were right about Darla's motives, my father would be coming under additional pressure. Leon was getting him out of the house more often, meeting him for lunch and such, but nothing was working. He and Louise were at each other's throats. They wouldn't even stay in the same room together.

In one of the last conversations I had with Louise, she sounded as though she thought the situation was hopeless and that the marriage could not be saved. I called my father: "I'm at the end of my rope, Mike. I told Louise I won't let her do to me what she did to her father," there was deep anger and resolve in his voice.

I asked him if he had been to the doctor to have his blood pressure checked. He had, and it was sky high. Now I was *very* concerned.

In my last conversation with Louise, she was resolute:

"I've been through this before, Michael," she threatened, referring to divorce. "The thought of being in this house alone, *uhhh*," she interjected in angst, visualizing living alone and no longer thinking about saving the marriage. "So this is goodbye, Michael," she said resentfully, merely a hint of sadness in her voice.

"Oh Louise, don't say that, thirty-six years..."

"Don't bother, Michael," she interrupted "It's over. He left me before...for two weeks."

Louise was referring to the time when more than two decades earlier I heard my father tell her off. The remark revealed a deeply emotionally disturbed woman. But that statement paled in terms of abnormal psychological significance as compared to what she said next:

"I'll just tell you one thing, Michael, one thing, marriage is sacred."

Louise, the woman my children called 'grandma,' was blaming me for the failure of her marriage *after* telling me that I shouldn't try to save it. It later occurred to me that maybe this disturbed thinking was somehow connected to her older daughter's asking me if I wanted to "rescue" my father.

I called my father: "Come live with us, Dad. We'll build a room, you'll be with your family, the kids, Sharon and me, we want you with us, Dad, we want you with your family," I said.

In a slightly shaky voice he responded, "Ok. Whatever time I have left, I want to be with my family."

Fearing that something might happen, I called Leon: "Get dad out of there right away."

My brother picked up my father and his two suitcases the next day and brought him to his house in Agoura Hills, where he stayed for a few days while getting his affairs in order. It wasn't the way I wanted it to happen, but at eighty-five years old, in the spring of 2001, my father was finally coming home...my *dad* was coming home...home to his family that loved him so very, very much.

Chapter Thirty-Eight

"Home is the place you grow up wanting to leave,
and grow old wanting to get back to."
— John Ed Pearce

Sharon and her mother left for the airport while I worked on finishing wallpapering the den and fighting an increasingly painful toothache. Since our daughter was relinquishing her room for her grandfather, I wanted her new sleeping area to look nice. Also, because it was the only room with a television, it would be where my father would be spending a lot of time until his new room and bathroom were completed.

His flight was scheduled to arrive around 6:00 P.M., but when Sharon and Ruth got to the airport, they were informed that the flight was delayed until midnight and they returned home.

By eleven o'clock my toothache was even worse; I couldn't go anywhere. Sharon returned to the airport alone. When she arrived there, no one knew anything about the flight. After about four hours of back and forth calls and dozing off in an empty terminal, Sharon called with the good news: "I got him. Everything's fine.

What a nightmare. But I got him! He looks great and we're on our way."

I greeted my father as he and Sharon came walking up the concrete pathway of the house. Despite the all-night excursion and the traumatic circumstances, he showed not a trace of fatigue. He was smiling and looking as strong and robust as ever. And for the first time in several years, he looked untroubled.

After serving him breakfast and helping him get settled in, I took my father with me to the dentist's office to have my cracked molar extracted.

Over the next three months, while I worked during the day and then helped my close friend, Rusty, the Irish contractor, and his rugby buddies build the new bedroom and bathroom into the evening hours, my father went to work settling into his new home. He opened a bank account, obtained a Maryland Drivers License, bought a car, and using maps and a GPS-like device, learned the area. It wasn't long before he was running errands and driving the kids' carpools.

Meanwhile, my brother was handling the divorce proceedings in California. Leon had built up a successful practice and was one of L.A.'s top family law attorneys. Besides the regular turnover of divorces and child custody cases, he accumulated an impressive stable of dysfunctional Hollywood celebrities and sports figures that couldn't seem to stay out of trouble.

Louise turned to her first ex-husband, also a lawyer, to handle the divorce from her side.

Despite supporting Louise and her daughters for decades, my father wasn't claiming any community property. He wasn't vindictive, and he especially didn't want to hurt Louise's children.

By mutual agreement, my father had left the marriage with a small annuity that he and Louise jointly held. The annuity, his two suitcases, and the clothes on his back were all he took with him. Louise, on the other hand, had the house and everything in it, the car, and about $200,000 from her father's estate. Nevertheless, she was now claiming having never agreed to relinquish the annuity, plus she wanted my father to pay her credit card bills. "If she tries that, I'll go to the mat," my father said upon learning of Louise's greedy intentions.

Completing the divorce documents was dragging on, but for no other reason than my brother was being overwhelmed with work at the time. Louise's youngest daughter, Janet, who was especially close to my father, as he had effectively raised her like he had done with Claire's son Wayne, phoned one day. "Why haven't you called me?" she tearfully asked my father. "I don't know, I guess it's just awkward that's all," he replied sedately. Janet admitted that her mother was pushing her to call in order to lean on him to expedite the divorce papers. "Leon is taking care of that," he told her. With that, the conversation ended. My father seemed a little saddened by the exchange. To my knowledge, Janet never called him again.

The divorce papers were eventually completed. Louise sold her house for over a half a million dollars and moved near her daughters.

My father had some odds and ends still at Louise's house and Leon made arrangements with Darla, Louise's oldest daughter, to pick them up. While he was there, he called my father asking what to do with certain things. During their conversation, he heard Darla bark in the background, "Leon! Get your father's junk out of here!!" For my father, the comment was the last bitter dregs of a thirty-six year relationship.

⚜ ⚜ ⚜

Although my father was not religiously observant, he was respectful of those who were, despite his past experiences with religion and years of listening to Louise's ridicule of religious Jews. When it looked as though his only viable option was to move to Baltimore, I had some reservations about how he would acclimate to our lifestyle. In addition, his going from a house occupied by just him and Louise to one with five children concerned me.

But my father integrated himself into the family and our lifestyle seamlessly. He exhibited no signs of inflexibility. He loved his grandchildren, and they accepted him with loving, open arms.

The only kink in my father's move to Baltimore came weeks after his arrival when he developed a persistent, dry cough. I strongly suspected that since it was the time of Maryland's spring pollen blizzard and since he had no other symptoms, the cough was probably allergy related. But after several days had gone by and it continued, I became concerned. Because it was the Sabbath, I could not take him to a doctor except in an emergency. The synagogue I attended, which was practically around the corner from our house, counted a number of physicians as members. I headed over there to see if I could enlist the help of one. On my way I spotted a doctor I knew. After explaining what was going on, I asked if he could take a look at my father. "I'm an anesthesiologist. Why don't you ask Jerold Maisef, he's a member of your [synagogue], and he's a *great* doctor," he suggested.

At the synagogue, I was directed to a ruddy complexioned, middle-aged man sitting in the sanctuary. I approached Dr. Maisef and after explaining my father's problem, asked if he could stop over after services to see him for a minute. "We can do that," he said.

Our family had been members of that synagogue for a number of years. But with a membership of some three hundred families I didn't know everybody and I had never heard of Dr. Maisef. I was grateful that he agreed to walk over to see my father.

At about noon, I escorted Dr. Maisef to our house and introduced him to my father. Using Sharon's stethoscope, the doctor examined his breathing. "I'm not hearing anything. It's probably an allergy. If you want I can call in some medication to the pharmacy," Maisef said. After thanking the doctor and asking him if he could see my father as his patient, I made arrangements to pick up the cough syrup and allergy medication he had ordered. I was impressed with the doctor's kindness and so was my father, who never forgot anyone who helped him in a time of need.

His cough soon cleared up and he followed up with an appointment with Dr. Maisef. I went with him for that initial visit and remember how after the doctor asked my father to take off his shirt, he laughed in wonder at an eighty-six-year-old physique that undoubtedly looked better than his own. When he tested his blood oxygen saturation, Maisef remarked, "Wow! Ninety-nine percent! That's probably better than mine."

It took a few months to complete the new room and bathroom. In the interim, Leon's daughter graduated from high school and he flew my father and me out to California for the ceremony. After three days in L.A., he was ready to get back to his new residence. It turned out to be the last time he would see California, the place he had called home since Harry brought him there from the orphanage in 1933.

My father's new bedroom was spacious, about 10' X 18', not including the large closet. It had dedicated heating and air-conditioning systems, an overhead fan with dark-cherry wood blades, and two windows with a view of the backyard. I painted the walls a soft, creamy gold, to go with the slightly darker new carpeting. He and I shopped for a couple of pieces of new furniture and settled on a dark cherry dresser and nightstand. I installed matching wooden blinds in the windows. A friend of mine from New York who was an expert in ceramic tile came down and spent several days installing a handsome motif in the new bathroom and shower. To forestall any problems with insufficient hot water, a distinct possibility in a house with five kids, four of whom were teenagers, I installed an oversized water heater. I finished off the room with a burgundy and gold bedspread, matching towels and rug for the bathroom, and a painting of a golden, sunlit path winding through the countryside as the sun set over distant hills, which I hung above his bed. I knew my father was in the sunset of his life and I wanted it to be a beautiful one.

The new facilities suited him well. He had all the amenities he needed. More, he felt at home and loved. When I visited him in California, I would hear him moan in his sleep. The first time I heard this, it scared me. But Louise assured me that he did it all the time and attributed it to "his childhood." After he took occupancy of his new room, I never heard my father moan again. However, he still rose every morning at six o'clock, undoubtedly to the Rising Bell that continued to ring in his subconscious mind.

To keep fit, my father used the treadmill that Sharon had bought the year before. He also joined Ruth in early morning walks through the local malls, which opened before store hours to accommodate seniors for that purpose, and he joined the local JCC.

The high point of my father's day was when our youngest son, Yoni, came home from school. *"Whadda'ya say, pal, put it there!"* he'd growl, extending his hand for a low five. *"How'ya doin, Grannypa?"* Yoni would squeak, and then slap his grandfather's upturned palm as hard as he could. "Don't call me Grannypa!" he'd sarcastically admonish his little buddy. Indeed, they became buddies. If you wanted Yoni, you'd usually find him in his grandfather's room watching sports on TV.

Still handsome and now available, my father became something of the talk of the community and people started trying to set him up on dates. Sharon and I frequently hosted singles for Sabbath meals and a few of the fifty-to-sixty-year-olds were interested in dating him as well. While he went out a couple of times, he didn't have a mind to start any new relationships. Nevertheless, it was good to know that he still had that unique attraction that my childhood friends' mother's adoringly cooed over.

He also went to occasional shows at Baltimore's premier concert halls, and frequently took friends out to lunch. When our son Yehuda became friendly with a local girl, Leah Shefter, my father sometimes picked them up from school to take them to lunch, driving them back in time for the start of class.

He was energized by his grandchildren and mentored them the way he had mentored Wayne, Roger Mobley, my brother and me, and Louise's daughter. He taught Yehuda how to drive, and six-year-old Yoni how to play golf, ordering a "midget-size" club for him as he had done for Leon and me when we were that age. Watching those two at eighty years age difference interact as though they were best pals was heartwarming beyond description.

When I heard the news on the morning of September 11, 2001 of the attacks on the World Trade Center and the Pentagon, I called my father on my cell phone for his advice on whether I should pull the kids out of school early. No one yet knew the extent of the situation and I was concerned that if a state of emergency was called, getting to the children might be difficult. I sought the advice of the veteran who would know best on how to deal with that level of emergency. "Pull 'em out," he said. I did. He was right. The school principal initially opposed what I was doing, but shortly after I left with the children he called an early dismissal, which resulted in a traffic jam of panicked parents.

The only thing about Baltimore that seemed to crimp my father's lifestyle was extreme inclement weather in the wintertime. When the roads became heavily inundated with snowdrifts or covered with ice, he stayed home.

Sharon worked a pretty full schedule at the hospital and with chores such as laundry, cleaning, and cooking, her days and nights were hectic even before my father came to live with us. Now she had the added burdens of additional laundry and making special meals to accommodate her father-in-law's strict diabetic diet. But Sharon didn't miss a beat and she took on the extra work with the same remarkable energy and good cheer that she always had. Although she didn't know many details, Sharon knew that he had had a rough life and was committed to making him happy and his life with us stress free. She treated him as though he was her own father, and she loved him deeply.

My father was crazy about Sharon and would have loved her no differently had she made no special efforts for him. And he always took notice of what she did on his behalf and expressed his appreciation. He was never demanding, always appreciative. In fact, part of him felt undeserving of the attention and care. But he deserved whatever we could do, and more.

The one peculiarity that my father had, if you could call it a peculiarity, was his concern for cleanliness. He wasn't obsessive-compulsive, but he was focused on cleanliness to a greater degree than perhaps the average person. The first mention of this trait appears in the HOA caseworker's report, which stated that his foster parents wanted more money because "Irving insists on wearing a clean shirt every day." Growing up, I had come to expect his inspections of the dishes I had washed. He'd rub his hand over a plate to check for unseen, caked-on food, or hold a fork up to see if it was clean between the tines. His habit could be annoying and a little insulting at times. It had also irritated Louise, who facetiously referred to him as "the pot fairy." My father considered clean eating utensils as essential to staying healthy and avoiding illness as personal hygiene. And if one of the kids had a cold, he'd ban that one from his room. It was hard to argue the point no matter how put off you might have felt by his attention to hygienic detail.

I had a profound sense of love for my father and was ever grateful to see him spend what I knew were the final years of his life with those that loved him the most and that he loved the most. I sensed what made him tick, including the deep pain that lay beneath his exquisite exterior. I didn't understand the source of that pain because, as I've said, I knew little of his background, but I had felt it since I was young.

My dad was home, finally home, and living a life that he had for too long been denied.

Chapter Thirty-Nine

"Getting old is not for sissies."
— **Bette Davis**

At eighty-six years old it's hard to avoid health issues. And as a diabetic, it was likely that he would eventually suffer some repercussions of the disease despite his unflagging commitment to diet, exercise, and doing what the doctor advised. But my father had managed to avoid any complications thus far. His worst ailment was a knee that pained him as he stood from sitting. In response to his complaints, Dr. Maisef referred him to an orthopedist.

Like Dr. Maisef, the orthopedist was pleasantly shocked at learning my father's age after meeting him. He took the doctor's reaction as a compliment.

Despite a cortisone injection the pain in his right knee persisted, and in late January my father underwent arthroscopic surgery to repair his torn meniscus cartilage. It was about an hour-long procedure performed at an outpatient clinic five miles from where we lived. After the surgery, I helped him walk to the car and we drove home.

The doctor recommended some physical therapy and within days of the surgery my father began attending twice weekly sessions, where he would essentially ride an exercise bike for about a half hour. He always scheduled his appointment so that after therapy he could head straight to the bagel shop or the local bistro where he would meet Ruth or a friend for lunch. The therapy became part of his weekly routine for a couple of months. However, he still suffered from some discomfort, as it turned out he also had some arthritis in that knee.

His sixty-odd years in the California sun had also created an issue with skin cancer. These basal cell carcinomas were tiny lesions that would appear from time to time on his upper cheek or nose. Fortunately, a dermatologist easily removed them without the need for medication or even a follow-up appointment.

My father also had difficulty with tingling in his feet, medically referred to as *diabetic neuropathy*; a problem that occurred only at night and sometimes prevented him from sleeping. To give him some relief, Dr. Maisef prescribed a sleeping pill and a drug called Neurontin.

From time to time I would go with him to his routine doctor's appointments. Maisef, if not a dynamic personality, was a pleasant man and he always gave my father priority consideration in scheduling appointments.

However, there were things that increasingly troubled me. Most prominently was what I perceived as Maisef's lackadaisical attitude and overreliance on routine. For example, my father was still taking the allergy medication he had prescribed some two years earlier, regardless of whether it was allergy season or not. When I asked my father about whether he should be taking the drug all year round, he responded, "Absolutely! If the doctor didn't want me to keep taking it, he would say so."

Another issue that bothered me was Neurontin: he was taking ever-increasing doses of the drug yet still complaining about how his feet felt at night.

Despite my concerns I remained silent, not wanting to interfere with the relationship between him and his doctor. Maisef had been the one to help him when he first came to Baltimore and my father liked him and trusted him.

Then again, he trusted all doctors.

I discussed my doubts about Dr. Maisef with my wife, who had been in healthcare for thirty years and I respected her levelheaded attitude. Sharon expressed her concerns as well.

Since his diabetes was the most important health issue he had and I was losing my confidence in Dr. Maisef, I pushed my father to see an endocrinologist. This was actually something I picked up from Louise. Although her motivations were rooted in neurotic fears, Louise had micro managed anything involving my father's medical care for years, which compensated for his naïveté when it came to trusting doctors.

Early in 2003, my father began to develop some additional, minor medical problems that were easily treated. None of the issues interfered with his daily routine and he was as engaged as ever with the family.

"I don't know how much time I have left," he unexpectedly said one night while I was with him watching the television news. It bothered me when I was a kid when he said things relating to his mortality, and it still bothered me as an adult with five children. But I always knew why he said such things: he was trying to prepare me, as well as himself, for that fateful day.

He began feeling weak and experiencing a tremor in his right hand when he tried to write. To treat the weakness, Dr. Maisef recommended a transfusion to "give him some pep."

My father drove himself to Sunnyside Community Hospital where he sat patiently for about five hours receiving a transfusion, before driving himself home for supper.

Not long after that, something else started to happen that was most alarming.

My father's day always began the same: he'd wake up every morning at six o'clock, shave, dress, and eat breakfast, before settling in to watch the business news. It was his adherence to routine that prompted my intervention one morning.

When I walked into the kitchen to prepare his meal, I didn't hear the usual sounds of his morning ritual coming from his room, which adjoined the kitchen. After knocking on his door, I went in to investigate. He was lying on the floor next to his bed. He was conscious, but his speech was slurred and he couldn't seem to gain full control of his muscles. I managed to get him up in his chair and immediately went for a glass of orange juice. I checked his blood sugar; it was normal. About an hour after the episode, the symptoms dissipated.

My father never allowed his blood sugar to get out of control. For many years, however, on occasion he experienced what he called "a reaction," which meant he was getting the shakes—a typical symptom of hypoglycemia or low blood sugar. A couple of glucose tablets, which he never failed to carry with him, or a glass of orange juice would always do the trick. Hence, I speculated that this was what was happening when his legs buckled as he was getting out of bed. However, the confusion and lack of muscle control that accompanied the episode didn't make sense. Later that day, I took him to the doctor's office to get checked out. Maisef felt that he was developing an infection of some sort that may have been the underlying cause of the episode and he prescribed an antibiotic.

Around this time, my brother came to Baltimore for a few days. He had another morning episode while Leon was there. Once again, a glass of orange juice and an hour or so later he was back in shape.

Leon took him out for lunch later that day.

But it happened again a few days after that. "What do you think is causing this?" I asked Maisef over the phone. "It's probably from a lot of things," is all he said.

Sharon wasn't satisfied; she thought the incidents were medication related.

The next such episode caused me to take my father to Beauford Hospital, where he was admitted with "possible pneumonia." He was released after two days.

Another such incident occurred several weeks later, again in the morning. This time I called 911. While my father was being assessed at Beauford, one of the doctors asked me some questions about his recent history. I told the doctor about the incidents and the previous hospitalization. I explained that he was initially admitted for possible pneumonia, but that I didn't think that was ever confirmed. After checking the record, the doctor reported, "You're right, there was no pneumonia." But, she said, this time they were going to keep him in the hospital longer in order to run tests and try to get to the bottom of what was happening.

I went to the hospital every day. Sharon, Ruth, or I brought him chicken soup daily. I came into his room one day to find him looking depressed. "The doctor told me I have leukemia. But he said it's treatable." "Whatever it is we'll deal with it and get through it, Dad," I said, trying not to convey my worry.

After about ten days, my father was discharged to the sub-acute rehab unit at Sunnyside Hospital.

The statement he made about leukemia remained foremost in my mind.

After his transfer to Sunnyside, I was sitting in the room with him when I noticed a small piece of note-paper on the nightstand with the word 'Myelodyspla-sia' written on it. As I was looking at the paper, I heard Dr. Vietik, Dr. Maisef's associate, being paged over the intercom. I waited a few minutes, and then called the switchboard:

"Hi Dr. Vietik, I'm Mr. Bennett's son, Michael. My father was given this piece of paper that says "Myelodys-plasia," "It's nothing," Vietik said, her voice was raspy to the point of being froglike. "Then why would someone write this down?" I asked. "It's nothing, forget about it, it's nothing," she insisted.

Dr. Vietik's reaction relieved me. If a doctor wasn't concerned, why should I be worried? I conjectured that some doctor at the other hospital had made a mistake or was perhaps premature in telling my father he had the disease before a test came back. Nevertheless, I was glad that he didn't have leukemia and that myelodys-plasia, whatever it was, wasn't something to be con-cerned about. However, now I was angry that my father had been unnecessarily distressed.

I visited him at Sunnyside every day. After kissing him on the cheek, I would ask him the same questions in order: "How was the day?" "Was the doctor here?" "For how long?" Some days were better than others; Maisef hadn't been there, but Vietik had, and her visits never lasted longer than a few minutes. I was starting to get angry and I called Dr. Maisef:

"Dr. Vietik is an excellent doctor," Maisef said, responding to my concern that he had not seen my father.

"But you're his doctor. He looks up to *you*," I said.

"Ok. I'll get over there tomorrow," Maisef begrudgingly stated.

Dr. Maisef did see my father the next day, but I had a bad taste in my mouth at having to call to get him to see his patient in the hospital.

I remained concerned about my father's condition. He didn't seem to be making good progress and the hospital was a dreary, slightly dirty place. In addition, he was complaining about the treatment, saying he wasn't being attended to properly, and that he was being brought meals not appropriate for a diabetic. My father wasn't a complainer. But if you treated him poorly, especially if he was sick, you had best be prepared to feel some heat. Conversely, if you did something right, you would receive his abundant appreciation.

He remained completely lucid, which made what I am about to relate all the more peculiar.

While my daughter and I were visiting him one evening, my father complained to us that he couldn't sleep at night "because of the music." "What Music?" I asked. "Religious music, there it is again," he said. Neither my daughter nor I could hear anything. "I guess I'm the only one that can hear it," he said dejectedly.

After two weeks of rehab, my father came home. I was just glad to get him out of that place. No one ever informed either him or me as to what had caused the incidents that led to either hospitalization.

The winter had set in and there was about six inches of snow on the ground. My father spent his days watching the stock market, the news, or the golf channel. To stay in shape, he walked laps around the house, pacing off the distance to determine how many laps would make a mile, as he had paced off the length of the Momote airstrip in March of 1944.

Just about every night I'd poke my head into my father's room and say, "How about some back work?" He loved to have his back massaged and I was happy to give my father that pleasure. I had been doing it on and off since he moved to Baltimore and now that he was housebound with the snow, I felt he could use the stimulation and attention more than ever. He'd lean forward in his leather chair and, sitting aside him on the edge of his bed; I'd squirt a dollop of lotion on his back and as he would say "get to work." He liked nothing better and the sessions would always end the same: I'd kiss him on the cheek and wish him a good night.

Sharon was growing increasingly concerned about my father's medical care. An earlier lab report indicated that he was having kidney trouble, yet Dr. Maisef hadn't referred him to a nephrologist.

Eventually my father did see a nephrologist, but it wasn't at the behest of Dr. Maisef; it was through his endocrinologist who had been following his blood tests. When he realized that Maisef wasn't doing his job, he took the initiative.

When my father suffered yet another morning episode of weakness and ataxia (extreme lack of muscle coordination), Sharon called the nephrologist, Dr. Chen.

Sharon recently had an elderly patient who called to cancel his therapy session due to having an episode that sounded identical to what my father had been experiencing. When the doctor of her department was told of the patient's symptoms, he categorically told the nurses and the therapists that the man should "Stop the Neurontin!"

When Sharon told Dr. Chen what was happening and relayed her concerns about the drug, Chen emphatically stated, "He should absolutely not be taking Neurontin."

The same day, I called a neurologist friend of mine seeking an alternative therapy. He prescribed a different medication for my father's tingling feet, which was effective. The stroke-like episodes stopped, as well as the intention tremor in his hand.

My concerns about Dr. Maisef were intensifying.

In early January 2004, my father started complaining of blurred vision in one of his eyes. We knew a good retinologist in the area and made an appointment with him. Tests revealed that he had developed some leaking of small blood vessels in his eye that was causing minor swelling in his macula, the area of central vision. It's a common problem, especially among diabetics, and it was effectively treated by simple laser therapy and some eye drops.

About the same time, he developed a blister on his heal from accidently banging it into a piece of furniture. The blister looked like any other and would ordinarily be nothing to worry about. But since he was a diabetic, and I had now adopted more of Louise's proactive position on my father's health care, although sans neurosis, I wanted to be cautious and took him to the dermatologist.

While waiting in the doctor's office, my father became somewhat solemn:

"You know, Mike, I have a lot of time to reflect upon my life these days. I've made some mistakes…"

"You'd be the first person in the world not to have, Dad," I interrupted, uncomfortable with the pending revelations.

"No, it's important to talk about," he asserted. "I shouldn't have gone to dramatic school."

"It seemed like the right decision at the time, Dad. And if you hadn't done that, maybe I wouldn't be here," I reasoned, trying to ease his pain.

"I shouldn't have stopped speaking with Aunt Claire..."

The receptionist interrupted his confession by announcing the doctor was ready to see him.

I waited in the lobby not knowing what to think about what my father had just said.

The blister turned out to be nothing.

Chapter Forty

February 2004 rolled in with freezing temperatures and six inches of snow still on the ground. My father had no intention of venturing outside, especially not after what he had been through over the last several months.

Concerned that my father might start feeling depressed with nobody to keep him company during the day, I enlisted the support of our rabbi and asked if he wouldn't mind stopping by the house to visit with him from time to time.

At twenty-nine years old, Rabbi Dov Hesed was younger than most rabbis, but he was remarkably learned, and one would be hard pressed to find a more sincere and friendly person. He and my father hit it off right away.

At the end of the first week of February, my father started developing another cough; this time it didn't sound like an allergy. I called Dr. Maisef and suggested that perhaps he should begin my father on a prophylactic antibiotic. The doctor agreed. But by the third day after starting the drug my father wasn't feeling any better. He had no real fever, but his cough, and now other symptoms—general malaise, body aches, lack of appetite—made it seem as though he had the flu. My father thought he had pneumonia. I called Maisef again. This time he phoned in an order for a chest x-ray at a nearby radiology clinic, but no pneumonia was seen.

By Friday, February 13th, his cough and malaise had worsened and he was hardly eating anything. I wanted to be ready in case I had to take him to the hospital on the Sabbath so I contacted Maisef again and explained the situation. "If he's no better by tomorrow night, take him to Sunnyside. Call me and I'll meet you there," he said.

Sharon had prepared a large pot of chicken soup, but my father couldn't drink or eat anything over the entire Sabbath.

At sundown Saturday night, I phoned the doctor to tell him that we were going to the hospital.

Dr. Maisef came into the exam room at Sunnyside as my father was being prepped for a chest x-ray. I chatted with him for a few minutes while the test was being done. My father was a little more talkative than he had been in several days, perhaps because he had his doctor with him. He pointed out what felt like a small protrusion in the area of his breastbone that seemed unusual. "That's an area that becomes enlarged when we get sick. You should have gone into medicine," Maisef said. He could have no idea how painful those last words were.

Maisef read the x-ray report and although he didn't seem worried, he admitted my father.

"I love you, Dad. I'll see you in the morning," I said, as I kissed him and left the hospital feeling reasonably comfortable that he was in medically competent hands: If I only knew...*if I only knew.*

Over the next couple of days my father seemed to improve, although he was again complaining about hospital staff not doing their jobs. I listened to his complaints but felt they were overblown due to his being sick; things tend to get magnified when you're not feeling well.

The one disconcerting thing that *I* found had to do with the patient in the next room.

The gaunt look and yellow pallor on the face of the emaciated figure in the bed was that of a nursing home patient. As I was doing with my father, the man's son visited his father every day. The son said his dad had been admitted to the hospital for pneumonia a total of thirty-seven times. He couldn't believe he was still alive. Displayed on the door to the man's room was a large green sticker that read, "CONTACT ISOLATION." I had no idea what that meant, but the ominous sounding words and the condition of the patient inside the room made me feel very uneasy. The room was just inches from my father's, the emaciated patient just feet away.

After about the third day, my father's condition seemed to reverse course. He said he was feeling "washed out." And his complaints about hospital staff were increasing, "Look at what they give me to eat, I'm a diabetic, I'm not supposed to have sugar!" he protested, as he pointed to the uneaten, melting ice cream and sealed packets of sugar sitting next to the empty coffee cup on the food tray. "I'll talk to them, Dad," I assured him. The nurse looked up the dietary orders, which simply stated "No concentrated sweets." I explained to her that my father was a diabetic and that he was meticulous in watching what he ate. "Could you make sure that he gets the right meals?" I asked politely.

Day after day went by and day after day my father complained to me about his treatment, "I'm being absolutely neglected," he said at one point, frustrated and feeling helpless. "I'm sick and nobody is doing any-thing," he added, turning his face to the side.

I didn't know what to do. I was afraid to bother the hospital staff and I had already complained to Dr. Maisef.

Every morning I called my father and asked him how the night was. His responses ranged from "alright, I slept on and off" to "not good, I couldn't sleep, I can't get comfortable." Every evening after work I came to his room, kissed his cheek, and started my visit with the same questions: "How was the day?" "Was the doctor here?" "Which doctor?" Some days were "ok," most were not. My father carefully thought about the doctor's visit of the day and was specific in his answers: "five min-utes," "three minutes," "seven minutes," and the like. The doctor was always Dr. Vietik. After about five days of this, I called Dr. Maisef:

"Dr. Vietik is an excellent doctor," Maisef said, using the same line as he did before. His tone of voice had markedly changed, he sounded arrogant and resentful.

"I'm not complaining about Dr. Vietik. I've never met Dr. Vietik. I'm complaining about you. You're his primary care doctor. Why aren't *you* here treating my father?"

After a brief pause, Maisef said he would try to get to the hospital in the next day or so.

After another week of the same trend—my father having more bad days than good ones, looking like he wasn't making progress and complaining—a green sticker appeared on *his* door. I called Sharon:

"What does this mean?"
"He probably has MRSA," she said.
"What's that?"
"It's something you get in the hospital. Is there a bag hanging on his IV pole that says Vancomycin?"

"No."

"That's weird," Sharon remarked.

My father had no idea what the sticker was about.

As I left the hospital that evening, I noticed the same type of green sticker on the doors of other patients' rooms. I thought to myself, "Well, whatever it is, it must be common."

When I returned to the hospital the following evening, I found my father's room empty. Starting to panic, I went to the nurse's station:

"Excuse me; do you know where my father is?" I asked.

"Let me see...Bennett...he's been moved to room.... It's down the hall," said the on-duty nurse.

"Why was he moved?" I asked.

"I don't know."

Two weeks after his admission, my father was transferred to the hospital's sub-acute rehab unit, the same unit he had spent two weeks in a few months earlier. The green sticker remained on his door. Still, no one had told my father or me anything as to why it was there.

The week of March 7th a nurse informed me that my father would be discharged that Thursday. Two days later, without explanation, his discharge was changed to sometime the following week.

At about seven o'clock on the morning of March 11th, I called my father. I could hear that he was in extreme pain:

"What's wrong, Dad?"

"My leg is killing me."

"I'll call the doctor and I'll call you right back."

I left a message with Maisef's service. The phone rang a few minutes later. It was Sharon. I explained what was going on and that I had called the doctor and was waiting for a call back. "They should be doing a Doppler,* he could have a blood clot," Sharon said, sounding very concerned. I had no idea what a Doppler was. The call waiting beep sounded and I switched over. It was Maisef:

"I just spoke with my father and he said that his leg is killing him. He could hardly talk. My wife suggested a Doppler."

After a long pause, Maisef said, "I would have ordered a Doppler with or without you or your wife's suggestion." His voice was saturated with arrogance.

I thanked him and ended the phone call. My father was vulnerable; I didn't want to get into an argument with his doctor.

After work that evening, I picked up Yoni and we went to the hospital.

My father was sitting in a chair; his left leg was double its normal size and was covered with red marbling from his ankle to his knee, a series of connected, dark purple patches over the area of his shin; he was in intolerable pain...the kind of pain one cannot talk through.

"What's happening with my father's leg?" I asked the on-duty nurse at the station next to my father's room.

"I don't know, been like that since I came, I give him the pain medication," the heavily accented woman casually answered, her eyes never leaving the papers she fumbled with on the counter.

I called Sharon and after explaining what was happening, told her to call Dr. Maisef right away and tell him the situation was urgent. I returned to my father's side, Yoni was sitting on his bed.

---

* A radiological test used in this case to determine blood flow.

A few minutes later the phone at the nurses' station rang. Overhearing the nurse's muted description of my father's leg; I asked to speak to the doctor:

"Son want to talk to you," the nurse relayed over the phone.

"Doctor say if you want to talk with him he be here in forty-five minute," she reported back.

After she finished speaking with the doctor, I asked the nurse about the results of the Doppler: It was negative.

I waited and anxiously paced as my father writhed in pain.

Spotting Maisef strolling down the hall, I walked to meet him.

"Thank you for coming," I said.

"I'm not supposed to be here," Maisef arrogantly replied, averting his eyes.

"The Doppler was negative," I offered.

"I know. I expected it to be positive," Maisef said, trying to sound confident.

Stopping in the doorway of my father's room, Maisef glibly remarked, "Yuk! That doesn't look so good," as he gazed at the enormously swollen and horribly discolored leg, while my father grimaced and struggled.

"Does this hurt here?" Maisef asked, now sitting in a chair beside my father, as he touched an area on the obviously diseased leg.

Instantly recoiling at the doctor's touch, my father shot his upper body backwards into the chair, violently sucking in air, his muscles contracting as though he had been hit with fifty thousand volts of electricity.

"Hmm. Looks like some sort of cellulites," the doctor said, sounding a little concerned, and obviously uncertain.

Maisef proceeded to write what looked like a pre-scription, which he handed to the nurse and instructed her to get my father in bed and elevate his leg.

As I escorted Dr. Maisef down the hall, I again thanked him for coming. Looking more concerned now, he said, "I wouldn't have been able to sleep. I'll have Dr. Vietik see him first in the morning."

Thinking he would be all right, as the nurse was helping my father back to his bed, I said goodnight to him and left with Yoni. It was about 10:00 P.M.

The following morning, Sharon went to see my father:

"I went straight to the hospital after doing carpool. I got there about nine, nine-thirty. As I approached the room, I saw Dr. Vietik sitting at the desk. She was very busy writing and looking through the chart I guess. I went into the room. Dad was in bed. He was telling me he was in excruciating pain and didn't sleep the whole night, and he is not one to complain. His leg was blown up like a balloon and the flesh was totally red and looked like it was being eaten away. It was horrible. There were enormous bubble blisters. I don't remember ever seeing a leg like that. It was horrible. I ran to get the nurse. There was nobody else in the room.... dad was moaning, he was in horrible pain. A well-dressed woman, whom I assumed had something to do with infectious disease, came into the room. She started asking dad questions and he was answering. She didn't seem to have an ounce of compassion and looked like she didn't want me in the room, so I stepped out. They gave him medicine, but it didn't work. He was moaning and groaning."

After stepping outside of the room, Sharon called me:

"I'm at the hospital. You better get here right away. Your father's leg is...is... I've never seen anything like this."

I rushed down the hall toward my father's room as fast as possible without breaking into a run. A short woman with long, straight, reddish-brown hair wearing a white lab coat emerged from a niche near the room:

"Dr. Vietik?"

"Yes."

"I'm Michael, Mr. Bennett's son."

We shook hands. She would not initiate conversation and just stood there, vacuously looking at me.

"What's happening with my father?" I finally asked.

"We're sending him to the University of Maryland; we're just waiting for transport."

"Should I call my brother to come in from California?"

"I don't think it's grave," she answered, her voice as croaky as it sounded during the phone call about the myelodysplasia note. I could tell Vietik was suppressing her anxiety.

"Are we talking about trying to save the limb?" I asked, attempting to sound clinical so she would feel comfortable talking to me.

"Yes," she said without emotion.

I was definitely going to call Leon.

After thanking Dr. Vietik, I went straight to my father. He was outside the room, wrapped in a sheet and strapped on a gurney. He had the traumatized look of someone who has survived a terrible ordeal but knows the crisis isn't over yet:

"I'm here, Dad," I said, as I rubbed his shoulder, trying to comfort him.

"We're gonna get through this. We've gotten through everything before. I'm right here, Dad. I'm not leaving."

"The nurse said, 'You're going to feel worse before you feel better.' I don't know how I could feel any worse," my father softly said, as he closed his eyes and gently shook his head.

After about two hours of waiting, the transport driver arrived. I walked next to my father while he was wheeled to the ambulance and helped load him inside, before I ran to my truck and headed for home.

I was rushing to change from my painting clothes and grab a few essentials, as I knew I'd be spending the Sabbath at the hospital, when my cell phone rang:

"Mr. Bennett, this is Dr. Sharon Henry from the University of Maryland Shock Trauma. Your father's leg looks horrific."

Trying to remain composed I asked Dr. Henry what the options were.

"I've explained to your father that there are two options. One is called debridement, which is where we remove layers of tissue to try to eliminate the infection; it usually takes multiple surgeries and there is an increased risk of further infection. I'm anticipating not being able to extubate him, his kidneys shutting down, I've seen it before. I told your father that I did not recommend it."

"What's the other option?"

"Amputation"

"What did my father say to that?"

"He said, 'I would rather die.'"

It was the second time in my father's life that he uttered those words; the first was when his position was being overrun at the Momote airstrip in 1944. I lost my composure. I had not cried since my mother's death twenty years before.

"What can I do?" I asked, struggling to speak through my convulsing sobs.

"Come here and be with your father," Dr. Henry said, not understanding what I meant.

"I'm on my way now, Dr. Henry."

As I walked through the double doors of the Shock Trauma unit, I was met by a trim African American woman. Exuding both competence and compassion, two traits that my father valued highly, Dr. Henry said that my father had something called necrotizing fasciitis or what is commonly called flesh-eating bacteria.

As she was explaining things to me, I looked past Dr. Henry and saw my father lying in a bay about fifteen feet away. He was wrapped in white hospital linen, a bank of machinery behind him. I felt myself loosing composure again and excused myself before rushing into a nearby restroom. After getting myself together, I emerged from the restroom and approached my father, kissing him on the cheek:

"When they first told me..." my father said, closing his eyes and gently shaking his head.

"...the shock," he continued.

"I'm a diabetic. I should have known." Incredibly, he was blaming himself.

"You know, I've lived longer than most people, Mike. I've got nothing to complain about [so let's get it over with]."

A nurse approached to tell my father there was a phone call for him. She reached behind the bed and handed him the receiver.

"That's alright honey, everything's gonna work out. I understand. Thank you. I love you too," he softly said.

The nurse returned the receiver. My father smiled and closed his eyes again. "Sharon, she was crying," he softly said, as a smile of love came across his lips.

I sat beside my father for about two hours...waiting. During that time, he asked about the kids and little else. He showed me the morphine pump he held in his right hand and said, "If I have any pain, I just push this and *thtttt...*"

Two nurses came: It was time.

I walked beside my father as he was being wheeled to the doors of the operating room where they would remove his left leg.

A male nurse and the hospital chaplain met me in the waiting area; both offered comfort and compassion. I explained to the chaplain that according to Jewish law my father's leg must be buried and that I'd like to make certain that it would be released to the Jewish Burial Society for that purpose. The chaplain and the nurse acquired the proper release. Since I could not sign the document on the Sabbath, I gave the nurse permission to do so and the chaplain to act as a witness.

After four hours of alternately reciting Psalms and pacing back and forth, Dr. Henry came briskly striding into the waiting room:

"Your father's a miracle man," she excitedly said.

"He came off the breathing tube fine and he's already asking for things," she added, taking hold of my hand as I thanked her, tears streaming down my face.

"Would you like to see him? Stupid question, c'mon."

My father was lying on his back in the recovery room. He wasn't quite awake and slightly moaning. It wasn't what I expected to see after Dr. Henry's upbeat report, but I was just so grateful that he was alive. I softly told him I loved him and rubbed his shoulder as he drifted off to sleep.

A taxi came at 4:00 A.M. and took me home.

At 11:00 A.M., a black limo pulled up to the house and Leon emerged. He had taken the first flight out of L.A.

My brother and I were sitting in the den at around noon when there was a knock at the door. It was Dr. Maisef. I invited him in. Sharon brought a folding chair. With Maisef facing us, I began the dialogue:

"They cut off my father's leg."

"I know, Dr. Vietik called me," Maisef said. "I would never bet against that man. I would never bet against that man," he emphatically stated. "This is something you see as a physician once in ten or fifteen years," he added, obviously nervous.

Then, with his eyes scanning as if he were trying to read me, Maisef incongruously said, "It was the right antibiotic."

I had no idea what he was talking about, and I was too stunned to ask. All I could think of was my father.

Maisef then turned to Leon: "What do you do?"

"I'm an attorney," my brother plainly replied.

"Please go see my father," I tearfully pleaded.

Maisef said he would, and then added, "I have to get back [to the synagogue,] I have a Bar Mitzvah," and then left.

The entire bizarre meeting lasted about ten minutes. Afterwards, I went out back and stood on the deck, my head leaning against a post, and cried for my father.

As soon as the Sabbath ended, Leon and I drove straight to the hospital.

My father was lying on the unusually high hospital bed with a facemask covering his mouth and nose, vapors of oxygen escaping from the sides; a vacuum device was suctioning blood and fluid from the wrapped stump of where his left leg had been. "Hi Lee, hi Mike," he said, his voice muffled by the mask and the *whooshing* sound of the escaping gas. Leon stood by his left shoulder and rubbed his arm. I stood next to him. "I can still feel my toes," he said with surprise. My eyes began to fill, but I managed to hold back this time.

He wasn't allowed to eat or drink anything but I could see he was parched, so I lifted the mask and placed small amounts of crushed ice in his mouth as the nurse had instructed.

The following day, Leon and I returned to Shock Trauma. While in my father's room, I noticed a small piece of paper torn from a pocket notepad lying on the counter near the foot of his bed. The note read, "Mr. Bennett. I was here to see you but you were in hyper baric [sic]. Jerold Maisef." I read my father the note and put it back on the counter. After several days, when the note had not been moved and Maisef had not been back to see my father, I dropped it in the garbage can.

My father was receiving treatments in a hyperbaric chamber. Every day, he was placed inside a cylindrically-shaped tube where oxygen-rich air was pumped in. The treatments were meant to augment his body's immune system in destroying the bacteria that he had been inundated with, and to speed healing. The treatments played havoc with his claustrophobia and he had to be given a sedative in advance of every visit to the chamber.

One day I arrived at his bedside to find a nurse adjusting his oxygen mask and my father looking angry and agitated: "She said, 'I don't want you to die!'" he growled in a muffled voice. "You've gotta keep this thing on properly, Dad," I said in support of his nurse. He just shook his head.

The following afternoon, I phoned my father's room in advance of my visit:

"Lieutenant Bennett's room," the female voice said.

"Uhh, this is Lieutenant Bennett's son. Who is this?" I said suspiciously. I had never heard anyone refer to my father as Lieutenant Bennett.

"This is Sheila. I'm his nurse." It was the same nurse who was aggressively adjusting his facemask the day before.

"Why did you refer to my father as Lieutenant Bennett?"

"I'm military," she said.

Ok, I thought, she's military, but what does that have to do with anything? Shock Trauma was not a VA facility, and how would she know that my father was a lieutenant? He never spoke about his military service. A few days later I discovered the amusing source of Nurse Sheila's comment:

A close friend in the military, Major Jason Saver, had gotten to know my father and looked up to him as a World War II combat vet. Major Saver had come to the hospital to visit my father but was told that he was in hyperbaric. So, the major went to the hyperbaric room, arriving there just before the treatment began. Wearing his full dress uniform, Major Saver leaned over the tube where my father lay and in a voice loud enough for everyone in the room to hear, said, "Lieutenant Bennett, the President and the Joint Chiefs of Staff send their best wishes for a full and speedy recovery!"

Subsequent to Major Saver's visit, Sheila, the military nurse, was assigned to "Lieutenant Bennett."

When I met Sheila the next time, she explained to me that she had been forceful with my father insofar as his oxygen was concerned because she was committed to his care. Indeed, Nurse Sheila cared for him with more competence and attention than any other nurse I have ever seen care for a patient. During breaks in her shift, she would step outside for a cigarette, and while looking up at the night sky, Sheila would pray for my father, her lieutenant, not to die.

As my father grew stronger he was weaned off the oxygen. But he remained very sick. When he was transferred from Sunnyside he was in septic shock, which in simple terms means that his body was turning on itself in the face of a massive infection. Although past the most imminent danger, he was far from out of the woods.

After my father had been at Shock Trauma for ten days, I received a call from a case manager telling me that they would like to send him to Kernan Rehabilitation Hospital, arguably the area's premier rehab facility. I questioned the move, feeling that my father was not yet in physical condition for rehab and should go to a step-down unit at the University of Maryland Hospital first, as I had been told would be the case by one of his nurses.

Responding to my skepticism, the case manager said, "Mr. Bennett, if I could physically implant the confidence in your mind that this was the best possible thing you could do for your father, I would. And the University of Maryland owns Kernan, so it's like still being with us and if something goes wrong, and they can't handle it, we can get him right back here!" The words and how they were delivered were convincing. I agreed to the move, although I still harbored doubt.

Chapter Forty-One

Pacing by the door to the ambulance bay for two hours, I couldn't imagine what was taking so long. The drive from Shock Trauma to Kernan is no more than thirty minutes and at night there wouldn't be traffic. At about 10:30 P.M., the ambulance began backing into the bay. When I opened the door to go out to my father, I was jolted by the deafening sound of a screaming siren. A guard keyed off the alarm and admonished me. As the ambulance driver and his assistant removed the stretcher with my father on it, the driver, pursing his lips and shaking his head, looked at me as if to say, "Why are we moving this man?"

My father was moaning in deep suffering, the stump of his left leg was oozing blood through the thick black cord holding the skin flap closed, his three remaining limbs were swollen, and fluid was weeping through the skin of his arms, leg, and chest.

My father had been betrayed, and I had been lied to.

"Can't somebody give me a shot or something? I'm in agony," my father groaned. "Get a doctor, now!" I ordered the guard.

After helping get my father to a room and into bed, I was approached by a man in a white lab coat:

"My name is Doctor Rakhmanin," said the tall, stocky man with the thick Russian accent.

"Are you familiar with your father'z medeecationz?"

"Somewhat," I said.

"Feefty seex units insulin?" Rakhmanin said, sounding doubtful.

"No. That doesn't sound right. My father took fourteen units in the morning and sixteen before dinner when he was home."

"Thirtee fife meelleegrams Ambien?[99] Thees iz dose for elephant," Rachmanan added.

"No. I think it was 10 milligrams."

"Neurontin?"

"No! My father was hospitalized twice from that drug. He should absolutely not be given Neurontin. Can you call Shock Trauma to get this clarified?"

"I deed, no one ansurz da phone, and medeecation orderz not signed."

His accent notwithstanding, Rakhmanin turned out to be a good doctor who wisely used his discretion and ordered more appropriate doses of medications. But even half the originally ordered dose of insulin sent my father into extreme hypoglycemia and he had to be given glucose intravenously to get stabilized. Had either of those drugs been given as ordered, it would likely have been lethal.

The doctors and nurses at Shock Trauma were beyond reproach. They had performed flawlessly as far as I was concerned. They had saved my father's life. But the deception and negligence involved in his transfer combined with everything else that had occurred in

---

99 Ambien is a sleeping medication that is commonly prescribed in a 10-milligram dose.

hospitals had left him without a leg and in unspeakable pain. I found myself now fighting for my father's life against the very system that was supposed to help him; the system and the people that he trusted.

Before leaving my father for the night, I wanted to somehow ensure his safety. I spoke to the night-duty nurse. After explaining to her what had happened with Neurontin, the nurse agreed that the reactions I described were typical for an overdose of Gabapentin (the generic name for Neurontin) and said that they should have been monitoring the levels in his blood.[100] It was time to address the pain issue:

"My father is a very reasonable person. If you treat him with a modicum of respect and competence, he'll be forever grateful. If he is left in pain, I will bring the entire cavalry."

The nurse nodded in acknowledgement, while looking as though a lunatic was addressing her. I didn't care anymore what they might think of me. I was too trusting before, and I had allowed myself to be intimidated. I had to protect my father.

The daytime doctor at Kernan, Dr. Booth, phoned me the next morning asking about my father's medications and who his primary care physician was; she wanted to talk to him. I didn't want any delays and I didn't know Dr. Booth so I volunteered to call Dr. Maisef myself and have him call her.

I reached Dr. Maisef and he said he would call Dr. Booth right away. When I offered him the phone number, he declined, saying he had it.

Several hours later, Dr. Booth called me back:

"Did you speak with your father's primary?"
"Yes, why, hasn't he called you?"
"No."

---

100 The nurse was wrong in her analysis as Neurontin is not measured this way. The dosages are adjusted for renal patients according to a standard formula.

"I'm calling him right now," Dr. Booth said, sounding very perturbed.

Over the next five days my father improved slightly, if at all. But the edema weeping from his limbs was even worse. Plastic bags had to be taped to areas of his body to keep the fluid from soaking the bed. The condition is called *frank anasarca*, which, in my father's case, meant that the proteins in his body were breaking down into liquid due to severe malnutrition.

The treatment at Shock Trauma had left him practically deaf, which could have been from the hyperbaric treatments, or perhaps a side effect of antibiotics. I didn't know. But whatever the cause, the case manager at the University of Maryland had promised me that an ENT would see my father at Kernan. To date, no one had shown up.

My father started again complaining about the care he was receiving, saying he was in pain and being forced to sit in a wheelchair "with this stump for hours." On one occasion, as I was walking down the corridor to his room, I could hear him howling in agony from fifty yards away. And there were other issues. But the biggest insult of all came when I entered his room one day to find two crude cardboard signs suspended over the bed. One read, "I have no leg," the other, "My left foot is gone."

However, the final straw that moved me to action came after calling his room one afternoon hoping that someone would be there who could hear the phone ring. My father unexpectedly answered: "I'm being tortured, I'm being tortured," he kept repeating, the abusive shouts of an angry male nurse in the background. "I'm coming, Dad! I'm coming, Dad!" I said loudly again and again. But he could not hear me and just kept repeating, "I'm being tortured," with the nurse still yelling in the background. Then, for the first time in my life, I heard my father break down and cry.

It's impossible to describe the feeling of helplessness in having to hang up on one's father under those circumstances, but there was no choice, he couldn't hear me. Leaving my customer's house in disarray, I sped to Kernan. En route, I called 911:

"My eighty-eight-year-old father is being abused and neglected in a rehab facility. I'm on my way there now and you better send an officer right away or there's going to be an incident!" I had completely lost it.

"We don't want any incidents. What is the name and location of the facility?" the dispatcher asked.

After providing the police with the information, I called Kernan and asked for the director of the unit my father was on. My call was transferred to Linda Bland. In very emotional terms, I told Ms. Bland what had been happening with my father and that I was on my way there and so were the police. Poor Ms. Bland, even if she lives to be as old as Methuselah she will not forget that phone call.

When I arrived at my father's room, he was lying in his bed, neatly tucked in, and he was trying not to cry. The place had obviously been cleaned spotless. "I'm here Dad," I said as I rubbed his shoulder. "I called the police, they're on their way." About a half hour passed before the phone in his room rang. It was the lobby guard: "The police are here, can you come to the lobby please?" "Tell the police that I'm waiting for them in my father's room," I said, and hung up the phone.

A lone Hispanic police officer entered the room; Ms. Bland and a phalanx of what looked like executive staff accompanied him.

As the officer stood at the foot of my father's bed, the suits on one side, me on the other and close to my father, I delivered a long, impassioned dressing-down of what had happened to my father and the neglect and abuse he was now suffering at Kernan. I concluded my furious tirade thusly:

"This police officer is going to take a report and that is going to be my guarantee that my father will not have to suffer another moment of abuse or neglect. The only thing it seems that you people understand is the threat of a lawsuit. Is this how you would want your father treated?"

There was stunned silence. Ms. Bland and the suits looked down at the floor like scolded puppies. My father didn't move.

The police officer began to speak:

"This is really an internal matter..."

I stopped him.

"Is there a department policy that you cannot take a report, officer?"

"Oh no, I can write anything I want," he responded.

"Good. Then get out your pen because you're taking a report. And when you're finished with my father, you'll go down the hall and take reports from the other patients too!"

The male nurse whom I had heard berating my father and who had rigged up the unbelievable signs dangling in front of his face was summoned to the room and questioned about why he had done such a thing. "It's a modality I've used..." he started to say sheepishly. "A MODALITY!" I shouted, cutting short the now mealy-mouthed man's lame excuse.

"I don't want this guy anywhere near my father," I commanded.

Ms. Bland asked him to leave.

The entire episode lasted about two hours. The officer took a statement from one other patient, which supported what I had alleged vis-à-vis the abusive nurse.

After everyone cleared the room, I remained beside my father:

"Things are gonna change now, Dad," I assured.

"I love you so much, Mike..." my father said, the emotion in his voice subsiding.

"I love you too, Dad."

I stayed with my father a while longer before heading back to the house I had left upside down and covered in drop cloths.

Minutes after pulling out of the facility's parking lot, my cell phone rang:

"Mr. Bennett, my name is Dr. Flynn, I'm the Vice President of Medical Affairs of the University of Maryland Medical System."

"What do you want Dr. Flynn? Am I supposed to be impressed with your title?" I was angry, very angry.

"I want to apologize for what happened at Kernan. Your father and you should never have had to endure anything like this and I'm going to Kernan tomorrow."

I wasn't completely disarmed, but Dr. Flynn said all the right things and he sounded sincere. He also said that he would call me from Kernan the next day.

The following day, Dr. Flynn called from the parking lot of Kernan. He said that the issues had been addressed and that there would be changes. He gave me his cell number, saying, "Call me anytime and for any reason. If something is wrong with your father's care, I want to know about it and I'll take care of it." I believed him.

Later that day, I went to Kernan and apologized to Ms. Bland. "It's your father, I completely understand, you did the right thing, you were right and I would never want my own father to be treated like that..." she gushed.

Ms. Bland turned out to be a nice lady. But she was the wrong person for the job. She was an occupational therapist in charge of a dysfunctional nursing staff over which she had little control. In a sense, she too was a victim of a broken medical system.

To provide my father with additional care, I hired a private nurse to stay with him on certain days.

For the rest of time that my father was a patient at Kernan, the staff cared for him in the manner that every patient deserves: his room was clean; his care was timely and consistent, and his caregivers were competent. He was even examined by an ENT who easily restored his hearing by simply cleaning out his ears, something that could have and should have been done a week earlier. My father told me that he felt guilty about the good treatment he was now getting. "You deserve it, Dad. It's what should have been all along," I responded.

I called Dr. Flynn's cell number intending to let him know how things had changed and to thank him. I received his voice mail and simply left my name and phone number. He never called back.

Once my father was medically stable and had regained some strength, the therapy sessions began.

With enormous effort he was able to transfer from the bed to a wheelchair by sliding across a board. Summoning samsonean strength, despite his horribly ravaged condition, he went from lying on his back on the floor to standing on his one leg by pulling himself up on parallel bars. My father was determined to overcome his new handicap and get well. He was eating more and mostly pain free. He wanted to live. He wanted to go home.

But after about two weeks he wasn't making enough progress to satisfy his insurers and I was informed that his being able to remain at Kernan was in jeopardy. Fearing what might happen, I related to my father what the therapists were saying and tried to coach him into giving even more effort. "Mike, I'm trying as hard as I can. I can't do anymore. What do they do, throw you out on the street?" he anguished, as he closed his eyes and struggled not to cry. "You're doing great, Dad. I just want to get you home. I'm sorry. I shouldn't have pushed," I said, feeling terribly guilty.

At a subsequent meeting with the therapists I was told that while my father was doing all that he could do, they would not be able to keep him. He was just too debilitated for the rigors of an acute rehab facility. It was no surprise and it made me even more resentful of what the University of Maryland case manager had done. Now I needed to find a sub-acute facility.

None of what was available was satisfactory. Every place I went to was depressing; they looked like stereo-typical nursing homes of the worst kind. But there was no choice.

I settled on the least objectionable facility that was closest to our house, Pleasantville Rehab. I also arranged for the private nurse to accompany my father and continue caring for him, expanding her hours and the number of days she would be with him.

Pleasantville sent a liaison nurse to Kernan to review my father's records. They wanted to be certain he was an appropriate candidate before accepting him.

Two days later, about half an hour after meeting with Pleasantville's director of admissions and signing the necessary papers, my cell phone rang:

"Michael, this is Dr, Booth. Have you spoken with Pleasantville?" the doctor asked, sounding distressed.

"I just left there, the paperwork's completed."

"They've rescinded your father's acceptance. They said it was because of his MRSA infection. This is highly inappropriate. I can see no reason why they should have done this. We were called after he was put onto the gurney and was about to be loaded into the ambulance. I've never experienced anything like this."

Dr. Booth went on to express how upset she was because of the additional trauma this was causing my father. And she remarked how much worse it would have been if he had already been in the ambulance and on the way to Pleasantville when his acceptance was rescinded.

Upset and not knowing what to think, I headed back to Pleasantville and walked straight into the office of the director of admissions, Fanny Bergoine:

"Your father was rejected because of his MRSA and VRE," the blond woman said. I could tell she was embarrassed. I had never heard of VRE, and but for Sharon's one comment, nor did I know about MRSA.

"Then why had he been accepted to begin with, all the information was exchanged and the liaison nurse has also been to Kernan?" I asked, feeling frustrated and increasingly angry.

"The nurse's notes were not written clearly and they were only discovered at the last minute by our medical director," she responded, averting her eyes. I didn't believe her.

Whatever the real reason, my father was suspended in limbo in American healthcare hell. He didn't deserve it.

When he was told about not being accepted, my father, feeling increasingly tormented and abandoned, simply closed his eyes, yet again, and sadly asked, "Why won't they accept me at Pleasantville?" My heart broke once more.

At a meeting with Dr. Booth, Ms. Bland, and my father's nurse case manager at Kernan, everyone stated that they did not believe what Pleasantville was saying. They thought it was an excuse, but could offer no explanation.

Consequential to the intervention of an influential friend, five days later my father was re-accepted to Pleasantville. The reason for withdrawing the approval, they were now saying was because there wasn't a private room available for a person with MRSA and VRE at the time. However, the influential friend who had intervened later said he was told my father was rejected because they feared his insurance would run out before he was well enough to return home. If that was true, why were they now willing to accept him? Nothing made sense; and my father was being treated like a pariah.

At Pleasantville, things seemed to go from bad to worse for my father. The private-duty nurse was reporting that when she arrived at his room each morning, she had to spend an hour cleaning the filth left by the night staff. "I would've thought that you're father being a Jewish man (Pleasantville was Jewish owned), they'd be treating him better than this," said Juanita Boyd, who had been an RN for more than forty years.

On two occasions, night nursing staff found my father lying on the floor.

When Ruth and I went to visit my father one day, as we approached his room, we heard a violent *bang!* As we entered, I saw a tech fumbling with the call button, trying to angrily shove it into its holder on the wall. "She ripped it out of the wall," my father said. The tech looked scared at my arrival. "She didn't rip it out, Dad," I assured him. Annoyed that he had summoned her, the tech had yanked it away from my father and slammed it into the holder.

Motioning to the woman in a friendly manner to step outside of the room, I tried to be diplomatic: "I know you've got a tough job and that it can be overwhelming with patients making demands and you not having enough help, but please understand that my father has been through hell. If he's ringing the call bell incessantly, just talk to him about it. He's really a very kind and compassionate person."

I was getting sick of having to give apologetic speeches to so-called caregivers.

"I'm one person and I'm running from room to room. One woman threatened to get me fired because I wasn't there as soon as her father rang the bell," the over-worked, under-paid, and obviously under-trained woman said.

After reassuring the tech that I understood and sympathized with her, I again asked for her patience and understanding in dealing with my father. We parted on good terms and I subsequently witnessed the woman trying to pay special attention to my father.

Friends and relatives visited my father regularly. Ruth came several times a week. Sharon kept making chicken soup. I was there every day.

But my father was getting depressed. At one point, while sitting up in his bed he tossed his arms and said to me, "Why can't we just end it all?" and then lowered his chin to his chest. With as much strength and sensitivity as he'd have shown had the situation been reversed, I replied, "It's not an option, Dad. It's not your time yet."

I requested a psychiatric consult, thinking perhaps he could get into a small therapy group or one-on-one session. The psychiatric social worker reported my father as saying, "I feel so helpless. I don't want to live anymore," but added that he would not take his own life. He was given a drug for depression.

While searching on line one evening, I came across an old piece of Yiddish sheet music titled *Die Spanishe*

Cholera, which means *The Spanish Flu*. It was produced in 1918, during the height of the worldwide influenza pandemic. On the cover was a picture of the young man who had written the lyrics: his name was Harry Boens. I printed out a copy and brought it to my father:

"Do you recognize this, Dad?"

"That's my father," he said with a modicum of surprise.

"Are you sure?"

"Absolutely, I never knew about this," he said, as he shook his head in disgust and handed the sheet back to me.

"Maybe it's time to get over that, Dad," I said.

Pursing his lips, he turned his head slightly, and then his face relaxed. He seemed pensive.

Two weeks into his stay at Pleasantville, Ruth and I arrived at my father's room to find him sitting up in bed, a pulse-ox monitor on his finger, and him trying to say something in a voice so raspy and distorted I would not have recognized it as my father's had I not been looking at him. When he tried to swallow, his entire body shuddered. A nurse and an administrator were in the room:

"What's going on?" I asked the administrator.

"We don't know. His blood oxygen suddenly dropped, but we don't know why."

"Why is his voice like that?" I said.

"Hmm, I'm not sure," the administrator said, looking indifferently puzzled.

"He's in pain, look at him," I implored.

"We gave him some crushed Tylenol in applesauce."

"Can't you give him something stronger?"

"Yeah, I guess you're right. Let me call the doctor and see if we can get him something," the woman said before leaving the room.

She returned about ten minutes later with some Oxycodone, crushed into more applesauce, which I fed to my father.

After about ten minutes of watching him sitting there, his chin on his chest, shuddering every time he swallowed, I turned to the administrator:

"There's something very wrong. My father needs to be taken to the hospital right away."

"Hmm, yeah, I think you're right, let me see if I can get it arranged," the unconvincingly concerned woman admitted.

Once again I helped load my father onto an ambulance while telling him I was with him. It had taken more than an hour and a half to get him to the hospital, which was literally across the street.

A CT scan showed that my father had epiglottitis;[101] his airway had closed to about five millimeters, the diameter of a drinking straw.

He spent the next week in ICU and then five more weeks on an infectious disease unit. I visited him multiple times each day. On Sabbaths, I walked three miles in each direction to visit him carrying a tennis racquet to beat back the swarms of large, red-eyed cicadas that emerge from the ground of Baltimore every sixteen years.

My father recovered to some degree. He asked about the kids and Sharon and I asked about the care and how he was feeling. He wasn't complaining much anymore. He was thinking about what the future might bring: "Where are we going next," he asked with his eyes closed. "No more hospitals, Dad. We're going home," I said. He smiled and gently sighed at the thought.

His pain and suffering were almost constant. The pain patches that were placed on his chest would put him to sleep sometimes for two days straight, and although he was receiving nutrition through a large bore intravenous line, he must eat to get the nutrients

---

101 An inflammation of the epiglottis that is usually caused by a bacterial infection, Epiglottitis is an *extreme* medical emergency.

his body needed to keep from wasting away. After getting the pain medication adjusted so that he would not be knocked out all the time, I told the private duty nurse to feed him whatever she could throughout the day and to keep a journal. I also arranged for special meals to be sent from the cafeteria.

The strategy worked to a degree and he became more awake and alert. But his suffering was still almost constant. And I suspected something new was going on. I suggested to his new doctor (I had replaced Maisef by then) that blood cultures should be taken. It turned out that the VRE he had been diagnosed with at Shock Trauma was now in his bloodstream and infecting his entire body.

I brought Yoni to the hospital almost daily. He remained my father's little pal, eighty years his junior. Seeing Yoni's face and hearing his squeaky voice always brought a smile of joy to my father's still handsome face. Nurses who entered his room to take his blood pressure or check his IV would often stand and gaze at him. Juanita was on vacation and the new private duty nurse who was with him now for six days a week seemed proud to be caring for him.

A neighbor's son who was soon leaving to join the army in Israel came to visit my father one evening. "Dad, Binyamin's leaving for Israel soon. He's going into the army." "Keep your head down," my father advised him.

My father greeted the Filipino nurses who often treated him with "Mabuhay!" the native salutation he had learned while fighting in the Philippines. Despite unspeakable pain from a stage-four pressure ulcer, he asked me to bring doughnuts for both shifts of nurses to show appreciation for what they were trying to do for him.

He often asked me to rub his shoulders and his arms.

"I know how hard this is for you, Mike," he said on more than one occasion. "You're my father, Dad," I always replied.

"I don't hate anyone," he said one night. I wondered whom he was thinking about.

At one point, my father said to me, "I would not wish this suffering on Adolf Hitler," then he added, "I'd shoot him, but I wouldn't wish this suffering on him."

Despite the private nurse's efforts he was still not getting enough nutrition. His new doctor had been recommending a feeding tube but I was hesitant. I was afraid that undergoing an invasive procedure would expose him to yet another infection. I called in an outside nutritionist to assess his caloric intake, which she confirmed was insufficient. My father had told me years ago that he did not want any "heroic measures" taken if he were to become hopelessly ill. I asked him about the feeding tube and he replied, "Maybe it's the best thing."

As I was escorting him to the pre-op area, my father instructed me, "Don't make any hasty decisions."

After he returned from the surgery, he never fully woke up. He could hear, but he was too weak to speak, or even open his eyes.

On June 11th, his eighty-ninth birthday, our five children came to his room with balloons and a piece of strawberry shortcake, one of the few things for which he would rarely cheat on his diet. Hearing his grandchildren's voices, my father struggled and opened his eyes. I convinced him to taste a morsel of cake from my fingers.

After the feeding tube was inserted, my father developed an irregular heartbeat—an atrial flutter. They planned on moving him to the cardiac unit later in the day.

As I was escorting him out of the room, I asked my father if anything hurt him; he shook his head 'no.' I then asked if he was comfortable, he nodded his head 'yes.' It was the last communication from my father to me.

That final Sabbath, struggling to endure the excruciating pain from the bedsore that had eaten a hole through his sacrum, as Sharon and our daughter, Meira, were preparing to leave his room they wished him "Good Shabbos." To my wife and daughter's astonishment, summoning his last ounce of strength my father responded in a loud voice, "Good Shabbos!" Those were the last words he uttered to anyone on earth.

That Sunday morning was our son Yehuda's high school graduation. My mind was on my father, but I knew being with our son on his special day was important. I planned on going straight to the hospital the moment the ceremony ended. As it concluded, my cell phone vibrated. It was the doctor from the cardiac unit: "You better get to the hospital right away. Your father's breathing pattern is like what we see before people pass away."

Running through the parking lot of the hospital, I kept saying, *"C'mon Dad. C'mon Dad. I'm coming, Dad. I'm coming Dad...."* I didn't want him to leave before I got there. I knew he didn't want to leave without me there.

On the afternoon of Sunday, June 13, 2004, Sharon, Ruth, and my five children and I gathered around my father's hospital bed reciting from the book of Psalms. My brother's wife, Karen, and their son, Blair, came to the room. Leon, who was in Washington, had been there the night before. Blair slowly, carefully approached the bed and said, "I love you grandpa." Ruth walked to the side of the bed where I was standing, bent over, and gently kissed my father on the cheek. His breathing was labored. Time was running out. Rabbi Hesed was summoned to his bedside and recited the Viduy, the final statement before someone passes away. At just after 9:00 P.M. with my daughter sitting beside the hospital bed, still reciting prayers for her grandfather, my father's soul left this world as I softly told him over and over and over again, "I love you forever, Dad; I love you forever, Dad; I love you forever, Dad...."

Chapter Forty-Two

I t's Robert Malinow from Levinson's," Rabbi Hesed said, as he handed me his cell phone outside the room where my father's body remained with Rabbi Nelkin from the Chevra Kadisha. Levinson's is the Jewish funeral home in our area of Baltimore. "Malinow," the name sounded familiar. "Are you related to the Malinows in California?" "Yes," he said. "Alvin Malinow?" I asked, the name popping into my head from some murky place. It had been more than thirty years since my tangle with the Hollywood funeral director. "That was my father," he responded. It all came back to me.

Despite my clash with Alvin Manilow over my mother's funeral, in a surreal way, having the son of the man who handled the final arrangements for my grandparents and my mother taking charge of my father's service was comforting at that moment of profound grief and shock.

I escorted my father's body out of the hospital, to the waiting hearse, and then the funeral home.

No more hospitals, Dad, no more hospitals; we're going home.

My Father

As my brother and I conducted the morose business of a funeral, the volunteers from the Chevra Kadisha were performing the final preparation of my father's body: washing and then dressing him in the eight, natural linen garments; a small amount of the sacred soil of the land of Israel was placed over his heart, and his body was wrapped in my tallis. Finally, with special reverence, the men lifted his body and placed it in the casket. His disinterred leg was returned to him. During the entire ancient ceremony, the men of the Chevra Kadisha exchanged no extraneous words; they only recited special prayers and verses from the book of Psalms for my father's soul. At the completion of their Holy work, these deeply religious men who never knew my father asked him for forgiveness if they had in some way not shown him sufficient respect.

Leon and I entered a small room off to the side of the large chapel. Behind a partially-open black curtain stood my father's casket. It was draped in the American Flag.

Rabbi Hesed, Rabbi Nelkin, Ruth, Sharon, and Karen were already there. As Rabbi Nelkin escorted each of us to the casket, he advised, "The soul hears."

I stood alone with my father, seeing only the flag, but feeling his presence. I asked him to forgive me for anything that I ever did to hurt him or wrong him or for not showing him enough respect. And I told him that I loved him forever.

The bier was wheeled into the chapel and positioned to the front of the dais. Two highly decorated soldiers in perfectly pressed uniforms moved into position, standing guard beside the casket. About seventy people whose lives were touched by my father in the short time that he lived in Baltimore were in attendance.

Rabbi Hesed recited prayers. Then, with tears streaming down his young face, he delivered a heartfelt eulogy of the man he had only recently come to know.

My brother began his eulogy by saying, "My father planned this day," referring to the fact that he, Karen, and Blair happened to be in Baltimore at the time he passed. Leon went on to speak lovingly, reminiscing of the good times they had together, and how his father was there for him when he needed him the most.

After the children spoke briefly about their grandfather and their love for him, Major Saver approached my father's flag draped casket, saluted, and then mounted the dais. He retold some of the history of my father's military service, and then spoke about "the man I came to know and love..."

Rabbi Hesed called on me to speak. I struggled with emotion:

"I tried to write something to say...but I couldn't. Even the simplest of lives cannot be adequately conveyed in words and my father had anything but a simple life. From the orphanage, through the Great Depression, World War II, and many other difficulties throughout his entire life, my father overcame it all, and he did it with class...he was a stunning human being and I am the luckiest of sons. As is our tradition, my lapel is torn. It represents my broken heart; one side is filled with pride, the other is filled with love."

Then, with tears streaming down my face, my voice choked with emotion, my daughter sobbing loudly, I shook my finger in defiance and concluded:

"I will love him forever!"

When we arrived at the cemetery, I exited the hearse to find another contingent of soldiers standing at attention. They marched behind the casket as it was brought to the graveside. A tent had been erected over the grave and the seating area.

Robert Malinow loudly announced, "PREPARE FOR MILITARY HONORS."

As I sat with Yoni on my lap, my brother to my right, a female soldier and a male air force officer in immaculate dress uniforms, their breasts adorned with colorful ribbons and brass decorations, marched to the front and rear of the casket. Grasping the ends of the flag, the two American soldiers raised it, pulling it taught before stepping one pace to the side. In flawlessly regimented movements, the air force officer folded the flag, section-by-section, stopping to smooth it with his white-gloved hands after each triangular fold. With the perfectly folded flag resting reverently on one white-gloved palm, the other on top, the female soldier turned right face and slowly marched toward me. Kneeling down, she presented the symbol of America and said, "Please accept this flag in memory of your father On Behalf Of A Grateful Nation." I lovingly took hold of the flag. The young soldier slowly stood, and with her eyes riveted on me, her face proud, she saluted. I saluted back, as I looked at her through pools of tears. Out of nowhere and everywhere came the haunting sound of TAPS from an army bugler. Each note pierced my shattered heart. I stood by the open grave as the casket was lowered. Leon and I slid the first few shovels of earth into the grave. As my friends continued, kneeling beside the opening, part of me wanting to jump in, I took handfuls of earth, each one embedded with my love and tears, and dropped them onto my father's casket, in his final resting place.

During the shiva period, friends and neighbors, as well as numerous rabbis, and a few doctors who had treated my father, filed in an out of the house from morning until night. As I sat on a low chair, I tearfully related stories about my father's life to those who came to pay their respects; many wanted to know what had happened to him. Sharon, Ruth, and the children worked tirelessly to welcome people and serve them food, which had been generously donated by friends. The flame from a seven-day memorial candle glowed in its red glass container on the mantle, pictures of my father surrounding it. Even after he was gone, people remarked in awe about how handsome he was. I often retreated to my father's room, closing the door, pressing myself into the farthest corner and crying in overwhelming anguish: *"WHERE IS HE? IS HE ALL RIGHT? YOU GAVE ME MY BEAUTIFUL FATHER...PLEASE G-D... PLEASE LET ME KNOW THAT MY DAD IS OK. I JUST WANT TO KNOW THAT HE'S OK..."*

Staring at the painting above my father's bed, I yearned to see him walking into that sunset.

Silent tears soaked my pillow every night.

The funeral had taken place on Monday, that Friday was the first time I left the house since returning from the cemetery. Jewish law prohibits mourning on the Sabbath. I would attend services and do my best not to mourn, knowing that would be impossible.

As I headed to the synagogue, a man whom I recognized, but did not know, followed me out of the house: "You shouldn't talk about what happened to your father," he said while walking beside me. "Why?" I asked. "When I was practicing medicine, just like I didn't say, 'this one had a heart attack, this one had a stroke,' you shouldn't

say anything," he reasoned. Learning that he was a doctor from his strange remark, I failed to see the connection between patient confidentiality and a son talking
about what had happened to his father. "But you had an
obligation," I replied. "That's right," he responded. The
discussion ended there. I knew something was wrong
with the encounter, but deep in mourning I hadn't the
mind to analyze it.

When shiva ended, Rabbi Hesed accompanied me
out of the house, offering me words of consolation and
instruction about how I was now entering a new phase
of bereavement called shloshim, a thirty-day period
where mourning is to be less intense, nevertheless ever-
present. The shloshim, Rabbi Hesed explained, would
be followed by another ten months of gradually reduced
sorrow. Just as I had done since the funeral, I would
continue to recite Kaddish for my father three times a
day.

Later that year Sharon presented me with an airline
ticket to Israel. Our son, Yehuda, was studying in Jerusalem at the time and she felt that the trip would do me
well.

I traveled around Jerusalem and its environs going
to sacred sites and praying for my father's soul. I
walked the streets handing money to beggars and giving twenty-dollar bills to rabbis and rabbinical students
asking them to dedicate some learning in memory of my
father. I visited Reb Noah who shook his head in disgust
at what had happened to my father, and consoled me in
a way that only a man with a heart so big and filled with
so much love could.

It was while I was in Israel that my father came to
me in the first of three radically different and unusually
dimensional dreams:

Standing near the curb of a street, a car pulled up along-side me. Although he was in the passenger seat, my father was driving. Appearing angry and looking directly at me, he simply said, "Michael!"

Toward the end of my brief visit to Israel, I was walking down King George Street in Jerusalem with Yehuda and his girlfriend, Leah, who was also studying there. We had just finished dinner at a local restaurant and were heading toward Jaffa Road to get public transportation back to where we were staying, when we came upon Dr. Maisef and his wife. I looked at him; he turned his head away. Tortured by the sight of Maisef, I walked away. Yehuda and Leah stopped to talk.

Neither of them knew what I had learned about this man's treatment of my father, or my growing rage toward him.

Chapter Forty-Three

After he was transferred to the hospital with epiglottitis and Dr. Maisef had long since remained conspicuously absent, I overcame my reservations about interfering with my father's doctor-patient relationship and signed him up with a concierge medical practice. For an upfront fee he would have a private physician available around the clock and would not have to rely solely on the overwhelmed house doctors.

Although he had effectively abandoned my father, and I was angry at what I suspected was his negligent care, at the time I still felt a need to personally inform Dr. Maisef that he was no longer my father's primary care physician. Buttonholing him in the synagogue one day, I told Maisef, "There's no way for me to say this without somehow hurting you, but I'm switching my father's doctor." Maisef looked unaffected by what I had just said. Instead, he responded by asking, "Can I still visit him?" Here was a doctor who had not seen his hospitalized patient in over a month, he had not even responded to a pressing need to clarify his medications, and now, after being fired, he was asking if he could *still* see my father! "I'd prefer that you didn't," I answered, and then added, "I have to think of my father's interests." As Maisef looked upward pondering what my final words might mean, I walked away.

Albeit he was eighty-eight years old, my father was a viable and independent man when he was admitted to the hospital with a respiratory virus that was burgeoning into pneumonia, a serious but treatable condition. At the time that I approached Dr. Maisef, my father, with one leg gone and the rest of his body morbidly devastated by bacterial infections, was fighting for his life. It screamed negligence.

But despite what I thought, not having the medical records at the time, it was far from certain that anyone had been negligent in my father's care.

After my father's death, I poured over his medical records and studied the complexities of various conditions he had developed while in hospitals, the standard treatments for those conditions, and the overriding issue of hospital-acquired infections.

I remembered my wife's relating of the scene that she had witnessed on that morning of March 12th and how the wound care nurses were photographing his leg. I called the hospital and spoke to one of those nurses and asked about the photographs: "Well, I don't know if we still have them. Bt if we do, they would be in the camera," the nurse said. "I need the photographs of my father's leg and I need you to make certain that they are not deleted from that camera," I told her. "I'll contact the other nurse and make arrangements for you to get your pictures," she replied curtly. The following day the nurse called saying that the photographs were available for me in the medical records department.

Through an acquaintance, I was referred to a well-known attorney with degrees from MIT and Georgetown and for twenty-five years represented only plaintiffs in medical malpractice cases. With such qualifications, I felt confident that Alison Kohler would know what to look for in my father's medical records and that if there was a case, it would be handled expertly.

But even if what happened to my father was caused by negligence, it was certain the defendants would do everything possible to exploit his age and underlying conditions to avoid responsibility at all costs. Because of that evil reality, I feared that no experienced med mal attorney would be willing to take the case.

Half an hour past our scheduled appointment time, Alison arrived at her firm's office and escorted me to a nearby conference room. She inspired my trust with her confident stride and a voice that conveyed intelligence, experience, competence, and compassion. I hoped that she would take the case.

I had brought along some of my father's medical records and the photographs I had retrieved from the hospital.

"Oh my G-d!" Alison exclaimed, as she looked at the twenty-one thumbnail pictures of my father's grotesquely rotting leg on the contact sheet. "This happened in a hospital?" she asked in disbelief.

At the conclusion of our hour-long meeting, Alison agreed to look at the case.

"We're having a rally in Annapolis to protest the governor's tort reform legislation. Would you like to come?" Alison asked.

I had been a supporter of the governor, and, before my father's tragedy, although abysmally ignorant of what victims of medical malpractice faced, I was also a supporter of tort reform. But after witnessing the dysfunction that occurred in five different hospitals and learning the reality of what victims of medical negligence go through, which is discussed further on, I wasn't any longer.

"I'll be there," I answered.

In the early winter of 2004, I found myself in paint-spattered work clothes standing behind a microphone before a crowd of demonstrators, politicians, lawyers, and television cameras telling the assemblage about what had happened to my father. In concluding my short remarks, I angrily said, "My father was betrayed by those he trusted the most: doctors and hospitals. I could go on, but it's not my place." Then, looking upward into the clear blue sky, my eyes filling with tears, and on the verge of yet again being overwhelmed with emotion, I added, *"That's for you, Dad."*

Famed Baltimore attorney Billy Murphy then stepped up to the microphone: "If it's not your place Michael, I don't know whose place it is."

Several days later, I carried blowups of my father and his grotesquely infected leg to Annapolis where I testified against the governor's proposed legislation. After summarizing my father's life, pouring out my anger and grief, and decrying the deplorable state of medical care and what victims of medical negligence face, before a group of politicians who may or may not have cared one iota about my father or what happened to him, I ended thusly:

"With deference to General MacArthur: Old soldiers never die, but they don't fade away; they leave behind sons who will fight for them. I will fight for my dad; I will fight for my dad."

A bevy of reporters converged asking my name and where I lived.

Having missed the last shuttle to the Naval Stadium parking lot where I had left my truck, with tears streaking down my face, I walked in the sub-freezing weather along the busy Rowe Boulevard, hugging the guardrail and struggling not to tumble over into the icy Severn River some thirty feet below.

Days later, my father came to me in a second dream:

The amorphous, golden sparks of my essence rose to greet the golden sparks of my father's descending essence. As my father's soul embraced mine, I heard his voice say, "I can't keep coming down," and our essences returned.

Over the next six years, I became an activist and patient advocate. Again and again I testified before legislative committees on patients' rights and safety issues and railed against the tort "reformers"[102] for trying to wrest justice or fair and just compensation from victims of medical negligence. I met with umpteen politicians and public officials on the state as well as the federal level, some of whom became outraged by what was happening; others simply remained complacent.

Almost a week did not go by when I wasn't in a studio or standing on a ladder or sitting in my truck doing interviews over my cell phone, or rushing home to change my work clothes ahead of an arriving reporter and cameraman. I didn't crave the limelight; I dreaded it. And every interview intensified my grief. But at the same time, like other victims in similar circumstances, I was grateful for the opportunities, because I was fighting for my father.

---

102 At one hearing, while waiting outside to testify against a piece of tort reform legislation, a doctor who was testifying in support of the bill, and whom I had similarly come up against at other hearings, told me, "We (doctors) hide our mistakes all the time." To which I responded, "Then how can you go in there and testify against victims?" The doctor did not respond.

Chapter Forty-Four

"A hospital is no place to be sick."
— **Samuel Goldwyn**

Among many other disturbing things, my father's medical records contained laboratory reports revealing that he had acquired at least six different strains of bacteria and a fungus over the course of his four-month-long nightmare through five institutions. Most of those pathogens were what are referred to as multi-drug resistant organisms (MDROs), or so-called "Superbugs," which simply means strains of bacteria that are resistant to multiple antibiotics, often including those normally used to treat infections caused by them.

Two of the most pervasive of these virulent MDROs that circulate in healthcare facilities are *vancomycin-resistant Enterococcus* (VRE) and *methicillin-resistant Staphylococcus aureus* (MRSA). Another nasty bug causing increasingly frequent hospital infections is called *Clostridium difficile* (C. diff). My father had acquired all three of these lethal pathogens, and more.

Background

In the 1960s, hospitals in the United States began noticing staphylococcal infections in patients that were not responding to penicillin and its synthetic relative, methicillin. These organisms were therefore termed methicillin-*resistant* Staphylococcus aureus, or MRSA.

For the next forty years, the rate of hospital-acquired MRSA infections steadily climbed. During the period from 1980-2000 alone, the rate increased more than thirty-fold. All the while, patients—legions of them—and their families were not told they had contracted MRSA, let alone that it had been spread to them in the hospital.

Normal staphylococcus bacterium becomes MRSA when it acquires a large genetic component called *Staphylococcal cassette chromosome Mec*, or *SCCmec,* a process that has rarely been duplicated in the laboratory. Therefore, *direct contact* with the already resistant bacterium accounts for virtually all MRSA infections. In 2007, a study[103] was published in the Journal of the American Medical Association stating that annually there were approximately 95,000 cases of sterile site[104] MRSA (a minority of all MRSA infections) accounting for almost 19,000 deaths, more than the average yearly number of people killed in the U.S. by AIDS. *The same study showed 85% of these infections occurred in healthcare facilities.*[105]

A plethora of studies have shown that the spread of MRSA in hospitals and nursing homes occurs predominantly through the contaminated hands, equipment, and/or clothing of healthcare workers.

---

103 A 2007 CDC study based on 2005 data.

104 Sterile site refers to a location in the human body where bacteria do not ordinarily live, e.g., the bloodstream.

105 The data also showed that Baltimore had the highest rates, by far, of any of the 9 sites participating in the study. In fact, Baltimore's rates were so high the researchers rechecked the data and their analysis looking for a mistake that might have caused the discrepancy; none was found.

MRSA can cause pneumonia, skin and soft tissue infections, as well as bone and bloodstream infections, which are often times deadly.

The drug of choice for treating MRSA infections for the last fifty years has been vancomycin, a powerful antibiotic that can cause kidney damage and hearing loss, among other serious side effects.

While the Centers for Disease Control and Prevention (CDC), and others who oversee public health, knew about the proliferation of MRSA in healthcare for decades, nothing effective to control its spread was implemented...nothing. And as the number of MRSA infections increased, so did the use of vancomycin, which fostered the emergence and then the proliferation of VRE.

Somewhat similar to MRSA, *vancomycin-resistant Enterococcus* (VRE) occurs when normal Enterococcus bacterium acquire genetic material making it resistant to vancomycin. Also like MRSA, VRE is virtually always acquired through contact. VRE infections occur almost exclusively in healthcare institutions, where the bug is acquired through contact with contaminated surfaces and equipment or spread via the contaminated hands or clothing of healthcare workers.

VRE primarily colonizes the gut through what is clinically referred to as the "fecal-oral route," which means bacteria from the feces of colonized or infected patients somehow gets into the mouths of other patients. VRE bloodstream infections, which my father had developed, are associated with a high rate of death.[106]

In 1990, VRE emerged in a single, world-renowned hospital in Baltimore, which, according to a high-level CDC insider, refused to allow the CDC to investigate and implement control measures. VRE was therefore

---

106 While VRE bloodstream infections are not as virulent as those caused by MRSA, the mortality rate is approximately double that of similar infections caused by *vancomycin-sensitive Enterococcus* (VSE).

not controlled, and it subsequently spread to hospitals and nursing homes throughout Maryland, and then across the entire country.

Clostridium difficile is an antibiotic-resistant, hospital-spread bacterium, which, like VRE, is also acquired through the fecal-oral route. It causes severe and potentially fatal colitis. Some strains of C. diff are associated with a 50% mortality rate; in other words half of the people that are infected with these strains die.

In the 1990s, around the same time that VRE emerged, new strains of MRSA started infecting otherwise healthy people who had no contact with the healthcare system. However, these so-called community strains were causing mostly skin and soft tissue infections and were susceptible to a wider variety of antibiotics than the hospital strains. But because hospitals were also not vigilant about keeping these strains of MRSA out of their institutions, they too gained a foothold in America's hospitals and nursing homes where they have now become endemic.

In 1997, the CDC funded a study in the Siouxland district of Iowa where an outbreak of VRE had been rampaging through the healthcare system for about two years, affecting patients in some thirty-two facilities. The intervention used in the study, which centered on identifying and isolating patients harboring VRE, eliminated the deadly bug altogether from all of the participating acute care facilities.[107]

When the results of the study came in, the then newly appointed head of CDC's Hospital Infection's program is reported to have stated that the approach was "a model" for the control of such infections in hospitals and nursing homes in all regions of the country,

---

107 Two facilities stopped participating in the study. Five of the nursing homes taking part continued to have a VRE problem due to poor compliance with the intervention.

and subsequently issued a press release trumpeting the intervention's success.[108]

But the CDC's enthusiasm for the method inexplicably disappeared, although the agency's push for vaccines for diseases that were killing far fewer people than MRSA and VRE, such as bird flu and swine flu, grew ever stronger.

The Saga of the 2003 SHEA Guideline

Practically two decades before the CDC helped fund the Siouxland initiative, a trim, blond-haired, young epidemiologist at the University of Virginia Hospital (UVA) had already witnessed how the same basic approach was effective in stopping the spread of MRSA.

When Dr. Barry Farr arrived at UVA in 1978 as a resident physician, the hospital was already several months into an outbreak of MRSA.

Interested in infectious disease, Dr. Farr joined the hospital's infection control committee.

After three years of seeing no improvement in the rampant spread of MRSA throughout the hospital using standard methods, the committee deployed a program that included actively looking for patients asymptomatically colonized[109] with MRSA and placing them in isolation. The scientific term for this approach is *Active Detection and Isolation* or ADI. After three years of steadily rising rates at UVA, MRSA began declining by the second month of the intervention's deployment; within eighteen months, MRSA had altogether disappeared from the hospital.

However, in 1991 the rate of MRSA at UVA inexplicably began to increase. After a careful analysis, Dr. Farr (now the hospital epidemiologist) and his colleagues

---

108 CDC Press Release of May 10, 2001.

109 Testing patients who are suspected of carrying MRSA but are exhibiting no signs of disease.

discovered that MRSA was being reintroduced into the hospital from patients who had been treated at health-care facilities in the surrounding area and subsequently admitted to UVA. It turned out that what was happening at UVA in the late 70s was also taking place at these facilities. However, because they had ignored UVA's success with ADI despite having access to the published results, those facilities had become saturated with MRSA.

As a consequence of his study, Dr. Farr believed that to maintain control of MRSA, regional deployment of ADI would be helpful and he began trying to convince other healthcare facilities in Virginia to adopt the approach. In the year 2000, he applied to the CDC for funding to help launch a statewide initiative: the CDC refused.

Undaunted, Dr. Farr continued his effort to convince his colleagues of the effectiveness of ADI in controlling MRSA and the urgent need to deploy such a program.

But Dr. Farr ran into strong opposition from people at CDC and elsewhere who had already established their careers in epidemiology while ignoring the proliferation of MRSA, arguing that MRSA was endemic and nothing could be done to eradicate it or that all that was needed was better compliance with hand hygiene.

Despite a growing body of scientific evidence supporting the effectiveness of ADI in controlling MRSA, opposition to Farr among a relatively small group of influential public health and infectious diseases leaders remained strong.

Eventually considered a radical about the need to control healthcare-spread MRSA, Dr. Farr continued to fight the battle virtually alone. That is until he found an ally at the CDC by the name of Dr. William Jarvis.

"Example is Leadership."
— *Albert Schweitzer*

A tall, slender man with a relaxed manner and a reserved personality, few people have reached the levels of achievement in the fields of epidemiology and infectious diseases that Dr. William Jarvis has. With degrees in medicine and specialties in pediatric infectious diseases, Dr. Jarvis was educated at prestigious universities in California, Texas, Toronto, and at Yale University in Connecticut. He has published more than four hundred peer reviewed papers, edited three books on infectious disease and infection control, given thousands of lectures, served on dozens of committees, and over the span of twenty-three years rose through the ranks of the CDC to Acting Director of the Hospital Infections Program and then Director of Extramural Research for the Office of the Director at the National Center for Infectious Diseases. Dr. Jarvis has supervised more than one hundred and fifty outbreak investigations (solved them all) and is the recipient of more than fifty U.S. Public Health Service citations and commendations for his work in infectious disease, infection control, and public health, to name a few categories. In 2003, Dr. Jarvis received the CDC Lifetime Scientific Achievement Award, the agency's highest honor; and in 2010 he received the CDC's Lifetime Scientific Achievement Award in Epidemiology.

At the time that Dr. Farr met him, Dr. Jarvis was Chief of the CDC's Investigation and Prevention Branch, Hospital Infections Program, the group responsible for the investigation of all healthcare associated outbreaks throughout the world. By that time, VRE had reared its ugly head in America's healthcare institutions and was already duplicating the same deadly path and steady rise as that of MRSA.

Responding to outbreaks of VRE, Dr. Jarvis and his CDC Epidemiological Intelligence Services (EIS) trainees traveled to some of the stricken facilities to investigate.

As Dr. Farr had experienced with MRSA, Dr. Jarvis found ADI successful in controlling and even eradicating VRE, such as had occurred with the hallmark Siouxland study, which he organized and conducted.

Unfortunately, just as Dr. Farr had experienced with his advocacy of ADI for MRSA, Dr. Jarvis found growing opposition to his proposals to expand routine use of the intervention for controlling VRE.

After Dr. Farr was elected president in 2002 of the Society for Healthcare Epidemiology of America (SHEA), a highly respected, private organization of primarily physician-scientists with members from around the world, he appointed a committee to draft a guideline to control hospital-spread MRSA and VRE. To make up the group, Dr. Farr chose scientists, such as Dr. Jarvis, who had experience in successfully controlling antibiotic-resistant infections. The committee's final product was an evidence-based guideline to control MRSA and VRE that included ADI[110] as the linchpin.

Predictably, the usual opponents went to work to derail the new guideline practically before the ink had dried. The attacks increased in both frequency and intensity and became so vituperative, one committee member resigned out of fear for his career in epidemiology.

But despite the fierce opposition, the guideline was eventually put to a vote before the SHEA Board and was approved by the majority. The SHEA Guideline for Preventing Nosocomial Transmission of Multidrug-Resistant Strains of Staphylococcus aureus and Enterococ-

---

110 Isolation, as advocated by the 2003 SHEA guideline, refers to "contact isolation," which means healthcare workers must use barrier precautions such as gowns, gloves, and sometimes a mask, a private room or cohorting with similarly colonized or infected patients, and dedicated personal equipment such as a thermometer and blood pressure cuff so that these items will not be used on other patients and spread the bacteria.

cus was published in the May 2003 edition of Infection Control and Hospital Epidemiology (ICHE).

The 2003 SHEA guideline, as it is called, is somewhat similar[111] to the Dutch method of "Search and Destroy" that had effectively kept MRSA out of Northern European hospitals for decades. A comparable approach was deployed in Western Australia where it was also impressively effective in protecting patients from disease.

But long before the 2003 SHEA guideline was published and even before the Dutch deployed their Search and Destroy program, the same basic approach was effectively used to prevent the spread of infectious diseases caused by smallpox, tuberculosis, and influenza. In fact, it was essentially the same method of control and prevention that Abraham Jacobi employed at the Hebrew Orphan Asylum where my father had spent his childhood, and it kept that institution virtually bug free even as epidemics raged all around, such as the 1918 Spanish Flu that Harry Boens, my father's father, lamented in his *Die Spanishe Cholera.*

In 2004, after my father's death, I came across an article about the scourge of hospital infections and specifically MRSA in which Dr. Farr was quoted as saying, "For years, we've been trundling the bodies of patients off to the morgue while infection rates got higher and higher." Thinking this is the man I need to speak with, I called Dr. Farr at his home in Charlottesville, Virginia. After he explained to me the basic principle of active detection and isolation, I commented that it sounded like common sense, to which he responded, "It's better than common sense *it is* science."

In the ensuing months, Dr. Farr patiently answered my numerous questions and referred me to various

---

111 The 2003 SHEA guideline is different from and *not* patterned after the Dutch approach in several ways. But it is similar insofar as it advocates identifying and isolating the entire reservoir for spread of MRSA.

sources where I could educate myself on the issue. He also referred me to Dr. Jarvis, who generously did likewise.

After discovering that these infections were preventable and that it was the failure and in some cases the refusal of public health leadership to recommend effective ways to control MRSA and VRE, I became incensed. How many people like my father had suffered and died for no legitimate reason?

Consumer Activism

The year before my father's tragedy, a popular movement to get hospitals to publically report their infection rates had been started by Consumer's Union (CU), the publisher of Consumer Reports. The director of CU's campaign, an indefatigable woman from Austin, Texas named Lisa McGiffert, spent much of the year travelling from state to state drumming up support and encouraging consumers as well as legislators to demand public disclosure laws.[112]

McGiffert's efforts paid off and by 2009, twenty-seven states had passed laws mandating hospitals publically report their infection rates.

I contacted McGiffert in 2004 and became involved in the CU campaign, which included testifying alongside her on the Maryland public reporting bill in 2005. The bill passed, but as long as five years afterwards

---

112 The CDC and others initially opposed public reporting laws. But as the consumer movement gained momentum, CDC leadership reversed their position. However, they wanted reporting done according to their formula. For a number of years the agency operated a *voluntary and confidential* hospital infection-reporting program called the National Nosocomial Infection Surveillance System (NNIS) with approximately 300 hospitals participating in it. The CDC reorganized and changed the name of the NNIS system to the National Healthcare Safety Network (NHSN), which, as a consequence of public disclosure laws, currently has about 4000 participating hospitals. Nevertheless, many consumer advocates remain unimpressed with the NHSN system and feel that most hospitals, particularly those in states that require public reporting, are woefully underreporting their infection rates.

no data on Maryland's hospital infection rates had yet been published.

While I agreed with CU that reporting laws would help put pressure on hospitals, I felt that would not be enough. Institutions which had for decades hidden a problem of their own making would not likely be forthcoming in disclosing their infection rates and would find ways to game the system. And the kind of culture change needed to stop the epidemic would take years of education. Meanwhile, more and more people like my father would unnecessarily suffer and die. I wanted a law that would force hospitals to do the right thing right away.

I had the idea to draft legislation to mandate the 2003 SHEA guideline in all of Maryland's hospitals and nursing homes. Because hospitals and nursing homes were still not implementing effective control measures, Drs. Farr and Jarvis thought it might be a good idea and pledged their support.

Introducing a bill mandating clinical guidelines was controversial to say the least, and passing such legislation thought to be a long shot at best. Right or wrong the medical powers that be would fight tooth and nail against any such proposal. Doctors and scientists do not like to be told what to do even by their colleagues, and they would certainly resent a consumer trying to do so through having a law enacted. Then again, I felt assured that with more than sixty studies supporting the approach and entire regions, such as countries in Northern Europe and the state of Western Australia, successfully employing it, we had a chance. But whether the bill passed or not, by simply introducing it we would increase the pressure on hospitals as well as public health leaders to finally do something meaningful about the epidemic. From that perspective it was a win-win proposition.

Early in 2005, after I had spent weeks collecting data and putting together a proposal, which included letters from Dr. Farr, Dr. Jarvis, and others, attorney Alison Kohler secured a meeting with the president of the Maryland State Senate, Senator Thomas V. Mike Miller. Alison joined me in the meeting during which we advocated for legislation mandating the 2003 SHEA guideline throughout the state.

Senator Miller was deeply moved by my father's story, expressing his regret that he did not have such a close relationship with his father. After quickly grasping the problem and appreciating the scientific validity of what we were trying to do, the senator promised to "get something done."

With the assistance of Drs. Farr, Jarvis, and others, I drafted the bill to mandate the 2003 SHEA guideline. Senator Miller facilitated getting sponsors for the bill and it was introduced during the 2005-2006 legislative session. It was the first legislation of its kind ever introduced anywhere in the country.

"No science is immune to the infection of politics and the corruption of power."
— **Jacob Bronowski**

After filing the bill, a storm of opposition erupted from practically every corner of America's infection control and hospital community. I was labeled "an angry radical" and accused of being "in the pocket of the trial lawyers," and "financed by corporate interests." And together with my scientific mentors and consumer supporters tagged "a group of vigilantes." The scores of studies and overwhelming data supporting the 2003

SHEA guideline approach were summarily dismissed as being "quasi-scientific."

By the spring of 2006, a panel of experts willing to testify in support of the legislation had been assembled. The group included: Dr. Farr; Dr. Margreet Vos[113] of Erasmus University Medical Centre of the Netherlands; Princeton trained and highly esteemed healthcare economist Dr. Ramanan Laxminarayan,[114] and former New York Lieutenant Governor, healthcare policy expert, and founder of the Committee to Reduce Infection Deaths (RID) Dr. Betsy McCaughey. Those who submitted written testimony supporting the bill included: Dr. William Jarvis; Dr. Carlene Muto from the University of Pittsburgh Medical Center and lead author of the 2003 SHEA guideline, and Dr. Leonard Mermel of Brown University Medical Center in Rhode Island, who had engineered the successful implementation of an ADI program in his state. In his testimony, Dr. Jarvis referred to the spread of MRSA and VRE in the nation's hospitals and nursing homes as a *"public health disaster."*

The press got wind of the bill sparking a flurry of stories in local, national, and international media.

Unsurprisingly, the legislative sponsors became targets of intense lobbying efforts by those challenging the bill, which included representatives of the state's hospitals, the Association for Professionals in Infection Control (APIC), and even SHEA. The opponents were so determined and their attempts to derail the legislation so unrelenting that but for the intervention of some of our more influential supporters, the main sponsor of the bill, Senator Paula Hollinger, a registered nurse and chairwoman of the Health Committee, would have

---

113 Dr. Vos traveled from the Netherlands; Dr. Farr came from Charlottesville, Virginia; Dr. Laxminarayan drove in from Washington D.C., and Dr. McCaughey came aboard a train from New York. All were unpaid volunteers.

114 Among his appointments, Dr. Laxminarayan is the Director of The Center for Disease Dynamics and Economic Policy. He has served as an advisor to the World Health Organization (WHO) and the World Bank.

withdrawn it. One sponsor reported being "stalked" by lobbyists, hospital representatives, and others at various meetings and appearances.

I reached out to public health officials, some of whom seemed sympathetic, but got no support. One of the most remarkable of those meetings took place with an official of the Maryland Department of Health and Mental Hygiene. In response to my arguments why the department should support the legislation, the official (a lawyer) uttered the most callous statements I could ever imagine a public health executive making: "We don't require best practices," said the Director of *Healthcare Quality*. "But people are dying from this," I pleaded. "People die from a lot of things," the bureaucrat retorted. "I knew you would say that, but this is preventable." All I got back was a heartless smile.

Hearings on the SHEA guideline bill were held on March 9, 2006 in committees of both the Maryland House and Senate. Dr. Farr was the first witness called to testify.

Before a packed committee room, with overflow spilling into the hallway where the hearing also was being broadcast, using Power Point charts, Dr. Farr launched into his testimony about the history of MRSA and VRE growth and the success of ADI.

But not five minutes into Dr. Farr's testimony, the chairman of the powerful Finance Committee suddenly interrupted him. Wanting to expedite the hearing, the chairman told Dr. Farr that since he had his written testimony, it was unnecessary to go into great detail at the hearing. The chairman's apparent impatience implied that he neither understood the urgency of the matter nor appreciate the remarkable panel of experts sitting in front of him. I was flabbergasted.

After Dr. Farr concluded his truncated presentation, Dr. Laxminarayan explained how unusual it was for an economist to support such a mandate but that because of the crisis of antibiotic resistance, he was willing to do so. He went on to warn the committee members that because of the failure to control these organisms, the country was moving in the direction of the days before antibiotics when bacterial infections were commonly a death sentence. Laxminarayan's only criticism of the bill was that it did not have enough "teeth" insofar as holding institutions accountable for not implementing its provisions.

In her testimony, Dr. McCaughey appealed to the committee members as "one lawmaker to another" to pass the bill and that if they were to ask, "Can we afford to do this? I say we cannot afford not to!"

The most dramatic testimony came from Dr. Vos. After describing to the committee how her country and others in Northern Europe had kept their MRSA infection rates down to a small fraction of America's, Dr. Vos, clasping her hands on the table in front of her, said, "I'm sorry to tell you that because of your country's failure to control these organisms, if any of you were to come to my country and be admitted to a hospital, we would immediately place you in isolation." I wondered if the committee members understood how damning Dr. Vos' words were.

When it was the opposition's turn to address the legislators, after stating in pious tones how they supported the *intent* of the bill, representatives of the Maryland Hospital Association, the Maryland Patient Safety Center, APIC,[115] and others, launched into a series of statements as to why it should be defeated. "It's too expensive," "too burdensome," "a one-size-fits-all approach that would deplete valuable resources from other infection control programs," "it's controversial," "we're [controlling] it

---

115 During a meeting with senior APIC leaders, which they requested, before hearings on the bill, I was lead to believe that the organization was going to support the legislation.

on our own," "the real problem is community-acquired MRSA," "placing patients on contact isolation endangers them because they get less adequate care," were just a few of their arguments. Some opponents even falsely misstated that the bill would require every patient enter-ing the hospital be tested at multiple body sites. Instead, they said, all that was needed was better compliance with hand hygiene (despite many studies showing that hand-hygiene campaigns alone didn't work in reducing the rates of MRSA or VRE infections).[116] The new Board of SHEA even came out against the bill, which prompted lawmakers to scratch their heads in confusion as to why SHEA was opposing the SHEA guideline. Representa-tives of the hospitals blamed the problem on nursing homes, while nursing home representatives blamed the hospitals.

Were it not a life and death issue, perhaps it all would have been amusing.

But *it was* a life and death issue and there was noth-ing funny about people protecting the failed policies that had resulted in the injury and death of untold numbers of hospitalized patients for close to half a century, one of whom was my father.

At the hearings, a number of committee members blasted the opposition witnesses for their failure to protect the public from these deadly diseases and now combating those who were finally trying to do so.

Nevertheless, the bill died in committee. We were not surprised and intended to file the bill the following year

---

116 A single negligent healthcare worker can spread bacteria to any number of patients. The CDC first issued guidelines for hand hygiene in 1986. In addition, healthcare workers had been federally mandated to be trained in hand hygiene and take an annual refresher course since 1991 yet the rates of MRSA and VRE continued to skyrocket. Several studies utilizing an enhanced hand-washing cam-paign component, such as the 9-year study conducted at Brigham and Women's Hospital (Huang et al), which improved hand-hygiene compliance from 40-50% (the national average) to 80%, failed to control MRSA infections until ADI was added to the bundle of interventions.

and every year thereafter until it passed or until hospitals were doing the right thing on their own.

After we submitted the Maryland bill to mandate the 2003 SHEA guideline, I received an email from a woman in Chicago who was starting a similar initiative in Illinois.

The woman had been infected in the hospital with a community strain of MRSA following surgery for a broken ankle caused by slipping on an icy patch of concrete. When she uncovered the cause of the surgical-site bone infection that had sent her into septic shock, almost killing her, the woman was angered by what she felt was the deceitful way in which the hospital and her doctors had treated her and was moved to action.

When she first contacted me, the woman was working with Illinois legislators on two pieces of legislation. One, if passed, would have mandated the CDC's Healthcare Infection Control Practices Advisory Committee (HICPAC) guideline for controlling MRSA.[117] The other would have mandated universal screening for MRSA. After I explained to the woman that the HICPAC guideline had not been effective in controlling MRSA and was therefore not the solution, and that universal screening was overkill and too costly, the Illinois bill was changed to screening high-risk ICU patients. Because the 2003 SHEA guideline had become a lightning rod for criticism since the introduction of the Maryland bill, the sponsors of the Illinois bill made no mention of it. Although I felt that the Illinois bill was not the optimum, it was a start and I pledged support.

The bill was submitted to the Illinois State legislature and wound up getting the backing of the state's hospital

---

117 Since the CDC is not a regulatory agency it cannot mandate practices. However, CDC recommendations are widely considered to be the basis for the standard of care in infection control practices.

association, which appreciated the money saving aspect of preventing hospital-spread MRSA infections.

But despite hospital support, opposition to the bill that was at least as virulent as what I had encountered in Maryland ensued, and state lawmakers came under intense pressure to kill it before it even came up for a vote. The new board of SHEA and the senior leadership of APIC, two organizations that had a history of being adversarial on many if not most issues now found common ground and joined in the fight to crush the legislation. APIC went so far as to have some of its members posted outside the legislative building handing out flyers urging its defeat to arriving lawmakers. APIC also distributed to its approximately fourteen thousand members a set of talking points on how to oppose similar consumer efforts.

In response to the Maryland and Illinois bills, SHEA and APIC even drafted a joint position paper, which was published in the SHEA journal, Infection Control and Hospital Epidemiology (ICHE), opposing all legislative mandates for infection control. The lead author of the paper was Dr. Stephen Weber of Chicago.

In reply to the SHEA-APIC position paper, I submitted a letter to the editor of ICHE drawing attention to some of the flaws in the published document, the most glaring of which was the invalid inference that the Maryland bill called for universal screening,[118] which I suspected was an intentional "mistake" meant to overstate the impact and cost of the bill and thereby discourage anyone from supporting it. I wrote that thirteen coauthors making the same fundamental error "cast a dark shadow of suspicion" over the paper's accuracy and objectivity. Not altogether surprisingly, the editor of ICHE refused to print the 744-word, thoroughly sourced

---

118 Universal screening means testing all patients upon admission to the hospital, as opposed to testing only those who are deemed at risk, based on local data, etc., for carrying the germ, as is advocated by the 2003 SHEA Guideline.

letter (titled *"Did Weber and His Coauthors Actually Read The Maryland Bill?"*) because there was ostensibly "insufficient space."

HICPAC published a revised MDRO isolation guideline[119] that recommended two tiers of measures for MDRO control. The first tier recommended scores of options. The second, only to be implemented if the first tier failed, recommended more than forty additional optional measures. Neither tier recommended ADI.[120] In effect, institutions attempting to control these deadly bugs and following the CDC's new HICPAC guideline could spend decades trying everything and still fail to achieve control of MRSA and VRE.

On the heels of the new CDC guideline, SHEA and APIC collaborated for a second time by drafting what amounted to yet another guideline, the SHEA-APIC Compendium, which mirrored the HICPAC guideline and was introduced at an elaborately staged press conference following an extensive media campaign.

But despite the fierce opposition, the Illinois bill unanimously passed both houses of the Illinois Legislature.

Similar bills started popping up around the country, four of which passed in other states over the next two years.[121]

When an MRSA control bill was submitted to the California legislature in 2008, APIC, in its panic to kill that legislation, circulated an internal memo calling on its members to do whatever was necessary to stop the law because it represented "another unfunded mandate." In response, I notified then California Governor

---

119 The CDC first published its MDRO guideline in 1986.

120 Ironically, the only control measure that received the highest level rating (category 1A), indicating the most support from scientific studies, was to isolate all colonized and infected patients. However, the only way an institution following the CDC's guideline could come to implement ADI would be through combining two separate options.

121 A similar bill was passed, but not yet implemented, in Pennsylvania just prior to the passage of the Illinois bill, which went into effect immediately.

Arnold Schwarzenegger of APIC's efforts to derail the legislation and sent him a copy of the APIC memo. I was told that the governor subsequently refused a meeting requested by APIC leadership.

The California bill passed largely through the efforts of Carole Moss, who lost her fifteen-year-old son, Nile (whom the law, "Nile's Law," was named after), to MRSA, and actress Alicia Cole, whose fibroid surgery turned into a lifetime nightmare when much of her abdomen had to be removed to stop the MRSA infection that was eating her alive.

The Maryland bill was reintroduced in 2007, 2008, and 2009 thanks to the persistent sponsorship of state Senator Lisa Gladden.

During the 2007 hearing of the bill, Kerri Cardello, a thirty-seven-year-old mother of four testified. Kerri had gone to the ER after accidentally breaking her nose while playing with her children. She was treated and sent home but readmitted several days later with MRSA in her lungs. While she was in a medically induced coma, both of Kerri's legs had to be amputated.

As she sat in her wheelchair, a bag of antibiotic dripping into her vein and a nasal cannula streaming oxygen to her lungs, Kerri removed one of her prosthetic legs to show the committee members the reality of MRSA. When the representative of one of the hospitals blurted out that Cardello was a victim of "community MRSA," not hospital-acquired (even though the representative knew nothing about Kerri's case), Kerri's strapping Marine husband shouted the opponent down, followed by one of the legislators shaking his finger at the opposition representative and yelling, "Had we passed this bill last year she would not have lost her legs!"

Ironically, Kerri Cardello's case can now be found in a medical journal where it is referred to as "hospital-acquired, community-onset MRSA."

But despite studies cropping up year-after-year that Baltimore had egregiously high rates of MRSA infections, the bill died in committee three out of the four years with only the same three legislators voting in favor of it. In the fourth year a vote wasn't even taken.

In 2008, the Chairman of the United States House of Representatives Committee on Oversight and Government Reform, Congressman Henry Waxman, conducted a hearing on the matter of hospital infections on the same day as the Government Accountability Office (GAO) released its report on the issue. The GAO report referenced the CDC's thirteen different guidelines that collectively contain approximately twelve hundred recommendations healthcare facilities can choose from in trying to control hospital-spread disease and the lack of prioritization for those recommendations. During a break in the hearing, I approached the main witness, a doctor who had recently gained notoriety (and lots of funding) for a checklist he compiled on how to safely insert a central line catheter.[122] The institution that the doctor was associated with had successfully used ADI for several years to control MRSA and VRE in its ICUs. I asked the doctor why his hospital was not recommending that all hospitals do likewise. He responded by happily saying, "I'm a fan of ADI!" "So why not recommend it for all hospitals?" I followed. "Well, [the head of infection control] is involved with SHEA..." he responded. "So you mean it's because of politics?" I asked incredulously.

---

122 The doctor's five-step checklist was based on the checklist Boeing Industries developed in 1935 after the maiden flight of the B-17. Shortly after takeoff, the aircraft stalled and crashed. The accident was attributed to the captain's failure to release a simple lock during pre flight preparations. Boeing instituted its checklist policy after a single incident. It has taken decades and untold numbers of lives for American healthcare to only begin to accept such things as a simple checklist that would save the lives of untold numbers of patients. That being said, according to recent data, most central line-associated bloodstream infections (70%) occur *after* the insertion period, or in what is called "the maintenance phase." The celebrated checklist did not include a "maintenance bundle." In other words, it did nothing to address the period of time during which 70% of the infections occur.

The doctor nodded in the affirmative. "But what about the patients?" To that, the doctor, appearing ashamed and saddened, remained silent.

Back in 2002, when Dr. Farr, as President of SHEA, began putting together the committee to draft the 2003 SHEA guideline, the opponents of routine ADI for MRSA and VRE began calling for an exclusive study that would supposedly settle the question of the effectiveness of the approach once and for all.

After British epidemiologist Sir Austin Bradford Hill proposed the use of randomized control trials (RCT) in the 1930s and helped pioneer their utilization to determine the best treatment of tuberculosis in the 1940s, RCTs became widely considered the "gold standard" of clinical studies. In simplified terms, by subjecting two random groups of patients to different strategies, RCTs reduce the possibly of bias, which can skew the results of a study.

However, no one had ever called for an RCT to see if isolation controlled hospital infections for several reasons; one of which was that other epidemiological studies made it clear that isolation worked; another was that ADI had been shown to work controlling very important hospital infections such as multi-drug resistant tuberculosis, SARS, and smallpox.[123] The multi-million dollar, taxpayer funded STAR*ICU trial, which was deployed in March 2005, was the first RCT using isolation to control any hospital infection.

But an RCT can yield false results if poorly designed or conducted. And that, according to at least some experts, is what occurred with the STAR*ICU study.[124] One of the most glaring examples of this was the more

---

123 The operative difference, it seems, between these pathogens and MRSA and VRE is their proclivity to infect healthcare workers and not just patients.

124 One doctor that took part told me that he voiced his objections to the study's design, which he called "awful," from the start. He said that he had been successfully using ADI along the lines of the SHEA guideline for years in his ICUs and went

than five-day delay in reporting the results of the screening cultures due to the use of a central lab rather than each facility's own lab. This meant that patients involved in the study went days without being placed in isolation (some were no longer even in the ICUs when the results came back) allowing for further spread of MRSA and/or VRE. Other design flaws included the extremely short duration of the study,[125] and limiting the study to a single unit in each hospital because surrounding units could have had poorly controlled MRSA and/or VRE, potentially contaminating the unit designated for the study.

After the STAR*ICU RCT was completed in August 2006, it went unpublished for more than four years.[126]

Instead of pushing for control of MRSA and VRE using methods known to be effective, other infection control groups lobbied congress for more taxpayer dollars to fund studies and development of a MRSA vaccine.[127]

In November 2010, the Office of Inspector General (OIG) of the United States Department of Health and Human Services (HHS) released a staggering report on the incidents of medical harm.[128] The HHS OIG report

---

back to that approach when the unit that was participating in the STAR study experienced a spike in MRSA infections.

125 Most similar studies run for a year or more. The STAR*ICU study's intervention phase was deployed for only six months.

126 The STAR*ICU study was finally published in the New England Journal of Medicine (NEJM) in April 2011. A co participant told me that the study was initially rejected and that he was "very surprised" that it was even published and chalked that up to "politics." In light of the Journal's own policy (NEJM November 16, 2000), which states, "When a manuscript is rejected, we are willing to entertain an appeal from the authors, although it is uncommon for us to change an editorial decision." and that a resubmission must be "...not 3 years later and with little change in the manuscript," it is indeed remarkable that the STAR*ICU study was ever published in the New England Journal of Medicine.

127 A vaccine that was purportedly effective in preventing MRSA infections failed in two clinical trials.

128 The report classified 128 "adverse events" into four clinical categories: events related to medication (31%), events related to surgery or other procedures (26%), and events related to infection (15%).

estimated that in 2008, 268,000 patients were harmed as a result of medical care every month! Those conditions, the report stated, contributed to the death of about 15,000 patients per month and that some 65,000 of the conditions were "clearly or likely preventable." What made the report even more shocking was that the numbers of incidents and injured and killed patients involved only those on Medicare, which account for a minority of all hospitalized patients.

But the HHS OIG report is only one of a number of similarly appalling studies or reports that highlight the systemic negligence in America's healthcare system and its adverse impact on patients.[129]

Much has changed since 2004 insofar as patient safety is concerned. The government has been little-by-little cutting payments to hospitals for preventable conditions, and more and more hospitals are instituting ADI programs. For example, the Veterans Administration deployed an ADI program that has reduced MRSA in all VA facilities by approximately 62 percent in the ICUs and 45 percent in other parts of the hospitals. And in 2011, the Maryland Healthcare Commission published a list showing almost every hospital in the state is now using ADI.

But there is obviously much more that needs to be done. Despite hundreds of studies now supporting the approach advocated by the 2003 SHEA guideline, the CDC still has not recommended ADI as a priority

---

129 The following are some of those studies: In 1999, the Institute of Medicine (IOM) reported that as many as 98,000 patients are killed annually as a result of medical error; in 2001, the CDC estimated that one in twenty patients are infected in the hospital, accounting for approximately 100,000 deaths per year; in 2007, the IOM estimated that the average patient experiences at least one medication error per day of hospitalization, resulting in 1.5 million injuries every year; in 2007, the Association for Professionals in Infection Control (APIC) released the results of the largest MRSA prevalence study ever conducted (conducted by Dr. William Jarvis), which suggested that approximately 1.2 million patients are infected with MRSA in hospitals every year; in 2008, the Institute for Healthcare Improvement estimated that there are approximately 15 million incidents of medical harm annually (40,000 per day), which account for some 100,000 deaths each year.

intervention and opponents of ADI are hard at work trying to prevent steps forward. Worse yet, some are even attempting to undo progress thus far made. For example, in June 2011, the California Hospital Association filed a lawsuit to essentially overturn Nile's Law.[130] The suit was joined by APIC and an amicus brief was submitted by SHEA. The STAR*ICU study is being used by opponents to try to discredit ADI. And despite the plethora of studies and voluminous data demonstrating the enormous extent of medical negligence and only the tiny fraction of victims that are compensated for their injuries or loss, the tort reformers continue to demonize plaintiff attorneys, whom they accuse of routinely filing frivolous lawsuits, characterize those seeking justice as blamers hoping to thrust their greedy hands into the deep pockets of the benevolent insurance and pharmaceutical companies and beneficent hospital corporations.

The lion's share of the credit for what progress has thus far been made unfortunately does not go to public health leadership. It goes to consumer advocates across the country that have suffered personal losses and who despite their pain and anguish have worked tirelessly and selflessly for change.

When Abraham Jacobi set up the medical system for the Hebrew Orphan Asylum he included the Reception House in his plan for a reason: by isolating all new admissions for a relatively short period of time, the general population of orphans was protected from infectious disease potentially being brought in. From the time that Dr. Jacobi's protocol was instituted, not a single outbreak of infectious disease occurred over the decades the HOA was in existence. While the Spanish

---

130 The lawsuit, which failed, challenged the state's requirement to report surgical site infections using the CDC's NHSN system. The plaintiffs argued that such reporting was "too burdensome."

flu raged and smallpox and tuberculosis claimed the lives of millions of people combined, thousands of children in the Hebrew Orphan Asylum were kept safe during those years because of Dr. Jacobi's insistence on placing the health and welfare of the children above all else, including money, ego, and politics.

If Rabbi Nelkin was right and the soul can hear, it's certain that my father preferred the sound of TAPS that he heard as a child of six years old, while peering down from the isolation ward of the Reception House in 1921 over the TAPS played for him on June 14, 2004, after his body had been ravaged again and again by diseases passed to him in hospitals.

I wanted to change the world for my father. I wanted to visit his grave and say, *"I did it, Dad; I changed the world for you."*

Chapter Forty-Five

What I sensed but did not fully recognize because of my intense grief during the encounter with the doctor who inappropriately said "You shouldn't talk about what happened to your father," was the attempted subterfuge: the man was Dr. Maisef's brother-in-law.

There were other things that raised my suspicions about Drs. Maisef and Vietik: It made no sense that neither doctor had called me on the morning of March 12th as my father was being readied for transfer to Shock Trauma. Why had neither Dr. Maisef nor Dr. Vietik not seen him or at the very least called to ask how he was during the three months after he was moved to Shock Trauma? Even more obvious, near the end of my father's life I was on my way to his hospital room when I ran into Dr. Vietik. Rather than greet me and ask how my father was doing, Vietik averted her eyes and continued on her way. Most remarkably, why had Dr. Maisef, who had regularly seen me at the synagogue after my father passed away, never expressed his condolences?

The incidents and behavior suggested guilt, but they proved nothing.

However, what my father's medical records revealed went far beyond mere suspicion. And in light of what eventually took place in a courtroom, Maisef and Vietik's behavior was both telling and consistent.

❖ ❖ ❖

"First, do no harm."

Hippocrates
460-370 B.C.

Even without the notoriously illegible handwriting of doctors, nurses, and therapists, attempting to understand a medical chart is a daunting task for a layman. But people who feel they have been wronged, or, as in this case, have lost a loved one due to what they believe to be negligence are angry, hurt, and are therefore very motivated. I spent night after night poring through my father's records and taking notes. And I spent an equal amount of time researching medical terms and conditions on the Internet and studying numerous reference books. What I learned was deeply disturbing, to say the least; and the negligence that I uncovered did *not* begin with my father's hospitalization of February 14, 2004.

After my father had developed the intentional tremor in his right hand, Dr. Chen, the nephrologist, suspected that it was due to the Neurontin that Maisef was prescribing. Dosing many medications for a patient with renal insufficiency is not the same as for someone with normal kidney function, and if this is not taken into consideration adverse reactions and even death can result; this is basic medicine. In my father's case, the Neurontin was building up in his system and causing what is referred to as *neurotoxicity*, or poisoning of the central nervous system. Dr. Chen believed the tremor was a sign of this and had informed Dr, Maisef via fax in May 2003, about six months before my father was stricken with stroke-like symptoms from the drug. She recommended the Neurontin be adjusted to a "renal dose." Subsequently, during my father's first hospitalization following a morning Neurontin attack, Dr. Vietik, Maisef's associate, who had only recently completed her medical residency, suspected problems with the medication as well. She noted that it was likely responsible for some of his symptoms and abnormal laboratory results and she significantly lowered the dosage. Dr. Maisef, who had been practicing medicine for more than two decades, had apparently not read Dr. Chen's fax or Dr. Vietk's notes in my father's chart. Instead, he had in fact *increased* the dosage of Neurontin, which he advised my father to take before bedtime, accounting for the morning attacks of *neurotoxicity*. In addition, remarkably, the only published paper I could find with Dr. Maisef as a coauthor was about *neurotoxicity*. From this one aspect of Maisef's negligence alone, my father had suffered two traumatic hospitalizations.

Furthermore, I discovered at least two other wrong or inappropriate medications that Dr. Maisef had my father taking.[131]

It got much worse.

The beginning of Dr. Maisef's negligence involving my father's February 14th hospitalization started with his admission order in which he wrote that my father had "No known allergies." My father was in fact allergic to penicillin, which Dr. Maisef absolutely knew as evidenced by his own office chart.

Several days after my father was hospitalized at Sunnyside, when his improving condition seemed to reverse course, a pulmonologist examined him and noted,

---

131 According to the Beers List which is a commonly accepted list of medications deemed "inappropriate" for older patients due to their side effects. As a physician whose practice largely consisted of geriatrics, Dr. Maisef should have been very familiar with the Beers List.

"Worsening pneumonia, possibly from nosocomial[132] organisms." The pulmonologist appropriately ordered a boost be added to his IV antibiotic and steroids to reduce inflammation. He also ordered sputum cultures to confirm what organisms were involved.

After the culture report came back positive for two different types of hospital bacteria, one of which was MRSA, days went by and neither Maisef nor Vietik did anything to address the antibiotic-resistant bacterial infection that was now eating away at my father's respiratory tract. A radiology report recommended a bronchoscopy, but neither Maisef nor Vietik ordered it. He developed a mass in his abdomen, a partial collapse of his distal trachea, and acute kidney failure. He was coughing up yellow, green, and rust colored sputum; his legs were beginning to swell; he was having trouble swallowing; his chest burned, "It hurts. It burns" he reported; his white blood cell count was skyrocketing, and his blood sugars were careening out of control. Despite all of this, and more, neither Maisef nor Vietik changed his antibiotic. When my father said to me that he was "suffering here and no one [i.e., Drs. Maisef and Vietik] is doing anything" he was right, and I should have become more aggressive.

Another radiology report recommended biopsy of the mass growing in my father's abdomen, which was now the size of an orange. Neither Maisef nor Vietik ordered the test.

My father's condition continued to worsen: his blood oxygen level began to drop precipitously; he was complaining of increasing pain in his legs, which were continuing to swell, his left leg more so than his right; his pancreas, gallbladder and liver were increasing in mass. Still, neither Maisef nor Vietik changed his antibiotic

---

132 Nosocomial is a Latin term that is usually translated as "hospital-acquired."

and they kept administering the now questionably necessary and otherwise harmful steroids.[133]

Ten days after his admission, a week since the prudent pulmonologist ordered cultures, when his white blood cell count had soared to more than four times the normal level, his blood sugar dangerously dropped to 45, and he was reporting that he was nauseous and weak, my father's antibiotic was finally changed to cover the MRSA that was in his lungs and destroying his organs. However, neither Maisef nor Vietik made the change; it was done by the pulmonologist who checked my father's chart during a follow-up visit two full days after the results were reported.

Over the next six days, a few of my father's symptoms improved, but the edema and pain in his legs continued to increase.

A respiratory therapist noted that my father did not receive treatment because he was "code blue."[134]

On February 29, 2004, Dr. Vietik scheduled my father to be transferred to the sub-acute unit. It was leap day, exactly sixty years to the day since he had landed on Los Negros Island. But this time, he had no idea that he was already in combat, or that there was even an enemy.

The following day, my father was unable to attend any rehab sessions and the swelling in his legs continued, the left still growing bigger than the right. Vietik wrote a note in the chart regarding his legs, stating, "Monitor Carefully." However, the swelling and pain continued to increase; the swelling on his left now extending to his hip and the leg was beginning to change color. Neither Maisef nor Vietik ordered a single test to determine the cause.

---

133 During this period, Dr. Vietik is seeing my father for mere minutes each day and, according to her later testimony, is daily reporting his condition to Dr. Maisef.
134 "Code Blue" means that the patient has stopped breathing. This could have been a mistaken entry. However, my father reported to me that a nurse informed him that he had indeed stopped breathing.

Two days later, Maisef saw my father and wrote a note in the chart to discontinue isolation, which was a clear violation of infection control guidelines,[135] and ordered sputum cultures, although my father was still on vancomycin making cultures practically meaningless.

On March 8th, my mother-in-law, Ruth, and her cousins, Lakey and Norman Kozak, visited my father in the hospital. Sharon and I had to go to the wedding of close friends in which I was asked to participate. It was the only day that I did not see my father. Ruth, Lakey, and Norman took seats around my father who was sitting in a chair, his left leg exposed and elevated and he was complaining about the pain. Ruth noticed the swelling and discoloration and asked him about it. "They're taking me to wound care to see what's wrong," he said. Norman, a World War II army medic, was concerned; he'd seen limbs like that before and he knew what could happen.

My father's white blood cell count was still extremely elevated and neither Maisef nor Vietik seemed to be doing anything. In fact, neither of them ever notified wound care.

The following day, my father's blood sugar dropped precipitously and he was experiencing "severe" abdominal and back pain. Ace wraps were placed on his inflated legs.

The next morning, the pain in his legs, back, and abdomen were increasing and he was "feeling cold all the time."

Later that day, he went for physical therapy, but he was in too much pain and too sick to participate and returned to his room.

On March 11th, the morning I called my father and then spoke with Maisef about his unbearable leg pain,

---

135 This violated the hospital policy, CDC recommendations, and state regulations.

his blood sugar plummeted into the 30s, he was "yelling out" in pain, and his leg was severely discolored, yet neither Maisef nor Vietik did anything despite an urgent call from the laboratory to the nurse and at least two calls from the nurse to Dr. Vietik.[136]

After reading my father's medical records, I no longer had the slightest doubt as to Drs. Maisef and Vietik's culpability. And I was as sick as I was angry; sick about the pain and suffering my father had gone through, and angry with these two doctors for their outrageous, prolonged, and indefensible negligence.

Despite being with my father every day with the exception of March 8th, he told me nothing about the conditions that were revealed in his medical records. I knew my father better than anyone in the world. I knew his medical history and he never failed to tell me what any doctor told him. Therefore, I have no doubt that he was never told by Maisef or Vietik about his increasingly serious condition. And neither Maisef nor Vietik had contacted me during those three and a half weeks... not even once.

In addition to everything else, Dr. Maisef had never ordered the Doppler. It became clear to me that he had come to the hospital on the night of March 11th out of guilt and concern for his own liability, not out of concern for my father. And he had given my father the wrong antibiotic as well as a contraindicated,[137] "whopping" dose of steroids, which only served to exacerbate the infection.

My father was as kind, generous, and forgiving as he was strong and principled. Despite all that had happened to him—the torture, suffering, and even the loss of his leg—had he known of the negligence and had

---

136 In later testimony, a third reference to Dr. Vietik having been called by the nurse that day becomes the subject of some debate.

137 Giving steroids to a hospitalized patient with this type of an infection can cause the bacteria to "gallop," like pouring gasoline on a fire.

Dr. Maisef and Dr. Vietik not abandoned him, he would likely not have wanted me to sue either of them. Had they admitted their mistakes and apologized, even after my father had passed away, he would definitely not have wanted me to sue them; and in either case I would not have simply because my father would not have wanted me to.

Was I supposed to absolve Jerold Maisef for his repeated acts of negligence and deceit simply because three years before he had walked two blocks to see my father? Was I supposed to ignore the months of torturous suffering my father endured, which had ultimately resulted in his death, and had come about largely through Vietik and Maisef's negligence? Was I supposed to pardon these physicians whom my father trusted implicitly but who had abandoned him? Was I supposed to forgive the man who came to my house to protect himself and who lied to me as I cried for my father while he lay in Shock Trauma with his leg cut off and fighting for his life and who had likely sent his brother-in-law to run interference for him while I was grieving for my dead father? Was this man even worthy of absolution? And what about Carmen Vietik who had watched my father suffering and getting sicker and sicker day-after-day yet persisted in giving him steroids and never changed the antibiotic or ordered certain tests or procedures including on his obviously infected leg?

Did I even have the right to forgive them?

I yearned for justice for my father.

Chapter Forty-Six

Deciding to file a lawsuit may come easy to some people; not for me, at least not as far as the doctors were concerned. However, when it came to suing the hospitals I never felt a shred of ambivalence. But even if I were to prevail in a suit, whether against the doctors or the hospitals, it would not bring my father back nor undo his suffering. At best, it would represent a semblance of justice, but justice nonetheless. And holding those accountable for what happened to my father in order to prevent the same from happening to others demanded that I do something. Unfortunately, I cannot go into any facts specifically relating to the hospitals' negligence and the monstrous suffering that my father endured as a result. Nor can I relate the details of the lies and deceit that followed or even why I can't go into all of that. I will say that I offered the hospitals a settlement if they would but implement the 2003 SHEA guideline, but they turned down the offer, saying they were "moving in that direction anyway." After three years of work and a score of depositions, the case against the hospitals was resolved. After the resolution, I said to the lead attorney for the hospitals, "This was never about money," to which the lawyer replied, "I know that," and then added, "but I can't say that about other cases."

Enough said.

Despite what I saw as clear and egregious negligence by Drs. Maisef and Vietik and their abandonment of my father, and more, a part of me remained hesitant to file a suit against them for several reasons: neither of those doctors had acted out of malice and people make mistakes; given the lousy state of healthcare institutions in general, it's clear that doctors who do care about their patients and cannot control what goes on in hospitals are often victims of the same dysfunctional system. And there was another issue that I needed to deal with, one that involved my faith; Jewish law prohibits taking a coreligionist to a secular court in many types of cases without first seeking remedy in a rabbinical court.

To that end, I called the local Bais Din[138] or rabbinic court. But after leaving several messages, no one called me back. Rabbi Hesed suggested that I fax them a brief letter describing what I believed the doctors had done, which I did, and subsequently received a call from the secretary.

After briefly describing what had taken place with my father, the secretary, a kind and elderly-sounding rabbi, was sympathetic and even related how he believed that doctors had negligently killed his wife some years earlier. However, he said, "The Bais Din is not equipped to handle a medical malpractice case. We mostly handle disputes involving money."

Subsequent to my conversation with the Bais Din, Rabbi Hesed suggested that he go with me to meet with whom I will identify as The Esteemed Rabbi. I respected The Esteemed Rabbi and had in fact unsuccessfully tried to reach him several times. Rabbi Hesed, being

---

138 "Bais Din" literally translated from the Hebrew means "House of Law."

a rabbinical insider, had better luck and scheduled a meeting with him.

At the meeting, I related to The Esteemed Rabbi what had happened to my father including the months of torture he was forced to endure and how this was not the result of a single mistake. Then, with tears streaming from my eyes, I tendered an offer to The Esteemed Rabbi: "If the doctors apologize to my family, go to my father's grave and ask for forgiveness, and do something charitable for the public in my father's memory, *there will be no lawsuit.*" I then added, "*But you cannot initiate the offer. You can relate it only if there is an expression of remorse.*" It was the same proposal that I had already conveyed to Rabbi Hesed and two others.

"Give me one day," The Esteemed Rabbi said.

Weeks went by and I heard nothing from The Esteemed Rabbi and the statute of limitations was closing in. The lawsuit was filed.

More than a month later, The Esteemed Rabbi finally called. After apologizing for the long delay in getting back to me, the rabbi said that he had met with Dr. Maisef, but instead of expressing any remorse, according to the rabbi, Dr. Maisef felt he had gone above and beyond in his care for my father.

The lawsuit was indeed going forward.[139]

In preparing the case the first item on the agenda was to get experts to review my father's medical records. For defendant doctors this is easy. They can practically close their eyes, point to a spot in a local physicians'

---

139 The Esteemed Rabbi phoned me a second time several weeks later saying that he thought Maisef was "a nice guy" and that maybe I shouldn't sue him. I reiterated my offer and now added reasonable attorney's fees to it. After he repeatedly pressed me as to how much I thought that might be, of which I had no idea, I threw out what I thought was a reasonable guess, "Ten thousand dollars." I never heard back from The Esteemed Rabbi after that.

directory and are likely to find someone willing to testify that they did everything within the standard of care, regardless, that is, of how egregious the negligence really was.

Plaintiffs, on the other hand, have a much greater burden: Doctors are rarely willing to testify against a colleague, which would surely invite scorn and alienation from others in the medical community. Consequently, victims of malpractice must search for experts from far and wide, regardless of the validity of their case.

In addition, plaintiff attorneys work on contingency, which means they pay all expenses, including expert fees, and are only reimbursed if they prevail in a lawsuit or if there is a settlement. Understandably, even if a case has merit, unless there is a strong likelihood of a significant settlement or a large judgment, plaintiff attorneys will usually reject the case. Defense lawyers don't have that problem; the malpractice insurer pays them no matter what the outcome and will often choose to fight regardless of their client's negligence.

The defendants in my father's case listed some fifteen doctors, all locals, as their experts.

We had two: An infectious diseases expert and board certified in internal medicine, after his fellowship at Stanford University Medical Center, Dr. Larry Rumans spent thirty-two years with the United States Navy as the Commanding Officer of two combat zone fleet hospitals. He also served as the Medical Director of the Shawnee County Health Department in Kansas, and then again with the military as an infectious disease expert during the first Gulf War. With his white hair and mustache, and stalwart bearing, Dr. Rumans looked like a robust version of Marcus Welby, MD. Our other expert was Dr. William Jarvis. Dr. Jarvis' résumé for just the previous ten years totaled seventy-one pages, including a list of four hundred and seventeen published articles, fifty-eight book chapters, three books edited, sixteen editorials, and twenty-nine published letters in prestigious journals, such as the New England Journal of Medicine and the Journal of the American Medical Association, among others.

Combined, Dr. Rumans and Dr. Jarvis found more than a dozen deviations in the standard of care during the three and half weeks my father was hospitalized under the care of Drs. Maisef and Vietik.

Once the experts had been identified and the case filed, depositions of the experts and the fact witnesses began.

When attorney Kohler deposed the defense witnesses, she was generally short and to the point, usually taking little more than an hour and a half. Both Dr. Maisef and Dr. Vietik's depositions, which I attended, were videotaped.

The defendants' attorneys, Bruce Orko and Helga von Flancelaut,[140] weren't so kind. My deposition alone took more than seven hours over a two-day period. Dr. Jarvis' also went on for two days, as did Dr. Rumans' deposition.

Both Dr. Rumans and Dr. Jarvis testified that had it not been for Drs. Maisef and Vietik's negligence, my father would not have lost his leg, and then his life.

From Dr. Jarvis' deposition:[141]

Orko: If Mr. Bennett were diagnosed by Dr. Maisef on the evening of ...March 11th... do you have an opinion as to what Mr. Bennett's outcome would have been?

Jarvis: I think if he would have made a [correct] diagnoses on the night he came in and immediately obtained

---

140 Von Flancelaut, who was the lead defense attorney for the doctors, was not directly involved in the depositions.
141 On the errata sheet, Dr. Jarvis noted 39 errors and/or omissions before signing off on the deposition transcript.

ID (infectious disease) and surgical consultation and the appropriate antibiotic was given and steroids weren't given, that more likely than not Mr. Bennett would not have lost his leg.

Orko: Do you have an opinion whether it would have any effect on his outcome?

Jarvis: Oh, absolutely, because I think as a result of the amputation it led to prolonged hospitalization that he may have avoided if he had not had his leg amputated.

Orko: OK, Any other changes in his outcome?

Jarvis: He would be alive.

Orko: What?

Jarvis: He would be alive.

As the trial date approached, I asked attorney Kohler to relay to the defense counsel my long-standing offer for the doctors to avoid the trial. Concerned that it would only be perceived as weakness, she advised against it. There was no weakness. There had been no let-up in my grief *or* my determination to get justice for my father.

The Trial

Before opening statements, the court needed to hear arguments and rule on motions to limit testimony or evidence. These so-called *motions in limine*[142] are standard fare in the American judicial system. Their purpose is to keep the trial focused on the allegations and the facts of the case. However, lawyers routinely file *motions in limine* in an effort to prevent evidence or testimony that does not serve their client's interest from coming before the jury. Lawyers von Flancelaut and Orko filed eight such motions, some of which contained multiple subdivisions:

---

142 Latin for "At the threshold."

- To preclude the plaintiffs from mentioning that Norman Kozak was an army medic and therefore an expert familiar with wounds.
- To exclude Dr. Jarvis from testifying as an expert witness.
- To exclude the claim that Dr. Vietik did not have a medical plan of action regarding Mark Bennett's infected leg.[143]
- To preclude eliciting any testimony about Michael Bennett's efforts to fight tort reform legislation and to pass infection-control legislation because "...a jury might infer from those activities that he has more knowledge than a layperson or that his suit has merit."
- To preclude plaintiffs from eliciting testimony about Dr. Maisef's prescribing overdoses of Neurontin.
- To preclude plaintiffs "...from alleging numerous infection related allegations...."
- To preclude suggesting that Drs. Maisef and Vietik failed to control Mark Bennett's blood sugars.
- To preclude "Plaintiffs from eliciting testimony that Mr. Bennett had an abdominal [mass] whose etiology may not have been definitively diagnosed or from suggesting in any way that Drs. Maisef and Vietik acted inappropriately by failing to determine the source of Mr. Bennett's abdominal mass."[144]

---

143 This is to block statements made by Dr. Vietik to Sharon Bennett when she arrived at the hospital on the morning of March 12th.

144 In her deposition, Dr. Vietik testified that she did not order the recommended test because my father had "declined it." When asked for something in writing to that affect, Vietik stated that it was only a verbal agreement! When asked why she did not contact Michael Bennett about this or any other issue during the entire hospitalization, Vietik, in stark contrast to her prideful pronouncement of communicating with patients and their families, said that she assumed Dr. Maisef was doing that, despite the documented fact that she was the admitting as well as the treating physician in the sub-acute unit. There were also indications during her deposition that Vietik was willing to throw Maisef under the bus, particularly on the matter of his prescribing a stress-dose of steroids on the night of March 11th, which she called

Based on the questions that the defense attorneys had asked at various depositions, attorney Kohler filed two *motions in limine*:

- To preclude the defense from asking lay witnesses about medical conditions or scientific evidence.
- To preclude any contributory negligence by Mark Bennett for the loss of his own leg because he allegedly "failed to keep his legs elevated."

Before ruling on the motions, the judge invites the attorneys to his chambers to explore the possibility of settling the case.

The conference begins with Judge Ralph Leslie Mudd making reference to my father's age: "Eighty-eight years-old! Maybe I should apply for a second mortgage?"

In his seventies and officially retired,[145] Judge Mudd is a scrawny, stoop-postured man with dingy looking hair on his balding pate and a sinus-clogged voice. My father could have run circles around him while singing a Broadway tune.

Acting on instructions from the insurance company she represents,[146] attorney von Flancelaut refuses to settle.

After returning to the courtroom, Judge Mudd asks that everyone be identified. When von Flancelaut introduces Dr. Maisef, Judge Mudd, seeking clarification on how to pronounce his name, inquires, "Mai-sef, with the three [sic] syllables?"

"unusual." She also opined that the swelling of my father's left leg was related to the arthroscopic knee surgery of two years prior. Ironically, that surgery had been performed on his right leg.

145 As of 2011, besides their generous pensions, retired judges in Maryland who process cases receive up to an additional 1/3 of their salaries.

146 The Medical Mutual Liability Insurance Society was a doctor owned company that insured approximately 85% of the physicians in Maryland, a virtual monopoly. It had a notorious reputation for not settling lawsuits as well as egregiously raising doctors' premiums (which sparked an insurance crisis in the state in 2005) despite diminished payouts and an ever-increasing surplus. Many of the state's defense attorneys refused to take Med Mutual's cases because they paid so poorly.

Judge Mudd next cautions against any demonstrations that might influence the jury: "I don't want any dramatic moments where the jury's attention [is drawn] to a person who...is not under oath on the witness stand." It is an appropriate admonition. However, in delivering it, the judge makes certain that it is directed to me above anyone else.

In arguing the defense's *motions in limine*, consider this exchange between Judge Mudd and attorney Orko on the matter of excluding testimony about Dr. Maisef ordering the "whopping dose" of contraindicated steroids on the night of March 11th for what he believed to be typical cellulitis:

Orko: At the end of the day it doesn't matter what it was for, because the issue is whether or not it caused damage.

Mudd: By suppressing the immune system excessively?

Orko: Or doing anything! Or whether turning green, or purple, or...

Judge Mudd reaches the matter of contributory negligence, i.e., that my father was responsible for losing his leg:

"There is a sub, quasi, a faux allegation that the decedent did not at sometimes elevate his legs. Is that not with tongue and cheek?" asked the judge with a chuckle.

"I wouldn't call it faux because that's French for false..." attorney Orko began to say.

"Exactly, that's why I used it," interrupted the judge.

"I don't believe it's a faux allegation," Orko pressed.

"F.A.U.X. is the one I meant," Judge Mudd stressed.

While attorney Orko, crossing his arms as if hugging himself, attempts to convince the judge that there is

evidence to support his premise, the judge again interrupts him:

"I can't hardly believe that you're going to present
a serious case on this...Do you have an expert that is
going to so say that based upon a fact that you can
assume will be in the record?"

Attorney Orko, nervously rubbing his hands together,
tries to respond: "I am your honor...plaintiff experts...
I...are willing to support...would certainly even agree
with my *premise*. Now I imagine that they don't think
that that's the case, but it's...I mean...this is...this is,
this is common knowledge. This is..." and the stum-
bling lawyer shrugs.

"The question is where is it common in the record?
That's what I'm interested in," inquires the judge.

"To the record," whispers von Flancelaut to her overgrown understudy, who makes a final, desperate, stammering attempt to salvage his sinking ship:

"A...I...I...I can't cite specifically as I stand here to
a...a...record of an expert, *but,* I believe the record, the
medical record, alone is enough...."

"I don't believe that it is. Thank you," Judge Mudd
concludes, ending the debate on this shameless attempt
to blame my father for his own death...but only for the
moment.

Judge Mudd's rulings on the motions:

- Motion to exclude Mr. Kozak as an expert witness granted in part and denied in part. [Kozak,
  the medic, could not say that Mark Bennett's leg
  "worried" him.][147]

---

147 What Kozak actually said was that it "scared" him. By changing the word to
"worry" the defense was making Kozak's statement sound more like a medical opinion, which the judge hastily disallowed. This type of subtle spin became a common
defense tactic throughout the trial

- Motion to exclude Dr. Jarvis as an expert witness heard and denied.
- Motion to exclude statement of daughter-in-law heard and granted.
- Motion to exclude mention of Michael Bennett as Patient Advocate heard and granted.
- Motion to exclude mention of over-dose [sic] given by Dr. Maisef heard and granted.[148]
- Motion to exclude mention that hypo glycemo [sic] can cause injury heard and granted in part and denied in part.
- Motion to exclude mention of abdominal [mass] heard and granted.
- Motion to use placards in opening statement granted in part [and] denied in part.[149]

Sitting at the plaintiff's table listening to attorneys von Flancelaut and Orko trying to stack the deck against my father and making disparaging references to him as a dying man with one foot in the grave and the other on a banana peel and who was "in denial," a "turkey baster" for infections, and responsible for the loss of his leg and his own death gave me an insight into why some people lose control and unfortunately take the law into their own hands. And listening as the judge excluded legitimate evidence while sounding self-righteous made me wonder about trusting the justice system.

The judge has precluded the jury from watching Dr. Vietik testify in her deposition that my father "declined" to have the growing abdominal mass tested. My father was more likely to have run the Boston Marathon than he would have refused *anything* a doctor recommended. Since his contracting malaria on Los Negros in 1944

---

148 This ruling excluded Dr. Chen's May 2003 fax to Dr. Maisef about reducing the dose of Neurontin from coming into evidence.

149 Defense counsel objected to use of the phrase "Rules of the Road" to describe standard of care to a lay jury.

because he did not take Atabrine, a doctor's advice was sacrosanct to him. "I don't question doctors," he often said, even toward the end of his fatal hospitalization.

The jury will also not learn about the overdose of Neurontin that Dr. Maisef had prescribed for eight continuous months after being advised not to by the nephrologist, Dr. Chen. Nor will they learn that the United States Department of Justice (DOJ) levied the largest *criminal* fine in history against a drug manufacturer in 2004 when it slammed Pfizer[150] to the tune of $430 million for off-label[151] marketing of the same drug.

From the DOJ press release on the matter of Neurontin:

"The Department of Justice is committed to rooting out health care fraud," said Associate Attorney General Robert McCallum. "It is of paramount importance that the Department use every legal tool at its disposal to assure the health and safety of the consumers of America's health care system and to pursue companies and individuals that steal from the taxpayers and inflict suffering on patients and families..."[152]

In 2010, Pfizer was ordered to pay an additional $142 million for violating the Racketeer Influenced and Corrupt Organizations Act (RICO)[153] for promoting Neurontin for unapproved purposes.

---

150 The fine was levied against Warner-Lambert and Parke-Davis, which were purchased by Pfizer in 2000.
151 "Off-label" is a term used to describe the prescribing of drugs for other than approved purposes. In this case, Neurontin, which is an expensive drug, was approved only for use as an anti-seizure medication for conditions such as epilepsy. Doctors all over the country were paid to attend lavish affairs where they were provided false or misleading information about the drug and otherwise induced into prescribing it to patients for a variety of unapproved purposes.
152 USDOJ Press Release of Thursday, May 13, 2004.
153 The same law used by federal law enforcement to prosecute organized crime figures.

Extracts from attorney Kohler's opening statement:

"We're in this courtroom today because in February of 2004, Mark Bennett, who you will hear was an 88-year-young gentleman, and I say he was a young gentleman because as you will hear by everyone's account he was "affable," he was "a wonderful man," he was "fully independent," he was "living independently with his son", "doing", "driving", "walking", "fully mentally competent."[154]

"In February 2004, he put his trust and his life into the hands of his primary care doctors...

"And you will also hear from the evidence that after four weeks under the care of Dr. Maisef and his colleague Dr. Vietik, when they were directing his care and managing his care, Mr. Bennett, who had walked into the hospital on February 14th, 2004, was rushed to Shock Trauma because his left leg, that had been perfectly normal when he came into the hospital, looked like this (shows poster of 21 thumbnail photographs; an audible gasp is heard from the jury box). He was rushed to Shock Trauma. And at Shock Trauma, unfortunately, because he had been taken there too late, his left leg was amputated...and for the next three months he went from Shock Trauma to Kernan to Pleasantville, and finally to Beauford Hospital.

"For three months, you will hear about the pain and the suffering and the torture that he underwent, until June 13, 2004, two days after his eighty-ninth birthday, he died...

"You will hear from every witness that knew Mark Bennett, including Drs. Maisef and Vietik, that Mark Bennett was an extraordinary man. You will hear that he was...a self-made man and he made himself over several times because of the adversities in his life. You

---

154 The defendant doctors themselves used all of these adjectives during their depositions.

will hear that he was raised in an orphanage from a very young age. You will hear that he served in the army during World War II. That he served in the Pacific. That he was injured in battle. That he came home and then he went to Hollywood and became an actor...

"In Hollywood, he met Michael and Leon's mother... they had these two sons, first Leon, and about twenty months later Michael came along...

"He did some producing and then he went into the Stock Market. Understand that Mark Bennett was a self-made man. He had not gone to college. He had come from an orphanage with absolutely nothing to his name and he became fairly successful...until the early 70s, when the Stock Market crashed...

"The other thing that you'll hear about Mark Bennett is that in the early 60s, his marriage to Michael and Leon's mother ended in divorce and there was a custody battle and Mark Bennett won custody of his two young sons, something that's a bit unusual in 2008 and that was highly unusual in the 1960s... and how that's a testament of his love and his affection for his two sons...

"...how after the Stock Market crashed and he just about lost everything and again he reinvented himself...

"He is a man whose optimism allowed him to overcome the adversities in his life...

"Everybody understands that everybody's life comes to an end. But there is a difference between walking to the end of the pier and being pushed off.

"Thank you ladies and gentlemen."

During attorney Kohler's presentation, Judge Mudd made a point of interrupting her three times, saying, in essence, to hurry along. Between his pre-trial conference disparaging remark, his rulings on the *motions in limine*, and now his unwarranted intervention in the plaintiffs' opening statement, it became clear that we were dealing with, at the least, a biased judge.

When during her opening statement attorney Kohler lifted a large poster of my father, remembering the judge's warning about dramatic moments drawing the jury's attention I struggled to contain my welling emotions. The image of my father being reduced to the two dimensional figure of a victim was overwhelming.

In contrast, ignoring Judge Mudd's admonition and clearly acting on the instructions of their lawyers, Drs. Maisef and Vietik engaged in a pathetic charade of pointing and smiling at the large photograph as if they were filled with joy at seeing the man they so fondly remembered.

Attorney Helga von Flancelaut, a barrel-shaped woman with a tight smile, husky voice, and a demeanor to match, ponderously walked to the front of the jury box to deliver her opening statement.

The following are extracts from her astonishingly fictional presentation, which was delivered with an abundance of cheap, transparent melodrama:

"Dr. Vietik is what I call a dynamo; she's a firecracker, wanted to become a doctor at age eight and did everything she could to get there. *Where she is!*

"Dr. Vietik is expecting her second child as we sit here today. You may see her leave from time to time. *Please forgive her.*

"Dr. Maisef in contrast, the elder statesman, is a Baltimore boy. He was born and raised here. His grandmother had a house over in East Baltimore and scrubbed the marble steps that we all know and love, in Baltimore...He is a quiet, unassuming man. He's not arrogant. He is not boastful. And even more than that, he's one of the only doctors I know that still makes house calls. That's who Dr. Maisef is. And in fact, in this particular case, what you'll hear is that the very first time that he met Mark Bennett he did it at the request of the family—for a house call. And he went over shortly after Mr. Bennett moved from California. And he went... because Mr. Bennett was having some breathing difficulties. Not unusual for an eighty-eight, uh, eighty-six-year-old man. Not terribly concerning. Dr. Maisef felt he should go over and see him...

"From that point on he had a relationship, a physician-patient relationship. And keep in mind that that relationship was between Mr. Mark Bennett and Dr. Maisef, because these were two individuals who were seeking and getting care. Now, that's sometimes one of those sticky lines that we all run into, cuz we take care of our parents, and we think that if we take care of our parents then *we have the right to know and do and be involved in everything!* But in actuality we don't. There's a relationship between a patient and a doctor and sometimes family members don't tell or don't want to tell other family members what's going on. And it's not unusual for that to happen with the elderly, *cuz they're proud and they're private and they're doing what all of us do and that is sort of to deny the inevitable, that our bodies are slowly breaking down and we're coming to the end of our lives...*

"You will hear that Dr. Maisef was *terribly upset* at Mark Bennett's death, as he should be...

"Now you've heard some offerings here that I believe the term was 'eighty-eight-years-young' and that he was a very kind and gentle man. From all the reports he was likeable, enjoyable, happy. *But he was eighty-eight,* and as in all *eighty-eight-year-old* individuals they start to fail and what you're gonna see in this case and it's gonna be important, because it's gonna give ya' context

516

and that's gonna be important in this case to keep it into CONTEXT...

"What you're gonna see...to me, and I don't mean to depreciate Mr. Bennett, it's sorta like a dam, you getta little trickle here, a little trickle here, a little trickle here, as the dam starting to fail and all of a sudden you have an overwhelming failure. And that's what was going on with Mr. Bennett toward the end of his life...

"Dr. Vietik...she's a young lady, attractive, Mr. Bennett sorta liked Dr. Vietik cummin in to work with him...

"Myelodysplastic Syndrome—that's a pre-leukemia... every infection that comes down the pike you get, and some that don't even come down the pike you get. And that's going to be *very* important in this case...

"Now the family all this time was under the belief that there was a drug that Mr. Bennett was on, Neurontin. Neurontin is used to give relief to the pain that diabetics can get in their hands and their feet...He was given this drug, the nephrologist was aware of it...

"What's go'in on with Mr. Bennett is what's go'in on with all of us, whether we like to admit it or not. So let me introduce the great elephant in the room, as they would say, and talk a little bit about that and dying.

"We spend most of our lives denying. That's our greatest ally...at some point after we get done denying we might move into blame. It's somebody else's fault, it's something else going on, it's... (Attorney Kohler speaks up, "I hate to interrupt, but I think we're getting well into argument, your honor." Judge Mudd responds, "Well, I think we're skirting on it, but we haven't crossed the slope yet." "I didn't think I was either," von Flancelaut says before continuing.) Once we get beyond blame, then hopefully we get to acceptance. Then, when we get to acceptance we start to pray for an easy death. Sometimes death isn't easy and sometimes it's not short, it's not quick and unfortunately that's what then happened to Mr. Bennett...

"...When he was on the MRSA Contact Isolation protocol that [they claim] Dr. Maisef (deep, sarcastic tone) violated hospital policy.... In 2004, people were just sorta figuring out, ya' know, what this MRSA thing was all about. At that time everybody thought it was to protect the healthcare workers from MRSA and the other bugs...'If I keep him on contact isolation precautions, he's not allowed to go to OT[155] and PT,[156] which means he will then get shipped to a nursing home. Or do I take him off of contact isolation thinking I'm not gonna hurt any of the healthcare providers because he's not coughing anymore, he's not gonna be contagious to them...' So Dr. Maisef made a decision, which he thought was in the best interest of his patient, and he did that. Course now he's getting accused of causing yet another infection, which brings us to VRE.

"Again, let's make it truthful and not exaggerated. What happened is that when he went to [Shock Trauma] he was found to be colonized with [VRE], which means that the bacteria was [sic] in his body BUT IT WASN'T MAKING HIM SICK! It was [just] there. The thing about being colonized is that you can be colonized anytime, anyplace, (chuckling) anywhere...to suggest that he was colonized in that little window when he was taken off contact isolation is nothing more than a great guess. And that's not legitimate in this courtroom. And it didn't make him sick...didn't make him sick.

"The issue is really what happened to Mark Bennett's leg... (holding up the photograph) My G-d! This is horrible! This is horrible! This is necrotizing fasciitis. IT IS RARE, RARE, RARE, some doctors will never see it in all of their years of being physicians. *This is horrible!* And I can tell you that Dr. Maisef didn't see anything like this

---

155 Occupational Therapy.
156 Physical Therapy.

on the 11th. *I can tell you that 'cuz neither did his son.*
WHAT SON (pointing an accusing finger at me) WOULD
LEAVE HIS FATHER WITH A LEG LOOKING LIKE THIS
AND GO HOME AND GO TO SLEEP!

"Now what did Dr. Maisef know? He knew he got a
phone call from the family...he could have easily called
his partner Dr. Vietik who I'm sure would have gone
in...but Dr. Maisef cares about his patients. And so he
left his family at eight o'clock at night and he came into
the hospital to see his patient, who he cares about...

"They [Maisef and Vietik] just happened to be there
when the dam burst...

"What you'll hear is that the family was quite upset.
Every family would be. You'll hear that they had issues
at Kernan. I believe they called a police officer on one
of the nurses there. They'll have issues at Pleasantville.
They'll have issues at Beauford...

"You're gonna hear from Dr. Jarvis, who they're
gonna bring in, and interestingly Dr. Jarvis, *he's a pediatrician and then he's going to testify in a case involving
an eighty-eight-year-old man...*I would ask you, listen to
his testimony, keep thinking in your mind, 'If I've got an
eighty-eight-year-old father in the hospital, do I want a
pediatrician to care for my dad...?

"The defense is going to bring up a number of experts
*that are community docs! They work in and around Balti-
more! This is what they do! They're doctors! They're not
'experts.' They don't have web sites in advertising their
services for hire coming into a courtroom...*

"They're going to be asking for money. We're going
to be saying *please don't, because there's no negligence
here.*

Switching now to honeyed tones, Von Flancelaut
concludes:

"This is a very important day for my clients. It's their opportunity to be redeemed. *Because they cared for their patient and to be accused of killing him is a really difficult thing to live with.*

"Thank you."

Judge Mudd did not interrupt a single time.

Chapter Forty-Seven

*"Better to reign in Hell than to serve
in Heaven, is that it?"*
—The Devil's Advocate, 1997

"**H**ave you ever been cultured for VRE or MRSA or any of those bugs?" attorney von Flancelaut, acting coy, asks Sharon; a *pffttt* of disgust is heard from the jury box. "No," she responds in a small voice, sounding perplexed. "Your house?" the defense lawyer shoots back. "No," she replies, now appearing a little intimidated.

During the direct-examination, Sharon's honest, sweet demeanor as she retold of her father-in-law's activities from running errands, doing car pools, taking people to lunch, playing golf, even joining the local JCC and exercising several times a week made her too sympathetic of a witness for the courtroom bully to attack head on. Instead, attorney von Flancelaut used Sharon's occupation as a set-up for one of the most shameful of the multitude of loathsome tactics she will eventually employ.

It had taken almost two days to get Sharon on the witness stand because of von Flancelaut's motions to exclude evidence and/or limit our experts' testimony. Drawing things out at this stage was to her advantage—all of her witnesses were *"community docs!"* Our experts, on the other hand, had traveled from afar and were staying in hotels.

After Sharon completed her testimony, Dr. Rumans enters the courtroom. While he waits to be sworn in, a bench conference is called. It is the first of what will be more than a score of such stoppages.

But before the conference begins, Judge Mudd calls upon a foreign observer—a young man from Germany that is interning at von Flancelaut's law firm[157]—to approach the bench. After chatting about Germany and commenting on the beauty of the language and the country, Judge Mudd asks the young intern if judges in Germany wear "those little bibs" on their robes. It is only one example of Mudd's frivolous time wasting. On other occasions during the trial he will take calls on his cell phone and invite the German intern to join him in his chambers.

Attorney von Flancelaut is asking the court to exclude three important pieces of evidence from the plaintiffs' case: one item is a widely used and highly respected reference book titled *Principles and Practices of Infectious Diseases*,[158] commonly referred to as *Mandell's*—the primary author's name; the second item the defense wants kept away from the jury is an equally respected physicians' reference book called *Harrison's*, and the third is the *Johns Hopkins Hospital ABX* (antibiotic) *Guide*.

---

157 Shortly before the trial, the law firm that von Flancelaut worked for experienced an upheaval; the entire medical negligence section of what was a long-standing and otherwise respected outfit walked out, leaving only von Flancelaut and Orko.
158 The fourth edition, published in 1995.

Von Flancelaut argues that the three books should be excluded because the plaintiffs failed to disclose them as potential reference sources during the discovery period before trial. Attorney Kohler counters that all three books should be allowed for the following reasons: Dr. Rumans had referenced *Mandell's* in his deposition as being "certainly reasonably reliable," which met the legal standard for use in court; Dr. Maisef in his deposition testimony referred to *Harrison's* as "the gold standard," and the *Johns Hopkins ABX Guide* was edited by one of the defense witnesses, Dr. Paul Auwaerter,[159] and authored by his boss Dr. John Bartlett[160], chief of infectious disease at Johns Hopkins Hospital. In addition, two days prior to Dr. Ruman's testimony, attorney von Flancelaut and attorney Kohler exchanged phone calls as well as emails on this very issue and both *Mandell's* and the Hopkins' guide were identified.

To appreciate the importance of these references and why the defense wants to keep them out of the trial, some background is needed:

Bacteria are divided into two large groups based on their reaction to a particular diagnostic test called a *Gram Stain*. Bacteria that turn a particular color when exposed to a dye are designated *Gram-positive,* and those that turn a different color *Gram-negative.* Not all antibiotics are effective against both groups of bacteria, whether they are resistant organisms or not. For example, an antibiotic that is effective against normal staph bacteria may not be affective against MRSA or e-coli, all three of which are *Gram-positive*. Also, an antibiotic that is effective against a *gram-negative* may not be effective against a *Gram-positive,* and vice versa.

---

159 Dr. Auwaerter was never called to testify, which was fortuitous for the defense. I discovered that he had been quoted in a newspaper article describing the appearance of necrotizing fasciitis almost exactly as that which Dr. Maisef had seen on the night of March 11th, and we had prepared a blowup of that quote.
160 I debated Dr. Bartlett on a 2005 cable television show.

During the time my father was a patient, *Gram-negative* bacteria caused up to more than 71% of the majority of hospital infections.[161]

The antibiotic that Dr. Maisef prescribed on the night of March 11th, the one that he made sure to tell his patient's housepainter son was "the right antibiotic" while my father had just come out of surgery to amputate his leg, was called Ancef. It is an antibiotic that belongs to a class of drugs called First-generation cephalosporins. Here is the pertinent reference from *Mandell's* that the defense wants kept away from the eyes and ears of the jury:

"...First-generation cephalosporins...because of their limited activity against Gram-negative bacilli are not appropriate choices for empiric[162] therapy of nosocomial infections."

The species of bacteria that had destroyed my father's leg was citrobacter, a *Gram-negative* bacterium. By the afternoon of March 12th when Dr. Maisef made his comment to me about "the right antibiotic," he knew that he had given my father the wrong antibiotic.

The reason that attorney von Flancelaut wants to keep *Harrison's* out is because the signs and symptoms of necrotizing fasciitis as described in this "gold standard" reference book are identical to Maisef's own notes from the night of the 11th, as well as what he had testified to in deposition. And the reference contradicts one of the main defense arguments—that necrotizing fasciitis could not have been reasonably diagnosed earlier than the morning of March 12th.

The *Johns Hopkins ABX Guide* clearly states that Maisef's use of Ancef for a nosocomial, complex soft-tissue infection was a breach in the standard of care.

---

161 Weinstein et al. Clinical Infectious Diseases, March 2005. Based on data from 1986-2003.

162 As it applies to treating infections, 'empiric' means choosing an antibiotic that would be effective on the pathogens likely to be causing the infection before positive identification is made through culture results.

Here is Judge Mudd's ruling on the motion, which he pointedly directs at attorney Kohler:

"I develop a bias, late arrivals, I can't come up with a polite expression. You would be outraged if this happened to you."

Needless to say, Judge Mudd grants the defense motion and excludes all three reference books from the plaintiffs' case.

Subsequent to yet another bench conference, during which Judge Mudd referred to him as "Rummage," Dr. Rumans is sworn in.

After establishing him as an expert by going through his credentials, attorney Kohler begins her direct-examination:

Dr. Rumans testifies extensively as to my father's general health and addresses the issues of his preexisting conditions: diabetes, which was very well controlled, and renal insufficiency, which he characterized as "minimal to moderate." He states that my father had no chronic lung disorders, no congestive heart failure (CHF) and that his ejection fraction, the rate at which the heart pumps out blood, was "normal."[163]

Dr. Rumans then addresses the issue of myelodysplasia (which von Flancelaut had sprung in her opening statement), saying that the condition "doesn't appear to have any impact" on my father having had a proclivity to infections.

As attorney Kohler is advancing on the question of my father's life expectancy prior to his hospitalization, attorney von Flancelaut objects and the judge calls for a bench conference:

---

163 These opinions were based on tests that were performed during my father's 2004 hospitalization and the accompanying reports, as well as the medical records, including those of Dr. Maisef.

Judge Mudd: You're asking a very unusual question...I am very uncomfortable with all of your questions about life expectancy...

Attorney Kohler tries to explain that doctors routinely refer to life expectancy and informs the judge that there is a universally accepted actuarial chart, aka "Life Tables," that is commonly used in courts and by insurance companies.

Von Flancelaut: Our testimony is going to be that he lived exactly what he was expected to live...

Judge Mudd: What would [Rumans] testimony be?

Kohler: 4-5 years (the actuarial chart stated 4.9 years).

Judge Mudd: That's ridiculous! You're making me regurgitate, to allow a witness to say that... [What is this] a new specialty, mortuologist? *I will not accept nonsense like that!!*

After the lunch break, attorney von Flancelaut introduces a motion to have the wrongful death charge dismissed because, as she says in so many words, Dr. Rumans cannot establish that the necrotizing fasciitis directly caused my father's death. Ostensibly, she bases her argument on the law, which she reads to the judge as stating the negligence must be *the* cause of death.

The problem with the defense attorney's rendering of the law, as attorney Kohler struggles to bring to the attention of the obviously slow-witted Judge Mudd, is that the statute actually states that the negligence must be *a* cause of the death not *the* cause of death, a critical difference. When that tact doesn't seem to be working for her, attorney von Flancelaut tries to define the statute as meaning "at least fifty-one percent," which is yet another fabrication.

After swaying in all directions for what seems an interminable amount of time, Judge Mudd finally, properly rules against the defense motion.

When testimony resumes, Dr. Ruman's states that by unnecessarily continuing the steroids Drs. Maisef and Vietik caused my father's blood sugars to run wild; fluid to collect in his limbs, and suppressed his immune system, all of which placed him at extreme risk for infection. Adding to the life and limb threatening combination was Dr. Vietik's failure to assess my father's leg when symptoms of pain and discoloration had been noted. And the coup de grace, Dr. Maisef's misdiagnoses of "cellulitis" and "vasculitis" and his administering of the wrong antibiotic and the whopping additional dose of steroids[164] on the night of March 11th.

Dr. Rumans concludes his testimony:

Kohler: In your opinion, to a reasonable degree of medical probability what if any treatment did Dr. Maisef prescribe on the night of March 11th that was effective for treating necrotizing fasciitis?

Rumans: *None.*

Kohler: In your opinion, to a reasonable degree of medical probability, by prescribing the Ancef and Solumedrol (the steroid), as you have already described, what if any damage occurred to Mr. Bennett?

Rumans: In my opinion, there was allowed progression of the infection, ma'am.

Kohler: Doctor, if both the correct antibiotic had been administered and surgery consult had been obtained, do you have an opinion to a reasonable degree of medical probability as to whether or not Mr. Bennett's leg would have avoided amputation?

---

164 Dr. Maisef testified that he prescribed this "stress dose" of steroids because he suspected "vasculitis," a condition that Dr. Rumans testified was "absolutely remote." Since my father was already on steroids, albeit improperly, he would not have had developed a condition, according to Dr. Rumans, "in the presence of the very medication used for its treatment."

Rumans: Yes ma'am. In my opinion Mr. Bennett would not have required amputation had those steps been taken appropriately on the evening of the 11th of March.

Kohler: Now, if Mr. Bennett had not developed necrotizing fasciitis and suffered his leg amputation, do you have an opinion to a reasonable degree of medical probability with regard to whether or not Mr. Bennett would have returned home?

Rumans: Yes ma'am.

Kohler: What's that opinion?

Rumans: In my opinion had he not developed the necrotizing fasciitis he would have completed the course of rehabilitation and he would have returned home at that point.

Attorney Kohler next addresses the issue of Dr. Maisef taking my father off of contact isolation in violation of the hospital's policy and how that had led to his acquisition of VRE:

Rumans: He had so acquired another type of resistant bacteria, which had been identified at the time of his admission to [Shock Trauma] called... *vancomycin-resistant Enterococcus*, V.R.E.... and he developed what we call sepsis as a result of the VRE infection...and he passed away.

Attorney Kohler proceeds to put the cork in the bottle by eliciting testimony on just how Dr. Maisef breached the standard of care when he violated the hospital's policy on infection control. To do so, she is going to produce the institution's written policy and procedures for controlling multi-drug resistant organisms, such as MRSA, VRE, and C. difficile. Naturally, attorney von Flancelaut objects and calls for yet another bench conference with the frequently eager-to-accommodate-the-defense Judge Mudd:

Judge Mudd: (laughing) Is this the right witness for that? Where does he live, Kansas?

Judge Mudd then questions as to whether or not this is even the actual document, stating, "It's not been authenticated," to which attorney von Flancelaut immediately echoes, "It's not been authenticated." Attorney Kohler explains that the document was produced by the hospitals in discovery and marked as an exhibit and that "it is consistent with the CDC guidelines." To that, attorney von Flancelaut intones, "That's (the CDC guidelines) not the standard of care!" Remarkably, Judge Mudd sustains the objection but grants the plaintiffs' some leeway in trying to bring the information (but not the document) in through some other line of questioning. It is probably the first time in history that a judge rules that the CDC guidelines, or even a hospital's own guidelines, are not the standard of care.

As attorney Kohler tries to restart her questioning by explaining the hospital's policy, attorney von Flancelaut objects and another bench conference is called:

Judge Mudd: I don't think this is salvageable
Kohler: In the infectious disease, contact isolation world, the standard of care with putting people in isolation is to follow the hospital's policy guidelines because they're there for a reason and there's no good reason *not* to do it.
Judge Mudd: I think that, frankly that makes not an intellectual sense to me.

Attorney Kohler, unable to reason with the illogical judge and therefore unable to even refer to the document's information, undaunted, pursues the line of questioning but without referencing the document:

Kohler: Now. Doctor, have you formed an opinion to a reasonable degree of medical probability as to what damage if any was caused by taking Mark Bennett off contact isolation in violation of the standard of care?

Rumans: In my opinion it resulted in the subsequent occurrence of VRE.

Attorney Helga von Flancelaut uses her husky voice, obnoxious personality, and rotund physique as weapons of intimidation and theatre for the jury. When arguing her motions to exclude evidence and such, the corpulent barristress stood behind the defense table raising her voice and punching the air in emphasis and often times even talking over the judge. When questioning the plaintiffs' experts, von Flancelaut will stroll around the entire area between the jury box and the witness stand to keep the jurors attention focused on her. She will antagonizingly get into the face of the doctor, bark a question, and then turn her back and walk away in contempt even before the witness begins his response. At other times, she will stand in the middle of the courtroom shaking her notes at the witness while cynically asking a rhetorical question, and then shoot back another before the witness has completed his response.

Cross-examination:

After a few questions about Dr. Ruman's professional history, which are meant to create the impression that he is weak in certain areas of medical experience, such as repeatedly asking about his three years with the health department in Kansas, attorney von Flancelaut goes to the issue of myelodysplasia, the syndrome that she promised the jury had played such an important role in what happened to my father by predisposing him to one infection after another, "even some that don't come down the pike."

Using an easel set up near the witness stand, von Flancelaut writes out the syndrome as she enunciates each syllable, "MYE-LO-DYS-PLAS-TIC-SYN-DROME." She intends to list a column of symptoms of this disease to demonstrate that my father was unavoidably susceptible to infection. Dr. Rumans asks her to make an additional column to list the conditions related to myelodysplasia that my father *did not have*. Von Flancelaut reluctantly agrees. Dr. Rumans adroitly answers each question and then pointedly pulls the rug right out from under the belligerent defense lawyer:

Rumans: You want to describe myelodysplasia syndrome as being what places a person at risk for infection and that occurs only when there is a reduction in the white blood cell count or in the neutrophil count, and Mr. Bennett *never had that.*

Von Flancelaut: So you would disagree that 40% of the deaths from myelodysplastic syndrome are due to infection, you would disagree with that?

Rumans: I don't know what the percentage is but it doesn't make any difference because Mr. Bennett didn't have that component.

Von Falncelaut: But he did have myelodysplastic syndrome?

Rumans: Yes ma'am. But he did not have leukopenia, he did not have neutropenia, and indeed he was able to respond quite well to situations where he needed an elevated white blood cell count *and he did that routinely.*

So ended von Flancelaut's promised demonstration of the importance of, as she called it, "myelodysplastic syndrome," her mostly vacant chart sat moribund on the easel.

The only area where von Flancelaut made some impact was on the issue of my father's kidney dysfunction, which Dr. Rumans had characterized as "mild" and then revised to "moderate." However, Rumans was not without a basis for his first opinion. My father's baseline kidney insufficiency was mild but had worsened due to dehydration caused by illness in the hospital, and, as Dr. Rumans had testified to, it rebounded to his baseline level.[165] Even Dr. Maisef in his deposition testimony admitted that my father could have gone years without the need for dialysis. But any small opening such as this gave rise to attorney von Flancelaut's bombastic pronouncements and exaggerated intonations meant to humiliate the witness in front of the jury and appear as though she had hit one out of the park.

After completing his testimony, disgusted by the affected behavior of the defense counsel, Dr. Rumans commented to attorney Kohler, "*She's blowing smoke all over the courtroom.*"

In substance, attorney von Flancelaut's cross-examination of Dr. Rumans was a failure. However, she succeeded in making certain the jury knew my father's age: she referenced it eighteen times during the approximately one hour questioning.

Before Dr. Jarvis is sworn in, the judge calls both attorneys to the bench:

Never one to miss an opportunity to turn the screws on the plaintiffs, Judge Mudd warns attorney Kohler not to be "laborious" when establishing Dr. Jarvis' qualifications as an expert. Attorney Kohler counters that while she will not be repetitious, she needs to preserve for what will be a likely appeal "no matter who wins" anything that the defense might attack so she has to be thorough:

Kohler: There is not one individual in the world that has done more investigations of MRSA and VRE and contact isolation and that's not just investigations, it goes to how the infections work…"

---

165 In his sworn deposition, one of the defense experts characterized my father's kidney function as "Borderline renal insufficiency."

Judge Mudd: What are you going to give him saint-hood or something? You wanna make him a saint?

Kohler: I want to make him the most highly qualified expert they're (the jury) going to hear from on certain issues in this case.

After Dr. Jarvis is sworn in, attorney Kohler hurriedly goes through his training as a physician, his experience, his work with the CDC, his investigations of outbreaks, and so on. Judge Mudd interrupts the questioning several times and repeatedly telegraphs his sighs and seat-shifts of annoyance and impatience to the entire courtroom.

In concluding her direct-examination for the day, anticipating von Flancelaut's attack on one area of the doctor's specialty, attorney Kohler asks the following:

Kohler: With regard to the diagnoses and treatment of cellulitis, necrotizing fasciitis, VRE, pneumonia, C. difficile, citrobacter, what, if any, difference is there in diagnoses and treatment approach between pediatric patients and adults?

Jarvis: None

During her cross-examination, attorney von Flancelaut asks Dr. Jarvis a litany of questions (while liberally employing her scowling, air punching, note waving, exaggerated intonations, cutting off the witness' answers, talking over the judge and contemptuous laughter) as to the doctor's clinical experience with adults, including such irrelevancies as surgery. Despite multiple objections from attorney Kohler (particularly regarding von Flancelaut's not allowing the witness to finish his answers), Judge Mudd does little to intervene. And this time, during her fifteen minutes of fame, attorney von Flancelaut manages to reference my father's age thirteen times.

The trial convenes for the day.

The following morning, the defense calls for a bench conference prior to the start of Dr. Jarvis' direct examination. It is a final attempt to have him excluded from testifying specifically about Dr. Maisef's use of the steroids and the antibiotic Ancef on the night of March 11th as having *caused* any direct damage. Dr. Jarvis' vast knowledge of infectious disease diagnoses and treatment notwithstanding, the judge rules in favor of the defense thusly:

Judge Mudd: I think the issue is very clear Ms. Kohler and I may be wrong. It may be wrong of me to isolate these meds...these bad med decisions, uh, and say that they're unacceptable because they do not contribute to the causal relationship in this case. I may be wrong because making...presenting the wrong meds to a patient paints a picture of a negligent doctor in general...[166]

Oh how true Judge Mudd's last words are, "a negligent doctor in general," indeed.

Attorney von Flancelaut next attempts to, yet again, prevent Dr. Jarvis from testifying about the standard of care. When it doesn't look like the judge is going to rule in her favor, von Flancelaut shifts to a different strategy—she asks attorney Kohler to stipulate to a standing objection to any testimony by Dr. Jarvis on the standard of care. According to attorney von Flancelaut, making one objection after another will delay the progress of the trial and that is something she does not want to do!

---

166 Mudd is saying that these drugs may have been wrong but testifying as such would unfairly imply that Maisef was a negligent doctor! This is similar to Mudd's reasoning for excluding Maisef's overprescribing of Neurontin by not permitting Dr. Chen's fax into evidence.

Attorney Kohler is happy to stipulate. What will actually take place during Dr. Jarvis' testimony, however, is revealing insofar as von Flancelaut's true motive in asking for the stipulation.

Dr. Jarvis' testimony should have taken little more than an hour. Instead, it went on for two days due to the twenty-two defense objections, thirteen bench conferences, and Judge Mudd's numerous interruptions of attorney Kohler's questioning of the doctor. It appeared that von Flancelaut's motion for a standing objection was to throw the plaintiffs, and perhaps the judge as well, off-guard and cause such havoc with Dr. Jarvis' testimony so as to make it incomprehensible to the jury and unbearably tortuous to sit through. The constant attacks by the defense made it impossible for attorney Kohler to establish momentum. And Judge Mudd's frequent inability to grasp or remember the arguments, or even his previous rulings, kept jamming her; one minute she was permitted to pursue a line of questioning, the next minute she was not.

Nevertheless, it was attorney Kohler's dogged persistence and reminding him about the issues and his rulings that brought Judge Mudd back to earth on several occasions. But insofar as the jury, who had no idea why she kept getting interrupted, was concerned, attorney Kohler appeared unable or unwilling to follow the judge's instructions or that perhaps she was trying to pull something over on the court.

Whether because of bias or some other syndrome, Judge Mudd not only aided and abetted von Flancelaut by allowing her to bully the court, at times he became an active participant by attacking attorney Kohler in the presence of the jury.

Dr. Jarvis' direct-examination:

Dr. Jarvis testifies at length that Drs. Maisef and Vietik's use of the steroids was inappropriate for virtually the same reasons that Dr. Rumans had testified. He also goes into detail about the risk of high blood sugars predisposing the patient to infections and how combined with the immunosupression caused by the steroids my father was at even greater risk. To emphasize the point, Dr. Jarvis explains to the jury that Drs. Maisef and Vietik had a particular duty to be vigilant about infection in a diabetic under any circumstances.

But Jarvis is prohibited by the judge's ruling from offering his opinion on all of these matters as being a *breach of the standard of care*. He can simply state his opinion.

Bolstering the argument about Drs. Maisef and Vietik's failure to rapidly taper and stop the steroids, attorney Kohler asks Dr. Jarvis, who authored an entire book on nosocomial pneumonia, the following:

Kohler: In Mark Bennett's case, when he was moved to the sub-acute unit on March the 1st, what if any respiratory problems was he having at that time?

Jarvis: I don't believe he was having any respiratory problems at that time

Kohler: What if any risk would there be to have stopped the steroids [on March 1st], as you have said, "cold turkey"?

Jarvis: ...he could have been off at that point.[167]

Attorney Kohler then focuses attention on Dr. Vietik's role in my father's care on the 11th of March, the same day when at about 7:30 A.M. I contacted Dr. Maisef about my father's complaint of excruciating pain in his leg. The medical chart indicated that the nurse had

---

[167] Patients who are on prolonged steroid therapy (months, or even years) must be slowly weaned lest a potentially lethal condition called "adrenal crisis" develops. The defense was planning on using this argument to justify Maisef and Vietik's continued use of the steroids, despite the fact that my father had been on them for mere days.

called Dr. Vietik at least two, and possibly three, times that afternoon about pain and the precipitous drop in his blood sugars:

Kohler: Do you have an opinion to a reasonable degree of medical probability as to whether Dr. Vietik met the standard of care in her treatment of Mark Bennett on March 11th?
Jarvis: Yes.
Kohler: And what is that opinion?
Jarvis: That she should have seen the patient.
Kohler: Why?
Jarvis: Because the patient had changed, *dramatically*. And not just on the 11th, but it had been going on intermittently on the 8th, 9th, and 10th, and [on the 11th] it's going on continuously.

Attorney Kohler is getting ready to have Dr. Jarvis read the nurse's notes about calling Dr. Vietik that day when attorney von Flancelaut calls for a ruling from the bench:

Judge Mudd: ...you have low blood sugars and you have pain, wouldn't you think low blood sugars would bring in the doctor...lickety-split?
Von Flancelaut: No! No!
Judge Mudd: With the numbers I've heard....
Von Flancelaut: No!
Judge Mudd: (chuckling cynically) I don't like your choice of doctors.
And then the frequently arbitrary and capricious Mudd rules thusly:
"Just because something is in the [medical] record doesn't mean you have to read it."

While attorney Kohler is attempting to elicit testimony from Dr. Jarvis about what my father's leg would have looked like on March 11th had Dr. Vietik responded to any of the phone calls from the hospital nurse that day, Judge Mudd, who had permitted the line of questioning at a bench conference, interrupts attorney Kohler as soon as she asks her first question, saying, "See, now you're doing what we talked about. I think you've polluted the pond, [you] can't swim in it." Attorney Kohler struggles to maintain her composure.

When attorney Kohler moves to the subject of VRE that my father had acquired and how that led directly to his death, following a defense objection, the jury is asked to leave the courtroom and attorney von Flancelaut argues that Dr. Jarvis should not be permitted to testify on the matter, again, ostensibly, because he lacks experience. When Judge Mudd appears as if he is going to rule in favor of the defense, attorney Kohler's emotions almost overcome her as she implores, *"Your honor you're taking away my entire case!"*

In his magnanimity, Judge Mudd allows attorney Kohler to question Dr. Jarvis on an issue about which he is quite literally the world's foremost expert:

Kohler: Can you describe for us, in the general population, what is the likelihood that any folks [are] walking around being colonized with VRE?

Jarvis: It is extremely rare particularly in the United States to have anyone outside of the hospital setting to be colonized with VRE.[168]

Kohler: Doctor, can you tell us to a reasonable degree of medical probability as to what the likelihood was of Mr. Bennett [becoming colonized] with VRE in the first ten days of his hospitalization?[169]

---

168 Dr. Jarvis also stated that in Europe, about 20% of pig farmers were found colonized, but never infected, with VRE consequential to the use of an antibiotic in animal feed that has "never been used in the United States."
169 When he was not on vancomycin.

Jarvis: I think the likelihood of his being colonized was very low.

Dr. Jarvis goes on to describe how VRE is not part of normal intestinal or "gut" flora, and that people who may acquire the bacteria but are not exposed to vancomycin do not harbor VRE, as the normal bacteria in the GI tract overwhelms the bug.

Attorney Kohler then sets up the argument for Dr. Maisef's improper removal of my father from contact isolation contributing to his acquiring VRE:

Kohler: Dr. Jarvis, have you had occasion over the years to study the literature as to the effectiveness of contact isolation in controlling the spread of VRE and MRSA?
Jarvis: Yes.
Kohler: Tell us a little about that experience.
Jarvis: There have been a number of studies looking at transmission of VRE and MRSA.[170] One study at the University of Virginia[171] found that the risk of transmission if you did not place a patient in contact isolation if you didn't have MRSA versus if you did, the risk is of transmission is sixteen-to-twenty-fold higher....

Defense cross-examination:

"I've got some questions for your *boy*," attorney von Flancelaut snarls at attorney Kohler before beginning her cross-examination of Dr. Jarvis.

Von Flancelaut goes right to work challenging Dr. Jarvis' statements that people who have had no contact with the healthcare system are not colonized with VRE. In so doing, she produces a CDC publication from

---

170 As of 2004, there were more than 60 such studies supporting the effectiveness of contact isolation in controlling MRSA and VRE. To date, there are hundreds of such studies.

171 Here, he is referring to the study involving Dr. Farr that gave impetus to the drafting of the 2003 SHEA guideline for controlling nosocomial MRSA and VRE.

1994 of a study that Dr. Jarvis took part in. The study simply states that they considered people with certain risk factors who might be in jeopardy of acquiring VRE. The fourteen-year-old study, which was written at a time when VRE was relatively new, does not contradict anything Dr. Jarvis has said and in no way supports what von Flancelaut is trying to establish—that practically anyone can become colonized with VRE.

When that scheme fails, she switches to the issue of vancomycin exposure:

Von Flancelaut: What information or knowledge do you have regarding Mr. Bennett's health history and antimicrobial therapy prior to the time he came to Maryland?

Jarvis: None.

Von Flancelaut: Did you go back as part of your (sarcastic) *epidemiological study* on Mr. Bennett and determine whether at ANY TIME in his life prior to 2001 if he had exposure to vancomycin?

Jarvis: No I didn't look at that but there's no reason to look at that because vancomycin is not a risk factor [for acquiring VRE] if I received vancomycin when I was two years old I wouldn't have VRE now. It's proximity to the time you have the infection, usually within a matter of weeks within the time you have the infection not six months before.

Failing again, she throws out a flare:

Von Flancelaut: You would agree doctor that once colonized with VRE you have it indefinitely.

Jarvis: No I would not agree with that.

Abandoning her attempt at discrediting Dr. Jarvis' statements on VRE and her client's violation of infection control procedures, attorney von Flancelaut, banking on a gullible jury, sets up a straw man and asks Dr. Jarvis a series of questions about his experience as a surgeon, and in so doing hits on my father's age several more times before ending her cross examination.

In addition to her failure to shake the witness, attorney von Flancelaut also made one major mistake: she asked Dr. Jarvis whether or not Ancef is the proper drug to treat a strep infection. We will see later her devilish reason for doing this.

Plaintiffs' redirect-examination:

Attorney Kohler proceeds to walk into the door that the defense had just opened, and that Judge Mudd had previously closed:

Kohler: Doctor, in your opinion to a reasonable degree of medical probability was Ancef the appropriate drug...?
Jarvis: No (goes on to explain that my father was in the hospital for several weeks at that point and that Ancef does not cover many of the hospital bugs).
Attorney Kohler asks Dr. Jarvis to further explain Ancef and how it "failed on the job with Mr. Bennett."
Jarvis: Ancef is relatively narrow. It's an older drug, a first-generation cephalosporin [now we are on] fourth-generation [cephalosporin]... [Ancef] would not cover MRSA, VRE, *gram-negative* organisms, such as citrobacter...there's a lot of organisms that you're not covering when you choose Ancef.

With doctor Jarvis' testimony completed, it is time to turn to the fact witnesses:
Leon is called first. His testimony is relatively brief and focuses on his description of my father's activities in California as well as in Maryland, to where he had

made several visits over the three years that my father was living with us.

When Leon's testimony is completed (the defense did not cross-examine him), Judge Mudd is informed that a judge in Los Angeles was ordering Leon back to California for a custody trial that awaited resolution before the school year started. Before leaving for Maryland, Leon had notified the court of his father's trial and that it was reasonably expected to last five days. The California judge agreed to recess the case for that period of time. However, at this point, thanks to the defense's strategic delays, the case has already taken five days and the plaintiffs' case is not yet finished. Attorney Kohler wants Judge Mudd to inform the jury as to the reason why Leon will not be in court the following week so that they should not infer anything else from his absence. The judge agrees and so instructs the jury. Nevertheless, predictably, attorney von Flancelaut plans to use Leon's absence to her clients' advantage.

Ruth is the next witness to testify. She is questioned by nurse-attorney Elizabeth Frey, attorney Kohler's capable second-seat. After describing my father's viability and his activities, such as luncheons, playing golf, driving car pools, caring for the kids when they were home from school due to illness, and so on, eighty-four-year-old Ruth, five feet tall, her head appearing barely above the top of the witness stand, with a pronounced southern drawl describes what she saw and heard on March 8th while visiting my father together with her cousins, Lakey and Norman Kozak:

Ruth: He was sittin in this chair and he had his legs up on this stool, and one [leg] was a lot more swollen than the other and he kept saying that they were going to take him up to the wound center, whatever that was. I guess the hospital had one; they'd been sayin that for a few days cuz his leg was swollen and it didn't look good, it was...dark color...it didn't look good at all...it's hard to describe, but it was a lot bigger than the other one...it didn't look good at all, it was a dark color in relation to the other [leg]...it was...I don't know how to describe it, brownish, dusty, whatever. It didn't look good to me, it hurt him and he was concerned and he kept sayin they were going to take him to the wound center.

Responding to attorney Frey's questions, Ruth goes on to describe the pain and sufferings that she witnessed my father endure throughout the rest of his hospitalizations before concluding thusly:

Frey: How has Michael been affected by his father's death?

Ruth: You know, anybody who has lost a parent is in a pretty bad way, but Michael took it even harder because he really felt that his father didn't have to die because of everything...

Von Flancelaut: Objection.

Judge Mudd: Sustained, any cross-examination?

Orko: While I'd love to continue a conversation with Ms. Leibowitz, I think we'll just leave it alone. No questions.

The court adjourns for the weekend.

Monday morning:

Kohler: The Plaintiffs call Michael Bennett.

For the next four hours, I will testify about my father's life history from early childhood until his move to Baltimore in 2001 and my relationship with him. Things are moving at a good clip with few interruptions by either the judge or the defense until we reach the time frame when my father suffered from the effects of the drug Neurontin. Attorney von Flancelaut asks to approach the bench.

Von Flancelaut has already managed to get the obtuse Judge Mudd to exclude the nephrologist's report of May 2003, which confirmed Dr. Maisef's negligence in prescribing overdoses of Neurontin and its toxic effect on my father. Now, she is determined to prevent me from testifying as to what I witnessed insofar as the drug's devastating effects, which would undermine her theory that my father was a sick, old man knocking on death's door, while her clients, Drs. Maisef and Vietik, are in fact heroes.

In the face of attorney von Flancelaut's demands, Judge Mudd states, "I cannot prohibit this witness from testifying to the facts." But those words, coming from the erratic judge, soon become meaningless. As I testify of my father's independence, Judge Mudd, as opposed to the defense counsel, interrupts and calls for a bench conference. The conference goes on for almost an hour. Rather than suffer you, dear reader, through all of Judge Ralph Leslie Mudd's tortured logic, here is a summary, spiced with just a little satire, of what took place:

Judge Mudd: You're aware, Mr. Bennett, that we have a very serious issue here with Neurontin. I say serious because the defense doesn't want you talking about it.

Bennett: Yes sir, I know they don't. But it happens to be a fact.

Judge Mudd: Now you've said that your father was independent and I believe that, by the way, you speak very succinctly, but if he's independent, how could you know anything about Neurontin?

Bennett: We'll, sir, when we built a room for him after he came out from California he didn't remain locked in it for three years.

Judge Mudd: Yes, but his decision to leave his room was his own. You've testified to that. See the conflict?

Bennett: Huh?

Judge Mudd: You can't debate that now, no Neurontin talk, Mr. Bennett I know you like to debate, I've noticed that.

Bennett: Huh?

Judge Mudd: You should have been a lawyer.

Bennett: Not after what I've seen take place here (everyone laughs).

Kohler: Judge; he knows exactly what happened with the Neurontin. He was there! He called the neurologist! He picked his father up off the floor. He picked up the new prescription; he even has it with him here in the courtroom, his wife spoke with the nephrologist. *He knows the facts because he was intimately involved!*

Judge Mudd: Oh that's convenient. Just so happens that he knows the critical issue of this case, what a coincidence, because of good trial preparation?[172]

Kohler: It's factual testimony your honor. IT IS THE TRUTH!

Judge Mudd: You're telling me the decedent was independent and then he wasn't independent. Don't you see the problem with that Ms. Kohler?

Kohler: It was different times and different circumstances your honor.

Judge Mudd: What time is it?

Kohler: January 2004.

Judge Mudd: You have no basis for that.

Kohler: I haven't gotten there yet your honor. I'm laying the foundation.

Judge Mudd: My notes don't say anything about 2004.

Kohler: I haven't gotten there yet your honor.

(Attorney Kohler repeats the sequence of events involving the Neurontin overdoses.}

Judge Mudd: I've heard you say that. But how does this witness know that?

---

172 In fact, attorney Kohler and I never discussed any of my testimony before trial. We had one brief meeting during which she advised me to tell the truth, be myself, and not to "guild the lily," in other words don't embellish on anything.

Kohler: HE KNOWS THE FACTS YOUR HONOR.

Judge Mudd: On what basis?

Kohler: HIS FATHER LIVED WITH HIM. HE WAS INTIMATELY INVOLVED.

Judge Mudd: There you go again. How could he be independent and still live with his father? Don't you see the logic?

Kohler: No.

Judge Mudd: I'll explain it to you. We know that Mr. Bennett was in-de-pen-dent. Therefore, he could not have been de-pen-dent. When he collapsed from Neurontin and suffered two hospitalizations and was found not to have pneumonia, he did it all by himself. And as far as the nephrologist and the neurologist are concerned, I've already ruled that those facts aren't permitted even though they're relevant and part of the medical record. Don't you see that Ms. Kohler? It's obvious.

Kohler: I'm trying to explain to you, *your honor*, that Mr. Bennett didn't stop taking Neurontin after suffering stroke-like symptoms in a vacuum. But if you insist that was the case, I'll have to live with that. It is what it is.

Judge Mudd: Listen. Michael Bennett can't talk about Neurontin no matter what he knows. He can't simply relay facts just because he was involved and even though I said I couldn't prevent him from relating facts. Did I say that? Only the defense can talk about Neurontin and only to support their allegation that your client and the decedent are in denial...uh...I mean *were* in denial...uh...whatever. That's the end of it...final...period. I've tried my best. I've got to be fair to the defense. But I do find this case very interesting.

Von Flancelaut: Does that mean he can't talk about the Neurontin?

Judge Mudd: No, he can, but only *after* the trial.

When testimony finally resumes, attorney Kohler asks me to relate the conversation about the myelodysplasia note with Dr. Vietik.

As I retell exactly what had happened and the doctor's shoving the issue to the side by repeatedly telling me "It's nothing, forget about it..." my attention is drawn to Dr. Vietik, who is flapping her hands in protest and croaking, "It's not true!"

No one other than Dr. Vietik can say if she was lying or if she honestly did not recall the incident. But not even she could deny that Judge Mudd had warned everyone at the beginning of the trial against any demonstrations or outbursts that might influence the jury. Just as her and Dr. Maisef's pantomime charade during attorney Kohler's opening statement went unpunished by the chronically mucus-impacted Mudd, Dr. Vietik's obvious eruption, whether real or contrived, provokes no judicial response. Although, as you dear reader will soon be stunned, Judge Mudd will see fit to launch into a vehement pontification against a plaintiffs' witness for something that allegedly takes place *outside* of the courtroom during a recess.

Attorney Kohler closes in on the events of March 11th:

Kohler: When if at all did you become aware of any complaints your father had about his lower extremities?

Bennett: The first that I can recall was on the 10th of March.

Kohler: What contact were you having with your father at the point in time that you became aware of these complaints?

Bennett: I was with him in his room on the night of the 10th of March.

Kohler: Did he tell you how he was feeling?

Bennett: Yes.

Kohler: What did he tell you?

Bennett: He said he was absolutely miserable, he was in pain, he was cold, he had intense abdominal cramping, *just awful*.

Kohler: Did he tell you where the pain was?

Bennett: He said his leg hurt.

Kohler: Did you visualize…did you look at the leg that night?

Bennett: No I did not.

Kohler: Did you leave the hospital that evening?

Bennett: Yes.

Kohler: Did you talk to your father the next morning?

Bennett: Yes.

Kohler: And at that point in time did he tell you how he was feeling?

Bennett: Yes.

Kohler: And what did he tell you?

Bennett: He told me he was in excruciating pain from his leg.

Kohler: What did you do if anything with that information?

Bennett: I called Dr. Maisef's office number, his exchange.

Kohler: Were you able to reach Dr. Maisef right away?

Bennett: No.

Kohler: Were you able to reach Dr. Maisef at all that morning?

Bennett: Dr. Maisef called me back.

Kohler: Did you talk to him?

Bennett: Yes.

Kohler: Tell us what you said and tell us what Dr. Maisef said.

Bennett: I told Dr. Maisef what was reported to me by my father and I made the suggestion that a Doppler should be done on his leg.[173]

---

173 Because of the hearsay rule, I was not permitted to relate my conversation with my wife, Sharon, who said to me, "They should be doing a Doppler."

Kohler: And what did Dr. Maisef say in response?

Bennett: Dr. Maisef said, "I was going to order a Doppler with or without you or your wife's suggestion."

Kohler: Now. Did you see your father on the 11th?

Bennett: Yes.

Kohler: So this phone conversation was on the morning of the 11th?

Bennett: Correct, about seven-thirty eight o'clock in the morning.

Kohler: And you went to visit your father that evening in the hospital?

Bennett: Yes.

Kohler: About what time did you get to the hospital?

Bennett: Approximately eight o'clock in the evening.

Kohler: And did you see your father at that time?

Bennett: I did. I came with my youngest son, Yoni.

Kohler: Tell us what you saw when you get to your father's room.

Bennett: I saw my father sitting in a chair, his leg severely discolored from his ankle to his knee and he was in excruciating pain, the kind of pain that he could hardly talk through. His leg was swollen.

Kohler: At any point in the few days leading up to March 11th did you have occasion to visually see your father's left leg?

Bennett: No. I don't recall seeing his leg earlier that week.

Kohler: Did your father say anything about how he was feeling on the evening of March 11th when you saw the leg?

Bennett: He said he was in extreme, excruciating pain.

Kohler: What did you do?

Bennett: I asked the nurse what was happening with my father's leg.

Kohler: You can't tell us what the nurse said.[174] What did you next do?

Bennett: I called my wife and asked her to call Dr. Maisef.

Kohler: Did you ask her to do anything else when you asked her to call Dr. Maisef?

Bennett: I explained to her what was happening with my father's leg, what I saw, the pain that he was in and that Dr. Maisef should come down to the hospital right away.

Kohler: Did you yourself talk to Dr. Maisef by phone?

Bennett: No.

Kohler: Did Dr. Maisef arrive at the hospital?

Bennett: Yes.

Kohler: About when did he arrive at the hospital?

Bennett: Approximately a half hour to forty-five minutes after I made that initial contact with my wife.

Kohler: How was your father doing in that half hour to forty-five minutes between the time you first made the call to Dr. Maisef and Dr. Maisef arrived?

Bennett: Exactly the same. He was in extreme, extreme pain.

Kohler: When Dr. Maisef arrived, did you see him arrive at the hospital?

Bennett: Yes.

Kohler: And how was it that you saw him arrive?

Bennett: I saw him coming down the hallway.

Kohler: What did you do next?

Bennett: I walked towards him to greet him.

Kohler: What happened next?

Bennett: I said thank you for coming.

Kohler: And did he say anything in return?

---

174 Again, because of the hearsay rule I was not permitted to relay that the nurse had said, "I don't know, it's been like that since I came here," and that the Doppler was "negative."

Bennett: He said, "I'm not supposed to be here." I said nothing in return to that and I just walked with him towards my father's room.

Kohler: And after he said, "I'm not supposed to be here" what did he say next or what did he do next?

Bennett: He walked towards my father's room, as soon as he could see my father, maybe several feet away, he looked at him and he looked at his leg and my father was trying to get relief by standing or sitting...there was a walker in front of him, he was trying to get some relief, he couldn't get any relief, and Dr. Maisef looked at this, and looked at the leg, and said, "Yuk, that doesn't look too good."

Kohler: And what happened next?

Bennett: Dr. Maisef bent down next to my father's leg and he said, "Does this hurt here?" and he pushed on a spot or he touched a spot on my father's leg and my father shot back in even greater pain the way that you would recoil if you would bang your finger with a hammer. And Dr. Maisef then said, "This looks like some sort of cellulitis."

Kohler: And what did Dr. Maisef do next?

Bennett: Dr. Maisef wrote a prescription, gave it to the nurse, told the nurse to get him in bed, elevate the leg with pillows, and that's what he did.

Kohler: And what if anything did Dr. Maisef do next?

Bennett: He wrote a note of some sort and I escorted him down the hall to a door where a physician would exit that unit. I thanked him for coming and he said, "I'll have Dr. Vietik see him first in the morning."

Kohler: Were you with Dr. Maisef the entire time when he was evaluating and examining your father?

Bennett: Yes.

Kohler: Other than touching your father's leg, as you have already described, what if anything did Dr. Maisef do—writing kind of marks on the leg, drawing on the leg—anything like that?

Bennett: Nothing.

Kohler: You described to us that your father's leg was discolored, can you describe for us with precision what you remember about that?

Bennett: His leg was *severely* discolored—red, fairly dark red, marbled red from his ankle to his knee. There were dark purple patches throughout that same area (gesturing in a vertical motion along the front of the shin bone) and the leg was exceedingly swollen and he was as I've stated in *extreme pain, extreme pain.*

Kohler: Now I want to show you what has been marked as exhibit 1-A (the contact sheet of 21 photographs). Do you recognize this?

Bennett: I do.

Kohler: And how do you recognize it?

Bennett: Because I know my father's leg.

Kohler: This contact sheet, this contact sheet. Do you recognize that?

Bennett: Yes

Kohler: How do you recognize this contact sheet?

Von Flancelaut: Objection.

Judge Mudd: Overruled.

Bennett: I've seen it.

Kohler: Ok. And when did you first see it and how did it come to be in your possession?

Bennett: I first saw it at the hospital in the medical records department and it came into my possession through my requesting of the wound care nurses who treated my father on the day that was taken.

A bench conference is called to address the defense objection that what I saw on the night of the 11th was not the same as the photographs, which were taken on the morning of the 12th:

Judge Mudd: I suppose he can say what he saw on the 11th?

Von Flancelaut: He didn't see the leg on the 12th.

Attorney Kohler tells the judge that Michael Bennett is going to describe what he saw on the night of the 11th as compared to what is depicted in the photographs. Judge Mudd overrules the defense's objection.

Attorney Kohler asks me to come off the witness stand and, using large blow-ups of the contact sheet, describe to the jury what I saw on the night of the 11th as compared to what was depicted in the photographs of the morning of the 12th.

The purple patches, the red marbling, the extreme swelling are virtually the same. What is different however, are two large blisters, an area of broken skin, and what appears to be a bluish tinge on the underside of my father's toes. All in all, I state that what I saw on the night of the 11th was about 75% of that which is depicted in the photographs.

Attorney Kohler asks me to retake the stand and continues the questioning:

Kohler: After Dr. Maisef left the hospital that evening, what did you do next?

Bennett: I returned to my father's room, with my son Yoni, and I saw the nurse putting my father into the bed, getting him situated and I said 'Goodnight Dad. I'll talk to you in the morning,' and I left and I went home.

Next, attorney Kohler walks me through the events of March 12-13. After I retell of Dr. Maisef's house visit and his statement "I would never bet against that man. I would never bet against that man," I turn to face Maisef whose elbows are on the defense table, hands steepled in front of his mouth, and I accusingly state, "*And then he said, 'It was the right antibiotic.'*" Maisef shows no emotion.

After a long question and answer session retelling the story of my father's hospitalizations following the amputation of his leg, attorney Kohler asks about my father's condition when he was finally admitted to the Pleasantville rehab facility:

Kohler: Can you describe for us your father's physical condition at Pleasantville both from your observations and from what your father related to you?

Bennett: My father was exceedingly sick. He had grown even more debilitated...he began to become depressed and at one point said, "Why can't we just end it all."

Kohler: Is that a sentiment that your father had ever expressed to you?

Bennett: *Oh no.* My father had been kicked down in life from the time he was a little kid and he *never* gave up. That's one of the things that made him my hero. This was a complete turnaround. This destroyed him.

Attorney Kohler continues to question me about all of the events leading up to June 13, 2004, the day my father passed away.

The hours long testimony, which is punctuated by periods of raw emotion as I relive the events surrounding the unnecessary and horrific death of my father, the father whose soul was bound together with mine, concludes thusly:

Kohler: Now. Can you describe for us, Mr. Bennett, what impact your father's death has had on you?

Bennett: *It's not just my father's death; it's how my father died. It's because of how my father died; the torture that he went through over those four months. The impact that it has had on me is beyond anything that I would have ever expected from losing my father, which I was never in denial about. I walk around in grief. I walk around in anguish. I go to bed with it and I wake up to it. I drive down the highway or the street and I start crying like I'm crying now and I have to pull over because I can't see. I still have to function, I have five children. My wife, who is an incredible human being...but it's affected me and I know it's affected them because they see me; they see I'm not the same person. So you ask how it's affected me. It's affected me in a myriad of ways and none of them good....*

Kohler: Now Mr. Bennett, you recognize that your father was 89 at the time of his death...

Bennett: I absolutely do recognize that

Kohler: And did you know that he wasn't going to live forever?

Bennett: Of course I knew my father wasn't going to live forever. In fact, one of the great things about my dad is that *from the time that I was a kid, when we lived together in that one-bedroom apartment, he told me, he knew how close I was to him and he would tell me, "Mike, you know," he'd find occasion to say, "I'm not gonna live forever," and I knew it. I didn't wanna hear it, I loved my dad and I didn't want to hear that one day he was going to die. But he had prepared me that way. And so no, I was not in denial at any point in my life—and neither was my father.*

Kohler: Thank you your honor, nothing further.

The jury is dismissed for lunch, I am asked to leave the courtroom, and attorney Kohler motions the court to restrict what she suspects will be the defense's next strategy—to blame my father for the amputation of his leg because it was "his decision."

Attorney von Flancelaut argues that when Dr. Sharon Henry called me on the afternoon of March 12th as I was on my way to Shock Trauma, what she related about having told my father of the two options, debridement or amputation, meant that my father did not have to lose his leg but had in fact *chosen* to do so. Judge Mudd is not happy with the defense's argument and quoting my father's statement that, "I would rather die," draws the proper conclusion, for a change, that he was talking about losing his leg. Nevertheless, attorney von Flancelaut presses the point again, and again:

Judge Mudd: I don't think any of it makes any sense. What is the essential point? *Motion in limine* is granted, it's not relevant and not probative.

Von Fancelaut: Just so I understand, umm, uhh, I'm really struggling with this. It seems that every ruling that we ask for is...

Kohler: (interrupting) Oh come on!

Von Flancelaut: We have had one testimony after another from this family talking about this gentleman's health and who said what to whom and what decision they made based on what they were told and I've got...

Judge Mudd (interrupting) That's...

Von Flancelaut: (talking over the judge)...circumstance here where a surgeon calls up Michael Bennett has a direct conversation...

Judge Mudd: (cutting off von Flancelaut) I wish you had such a situation as you're dreaming of but you don't have it. Let's bring this witness (Michael Bennett) back please...

Von Flancelaut: We absolutely do your honor and I note my exception to that ruling and I think that you are...with that ruling...that it is (pointing at the judge) prohibiting us from being able to put on a very critical element of our case...

Judge Mudd: Well I'm sorry. You don't have the facts for it...

Von Flancelaut (interrupting again) Well, I believe the facts are there within the confines of the knowledge of this witness (grunting). Am I gonna be able to set it up that there was a choice...you say'in the entire discussion?

Judge Mudd: Unless you have a stipulation.

Kohler: No!

Von Flancelaut: (very agitated) Your honor I would like to ask a question of the witness. If she (attorney Kohler) wants to object...

Judge Mudd: (interrupting) You don't need to do anything like that and I'm telling you not to.

Von Flancelaut: Ok.

Judge Mudd: Because if the record's not preserved on this issue, nothing is.

Von Flancelaut: And are you finding that it is hearsay?

Judge Mudd: I'm finding that the substance of it is so vague and inconsistent and makes no sense for a jury.

Von Falncelaut: How is it inconsistent and vague?

Judge Mudd: No repetition. No repetition. The clock is ticking.

Von Flancelaut: But how...I don't understand how it is...how it is vague...that there was a choice.

Judge Mudd: I know you're upset.

Von Flancelaut: No. I'm tryin to understand so that if there's a way that I can...

Judge Mudd: You do understand. You just don't like it.

Von Flancelaut: I don't understand your honor; with all due respect I DO NOT!

Judge Mudd: Of course another way to put it, which I think puts it in proper light, is there a witness out there in the world who could do this?

Von Flancelaut: Well I'll be glad to call Dr. Henry, *sir*, from Shock Trauma but that seems a little much to get in for something...pull her out of Shock Trauma, have her articulate that.

Kohler: It's up to you. That's the proper way to do it.

Von Flancelaut: (fuming mad) Well. There is yet another way. We'll read it from the informed consent documents. (Attorney Orko throws up his hands in exasperation, while attorney von Flancelaut angrily shuffles papers on the defense table.)[175]

I am called to retake the stand:

Attorney Von Flancelaut begins her questioning centered on what I saw on the night of March 11th and my description:

Von Flancelaut: You also described the color that you saw and you described it as a red...umm..."like a poinsettia color red," fair?

Bennett: I did refer to a poinsettia.

Von Flancelaut: And the color red that you saw on your father's leg on the evening of the 9th [sic] was a very red like a poinsettia color red, fair?

Bennett: Well. I don't think it's fair. I might not have been quite accurate. Poinsettias...I'm not very much into flowers....

Judge Mudd: ...sir, STOP! Whatever was said was said. I mean your referring to a deposition that's in black and white, are you not?

Von Flancelaut: I am!

Judge Mudd: It has words in English in it?

Von Flancelaut: Yes!

Judge Mudd: So I mean if it's a question if he said it, he said it.

Von Flancelaut: Right!

---

175 The defense's own expert, a surgeon, had already testified under oath in deposition that based on the photographs taken on March 12th, "It's not very likely that the leg [was] salvageable under any circumstances."

Judge Mudd: If the witness wants to challenge...if the witness questioned what he said and then there's a way to present that to him.

Von Flancelaut: Right!

Judge Mudd: Let's do it that way.

Kohler: Thank you.

Von Flancelaut: Well...

Judge Mudd: But I'd rather, sir, when if you are asked if you said such a thing in the deposition you either said it or you didn't say it and if you wish to question whether you said it, so say and the deposition will be presented to you.

Bennett: That's what I would like to do. I'd like to see exactly what I said, sir.

(Attorney Von Flancelaut hesitantly begins to approach the witness stand, and then she suddenly stops and reverses.)

Von Flancelaut: Uhh...I don't think it...

Attorney Kohler: Could you show him (the witness) where it's in the deposition...

Von Flancelaut: I will but...I...I really wanna get through...

Kohler: But you...

Von Flancelaut: Let me rephrase the question...do... I'll withdraw the question...

Kohler: Show him the deposition.

Von Flancelaut: (raising her voice) I'll withdraw the question. Was your father's leg red?

Bennett: Yes.

Starting her redirect, attorney Kohler brings my deposition to the witness stand:

Kohler: Mr. Bennett. Ms. Von Flancelaut asked you about whether in your deposition, at page 142, you described your father's leg as "red as a poinsettia," can you read for us what you said with regard to red as a poinsettia?

Von Flancelaut: Your honor I think I withdrew that question.

Kohler: Well, after the implication was there your honor.

Judge Mudd: (begrudgingly) I'll permit it. Go ahead.

Kohler: Thank you.

Bennett: (reading the text) "...it *wasn't* red like a poinsettia."

Kohler: Thank you.

Defense recross-examination:

Von Flancelaut: (holding the enlargement of the contact sheet). In fact, if you had seen anything that looked like this on the 11th you *never* would have left your father in the hospital that night, fair?

Bennett: I don't think that's fair.

Von Flancelaut: You would have left him even if his leg looked like this?

Bennett: If my father's leg looked like that and he was under the care of a doctor and in that setting (a hospital) and I thought he was being cared for I would have left just like I left that night.

(While I was saying this, von Flancelaut kept interrupting with "Ok, ok...")

Attorney von Flancelaut next sets the stage for a planned ambush that would surface at the end of the trial:

Von Flancelaut: When your father got to Kernan, you had an issue with the care that he received at Kernan as well, correct?

Bennett: At what point in time?

Von Flancelaut: At *any* point in time.

Bennett: There was a point in time where I did have issues with his care.

Von Flancelaut: There's a point in time in which you called the police to come to the hospital because you were concerned that a nurse was abusing your father, fair?

Bennett: Fair.

The defense attorney then begins a line of questioning that could potentially open the door for testimony about my activism to control hospital-acquired infections and a bench conference is called. During the conference, Judge Mudd comments on my having called 911: "Did he really call the police?" he asks incredulously. "Yes he did," von Flancelaut responds forcefully, and starts discussing an issue involving my activism,[176] to which attorney Kohler says, "If you do that, then I'm going into advocacy and I'll be glad to talk about that all day, your honor. He became an activist after they killed his father." "Please don't talk like that. It's silly; *you know it's silly*, saying they killed his father. Are we not all adults up here?" the judge intones bitterly. Attorney von Flancelaut then states she will not pursue the question.

When testimony resumes, attorney von Flancelaut proceeds to ask me a question eliciting testimony about Neurontin as it relates to the nephrologist's report which has thus far been excluded from the trial. Consequently, attorney Kohler attempts to revisit the issue in a motion.

But Judge Mudd again refuses to allow her to pursue the matter. He also refuses to allow her to elicit testimony as to what actually occurred with my call to the police so that the jury will hear the *entire* incident. "Are you trying to justify his calling the police, is that what

---

176 When my daughter gave birth in 2007, I tested the baby's bassinet in the hospital—one of the hospitals where my father had been infected—and grew out MRSA. And I photographed a housekeeping sign indicating that the room had not been cleaned in ten days. Von Flancelaut wanted to bring this up to give the jury the impression that I was a crazed fanatic.

this is about?" the judge asks attorney Kohler, and then adds, "The man overreacts by calling the police and you now justify [that] because a patient complains?"

After fighting attempts to blame my father for losing his leg and his own death, attorney Kohler also has to fend off an attack by the defense who argues that the case should be thrown out on the basis of contributory negligence because I delayed the placement of the feeding tube, instead hiring a nutritionist and instructing the nurse to increase her attempts at getting my father to eat.

The redirect concludes:

Kohler: Ms. von Flancelaut mentioned a number of times in which you voiced complaints about your father's care...did you voice complaints?

Bennett: I voiced complaints. Yes.

Kohler: And why did you do that?

Bennett: I was caring for my father and was trying to get him the best care I could.

Kohler: Thank you. That's all, your honor.

Attorney Kohler then plays for the jury excerpts from the videotaped depositions of several fact witnesses, including Norman Kozak, nurse Juanita Boyd, a hospital nurse, as well as Dr. Maisef and Dr. Vietik.

The videos were the subject of vigorous debate and the judge permitted only select snippets. The defense was not only successful in preventing the jury from hearing and seeing important testimony, von Flancelaut even succeeded in having the eighteen-inch video monitor moved as far away from the jury as possible—more than thirty feet—in an already dimly-lit courtroom. In so doing, she was obscuring from the jury the hard swallow, nervous smile, dry mouth, and other telltale signs of lying all of which Dr. Maisef and Dr. Vietik exhibited, plus one unique indicator of Maisef's guilty conscience: his ruddy complexion turned noticeably redder when he lied, although *not* as red as a poinsettia.

After Dr. Maisef's video deposition is completed, one of the jurors looks at me, purses her lips, and nods affirmatively.

Later that day, as we return to the courtroom following a recess, attorney von Flancelaut befuddles everyone when she loudly informs Judge Mudd that my son, Yehuda, has glared at her in the hallway, making her feel threatened. In a booming voice an angry Judge Mudd demands, "HAS HE BEEN SENT HOME? SEND HIM HOME! SEND HIM HOME! SEND HIM OUT-SIDE ON CALVERT STREET! AND TELL HIM THAT IF THERE'S EVEN THE REMOTEST CHANCE THAT WHAT HAS BEEN ALLEGED, not proven, HAS TAKEN PLACE, HE WILL BE BANNED FROM THIS COURTHOUSE AMONG OTHER THINGS!"

The judge goes on to deliver a ten-minute lecture that includes lessons in psychology, philosophy, "glaring," "glowering," and quotes from Charles Dickens, among other things. Judge Mudd has already established that he is unkindly disposed to the plaintiffs, so his willingness to take attorney von Flancelaut at her word and his bizarre overreaction to a strange accusation that has nothing to do with the trial or testimony is of no surprise. Attorney von Flancelaut's reaction to the alleged glaring, however, is curious: despite outweighing the 5'6" post-adolescent by at least a hundred and fifty pounds, she seems genuinely frightened. Then again, as my father always said, "Every bully is a coward."

Chapter Forty-Eight

The defense will call three experts: the chief of surgery of a 215-bed medical center, the chairman of the department of infectious disease of a 315-bed medical center, and the medical director of a 300-bed medical center: henceforth known as The Butcher, The Baker, and The Candlestick Maker.

Based on their earlier depositions, The Butcher will testify that my father's leg could not have been properly diagnosed before the morning of March 12th; The Baker is going to say that the right antibiotic was used, and The Candlestick Maker will state under oath that Drs. Maisef and Vietik had done virtually everything right, if not beyond.

Walrus-like in appearance, The Butcher admitted in deposition that, at a rate of three hundred dollars per hour, he had been involved in about a hundred medical malpractice cases—an expert for the defense in virtually all of them. He had also been sued for malpractice four times. He doesn't exactly fit the profile of *"They're doctors! They're not 'experts'"* that attorney von Flancelaut introduced to the jury in her opening statement: but the jury will never know.

In her direct examination, attorney von Flancelaut elicits testimony from The Butcher that my father lost his leg due to a strep infection. This of course supports Dr. Maisef's use of Ancef on the night of March 11th since Ancef, it just so happens, is effective on that bacterium. He also states that, "you can't just stop steroids," regardless of his deposition testimony that he would not be offering an opinion on that issue.

The Butcher, who has already crossed the line of his expertise by offering his opinion on how to treat infectious diseases as well as the use of steroids, also morphs into a microbiologist when he states that the cultures which grew citrobacter from my father's leg were faulty, despite two separate samples having been taken at two different facilities and processed at two unrelated laboratories producing the same results—facts the jury will also never hear.

But The Butcher is slick, and image, as opposed to substance, can be convincing. He delivers his perfectly supportive (of the defendant doctors) nonsense with an air of confidence. It isn't surprising; The Butcher stated in his deposition that he didn't rely on books or literature because, practically speaking, he already knew everything.

According to The Butcher, Drs. Maisef and Vietik had done everything right and necrotizing fasciitis could never have entered anyone's thinking before the morning of March 12th.

Attorney Kohler wastes little time in, pardon the pun, getting to the meat of the matter with The Butcher:

Kohler: You would agree with me, doctor, that according to everyone's description that on the evening of March the 11th...there were purple patches [on Mr. Bennett's leg], correct?

Butcher: I'm sorry.

Kohler: On the evening of the 11th there were purple patches.

Butcher: Well, throughout...when you look at the chart, he had some purple patches all over his body.[177] The question is are they the same purple patches that were seen with the necrotizing fasciitis? I don't think we should confuse the different purple patches.

Kohler: I thought I heard you say here today that you believe that even if Mr. Bennett had been taken to surgery on the evening of March 11th that you believe that amputation would have still been the result. Did I hear you say that?

Butcher: I'm not sure if I said that, but I believe that to be the case, yes. If I didn't say that, I'll say it now.

Kohler: Well then go to page 60, please, of your deposition.

Kohler: The question that Ms. Frey asked you was "I want you to assume that if Mr. Bennett was taken to the OR on March the 11th, if you assume that, based on his condition as depicted in the medical record, do you have an opinion to a reasonable degree of medical probability as to whether his leg would have been amputated...? *"I do not. Without seeing the leg, I don't know...I don't know without looking at it."* That was your testimony back on July 30th, 2008, correct?

Butcher: That's correct.

Attorney Kohler then moves on to the issue of Ancef, the antibiotic that Dr. Maisef prescribed on the night of March 11th:

---

177 In fact, there is no mention of purple patches anywhere in the medical record with the exception of those seen on my father's leg on the night of March 11th as noted by Dr. Maisef.

Kohler: Would you agree with me that when you're facing necrotizing fasciitis, you don't know whether you have a group-A Strep or a mixed organism type of necrotizing fasciitis, typically, until the cultures come back and therefore you're gonna use a broad spectrum antibiotic?

Butcher: No, I would not agree with that.

Kohler: Group-A strep is not typically foul-smelling, is it doctor?

Butcher: No, group-A strep is not.

Kohler: And you saw the record, did you not, that on March the 12th the leg was reported to be foul-smelling?

Butcher: That was on the 12th, yes.

Kohler: So in light of the fact that the leg was foul smelling on March the 12th, would you want to change your opinion with regard to this necrotizing fasciitis being group-A strep?

Butcher: No

With his ill-fitting, mismatched suit and tousled hair, The Baker looks like the prototype *schlump*. His fast talking-style and quirky demeanor make him as irritating to listen to as he is unpleasant to look at. Another of attorney von Flancelaut's altruistic "docs," The Baker has been involved in over a hundred malpractice cases. His charges of six hundred dollars per hour for review, seven hundred and fifty dollars per hour of deposition, and thirty-five hundred dollars per half-day of trial had admittedly earned him over two hundred thousand dollars the previous year alone. At the time of his deposition in my father's case, The Baker had already racked up about ten thousand dollars in billable hours: but the jury will know of none of this.

As The Baker approaches the witness stand, attorney Kohler hands me a slip of paper with one word written on it: "Whore."

"Doctor, you wanna raise your right hand and be sworn in by the clerk," Judge Mudd's voice echoes over the sound system.

"There's no jury!" attorney Kohler loudly informs the judge.

"Oh. This is a jury trial isn't it?" the judge observes, "So inconvenient," he adds facetiously, trying to recover.

During his direct-examination, The Baker testifies that virtually everyone is indefinitely colonized with VRE and that the bug is nothing to get all worked up about because "it doesn't make people that sick." He doesn't believe in contact isolation—MRSA is everywhere and you can't do anything about it—and that its main purpose is to protect healthcare workers. He's convinced that most MRSA infections are community acquired.

The necrotizing fasciitis that my father developed under the care of Drs. Maisef and Vietik was not caused by group-A strep and did not contribute to my father's death, according to The Baker. He theorizes that a bug called peptostreptococcos[178] caused the infection that ate off my father's leg, although no such organism was ever identified. The Baker confidently states that Ancef was "the right antibiotic," although he does own a copy of *Mandell's*.

Despite no evidence in the medical record to support his opinion, The Baker diagnoses my father with having had congestive heart failure for years!

He states that my father could have picked up VRE anywhere including, "If Michael Bennett had VRE, and Mark Bennett could have acquired it from him."

He insists that the litany of infections that my father acquired in hospitals did not contribute to his death.

Cross-examination of The Baker by nurse-attorney Elizabeth Frey:

---

178 The Baker admitted, however, that this bug also would not be "foul smelling."

Frey: Treatment for cellulitis is not steroids. Is that correct?

The Baker: That's correct.

Frey: And treatment for necrotizing fasciitis is not steroids. Is that correct?

The Baker: That's correct.

Frey: With cellulitis of a patient that's in a hospital, you cover that type of infection for both strep and staph. Is that correct?

The Baker: I'm sorry. I don't know what you mean.

Frey: The type of antibiotics you would prescribe...?

The Baker: Yes, that's true. That's the standard approach.

Frey: And to do that you need a broad-spectrum antibiotic. Is that correct?

The Baker: Well, you don't need a broad spectrum.

Frey: But it won't cover MRSA?

The Baker: No, it won't cover MRSA. That's true.

Frey: If you suspect cellulitis in a patient that already has MRSA, it's more likely that that type of staph infection that they have is not the normal staph...but the resistant staph. Is that correct?

The Baker: I don't know if that's true.

Frey: In 2004, MRSA was the most common type of staph infection. Would you agree?

The Baker: ...Yeah, that's basically true.

Frey: In 2004, Mr. Bennett did not have cellulitis. Is that correct?

The Baker: No, he had necrotizing fasciitis.

Frey: So what Dr. Maisef is looking at on March 11th was not cellulitis?

The Baker: It turns out it was not.

Frey: You would agree that steroids mask infection?

The Baker: Yes. Steroids can mask certain types of infections.

Frey: And steroids can cause certain types of infections to spread more rapidly?

The Baker: Yes.

Frey: Regarding the signs and symptoms of necrotizing fasciitis, have they changed from 2000 to 2008?

The Baker: No, I don't think so.

Frey: Would you agree that the signs and symptoms of necrotizing fasciitis are: initially erythema (redness), swollen, without sharp margins, hot, shiny, exquisitely tender, painful, the process rapidly progressing over several days with sequential skin color changes from red, purple, to patches of blue-gray? Do you agree with that description?

The Baker: Well, I think that's a description...there are certainly other descriptions. As you noticed it said indistinct margins, I think that's one of the things that fooled people this time.

Frey: Let's look at Dr. Maisef's testimony regarding demarcation. Is there anything in Dr. Maisef's note (from the night of the 11th) that says demarcation?

The Baker: No, it doesn't say...I don't believe there's anything in there.

Frey: And he's the treating physician. Is that correct?

The Baker: Right.

Frey: And that's his description of March 11th, is that correct?

The Baker: Right. I think...well yes...it says what it says.

Frey: Doctor...if you see demarcation don't you think it's a significant clinical finding?

The Baker: I...I..don't...I'm sorry, I don't.

Frey: Doctor you mention that if we don't get ahead of bacterium they will evolve and change over time. Correct?

The Baker: I think that's true.

Frey: And that's why we've gone from first-generation antibiotics to second, third, and fourth. Is that correct?

The Baker: That's true.

Frey: And Ancef is a first-generation antibiotic. Is that correct?

The Baker: That's true.

Frey: You have not studied VRE. Is that correct?

The Baker: Actually I did.

Frey: Where in your résumé do you refer to any studies on VRE?

The Baker: It's probably an abstract...uh...we never published the paper, but there...uh...uh...

Judge Mudd: (interrupting) Well, we don't want to have probabilities.

The Baker: Huh?

Judge Mudd: We don't want probabilities.

The Baker: No, no...if you give me my CV, I'll find the abstract in it.

Attorney Frey hands him his CV and he reads the title of the abstract.

Frey: That study was not published. Is that correct?

The Baker: Right. It never got published.

Frey: And therefore it wasn't published in a peer-reviewed journal, reviewed by your colleagues?

The Baker: No. It was one of...the many studies the fellow (his student) never published...uh...umm (incoherent mumbling). It's a sore subject, but the fellow's not getting... (more mumbling).

Frey: But you agree the folks at CDC have studied VRE more extensively than you have?

The Baker: I tend to have a lot of problem [sic] with the CDC. I'm sure they spent a lot of time...

Frey: (interrupting) Excuse me. The question is would you agree...

Von Flancelaut: (interrupting) Can he finish his answer?

Frey: It's non-responsive to my question your honor.

Judge Mudd: Not yet.

The Baker: I have a lot of problems with some of the CDC studies...

The judge interjects, "He's answering your question. He's answering your question."

The Baker: They have...

Judge Mudd: No. STOP, sir. *I dominate, I rule.* He's answering. So far the answer is 'no,' now he's gonna qualify it.

The Baker: Yes. They have probably done more investigations than I have.

Frey: Contact Isolation protects a patient in isolation from acquiring other organisms. True?

The Baker: Not...well it does to an extent...that's not really what it's for...it does to an extent...to an extent.

Frey: You mentioned that contact isolation policies are all the same?

The Baker: There's probably some fine differences, but yeah, they're pretty much all the same.

Frey: And that's because they're based on the CDC guidelines. Correct?

The Baker: Or the SHEA guidelines.[179]

Frey: Did I hear you testify before that it's silly to follow hospital contact isolation procedures?

The Baker, stammering and stuttering, goes on to qualify his referenced remark as only applying to certain aspects of the procedures.

Nurse-attorney Frey switches the subject matter:

Frey: Where in the medical records before Mr. Bennett's hospitalization in 2004 does it say that Mr. Bennett had chronic lung disease?

---

179 Here, The Baker is citing the 2003 SHEA guideline, which in fact he adamantly opposes.

The Baker: Well. It doesn't say that. You're absolutely right. It doesn't say that...I think more than likely he has chronic lung disease but I can't prove it by the medical record. But you're right. Maybe he doesn't have chronic lung disease.

Frey: Let's talk about diabetes. You would agree... well (pointing to Dr. Maisef) Dr. Maisef's [deposition] testimony that Mr. Bennett's diabetes was reasonably controlled before his admission of February 2004?

The Baker: That's true.

Frey: Mr. Bennett never had diabetic problems. He never had ulcers [or] lesions [in] his lower extremities before he's hospitalized in February 2004?

The Baker: I don't know about never. I didn't see anything in the medical records.

Frey: Mr. Bennett was never hospitalized for diabetic-type complications prior to his hospitalization in February 2004?

The Baker: Not that I was aware of. I only saw two other hospitalizations. I didn't even see much of those records...

Frey: Did you see [Dr. Maisef's records]?

The Baker: I did see those. You're right. I didn't...I didn't see anything particular to diabetes.

Frey: Vasculitis. That's treated with steroids. Is that correct?

The Baker: That's true.

Frey: Would you agree it's unlikely to get vasculitis when you're on steroids?

The Baker: (thinking out loud) Is it unlikely to get vasculitis when you're on steroids? I don't know the answer to that, I think it probably is but I really don't know. I think you're probably right on that one. I haven't thought about that one.

Frey: And is it your testimony that Mr. Bennett died of old age?

The Baker: Basically he died of old age...

Frey: Mr. Bennett did not have chronic heart failure before he was hospitalized in February of 2004. Is that correct?

The Baker: I think he did. He absolutely did.

Frey: Let's talk about chronic heart failure for a minute ok. But let's talk a little about the heart first.

Nurse-attorney Frey sets up an easel in front of the jury and calls The Baker off the stand. She takes him through a simplistic drawing of the heart and explains to the jury its basic function. The Baker agrees with her description and is asked to return to the witness stand:

Frey: And can we agree that the test utilized to look at the heart and see how it's functioning is called an echocardiogram. It's one of the tests you can use?

The Baker: It is a test. Yes.

Frey: And what the echocardiogram is, you use sound waves and a computer to see how your heart is functioning?

The Baker: That's true.

Frey: It will show how effective the heart is pumping?

The Baker: Yes...well, we, wah, there's lots of exceptions, but generally yes.

Frey: And the echocardiogram is used to diagnose heart problems. Is that correct?

The Baker: It's one of the techniques we use to detect heart problems.

Frey: And how the left ventricle functions, that's the most common way to measure that is by looking at it, the ejection fraction. Is that correct?

The Baker: Yes.

Frey: And the ejection fraction is a test that determines how well your heart pumps at each beat?

The Baker: Yes.

Frey: And a normal ejection fraction is about 50% or more. Do you agree with that?

The Baker: It's actually a little higher than that but yeah.

Frey: Mr. Bennett had an echocardiogram. Correct?

The Baker: When?

Nurse-attorney Frey hands him the medical record and directs him to the page.

Frey: What you're looking at is an echocardiogram done on Mr. Bennett on February 18, 2004 (four days into his final hospitalization).

The Baker: Yes.

Frey: And would you agree that the results show that his ejection fraction was normal?

Instead of answering, The Baker tries to divert the discussion by addressing other aspects of heart function[180] when attorney Frey interrupts him and insists he answer the question:

Frey: *The ejection fraction.*

The Baker: The ejection fraction is normal.

Frey: So the blood pumping through his body is being read as normal.

The Baker: That part is normal.

Frey: And the left atrium is also normal. Is that correct?

The Baker: Uh...I believe so. Yeah.

Frey: And when you have heart failure your ejection fraction is abnormal. Is that correct?

The Baker: No. Not necessarily...no...no...but ok.

Frey: Is it your testimony that the necrotizing fasciitis and the amputation...Mr. Bennett underwent did not contribute to his death?

---

180 The tests showed that my father had cardiomegaly or an enlarged heart, something he was known to have had for decades, if not his entire life. Cardiomegaly is not in itself a disease and is shared by millions of people, including athletes, with little or no impact on their health or lifespan.

The Baker: Yes. That's correct.

Frey: And is it your testimony that the VRE that Mr. Bennett developed did not contribute to his death?

The Baker: The VRE infection that he had did not contribute to his death.

Frey: And is it your testimony that the other hospital-acquired infections that Mr. Bennett developed had nothing to do with his death?

The Baker: ...this is a debilitated elderly man and things are deteriorating...he's going downhill; he's dwindling away. This is what happens with elderly patients.

Frey: I'm going to show you the certificate of death. Have you seen this document prior to today?

The Baker: Yes.

Frey: Would you agree with me that according to Mark Bennett's certificate of death the cause of death is "Vancomycin-resistant Enterococcus in Blood"?

The Baker: I agree that's what it says.

Frey: I have no other questions.

Before he was a doctor The Candlestick Maker was a lawyer who specialized in shopping center development. He admits to seeing patients for only about an hour and a half each day, not including weekends. His primary function, it seems, is to get money for his hospital. The Candlestick Maker has been involved in about a dozen malpractice cases, for which he charges three hundred dollars per hour. He has already billed the defendants several thousand dollars before trial. He knows The Butcher personally and attorney Orko's father is a colleague of his, a fellow physician in fact, and was the one who referred him to my father's case. He also went to the same medical school as Dr. Maisef, although he says he only vaguely remembers him. The jury, of course, will never learn any of this either.

The Candlestick Maker, under oath in deposition, stated that my father had a "50-pack-per-year smoking history" and a "2-pack-a-day" for "20-25 years" smoking history—simultaneously one supposes.[181] He testified that my father suffered from "lung disease," including "chronic obstructive pulmonary disease (COPD)," and "significant cardiovascular disease," among other phantoms. While he admitted that he knows next to nothing about infection control, necrotizing fasciitis, MRSA, or VRE, The Candlestick Maker didn't hesitate to offer an opinion on those subjects when it came to defending Drs. Maisef and Vietik.

During his direct testimony, parroting von Flancelaut in her opening statement, The Candlestick Maker states that in 2004, MRSA and other resistant bacteria "weren't so much of a problem in hospitals as they are in 2008."[182]

He strongly asserts that during my father's hospitalization, Drs. Maisef and Vietik kept my father's blood sugars under "good control" in the beginning and then "very well controlled" when he was transferred to the sub-acute unit.

Perhaps The Candlestick Maker—a nervous man who overuses hand gestures and head bobbing to emphasize his words—has reviewed the wrong person's medical records?

Attorney Kohler cross-examines The Candlestick Maker:

Kohler: You don't hold yourself out to be an infectious disease specialist?

181 Except for a short period of time when he was in dramatic school in the early 50s, my father had not smoked since he left for Australia during World War II.
182 According to CDC data, by 2003, 70% of hospital-acquired infections were resistant to one or more of the drugs normally used to treat them. From 1980-2000, the rate of hospital-acquired MRSA had increased more than 30-fold, also according to CDC data. By 2004, MRSA had reached over a 50% prevalence rate in hospitals, again according to the CDC. In reality, by 2004, MRSA as well as VRE were known to be running rampant in virtually every hospital in America.

Candlestick Maker: No. I'm not an infectious disease specialist.

Kohler: Now, you haven't spent any time in investigating or studying VRE, correct?

Candlestick Maker: I haven't.

Kohler: You wouldn't suggest that you have any particular expertise how frequently VRE occurs or under what circumstances?

Candlestick Maker: No, no, I don't have any particular expertise in that field.

Up to this point, Judge Mudd has found reason to interrupt attorney Kohler four times.

Kohler: You mentioned that Mr. Bennett had some underlying lung disease. Did I hear you correctly?

Candlestick Maker: That's right. I did.

Kohler: And you had carefully reviewed Dr. Maisef's office charts, correct?

Candlestick Maker: I looked at them, yes. I reviewed them.

Kohler: All right. And you would agree with me that *nowhere, nowhere* in Dr. Maisef's office chart is there a reference to an underlying lung disease, correct?

Candlestick Maker: Not in Dr. Maisef's charts but in other parts of the records.

Kohler: And Dr. Maisef was the doctor that was treating Mr. Bennett for three years and was his primary care doctor, correct?

Candlestick Maker: That's correct.

Kohler: And you would expect Dr. Maisef to have the most intimate knowledge of Mark Bennett's underlying health conditions in that three-year period?

Candlestick Maker: Well, I would expect him to have that knowledge and to treat those symptoms...if there were any symptoms.

Kohler: And you would agree with me that emphysema, COPD, or [any] other underlying lung disease is not in Dr. Maisef's charts?

Candlestick Maker: I would.

A bench conference is called. During the conversation, Judge Mudd admonishes attorney Kohler:

Judge Mudd: One of the questions, you laughed at him, for effect to the jury: *Don't do that* [again]!

When testimony resumes, attorney Kohler asks The Candlestick Maker to approach the jury box where she makes him confirm the three references of nursing calls to Dr. Vietik regarding my father's increased pain level (10/10 while on a double dose of Percocet), potentially lethal drops in blood sugar levels, and other issues. As The Candlestick Maker passes the defense table on his way back to the stand, he looks at the defendants and shrugs. Maisef and Vietik look disheveled and depressed.

Kohler: Did I hear you tell the jury today that you believe Mr. Bennett's blood sugars were in control?

The Candlestick Maker: Well, I believe that...well... umm...when   he...stoo...they...were...when...when someone is sick, it's difficult to control their blood sug... blood sugars, when this case, the acute-care hospital, when they started steroids there four or five days that they were really fluctuating, um...then they got more stable, then there were days they would jump up...umm, and ya' know might depend on what the patient's eating, if their appetite picked up, if they had a lot of sugar... and then...and then the sub-acute unit...umm...*they were very well controlled.*

Kohler: Now let's define what well controlled means. A well-controlled blood sugar is what?

Candlestick Maker: Well, as I said to you in my deposition, obviously 80-120 is a wonderful number. But in someone who's got Type-1 Diabetes,[183] where you require insulin, in the acute care hospital you might be satisfied with 150, something like that, 180, something like that.

Kohler: On February 19th, Mr. Bennett's jumps to 334 on one occasion?

Candlestick Maker: Umm...it...it...I agree it went up and down and you would expect that. Yes ma'am.

Kohler: Just the 20th: 334, 276, 351, 461, you agree with these?

Candlestick Maker: I...I...I agree those next few days after he started the steroids it was very hard to control the blood sugars.

Kohler: All right. On February 21st: blood sugars of 389, 280, 400, 444, you agree with that?

Candlestick Maker: As, I said, the, say, you, you still, umm, oooh, that was a difficult time controlling the sugar.

Kohler: All right. I'm just tryin' to make sure we all understand what happened to these blood sugars. On February 23rd: 336, 322, 330, 311, you agree?

Candlestick Maker: That was reminiscent of the flow sheet that I saw.

Kohler: Ok. All right, and did you create a flow sheet or was that given to you?

Candlestick Maker: No, no, I think, they kept a list of...I don't recall (looks to the defense table for guidance)...it was...I think they kept a list in the hospital.

Kohler: I'm just asking whether or not defense counsel provided you with any flow sheets of any sort at any time about Mr. Bennett's course whether or not blood sugars or anything else, did they?

---

183 My father had Type-2 Diabetes.

Candlestick Maker: (looks to the defense table again) the...the...

Von Flancelaut: (whispers loudly) the medical records.

Kohler: Ms. von Flancelaut the question is to the witness.

Von Flancelaut: Oh.

Candlestick Maker: The blood sugars...the flow sheet is always the medical records, umm...and...uh...ya' know...I...Mr. Orko might have...I remember him showing, not blood sugars, but showing, um, how, um, the... what we talked about in deposition...I remember him showing me a chart how once we started the steroids, with Mr. Bennett, that his oxygen levels got...um...got much better and that reflects exactly what you and I went through in our deposition.

Kohler: All right. Now let's jump just for a second to the sub-acute side. On March the 1st, when Mr. Bennett is transferred to the sub-acute side, the highest blood sugars ever, correct?

Candlestick Maker: Umm, I don't recall but I know that first day that he did have a way high blood sugar.

Kohler: 514, 503...

Candlestick Maker: And then for the remainder of the hospitalization, for almost all of the sub-acute unit, it was *very well controlled*!

Kohler: Ok. So blood sugars later on: 295, 216, 332, (the witness is repeatedly covering his face with his hands) those would be well controlled, sir?

Candlestick Maker: You...during the course of a hospitalization, someone recovering, they're eating varying foods, sometimes their diet is good, sometimes it's bad, usually blood sugar vacillates, but overall, looking at those numbers, yes, they were well controlled.

Kohler: Now I want to talk about isolation. Do you remember that?

Candlestick Maker: Yes.

Kohler: Now you also saw in the progress notes that Dr. Maisef in fact discontinued isolation. Correct?

Candlestick Maker: I think he dis...ice...he...um... stopped facemask. He stopped the facemask. That's the order I remember.

Kohler: Ok, and do you recall in the chart as well he wrote a note as well that said discontinue isolation?

Candlestick Maker: I don't re...I don't recall that. But it's the order that's important.

Kohler: So the notes themselves are paid no attention to?

Candlestick Maker: No...it's what, what nursing does is not what a doctor writes or half sentences, like we're sometimes guilty of writing, they look at the orders.

Kohler: So you're telling me that what he wrote is unimportant in terms of what he did with regard to contact isolation?

Candlestick Maker: They...uh...again...I've said this; the important thing is what the order...what he instruct [sic] the nursing staff to do.

Kohler: So if you assume that Dr. Maisef took Mr. Bennett off of contact isolation on March the 4th, you agree that that is a violation of the hospital policy?

Von Flancelaut: Objection to form and foundation.

Judge Mudd: I'll permit it. Overruled, go ahead, doctor.

Candlestick Maker: I'm not familiar with [the hospital] sub-acute policy...um...in 2004, but if you tell me that that's not what those policies said, then...then I'd have to believe that the policy was violated...although no harm as far as I was concerned came to Mr. Bennett.

Redirect-examination:

Von Flancelaut: Doctor is there anything in the record that suggest [sic] that Mr. Mark Bennett was unconscious when Dr. Maisef saw him on the night of the 11th?

Candlestick Maker: No, not at all.

Von Flancelaut: Is there anything in the record to suggest that Mr. Mark Bennett would not be able to communicate and articulate to Dr. Maisef what his issues were during the course of the day?

Candlestick Maker: No, not at all.

Von Flancelaut: Is there anything in the record to support that Mr. Michael Bennett would not be able to speak with Dr. Maisef the night of the 11th?

Candlestick Maker: No. I believe it was Michael Bennett was [sic] who called Dr. Maisef at home and said please come in and see my father; I'm worried about him.

Von Flancelaut: Ok. And…um…Dr. Maisef did write a note in the chart that Ms. Kohler showed that to you. Is that fair?

Candlestick Maker: Yes.

Von Flancelaut: And in reading the note, does he respond at all…what does he say?

Candlestick Maker: It says "Doppler negative."

Von Flancelaut: How would he have known that… that a Doppler would have been done?

Candlestick Maker: Well…there's…there's two ways; either he read the chart…um…or possibly nurses came by and said, "By the way, this what's happening (sic) all day."

Recross:

Kohler: In forming your opinion, you did review the testimony of Michael Bennett, correct?

583

Candlestick Maker: I did.

Kohler: What do you remember about Michael Bennett's testimony as to whether Dr. Maisef knew [about the Doppler] before he even got to the hospital?

Candlestick Maker: I don't recall.

Kohler: Ok. And assuming that he testified that Dr. Maisef knew the Doppler had been negative before he got to the hospital that would then not tell you anything about whether Dr. Maisef read the notes that night, correct?

Candlestick Maker: If...that's where he got the information, it doesn't mean he didn't read the notes, he didn't talk to the nurse, it's...just that the patient's family gave him that information.

Kohler: That's all I have.

(The Candlestick Maker walks out of the courtroom in disgrace.[184])

So went the testimony of the three defense experts; the "local docs" who weren't "experts" and didn't have "web sites advertising their services for hire," the professionals, the healers, these men of noble character.

Over his three-decades-long career in medicine, Dr. Larry Rumans had testified in a handful of medical malpractice cases for both the plaintiff as well as for the defense. After completing his testimony, I thanked Dr. Rumans for defending my father. In response to the obvious pain that I was in at having to relive the events that took my father's life and listening to all of the lies told so far in that courtroom, Dr. Rumans said compassionately, "It's worse when they try to cover it up."

---

184 Two of the attorneys representing the hospitals had entered the courtroom during the last part of The Candlestick Maker's testimony. They took seats on the plaintiff's side of the gallery from where they waved and smiled at me. After the Candlestick Maker finished testifying, both attorneys approached me, saying, "[The Candlestick Maker] wasn't a very good witness," and "Dr. Maisef doesn't look too good."

Dr. William Jarvis had never before testified in a medical malpractice case. His work as a consultant for hospitals and governments seeking his expertise in infectious diseases, infection control, epidemiology, outbreaks, designing and conducting studies and surveys, and public health, to mention a few of his activities, takes him across the country and to the four corners of the world[185] year after year, leaving him little time to be with his wife and two daughters. He didn't need to testify in my father's case; he believed in it.

At the time of their court appearances, neither Dr. Rumans nor Doctor Jarvis had received a cent for their work on the case. Both men had traveled across the country and had been staying in separate hotels for two nights due to the defense's delay tactics.

"Seek not the favor of the multitude; it is seldom got by honest and lawful means. But seek the testimony of few; and number not voices, but weigh them."
— Immanuel Kant

---

185 Working as a consultant on infectious disease issues, Dr. Jarvis often logs over 250,000 air miles per year and has in some years traveled to all 50 states.

Chapter Forty-Nine

Answer: The other staff that I interacted with was I believe the doctor of the unit.

Question: What was his name?

Answer: It was a lady and I don't know her name. But I came out of the room and I, sometime afterwards, and the rabbi was there, and this lady who was I believe a doctor in charge of the unit. I asked her what had been listed on my father's death certificate. She read something to me or recited something to me and it wasn't what had happened. I told her that wasn't accurate and that it should be changed. She responded to me by saying, 'How many death certificates have [you] reviewed?' And I responded to her words to the effect that 'What does it matter?' She said something to the effect of, 'What's the difference what it says?' I said, 'Because the truth matters,' and I said, 'you need to call the primary care physician and get that cleared up.' She came back to me sometime later, my recollection is maybe a half an hour or so, and said that you are right and the death certificate has been changed.

Question: What had she said was the cause of death?

Answer: Initially?

Question: Yes, sir.

Answer: I don't recall what it was. I just recall that it was not what my father died from.

Admittedly, it sounds a little strange, asking about my father's death certificate, but in light of what had taken place over the previous one hundred and twenty days it was appropriate. After seeing how the healthcare system and its employees had grievously injured my father in a multiplicity of ways and having been repeatedly deceived or kept in the dark altogether about what was happening with him, I had become an angry cynic. Hospitals and doctors had first tortured and then killed my father, ripping apart my soul; I didn't trust anybody anymore. It was in that context and with that mindset that I asked about my father's death certificate.

At the time of the deposition, I could not recall what the doctor had said to me about the cause of death; later I remembered: she had said, "Diabetes," which further angered me. It was another betrayal of my father by the people and the system that he had unbridled trust in, and it had occurred when he could not defend himself: he was lying dead in the next room.

The incorrect death certificate entry may have been simply the result of convenience and nothing sinister, but it carried with it the implication that my father had not cared for himself by allowing his diabetes to run out-of-control. I wouldn't allow that indignity to be a part of his legacy. I had no idea what should be written on the certificate and I suggested nothing. I didn't even see it until certified copies were mailed to me by the funeral home about a week later. I just wanted the truth because, as I told the doctor, the truth matters.

But the truth doesn't matter to everyone, and it certainly wasn't of concern to Helga von Flancelaut and

Bruce Orko and their liars-for-hire, and, as will soon be seen, Dr. Jerold Maisef and Dr. Carmen Vietik.

> *"Truth exists, only falsehood has to be invented."*
> — **Georges Braque**

After the conclusion of the defense experts' testimony, a hearing was convened on, among other things, a motion by attorney von Flancelaut to read my deposition testimony about the death certificate directly to the jury. In doing it this way the defense would preclude any further testimony on what had actually taken place—you can't cross-examine a deposition.

At the time, I could not fathom why the defense would want to do this. The jury, I assumed, would see it for what it was: another damning example of the same dysfunctional system that had been injuring and killing patients for decades while hiding it from the public.

Attorney Kohler wasn't so naïve. She had too much experience for that. She argued vociferously against the motion on the basis that it was hearsay.

In an attempt to bias the judge, von Flancelaut fabricated a most remarkable scene: "The family," she said, "[had been] once again, yelling and screaming...'you don't know what you're talking about,' and they pitched a fit [to get what they wanted]." Von Flancelaut went on to relate how out of compassion and to quell the irrational family-gang, the doctor changed the death certificate, which, she insisted, originally stated that the primary cause of my father's death was coronary artery disease and congestive heart failure![186] What the family wanted, according to von Flancelaut, was for the certificate to say VRE in furtherance of a malpractice case. In other words, von Flancelaut was suggesting, these

---

186 The actual death certificate in fact *ruled out* these conditions as contributing to the cause of death.

people are a bunch of troublemakers looking to make money off of the death of Mr. Bennett; we all know the type.

An angry Judge Mudd ordered that the doctor who signed the death certificate be brought into the court, commanding, "Get [the doctor] on the phone!"

But the judge who had loudly proclaimed "*I dominate. I rule*" was ignored. The doctor who signed the death certificate was never brought to the courtroom. No one even attempted to contact her.

The defense was going to tell the jury that I, in conspiracy with someone else no less, had altered my father's death certificate. And Judge Mudd was enabling this revolting lie to proceed unchallenged.

Here is the context of my testimony as it appears in the deposition. It is what neither the judge nor the jury would see or hear:

"Question: After your father passed, were the staff members at [the hospital] helpful or supportive to you?

Answer: No.

Question: What was their reaction? How were you treated?

Answer: I wasn't treated at all. Actually, let me qualify. There was one nurse. I still remember her name. Her name was Nurse Ann Patience and she was what a nurse should be. She was compassionate and professional. She was respectful. She was everything that I would expect a good nurse to be.

The other staff that I interacted with was I believe the doctor of the unit...."

The day before testimony ended and closing arguments were to begin, attorney von Flancelaut entered the courtroom and dropped three documents on the table in front of attorney Kohler: a chart, a graph, and a summary of oxygen saturation levels. The chart, according to attorney von Flancelaut, supported her claim that the use of steroids was necessary to keep my father off of a ventilator. The grossly exaggerated claim aside, it was a clear violation of the rules of discovery. And, even more remarkable, The Candlestick Maker had revealed under attorney Kohler's pressure that attorney Orko had shown him just such a chart while being prepped for his deposition—a glaring contradiction of von Flancelaut's claim that the documents didn't exist until shortly before she brought them into the courtroom.

But the judge who would not permit the plaintiffs to use the highly esteemed medical reference books *Mandell's* and *Harrison's,* as well as the *Johns Hopkins' ABX Guide,* despite their having been discussed months before the trial, had no such reservations about this obvious ambush. The strongest criticism Mudd could muster was to say, "I don't applaud it. I don't applaud it. I'm not giving it any kind of an award. I think it borders on unprofessionalism to do it the last minute like this."

Attorney Kohler persuaded Judge Mudd to forestall his ruling on allowing the material into evidence until she had a chance to check its accuracy. To that end, I spent the lunch hour poring through paperwork, flipping page after page to verify the chart and the graph's data points against the record.

Data point after data point on the defense chart proved elusive to locate in the medical record. In addition, many of the references to my father's oxygen saturation levels that I found in the record were not on the chart or the graph. Also, it appeared that the graph had been horizontally and vertically manipulated in order to exaggerate the peaks and valleys representing my father's blood oxygen levels in a way favorable to the defense argument that had it not been for the ongoing use of steroids, my father would have died.

When court reconvened after the lunch break, attorney Kohler explained the findings to the judge and called the material "so inaccurate as to be irreparably inaccurate."

Unconvinced by attorney Kohler's cogent arguments and examples of the graph's inaccuracies, Judge Mudd was going to allow the chart and the graph into evidence.

After he took the oath to tell the truth, the whole truth, and nothing but the truth on penalty of perjury, Jerold Maisef mounts the witness stand. The doctor bites his lip as the lead defense attorney, overacting to a degree that would have gotten her thrown off the set of even one of my grandfather's cheap B-movies, speed-waddles across the courtroom in full view of the jury to fetch him a cup of desperately needed water. As he states his name and address for the record, Maisef's voice sounds weak and shaky. Appearing anemic, shrunken, and somewhat sedated, attorney von Flancelaut's "elder statesman" looks like a pathetic, frightened man.

On direct-examination, Maisef predictably paints himself as the caring and competent physician whose family has "been [in Baltimore] for almost a hundred years" and who had been treating a man with so many medical problems it was practically miraculous he was still alive. He even goes so far as to suggest that my father had suffered a stroke, which, he infers, was what had caused the "stroke-like symptoms" instead of the Neurontin. He claims that he came to the hospital on the night of March 11th for no other reason than, "I felt

I wanted to see Mr. Bennett. He was my patient, wanted to see if I could help him."

Dr. Maisef states under oath that on the night of the 11th, my father had quarter-sized "bruises above and below the knee," which he surmised were from the ace wraps.[187] He testifies that had he seen purple patches he would have immediately suspected necrotizing fasciitis and called for a surgical consult. Incredibly, the "bruises," says Maisef, had somehow magically morphed into purple patches and became coalescent into a group in the middle of my father's lower leg along the shin area.

Keeping to the game plan, physician Maisef testifies that he prescribed Ancef because the infection looked like a "typical strep cellulitis."

To shore up any question as to whether he had considered the progression of symptoms that led up to his treatment plan on the night of March 11th, von Flancelaut asks the good doctor about his interaction with my father that evening:

Von Flancelaut: When you saw Mr. Bennett, did you actually have a conversation with him?

Maisef: With Mr. Bennett? Yes.

Von Flancelaut: Was he able to articulate to you the events, the progression of this angry cellulitis?

Maisef: (expressionless) Yes.

Disregarding the fact that he was in searing agony at the time and that I was there, Maisef states, under oath, that my father had provided a play-by-play description of how his leg had gone from practically normal to the abhorrently infected one he saw on that night.

---

187   The ace wraps only went from the ankle to the below the knee, a contradiction that Maisef, in his fabrication, failed to recognize.

He explains his visit to Mr. Bennett's family on the afternoon of the 12th, when he told his patient's house-painter son "it was the right antibiotic," thusly:

"I really had no agenda...just to talk to them to see how they were doing, them meaning the family."

And finally, here is how Maisef the healer justifies his failure to see his suffering patient for more than a month, *before* I took him off the case:

"I sp...spoke with Mr. Michael Bennett at one point and asked...he would...he had told me that his father was going through hell. I said...I wanna visit him... um...he told me that he would prefer if I not go...and I respected his wishes."

After listening to Dr. Maisef's testimony, attorney Kohler looks like a police German shepherd, focused and aching to attack the criminal.

But before cross-examination begins, von Flance-laut, fearful of what attorney Kohler might do to her weak, lying witness, calls for a bench conference. She petitions the judge to "limit Ms. Kohler's questioning" to what she covered in her direct-examination to the exclusion of his deposition testimony. When Judge Mudd sarcastically suggests that Ms. Kohler "forgo" her cross-examination altogether, von Flancelaut explains that her concern is the schedule, "I'd just like to finish this today, that's all I'm saying."

Attorney Kohler starts her cross-examination of the doctor by eliciting testimony that my father, up to and including the February 14, 2004 hospitalization, was "totally competent," "compliant" with following medical instructions, and had been a man who was "careful about his health and *taking care of himself.*"

After Maisef confirms that in the three-year period prior to the hospitalization he had seen my father an average of eight times per-year, attorney Kohler moves on to the conditions that my father had, and also the ones the defense wants the jury to *believe* he had:

Kohler: In that spring of 2001…you prescribed some allergy medicine and some nose spray for his nose, correct?

Maisef: (looks through his records) Correct.

Kohler: Baltimore is pretty famous for giving people allergies.

Maisef: Pretty much.

Kohler: I wanna talk a little bit about *lung disease.* It's fair to say, Dr. Maisef, that you never in any of your office notes diagnosed Mr. Bennett with any kind of chronic, long-standing lung disease.

Maisef: I…I'm…that's correct. It's not in my notes.

Kohler: And that's the sort of thing you'd be looking for when examining your patients, correct?

Maisef: Yes.

After getting the witness to admit that my father in fact had only two primary diagnoses, diabetes and osteoarthritis, attorney Kohler focuses on those conditions:

Kohler: Diabetes, we've heard a lot about that and we're gonna talk a little more about that. Now osteoarthritis, that's basically arthritis in the joints.

Maisef: Correct.

Kohler: And when you're eighty-eight years old it's probably likely to get some arthritis in your joints.

Maisef: I think that would be fair to say.

Kohler: Let's talk about diabetes for a minute. You performed these A1c tests on Mr. Bennett, correct?
Maisef: Yes I did.

Attorney Kohler goes on to explain how the test is designed to provide an approximate three-month view on the management of blood sugars. Dr. Maisef stated in deposition that my father's A1c results, of which he had ordered a total of eight in three years, showed "reasonable control." [188] She gets Dr. Maisef to agree that the diabetic related macular edema my father had in one eye had no bearing on the events of March of 2004. In fact, the condition was effectively treated by a simple outpatient procedure that is performed on millions of Americans every year.

Moving to the issue of kidney dysfunction, attorney Kohler elicits agreement from Dr. Maisef that my father's kidney dysfunction was at worst intermediate and that he was years away from even possibly needing dialysis. Then, she addresses the matter of my father's heart:

Kohler: Now we've heard some reference to congestive heart failure. Back in 2002, you ordered an echocardiogram on Mr. Bennett's heart.
Maisef: Yes.
Kohler: And on that his ejection fraction was 65-70%.
Maisef: Yes.
Kohler: ...and what you've written down [in your report] is that it's a normal echocardiogram. Correct?
Maisef: Yes.

Attorney Kohler takes Dr. Maisef through virtually every test performed on my father's heart from the day he became his patient up to and including the 2004

---

188 The highest test score was 7.3. All of the others were 7.0 or lower. In 2004, according to the American Diabetes Association, an A1c of 6.9-7.5 was considered "Excellent." The ADA subsequently recommended keeping the A1c below 7.0.

hospitalization and how they all showed no signs or symptoms of congestive heart failure or coronary artery disease.

Because the judge has precluded any mention of Maisef's prescribing overdoses of Neurontin, attorney Kohler can only focus on the drug having caused the intentional tremor that my father intermittently had in his right hand:

Kohler: Fair to say that tremors are a known side effect of Neurontin?

Maisef: It is a known side effect of Neurontin.

Kohler: It's fair to say that that nephrologist...in May of 2003 suggested that the Neurontin may in fact be the cause of Mr. Bennett's tremors?

Maisef: It did suggest that.

Kohler: And that report went directly to you?

Maisef: Yes.

Methodically hitting on the witness' direct testimony, attorney Kohler asks about Dr. Maisef's inference that my father may have had a "lacunar" stroke as an explanation to the two hospitalizations that were, in fact, caused by the Neurontin:

Kohler: Did you even write down "stroke" in your chart after that MRI report was issued to you?

Maisef: I don't recall.

Kohler: So whatever was going on with Mr. Bennett wasn't a stroke?

Maisef: At that time yes [meaning no, it wasn't a stroke].

The plaintiffs' counsel next takes aim at Dr. Maisef's failure to follow the hospital's policy on contact isolation. Maisef is adamant that he did not violate the policy

even though he wrote a note to discontinue contact isolation, which was in clear violation of that policy. He
tries to explain away his deposition testimony that he
didn't know anything about the hospital's policy because
"they have infection control people for that"[189] by saying
he was nervous and that the hospital had issued a new
policy in February 2004. He now claims he only meant
that my father could stop wearing a mask outside of his
room because it would interfere with his doing physical
or occupational therapy and that he had no cough:

Kohler: Now there's always been contact isolation
guidelines at the hospital haven't there, even before
February 2004?

Maisef: I can't remember what they were.

Laying the foundation for her attack on Dr. Maisef's
diagnoses of "cellulitis" on the night of March 11th, attorney Kohler addresses the veteran doctor's knowledge of
disease:

Kohler: You would agree with me that you knew...
back then in 2004...that necrotizing fasciitis begins
with an area that can be red, hot, shiny, swollen, and
exquisitely tender?

Von Flancelaut: Objection to form your honor.

Judge Mudd: Well, this is cross-examination.

Von Flancelaut: She's referring...she's referring to
his deposition, which is improper form I believe.

Kohler: No, I didn't say a peep about his deposition.

Von Flancelaut: No? I'm sorry. You're right. I apologize. I withdraw the objection. It just sunk in it was
2004. I apologize.

Kohler: Let me repeat [the question] so that we all
remember what it was. In March of 2004, you understood

---

189 A very damning admission since Maisef, at the time, was also the medical
director of the unit.

that necrotizing fasciitis can begin as an area that is red, hot, shiny, swollen, and exquisitely tender?

Maisef: Yes.

Kohler: And you also knew that if it is untreated, the overlying skin develops blue-gray patches after thirty-six hours?

Maisef: I'm not sure of thirty-six hours, but it can get patches...and bullae.[190]

Kohler: And did you know that necrotizing fasciitis can present after the red, hot shiny phase as blue-black patches?

Maisef: Yes.

Keeping the witness off balance, Kohler switches tracks and delves into Dr. Maisef's work schedule, which showed that he routinely made hospital rounds on Thursdays.

Kohler: Now we know that March 11th was a Thursday, don't we?

Maisef: Yes.

Kohler: And you did not see Mr. Bennett that Thursday?

Maisef: I wasn't in this...that day...I was having trouble walking. I just went to the office.

Kohler: When you came to the hospital that night at the request of Michael and Sharon Bennett that was the first time that you knew that Mark Bennett was in pain, correct?

Maisef: Yeah. I went there because he was in pain. Yes.

Kohler: When you got there, did you look back in the chart to see what pain he had on previous days?

---

190 By adding "bullae," which are large blisters, Maisef is trying to alter the definition so that on the night of the 11th my father's symptoms were not necessarily consistent with necrotizing fasciitis. In all likelihood, Maisef did not know what the symptoms of NF were and/or never considered the diagnoses that night. But he cannot admit this lest the jury infer he was either incompetent or that he should have called for an expert consultation.

Maisef: I looked at the...chart and the entries for the...few days before, three or four days before, which is what I usually do when I see a patient.

Kohler: All right. So then you would have known that he had pain in his leg on March the 8th.

Maisef: Yes.

Kohler: And you would have known that he had erythema [redness] in his leg on March the 9th.

Maisef: I don't recall.

Kohler: Ok. And would you have looked back on all of the notes that appear in the progress notes for those couple of days?

Maisef: Certainly the day before and the day of.

Kohler: All right. You also knew that the principal problem with Mr. Bennett was the edema in his legs, the swelling in his legs that was worse on the left than the right?

Maisef: I knew he had swelling because he had ace wraps.

Kohler: You knew when you got to the hospital that beginning about 13:15, sometime in that one o'clock-ish time frame in the afternoon Mark Bennett began to complain about the pain in his legs on March 11th?

Maisef: Yes.

Kohler: And you knew that a little while later he had additional pain and was given Percocet for that pain, correct?

Maisef: That was the order that was written prior to that "as necessary." But he had been given that.

Kohler: Wasn't there a second order written for Percocet that day?

Maisef: I really don't know.

Kohler: And you know that finally he was in such pain that he had taken the ace wraps off his legs [himself], correct?

Maisef: Yes.

Kohler: And you knew that [when] the ace wraps came off his legs that the leg was red with ecchymossis, or purple areas, according to the nurse?

Maisef: Yes. That's what I saw also.

Kohler: Now you didn't talk to the nurse did you?

Maisef: I...don't think so.

Kohler: Did you talk to anybody other than Mark Bennett and Michael Bennett when you went to the hospital?

Maisef: (shrinking and barely able to speak) I didn't but I made an entry in the chart.

Kohler: At five o'clock that night the Doppler was ordered, is that right?

Maisef: Yes.

Kohler: And did you have any role in ordering that Doppler?

Maisef knows that if he says "Yes," there is no documentation to support the lie. If he says "No," he can simply deny that the conversation on the morning of March 11th, when I suggested doing a Doppler, ever took place. He has already made his choice:

Maisef: N...n...no.

Kohler: And you knew that the Doppler had ruled out a DVT so that when you got to the hospital that swollen, red, and painful leg was not because of a clot, a blood clot.

Judge Mudd: What time did you say the Doppler? Remind me. What time did you say it had been ordered?

Kohler: The Doppler was ordered at about 5 P.M.

Judge Mudd: Five, and the results?

Kohler: By 8 P.M. I believe.

Judge Mudd: Next question.

Kohler: You knew that Mr. Bennett had reported that the leg was twice its normal size.

Maisef: It was swollen.

Kohler: When you got there the leg was hot and shiny.

Maisef: It was hot and shiny.

Kohler: And it had purple patches throughout it.

Maisef: It had ecchymoses, yes.

Kohler: And those ecchymoses were purple patches, *correct?*

Before we see Dr. Maisef's answer, let's look at his deposition of five months earlier:

Question: ...Can you describe for us what you were seeing there?

Maisef: Some purplish areas, like purple patches... with ecchymosis, which basically was redundant. It was saying the same thing.

Question: Right.

Maisef: Ecchymosis means bruising, *but it was purple* (emphasis added). And they were patchy, not coalescent.

Back to the trial:

Maisef: They were bruises.

Kohler: Did you describe them to me as purple patches?

Maisef: Yes, yes (nervous smile).

Kohler: So ya' had red, hot, shiny, swollen, exquisitely tender, meaning very tender, very painful?

Maisef: Yes.

Kohler: In fact, by the time that you got to the hospital, the Percocet was not controlling Mr. Bennett's pain and he'd now been given [morphine], correct?

Maisef: Yes.

Kohler: And even with that, by the time you got there, even getting the [morphine], it was still exquisitely painful.[191] And with that you didn't think about necrotizing fasciitis?

Maisef: I still thought he had cellulitis with bruising and it hadn't been treated yet.

Kohler: What you write in the note is that you think it has a vasculitic component, correct?

Maisef: Right, which is the small vessels that are inflamed right under the skin...from infection.

Kohler: And you thought the vasculitic component was what was explaining the purple patches, correct?

Maisef: One of the explanations.

Kohler: In fact that's why you gave the Solu-Medrol for treatment of the vasculitic component, correct?

Maisef: One of the reasons.

Kohler: The treatment for vasculitis is giving steroids, right?

Maisef: Yes.

Kohler: And Mr. Bennett was already on steroids as of March 11, correct?

Maisef: He was.

Kohler: And you would agree with me that the chance of Mr. Bennett having developed vasculitis while he is on a continuing course of steroids was about non-existent.

Maisef: It was not, not in light of an acute infection that was in the skin.

As the pressure on Dr. Maisef mounts, he becomes noticeably more nervous, he frequently sips water and his voice becomes so weak, the judge has to ask him to speak up and move closer to the microphone.

By moving to the issue of the doctor's treatment plan, attorney Kohler is effectively doing what General MacArthur had done in isolating the Japanese strong-

---

191 The chart states that even after the morphine, my father was reporting his pain level as being 10/10, which constitutes a medical emergency.

hold of Rabaul. And now, just like General MacArthur, she is about to complete the encirclement.

Attorney von Flancelaut knows exactly what is happening to her withering client. She spills a glass of water on the defense table and asks for a recess, which the judge is happy to oblige.[192]

Nobody's fool, when she resumes her questioning of Maisef, attorney Kohler feints in another direction, before returning to the subject of the doctor's treatment plan on the night of March 11th:

Kohler: You did not write in your note that there were lines of demarcation.

Maisef: That's correct.

Kohler: There were no lines of demarcation, were there?

Maisef: It was...it was quite well demarcated on the top and bottom with a little bit of pink on the foot.

Kohler: Now the fact that it was well demarcated, why didn't you put that in your note?

Maisef: Because it was cellulitis.

Kohler: And it wasn't important for you to know or the people coming behind you to know whether the "cellulitis" was progressing?

Maisef: It was important. I did convey that information to Dr. Vietik about the involvement.[193]

Kohler: *About the involvement?* In fact didn't you tell Dr. Vietik that you think he had "an angry cellulitis"?

Maisef: Yes.

Kohler: *And now you're saying that you told her there were lines of demarcation and where those lines were?*

Maisef: I think I recall I did.

---

192 Von Flancelaut claimed that attorney Orko had spilled the water.
193 In his deposition, Maisef said he had told Vietik that Mark Bennett had "an angry cellulitis." I suspect that he never used the word 'angry' in his description to Vietik. In fact, in her deposition, Dr. Vietik testified that Maisef simply said, "Mr. Bennett had cellulitis." It was another example, albeit a subtle one, of Maisef's dishonesty.

After attorney Kohler reads his deposition testimony about what he told Dr. Vietik on the night of the 11ᵗʰ, Maisef sticks to his new story that he described my father's leg in detail to Dr. Vietik that night:

Kohler: You would agree with me that your note says nothing about demarcated?

Maisef: I would agree with that.

Kohler: And your note talks about these purple patches throughout the leg, correct?

Maisef: That's correct.

Kohler: The house officer doesn't say anything about purple patches, correct?

Maisef: That's correct but it was quite an incomplete note.

Kohler: It was quite an incomplete note?

Maisef: About the exam.

Kohler: How do you know it was an incomplete note?

Maisef asks to see the house officer's note and while it is being retrieved states, "I don't think it gave a full physical description." Attorney Kohler asks the doctor to read the in fact thorough note to the court. After Maisef stumbles through the reading, Kohler returns to tightening the noose and asks if after reading the note on the night of March 11ᵗʰ he was concerned about progression of the disease:

Maisef: (long pause) I'm sure I was concerned about that.

Kohler: What did you do to try and figure out if it had progressed? You didn't talk to the nursing staff, correct?

Maisef: Correct.

Kohler: You didn't talk to the Bennett family outside of Mark Bennett. Correct?

Trying to figure an escape, Maisef isn't answering. Attorney von Flancelaut intones loud enough for the witness to hear "the patient." Angry at the dirty trick, attorney Kohler tries to drown out the contemptuous coaching by loudly repeating, "ABOUT HOW THE LEG HAD PROGRESSED?" Judge Mudd says nothing.

Maisef: (picking up on his lawyer's cue) The patient didn't offer those complaints.

Kohler: (incredulous) The patient didn't offer you a complaint how it had been progressing?

Maisef: The purple.

Kohler: Did you ask the patient that question?

Maisef: Don't recall.

Kohler: Ok. And you didn't talk to the nursing staff, correct?

Maisef: Correct

Kohler: And you didn't talk to [the house officer], correct?

Maisef: Correct.

Kohler: Now when you left you didn't draw any lines on the leg, correct?

Maisef: Correct

Kohler: You would agree with me that you didn't write any order for the nurse to do that, correct?

Maisef: That's correct.

By having elicited earlier testimony from the witness about the signs and symptoms of necrotizing fasciitis and making him read from his deposition testimony, attorney Kohler has forced open another important door that Judge Mudd had previously closed:

Kohler: Now, you're familiar with the textbook *Harrison's*?

Maisef: Yes.

Kohler: And you consider it as the "gold standard," reasonably reliable, correct.

Maisef: Yes.

Kohler: Doctor, you know that diabetics are at increased risk for developing necrotizing fasciitis, correct?

Maisef: Yes.

Kohler: (Attorney Kohler approaches the witness and hands him a copy of the pertinent page from *Harrison's*.) Directing your attention doctor, up in the right hand corner of that, you would agree that according to *Harrison's*, *the gold standard*, "The examination [of necrotizing fasciitis] first may be unremarkable except for soft-tissue edema with erythema," correct? "And the affected area is red, hot, shiny, and exquisitely tender..."

Maisef: Yes.

Kohler: "...and that in an untreated infection, the overlying skin develops blue-black patches after 36 hours..."

Maisef: That's what it says.

Kohler: "...*and that coetaneous bullae and necrosis develops after three to five days.*"

Maisef: Yes.

Kohler: Now. You mentioned that you were getting a history from Mark Bennett. At that point in time he was in *extreme pain* was he not?

Maisef: Yes. But he was still able to speak.

Kohler: (sounding incredulous) *He was able to speak and he was able to describe to you...what did he tell ya?*

Maisef: He was in pain and his leg hurt and he had...they had just...they had...they had taken off the wraps.[194]

Kohler: Ok. And you didn't ask him about the progression either, right?

Maisef: I don't recall.

---

194 Besides being another outright lie, Maisef has forgotten that he already testified that the nursing notes stated that my father himself had taken of the ace wraps.

Kohler: All right…you did physically examine the leg, correct?

Maisef: Yes.

Kohler: And when you touched his leg he recoiled in pain, did he not?

Maisef: Yes.

(In the face of all of this, Dr. Maisef did not call for surgical or infectious disease consults even though such were readily available virtually down the hall.)

Brilliantly, attorney Kohler returns to the subject of Maisef's treatment plan, which had been disrupted by von Flancelaut's water spill ploy. Point-by-point she shows how Ancef was not just the wrong antibiotic, but that the doctor would have likely done better had he closed his eyes and pulled almost any antibiotic off the shelf. Dr. Maisef can only agree with each and every point made by the well-educated lawyer.

Nevertheless, contrary to science, medicine, and logic, the defendant remains insistent that he had done no wrong and that what he saw on the night of the 11th of March was cellulitis caused by strep.

The one critical element that neither Dr. Maisef nor the defense experts considered was that under the circumstances, it was virtually medically impossible for my father to have developed a strep infection, as vancomycin, which is effective against that bacterium, was still coursing through his veins.

What Dr. Jerold Maisef had done on the night of March 11th sealed my father's fate: he prescribed the wrong antibiotic, even for empirical use, and he prescribed a massive dose of steroids that fueled an already terrible infection into a raging inferno.

During his time on the witness stand thus far, Jerold Maisef has engaged in an orgy of obfuscation punctuated by utter lies. But the most obvious of his perjury is yet to come.

> *"An abomination to G-d are lying lips:*
> *Faithfulness is His wont."*
> **— Psalms 12:22**

Redirect-examination:

Von Flancelaut: At the time that you came into the hospital and reviewed the chart on the evening of the 11th you noted in you...um...ah...record that the Doppler was negative?

Maisef: Yes.

Von Flancelaut: Did you receive that information from by [sic] virtue of any phone call or interaction with Michael Bennett?

Maisef: (pause) Not Michael, Shh...Sharon Bennett might have told me that but I also read it in the chart.

Von Flancelaut: Ok. Did they ever call you and ask you to do a Doppler?

Maisef: No.

Von Flancelaut: Did they ever call...uh...the conversation that occurred in the morning of March 11th, did that occur?

Maisef: No.

Enraged, I stare at Maisef. He tries to stare back, but he cannot keep eye contact.

When Dr. Carmen Vietik, the rail thin, but purportedly expectant, and diminutive woman was called to take the stand, the flat-affected person that I had met on the morning of March 12, 2004, and then again when present at her deposition months before trial, made an obvious but feeble attempt to fit the cartoon character of the "dynamo" and "firecracker" that Helga the story-teller had created. She practically danced to the podium as she aw-shucks sawed her arm across her chest. When she stated her name and address for the record, her frog-like voice was as smooth as polyester.

Nonetheless, Vietik was a better performer than her colleague, the "elder statesman," and she parroted her trainer's talking points with aplomb.

"It is better to remain silent and be thought a fool than to open one's mouth and remove all doubt."
— Abraham Lincoln

However, under cross-examination by nurse-attorney Frey, Dr. Vietik, her voice occasionally slipping from synthetic back to amphibian, stated that she had performed *a full body exam on my father while he was in physical therapy on March 10th, which included unwrapping his legs, and that she had seen him doing leg pumps!*

Remarkably, Judge Mudd, the one who said Dr. Ruman's estimate of my father's life expectancy made him "regurgitate," showed no sign of nausea at hearing Vietik's ridiculous, self-serving assertions.

Nursing notes attesting to my father's leg pain and erythema as well as therapy notes that my father was in too much pain to climb the practice steps and had to return to his room contradict Vietik's testimony on its face. The absence of a single piece of documentation from the therapist that she had even entered the therapy area that day, let alone performed a "full body exam" there, buttressed my opinion that von Flancelaut's "dynamo" was simply a liar.

Both Drs. Maisef and Vietik had become classic examples of people who make mistakes and then, out of fear and false pride, make it worse by choosing to cover them up and blame others. And in this case, among others, they were blaming my father, who could not defend himself. It is the very definition of cowardice, and the polar opposite of what my father stood for.

At the conclusion of the defense case, I sat alone in that courtroom reflecting on what had taken place there. I had told the truth and fought for my father the way he would have wanted me to—with honor. As for the defendants, regardless of the trial's ultimate outcome, Drs. Maisef and Vietik would not be redeemed. Instead, unfortunately, they had created for themselves shameful legacies and had disgraced their honorable profession.

A lot of iniquity had taken place in that courtroom thus far, but what the pathological lead defense attorney would do next, plumbed the very depths of evil.

Chapter Fifty

My father looked as I always envisioned him: dignified, robust, the definition of class, my hero. He stood to my right, his left arm around my skinny, eleven-year-old shoulders and his face beaming with pride, as I struggled out of shyness to stifle a smile.

As I dozed off in the empty courtroom waiting for closing arguments to begin, this was the third dream in which my father came to me. I had fallen asleep praying "bring it home Dad, bring it home..." I had spent four long years trying to change the world for him in every way I could think of. There were two more things I needed to do for my father; one of them was to get justice for him.

Before addressing the jurors, attorney Helga von Flancelaut lined up volumes of my father's medical records on a table directly in front of them. With the exception of Dr. Maisef's office chart, all of the records were from the medical care consequential to her clients' negligence. It was obvious what she was getting ready to do, despite her imploring the jury to put the evidence "into CONTEXT." I could only hope that during deliberations, the jury would merely open up the binders and look at the dates.

From the Defense's Closing Argument:

"I told you from the very beginning of this case that it was my honor to represent Dr. Maisef and Dr. Vietik. They're good people. They're good physicians. They care about their patients. They do what's right...

"I said in the very beginning that this case was going to be about the process of dying. That's what this case was before it was filed and that's what this case is today. We all die...we all do. And we all suffer from that condition that we sort of put away and that is the condition of denial. We don't want to. We're afraid of it. We are. We admit it...

"The other process that goes with the process of denial is the process of blame. Because if you can't get to the point where you can accept it's a lot easier to *blame someone else.* And that's what I suggest is happening in this case. "Eighty-eight years young"...You can see the volumes of records that we have on Mark Bennett just from the last four years of his life. VOLUMES!

"Mark Bennett had lived a full life. My clients loved Mark Bennett. They cared for Mark Bennett.

"He was just short of dialysis...he had diabetes... he had diabetic retinopathy that moved into macular edema...the signs and symptoms that a diabetic is reaching the end of his life...he was having a process on top of a process on top of a process that you'd anticipate someone would have when they're at the end of their life.

"He was a proud man...but he recognized that that (sic) he was going through the process of life and it was cycling toward the end.

"Dr. Maisef and Dr. Vietik were trying their best to keep things going with Mr. Bennett. It had just become overwhelmingly more difficult to keep him all patched up.

"He used the Neurontin to control the pain that he had in his legs and his arms from the diabetic reti-nopathy [sic]...it's this process of denial that maybe it's something other than my father is dying.

"If they hadn't given him steroids and he had died it would be an entirely different case...the steroids SAVED HIS LIFE! (shows oxygen chart to jury)...it's important because their whole case hinges on blaming Dr. Maisef and Dr. Vietik for giving him necrotizing fas-ciitis, hinges. When you give someone steroids it's like waiting for a hurricane. There isn't anything yer gonna do t'change it, it's commin, where it's gonna come, it's gonna blow where it's gonna blow, yer not quite sure how hard it's gonna be, yer not quite sure how the tides gonna be affected by it, but ya' know it's commin. One of the things ya' know it's commin, it's gonna alter you blood sugars, and yer waitin fer it...your ready for it... he had good sugar management a person that's in the hospital *with a pretty significant illness.*

"Ya then get confronted with what I would call...a side show, which is this whole VRE thing. I've never understood why that's been a part of [this case]...VRE is something that any one of us can have. You get colo-nized with it forever. It doesn't make you sick. For them to suggest that he contracted it [in the hospital]...is just insane.

"They wanna say that Dr. Jarvis is the world renown (sic) expert on the topic. The only person who called himself world renown is him [sic]. When I asked Dr. Jarvis, do you even know if he had vancomycin in California? Did you see any records from California? (sarcastically deep voice) *'Well, no, I have no knowledge of that.'* Well, yer gonna come in this courtroom and try to suggest that two doctors killed someone I would suggest that it would be important make sure that all the evidence is there.

"His daughter-in-law...*she brought something home.* It could'a happened anywhere. He got MRSA somewhere else. I wonder where he got VRE.

"This thing that he died from...*this death certificate that Michael Bennett and Leon Bennett told you that they had altered from the original one to say VRE!* [195]

"He didn't get VRE at [the hospital]. I suggest to that the VRE, no way, no way.

"We know that cellulitis and necrotizing fasciitis look exactly the same in the early stages. Every cellulitis case, if you believe Ms. Kohler, every cellulitis case you're gonna have to bring in a surgeon and bring in an infectious disease [sic] just to rule out necrotizing fasciitis cuz it's all red, hot, shiny with lots of pain.

Leg Pain on the Night of the 11th:

"Keep in mind Mr. Bennett didn't have his Neurontin [the family took it away from him]...

"Necrotizing fasciitis is rare...rare...rare...

"Michael Bennett and Jerold Maisef went to the same synagogue. They knew each other's lives!

Dr. Maisef's arrival at the hospital on the night of March 11th:

"He sees Mr. Bennett. He gets a history from Mr. Bennett. He sees Michael Bennett. Do you think that Mr. Bennett or Michael Bennett wasn't going to

---

195 Already fuming at the diabolical diatribe, when I heard this, I handed nurse-attorney Frey, who was sitting next to me at the plaintiff's table, a note that said, "Can I sue her for that?"

tell Dr. Maisef what had happened with his leg? He's in pain. It hurts.

"Dr, Maisef told you...that if I would have seen anything that looks like this leg I would have not hesitated to call in a surgeon or to call in infectious disease. *I suspect he would have put him in the car and taken him to Shock Trauma himself!* That's the kind of man he is...Dr. Maisef came to provide care and comfort for his eighty-eight-year-old patient.

"Everybody that came in [to the courtroom] said 'this is strep.' First line treatment for strep cellulitis is Ancef. Well, it could be penicillin. But that would have been a problem because Mr. Bennett was allergic to penicillin.

"Remember, every expert in this case said no way citrobacter caused this.

"Ancef was the right antibiotic.

"At the end of the day, if you're diagnosing cellulitis and it turns into necrotizing fasciitis it's not negligence.

"Eighteen-year-old football players get necrotizing fasciitis; eighty-eight-year-old diabetics do too; doesn't have anything to do with steroids.

"We know that he was seen at Shock Trauma. Dr. Henry called Michael Bennett and said 'Ya' know, I can try to do these things called debridements, but yer dad's gonna need a lot of surgeries and he's old and got all these other problems and if I try to it...he may not make it. I suggest an amputation.' That's the same discussion she would'a had on the 11th. That's the same discussion they would'a had on the 10th...

The Missing Witness Defense:[196]

"...and I suggest to you that's, that we know that because if it wasn't, I'm sure we would'a seen Dr. Henry in here...and I suggest that if their case is that it had

---

196 Long prohibited under Maryland law.

made a difference in terms of the diagnoses, then where's their surgeon...where's their surgeon. Who'd they bring in? The world renowned Dr. Jarvis THE PEDIATRICIAN! I have a little trouble with that when you're accusing two doctors of killing somebody...have a little trouble with that...where's their surgeon.

"I take nothing away from the Bennett family in terms of watching a loved one suffer. We have all been there. We don't get to pick how we die...Just because someone suffers does not mean the physicians caring for them caused it. And that's where I don't feel any comfort for the Bennett family. Cuz in their denial of their father's fading they cast blame. And blame is an evil and painful and wrong emotion. Acceptance; I hope they find it.

"My clients have been here every day. I don't discount the fact that Leon Bennett has clients in California, but he's not here in a trial that has to do with his father's death in which he's accusing two physicians of killing his father.

"Mr. Bennett, Michael Bennett has been here every day and I know he feels pain. But again, I'd like you to ask yourselves back in the jury room was that based on denial and blame in an avoidance of acceptance? If somebody's at fault is it easier to accept the passing of a loved one? I don't know. I don't know.

"Now when you go in and deliberate...I want you to think about all the other things that happened and all the complaints that went along with it. Remember the fact that the family called 911 at Kernan on a nurse cuz they said that the nurse was abusing and neglecting their father.

"Remember that he got one infection after another for the remainder of his life.

"Dr. Maisef and Dr. Vietik just happened to be there.

"You have two doctors in this courtroom who've dedicated their lives, their careers, maybe short, maybe

616

long. They did everything, dedicated their time to care for Mr. Bennett. Please get back and do justice by them. Please tell them that they gave good care.

"I promise I will never speak to you again other than in the hallway to say hello; I'm not sure you're glad, don't applaud too loud... I thank you.

"I won't get a chance to respond to [Ms. Kohler]. But I ask only that whatever is said...that you think about those arguments that I have presented to you and the *evidence* you're going to get a chance to look. Because as much as I feel for Judge Mudd, and I like Judge Mudd, in this case you are the judges. You are the judges of the facts.

"Thank You."

Alison D. Kohler: The Heart of a Victim's Advocate:

"After two weeks, now I know why we're here. Now I know what the argument is. What they are saying to you ladies and gentlemen is that an eighty-eight year-old man's life has no worth. It has no value. If you cut through everything, their defense is; he's old; it was his time; he was going to die; that the amputation of his leg, that the infections he contracted, and all the rest of what happened to Mark Bennett...had nothing to do with his death. He was simply old..."

"Ladies and gentlemen what you have just heard is a lot of smoke and mirrors and I'm going to tell you why.

"Blame someone else? Blame someone else? The family can't accept their father's death so they want to blame someone else. Well that's what you've heard ladies and gentlemen for the last two weeks. We're going to blame Sharon Bennett for bringing VRE into the household; we're going to blame the hospital staff; we're going to blame the community, in fact, we're going to base our entire defense on Michael Bennett's description of his father's leg on March the 11th. On Michael Bennett the untrained housepainter's description as opposed to what Dr. Maisef said he saw on March the 11th. We're going to blame everybody and everything other than the defendants.

"Necrotizing fasciitis is rare; nobody has ever seen it. The defense expert said he's seen it over a hundred times...Dr. Maisef and Dr. Vietik have seen it. They admitted that they knew about it. They admitted they knew the signs and symptoms. That's why you call in a doctor as opposed to a housepainter.

"I'm not here to tell you that Dr. Maisef is a bad man. But he was a bad doctor.

"Mark Bennett's death certificate does not say that he died of natural causes. It doesn't say that he died of old age. It says that he died of VRE in his blood, VRE sepsis.

"Let's take a look at who did what. Michael Bennett didn't write his father's death certificate. Did he influence the death certificate? When have you ever known of a patient dictating to a doctor what a death certificate should say? Remember what Michael Bennett said? What he said was 'I asked the doctor to call the primary to get it straightened out,' and the doctor said, 'Well what does it matter what the death certificate said?' You know what Michael Bennett said? He said '*the truth matters,*' *the truth matters.*

"Michael Bennett didn't give the whopping dose of steroids to his father.

"Michael Bennett didn't give the wrong antibiotic.

"Michael Bennett didn't miss the diagnoses of necrotizing fasciitis; that was Jerold Maisef.

"Carmen Vietik missed Mr. Bennett's leg getting bigger and bigger and redder and more painful, not Michael Bennett.

"Dr. Vietik testified that she saw Mr. Bennett in physical therapy and that she un-wrapped the Ace wraps. We know that's not in her notes and we also know there's not a single reference in the therapy notes that Dr. Vietik unwrapped the leg and stopped physical therapy in the middle of it.

"We know that on March 11th, Michael Bennett calls his father in the morning to ask how he's doing and when his father tells him that he's in pain, Michael Bennett calls his wife and then calls Dr. Maisef and after describing what was going on with his father suggests that Dr. Maisef order a Doppler.

"Now you've heard testimony from Dr. Maisef that that conversation never occurred. And you're going to have to be the judge of whether that conversation occurred. So let me throw out a few things for your consideration in that regard that will allow you to easily conclude that the conversation occurred and that Dr. Maisef ignored, once again, additional signs and symptoms that something was going on. Why would Michael Bennett, a housepainter, call up the doctor and suggest a Doppler? Michael Bennett doesn't know anything about Dopplers; he paints houses for a living. His wife knows. She's an occupational therapist. Think about Michael Bennett's testimony throughout this case. You've seen that almost everyone that's taken the witness stand [for the Defense] has been impeached... But Michael Bennett didn't say one thing different than he said in his deposition. The reason that there are no contradictions ladies and gentlemen is because Michael Bennett has been *telling the truth for the last four years.*

"Credibility is what this case is about.

"When Dr. Maisef came to the Bennett's home after Mark Bennett had lost his leg and said, "I wouldn't bet against that man," and "It was the right antibiotic," and he went there with no agenda...I find that to be incredible...you don't go to a patient's house the day after their father has had his leg amputated...and lecture on antibiotics unless you know you gave the wrong antibiotic. You don't go in there and tell a housepainter about antibiotics. There was an agenda.

"Let's talk about contact isolation precautions...

"Are you going to believe a fellow that is supposedly an infectious disease doctor who believes that contact isolation procedures are silly?

"Again, let's talk about smoke and mirrors...Where's Dr. Henry? Why didn't we bring Dr. Henry into the courtroom? Ladies and gentlemen, I think that you have your common sense appreciation for the fact that the plaintiffs in a medical malpractice case have an uphill battle. A doctor can call just about any doctor they want...

Von Flancelaut: Objection.

Judge Mudd: Well, overruled. I mean I don't want to go too far astray from this case now.

Kohler: All right. Well, Ms. von Flancelaut opened up "Where's Dr. Henry?"

Judge Mudd: So you can say that, but let's not dwell on it.

Attorney Kohler continues to address the jury while the judge is still audibly babbling about the issue...

"What did [Dr. Henry] say? Well she's certainly as equally available to the defendants as to the plaintiffs.

"Chronic renal insufficiency, myelodysplasia, COPD, underlying lung disease, leukemia, tremors, none of these conditions that the defense says Mr. Bennett supposedly had are in Dr. Maisef's notes; either this is smoke and mirrors or Dr. Maisef is so incompetent that he missed all of these things.

"Ladies and gentlemen, we call what has been going on in this courtroom the three-dog defense; my dog didn't bite you; my dog bit you but he didn't do any damage; my dog bit you and caused damage but you provoked him."

"You've heard that Mark Bennett was a man that had been kicked down and out a number of times in his life and that he got up every time and rebuilt himself...that he was a man of outstanding character, optimism, personality. I believe the proof of that sits in this courtroom today. That Mr. Bennett is with us today. I have never seen a son more devoted to his father than Michael Bennett. Michael Bennett's relationship with his father is something that we all hope to have with our parents. How do you value that? How do you value the love of a son for his father and the love of a father for his son?"

"There's no doubt that Mark Bennett began dying the day he was born. But as I said to you in opening statement, there's a difference between walking off the end of the pier and being pushed. Mark Bennett was *pushed.*"

"You cannot undo Mark Bennett's suffering. You cannot bring him back. You can give Mark Bennett back his dignity and his respect. And you can give Mark Bennett and his loving and grieving family justice."

The trial recessed for the weekend.

The following Monday, about an hour-and-a-half after they began arriving at the court, the jury of four women and two men returned a verdict in favor of the defense.

"Rather fail with honor than succeed by fraud."
— Sophocles

Conclusion

After we moved into that small, one-bedroom apartment, I was riding with my father down Coldwater Canyon and asked about his childhood: "I grew up in a home," he said curtly. When I asked about his parents, "Your grandfather was a cruel person," was his embittered initial response. "What happened to your mother?" "My mother died when I was a little boy," he said, staring intently at the road ahead. The question and answer session ended there.

Sometime after my father moved to Baltimore, I showed him a photograph that was sent from a long lost cousin who found me through the Internet.

Sharen Hogarth had been digging deep into family history for several years. As a part of her research she had a friend visit a cemetery on Long Island in search of a relative's grave. After the friend found what Sharen was looking for, he turned around to leave; staring him in the face was an upright marker with the following epitaph:

Dora Ladena Boens
Born 1893-Died 1973
MOTHER DEAR
WE BEG YOUR
FORGIVENESS
Rest In Peace

My father looked at the photograph for a moment, then, he silently stood up from before the computer screen, and quietly walked away.

After my father passed away, during a visit with my brother in California, I went through a box containing some old photographs and my father's personal papers that Leon had retrieved from Louise's house. What I found was quite remarkable. Besides pictures of my father, Claire, Phil, and Bud from their days in the orphanage, secreted away inside a hidden portfolio pocket were two envelopes addressed to Claire from the Rockland State Hospital and postmarked 1946. One envelope had never been opened; the other contained an invoice with a balance forward for services rendered to Dora Boens. The Rockland State Hospital was a sprawling psychiatric facility located in Orangeburg, New York.

Dora had escaped the pogroms of Kishinev and Kalarash and left her mother and family behind to start a new life in America. Instead, she wound up abandoned by her husband in the squalor of the Lower East Side and had her three children taken away from her; she survived the ghetto and the ongoing poverty caused by the Great Depression only to watch her children get lured away by their father, leaving her virtually alone; her mother, Esther, and other family members were murdered by the Romanian Nazis in 1942 and buried in a mass grave in an unmarked field outside Kalarash. Dora became depressed, and at a time when it took nothing more than a doctor's signature to do so, she was simply "put away." She spent some thirty years in a mental asylum that discouraged contact with the outside world, including family, and that routinely used ice baths, insulin therapy, shock treatments, and lobotomies to treat the inmates. She died the same year that I was asking my father about his childhood and his parents.

My father, his sister and brother had jumped at the carrot that Harry had dangled in front of them. Fleeing the stigma of being orphans and the children of despised

624

immigrants, they reinvented themselves in California. When their mother was institutionalized, they fled that stigma, and that pain, too. Understandably, if not completely justified, they blamed Harry for everything. Phil, the most introspective, sensitive, and the youngest of the siblings, was the only one, it seems, to have faced his ghosts; he came to view Harry in the context of his life and times. My father would not accept that. To him, nothing could rationalize abandoning one's children, and he viewed Harry's treatment of Dora as inexcusable cruelty.

But guilt festered inside all three of them. The inscription on Dora's tombstone says it all, "We Beg Your Forgiveness." My father's "reaction" to his father-in-law's film, *Shock Corridor,* and his succumbing to his wife's pleas after just one day in rehab perhaps had their foundation in that guilt. When he cried on the witness stand under questioning during the custody trial, there's no doubt that my father was feeling the pain of his children, but perhaps he was also thinking of Dora. When my father said that his mother died when he was a little boy, the only lie that he ever told me, he was hiding his pain, and, perhaps, his guilt. And guilt and frustration can turn into anger.

From practically the day he was born my father suffered one hardship, insult, or assault after the next: his childhood in the slum and then in the orphanage and foster homes; the abandonment and deceit of his father; the Great Depression; prolonged combat in World War II and all the related trauma; a tumultuous and insane marriage to my mother and a bitter divorce that included the betrayal of his in-laws and their attempts to destroy him; repeated financial difficulties; a decade-long marriage to a terminal cynic, and finally the negligence and abandonment by those he trusted the most—hospitals and doctors. My father fought through it all with class, dignity, and integrity. He shouldered his adversities and tried to protect and provide for his children and others so they would not have to suffer the same. He was a champion of the underdog and an advocate for the disenfranchised. Although he had no parental role model, he became one to me as well as others. He gave his all. Like the rest of us, he had his faults. He made mistakes, no doubt. But my father acknowledged his mistakes and tried to learn from them, as he would want his children and their children to do. I can only speculate what he might have revealed in that doctor's office in 2004 had his confession not been interrupted.

My father was a remarkable human being for more reasons than I could possibly express. His mentorship, support, guidance, and love were without measure or expectation of return. He was strong yet gentle; tough yet compassionate; smart, but a little naïve; a fighter yet also a lover; serious yet possessing a great sense of humor; a realist but still an optimist; thrifty yet generous; honest, loyal, trustworthy, dependable, and faithful. He left a legacy for generations to cherish and I am among the luckiest of sons.

"They that sow in tears shall reap in joy."
— Psalms 126:5

On June 2, 2007, our daughter, Meira, and son-in-law, Reuven, were blessed with a baby girl whom they named after Dora. On March 29, 2011, they had a baby boy whom they named after my father.

When the police and executive staff of Kernan left the hospital room that day in 2004 and I stood beside my father assuring him that things would be different from then on, after saying how much he loved me, with his eyes closed, he made this, his final request: "I want you to write a book about my life...and I want you to call it *My Father*."

Some might think such a charge narcissistic. In my father's case nothing could possibly be further from the truth. Yes, he was a romantic, but he wasn't an egoist. He had spent his life fighting for himself or for others. No one ever fought for him. I had; and in return my father was giving me all that he had left: he was giving me his life.

So here it is, Dad. I pray that I've done it right. And I end with the only possibly appropriate words—*I love you forever!*

Epilogue

Among the papers in that long forgotten box in Leon's garage was a diary that my mother kept from 1945-1949, a glassine envelope containing a lock of her hair was wedged between the pages.

The first read through the diary was disappointing. In the hundreds of entries over that five-year period my mother only pithily expressed her emotions a handful of times. It was more like a list of names and a calendar of events than it was a journal of a young girl's most intimate thoughts. But in subsequent readings and analysis, I found the diary revealing, not only because of what was written in it, but also because of what was not. Those revelations provided some insight into my mother and what, at least in part, led to her sad and tragic life.

Her diary was a list of all that had "meaning" to her. It was an expression of the emptiness of her privileged existence. Her life was defined by whom she met, where she went, and what she did; and practically all of it related to her parents in some way. Her identity was intimately linked to their identities, which were defined by "The Industry." She never developed a sense of self and a life of her own. But who and what were to blame for that?

I agree with Sam Goldwyn Jr's, observation that my mother was the apple of her father's eye. And despite my grandmother's domineering personality, I believe she also deeply loved her daughter.

When researching my grandfather's career, virtually everyone that I interviewed—actors, directors, technicians, and former executives, as well as a few lawyers—praised him. "He was a fine gentleman;" "a "producer's producer;" "a man who knew his business;" "someone with no enemies in an industry of hate," and "he treated everyone with respect" were just a few of the superlatives people related to me. When I told Samuel Goldwyn Jr. of the interviews and that no one had a bad word to say about my grandfather, he said, "You won't, you won't hear anyone say anything bad about Leon."

But when I asked people for their opinion of my grandmother, her overbearing personality and meddlesome ways was a consistent refrain:

Shirley Ulmer, wife of celebrated film director Edgar G. Ulmer who was "enormously fond" of my grandfather, had this to say: "I felt so sorry for that girl. Rita would not let her breathe. She dressed Maxine in adult outfits and wouldn't let her have any friends her age. She couldn't even walk to school with the other children." Shirley, who was a script supervisor at both PRC and TPA, also related how my grandmother would show up on sets and meddle in the filming, which "drove Edgar crazy."

Arianne Ulmer Cipes, the daughter of Edgar and Shirley Ulmer, said the following: "Rita was difficult. It was all her way and she was used to having a husband that indulged that...[Maxine] wouldn't have a chance because she wouldn't have any back up from her dad,

I'll tell you, no backup whatsoever, there was only one ruler in that household."

Sidney Salkow, a director with an impressively long list of credits in both motion pictures and television, referred to my grandmother as a "terror" and an "intimidating woman."

Gerri Firks Brawerman, the widow of Sam Firks: "Your grandmother was a very difficult woman."

Leon Kaplan, the granddaddy of legitimate entertainment lawyers in the 40s and beyond, recalled how my grandmother would show up at executive meetings (something that was unheard of in those days) and "often embarrass your grandfather."

Stan Neufeld, the son of Sigmund Neufeld who together with his brother, Sam, ran the western unit at PRC and later TPA's Canadian subsidiary, confidently blamed my mother's sad and tragic life on my grandmother and her "domineering" personality.

My father adamantly blamed Rita for her daughter's destruction and referred to her without question as "the villain" calling her "one of the three most hated women in Hollywood."

The list and the theme went on and on.

But serious questions remained: Where was my grandfather in all of this? Why would any man tolerate someone so reviled and at the expense of the apple of his eye? And what happened to his money? Such an astute businessman who played important roles in building companies like Columbia, Monogram, PRC, Goldwyn, MCA's Television Revue, TPA, and who produced scores of films and almost two-dozen television series should have left an estate worth millions.

The answer, perhaps, to the first question came from more than one person that I interviewed who referenced my grandfather's infidelities, which seem to have begun in the 40s and continued all the way up to the early 70s.

In light of his genteel, conservative persona and professional reputation, it was a shocking revelation. And it was so well hidden, not even my father knew about it; but others obviously did.

The most intimate source of that information was Monroe Sachson, the son of my grandfather's longtime film and television associate and relative of my grandmother, Arthur Sachson. In a 1999 interview, Monroe referred to Rita as "a barracuda" and that "Leon was not faithful to Rita... and Rita knew it." "Was she then a victim or a villain?" I asked. "She was a victim." Monroe replied, and then added "but she drove Leon to it."

But whether she was the ultimate cause of her husband's infidelities or not they certainly wreaked havoc with Rita and Leon very well may have tolerated her obtrusive behavior out of guilt. More importantly, if the affairs were know to my grandmother, they were likely known to my mother as well.

Arianne Ulmer Cipes, who suffered from her father's infidelities, offered some insight as to both why Rita tolerated her husband's indiscretions and how they in all probability affected my mother: "[Infidelity] was very acceptable in those circles, as long as you didn't shame your wife [publicly]." Divorce for such things in "those circles," according to Arianne, "was not an option." Then she added, "Daughter's of philanderers live in terror of losing them."

As for what happened to my grandfather's money, the answer to that came from a combination of my mother's diary, more interviews, and a stack of letters and telegrams he had sent to his then fiancée in 1927.

When I began researching my grandfather's career in 1998, one of the first people I located was Herb Baerwitz, his lawyer. When I called his law office, where he remained "of counsel," his secretary patched me through to him while he was on his yacht in Marina Del Rey.

In his eighties, still possessing the gravelly voice I remembered from decades before, Baerwitz was lucid, friendly, and seemed eager to speak with me.

He described my grandfather as someone who "... had a very varied career. He was a very important man in the business at one time. At the end of his career, he wasn't that important in the business, unfortunately."

When I raised the subject of what happened to my grandfather's money, Baerwitz said, "I don't know, I never counted his money. I don't know what he had. I know he died broke. If he had any money, I don't know what he did with it..."

Then Baerwitz added:

"Unfortunately, I don't know the stories that I hear, but I didn't know as to be *true*, that your grandfather at one time had some money, how much I don't know, but he was a *very* big gambler. And he lost all his money, is my best recollection."

Shortly after our conversation, I travelled out to L.A. where I met with Baerwitz and Leon Kaplan at the Friar's Club in Beverly Hills. Baerwitz demeanor at the meeting was markedly less friendly than during my initial conversation with him; he seemed suspicious and angry. Just before parting, he said something curious:

"When you first told me about what you were doing, I didn't think that that you would find much. I thought it would be too hard, but obviously it's not."

In a subsequent exchange of letters, Baerwitz lawyered up, invoking variations on the phrase "to the best of my recollection" eleven times in one, one-and-a-half-page letter. Ultimately he became hostile and denied that he was my grandfather's lawyer and that he was involved with or even aware of my parents' divorce at the time that it took place. My grandfather's will, corporate documents, testimony of friends, relatives and business associates, and the transcript of the divorce proceedings all contradict his assertions on their face. As just one example, in his will, besides appointing him co-executor and the trustee of his estate, my grandfather referred to Baerwitz as "my friend and attorney" and named his two children as contingent beneficiaries. Why Baerwitz would have denied all of that is a question yet to be answered. But Baerwitz' supposed speculation about my grandfather being a "*very* big gambler" turned out to be dead-on accurate.

In my mother's diary she makes multiple references to visiting her father while vacationing in Palm Springs at a place called The 139 Club, which, according to published reports, was a cheesy, mob-owned-and-operated gambling den that sported a gun turret outside its entrance.

Also according to my mother's diary, following the great success of *Best Years of Our Lives*, my grandfather took his wife and daughter on a trip to Las Vegas and then to Palm Springs where again he frequented The 139 Club. A little over a year later he sold his house. Right after that he bought a new Cadillac and took his family on a two-week long gambling tour that included Las Vegas, Palm Springs (The 139 Club) and a horseracing track in San Francisco.

According to my brother, who spent numerous vacations with the family in Las Vegas, routinely upon arrival at the Riviera Hotel Casino my grandfather would open a ten-thousand-dollar gambling account. If he won substantially—a thousand dollars and up—he'd have my grandmother deposit those proceeds with the cashier. The only explanation for this seems to be that he was paying off previous gambling debts.

My brother also recalled having regularly dined together with my grandfather and the Riviera's co-owner and powerful Hollywood attorney, Harvey Silbert. According to author Gus Russo and based on FBI documents he obtained through the Freedom of Information Act, Silbert, who was a close associate of the well-known organized-crime link to Hollywood, attorney Sidney Korshak, was suspected of using his prestigious law firm to launder the Riviera's skimmed casino profits. Russo's meticulously researched, thoroughly documented, and well-written book, titled *SUPERMOB*,[197] reads like a who's who of my grandfather's friends and associates. And among the names in Russo's book is the law firm of Ball, Hunt, Brown, and Baerwitz; Baerwitz being Herbert G. Baerwitz, and Brown being Edmond "Pat" Brown, the former governor of California.

Also, according to my brother, my grandfather bragged about being at the 1946 grand opening of infamous mob boss Bugsy Segal's Flamingo Hotel in Las Vegas.

And then of course there was my father's recollection of how "your grandfather loved the races" and his association with slot machine kingpin Bob Gans and Gans' former gambling syndicate protégé Sam Firks.

The first mention, if not the genesis, of my grandfather's gambling addiction appears in a 1927 letter that he wrote to my grandmother while on his last road trip as a travelling dish salesman, in which he writes, "I played cards with some of the boys last night. I lost eight dollars, but I really enjoyed it!"

Monroe Sachson offered another revelation: my grandfather's gambling addiction was the reason why he came out of retirement not long after the sale of TPA and began making feature films again. According to

---

197 *SUPERMOB*: How Sidney Korshak And His Criminal Associates Became America's Hidden Power Brokers. 2006 Bloomsbury.

Sachson, he would make a picture, gamble away all the money, and then make another picture, and so on.

Toward the end of my grandfather's career, as he became increasingly desperate, he not only continued his trysts and persisted with gambling, he also made foolish investments. For example, he purchased a huge block of stock in the Cinerama Corporation, which manufactured a wide-screen film system utilizing equipment so complex and cumbersome it was impractical for shooting on locations and required an equally unrealistic system for theatre projection, among other problems. But bad investments were not the only problem: he also engaged in shady transactions, such as buying and selling stock in a "new technology" company called Laser Power Industries, which ostensibly had "offices" stretching from Los Angeles to New Mexico to Texas. In reality, the company consisted of little more than a stack of batteries in a California warehouse. The principals involved with Laser wound up doing years in federal prison for securities and mail fraud.

Also, atypically for him, my grandfather embarked on poorly thought out movie ventures, which began with his partnership with Sam Firks in F&F Productions.

Sidney Salkow, who retained a very high opinion of and fondness for my grandfather, recalled how Leon had contacted him while he (Salkow) was in London making a picture. According to Sidney, my grandfather was enamored with director Sam Fuller, whose movies didn't make much money in the U.S. but were popular in Europe. It was an attraction that Salkow could not appreciate because of Fuller's unconventional cinematic style and volatile personality. My grandfather had just completed filming the F&F production *Shock Corridor* and was counting on foreign sales to recoup his negative costs. However, the censor in England would not approve the film for release because it appeared critical of psychiatric hospitals, a subject the Brits were very sensitive about. Even after Salkow offered, on my grandfather's behalf, to prominently display a disclaimer that the story was in no way a reflection of England's mental health system the British censor would not pass the film.

Shock Corridor was eventually released in the U.S., where it bombed, as did three other F&F films—another directed by Fuller and two directed by Salkow.

By all accounts, Sam Firks, his gambling-syndicate associations aside, was a well-liked and kind person. But Firks apparently felt that my grandfather had deceived him somehow and he became a very unhappy investor. Not long after the divorce of my parents, my father ran into Sam who told him that he was so angry with my grandfather he wanted to sue him. Gerri Firks Brawerman, Sam's young widow, dismissed that notion, claiming, "Sam didn't believe in suing."

But according to Herb Baerwitz and Stanley Sherdorf, Firks' accountant, Sam Firks and my grandfather indeed had a serious falling out and, although there is no record of a lawsuit, F&F Productions and all of its products, including the four feature films, wound up completely in Firks' hands.

After the F&F Productions debacle, my grandfather purchased his shiny, new, black Cadillac with the gold damask upholstery and embarked on what would be his last project, which, unfortunately, was an even greater fiasco:

Richard McDonald was a young CPA working for the prestigious accounting firm of Arthur Andersen & Co. One of his clients was oil baron J. Paul Getty—the richest man in the world at the time. When one of J. Paul's sons, J. Ronald Getty, asked him to draw up a list of possible investment areas, McDonald included motion pictures among ten options. The young Getty was intrigued by the idea and McDonald engineered a meeting between himself, my grandfather, whom he had met through social functions, and Getty. The three subsequently formed GMF Productions, with offices at Goldwyn Studios. My grandfather hired Morey Amsterdam's son, Gregory, as his executive assistant, and he called on Leon Kaplan to act as legal counsel.

Not long after GMF got underway, Kaplan cut bait because he "wasn't getting paid." The reason, Kaplan said, was "Getty didn't have any money."

Getty was one of five of J. Paul's sons, but to his second marriage, which, like his first, ended in divorce. Figuring that Ron was well taken care of by his mother, who was substantially wealthy in her own right, J. Paul provided his son with little support. But Ron's mother's money was tied up in East Germany and had been inaccessible since after the war. At least that was what Leon Kaplan believed to be the case.

But Dick McDonald explained things differently. In fact, said McDonald, Getty was funding GMF.

Around the same time as his involvement with GMF, my grandfather formed a corporation called Zenon together with a former cameraman of his by the name of Ralph Hogue. Hogue had developed a unique process for color correction and optical printing of theatrical film. My grandfather asked McDonald to find investors to fund the development of Zenon in exchange for an equity interest in the company. McDonald subsequently secured investors and became a stockholder.

GMF started making feature films in 1969. Its first picture, *Flareup*, was an exploitation piece about an exotic dancer in a seedy Las Vegas dive. The film featured shallow drama and dumb dialogue but relied on the star, Raquel Welch, for draw. It was shot on location in Las Vegas where Getty, McDonald, and my grandfather stayed at the Riviera Hotel, of course.

After completing a second film, another exploitation piece, titled *Honky,* my grandfather moved the company's offices to a bungalow formerly occupied by John Wayne and Frank Sinatra at Warner Brothers Studios.

GMF's third picture, *Zeppelin,* was shot on location in England and Malta. Not long after the picture got underway, technical difficulties cropped up[198] that were threatening the entire project and Dick McDonald was dispatched to Europe to help iron things out.

But two weeks after he arrived overseas, McDonald received a telegram from Leon informing him that he had been fired. According to McDonald, Getty was aggressively going after Zenon and he wanted McDonald out of the way. He (McDonald) surmised that Getty prevailed upon Leon to find a way of getting rid of him and that Leon, wanting to maintain his relationship with Getty, went looking for a pretext. He found it in a five hundred dollar check that McDonald had written as a reimbursement to himself for fifteen hundred dollars in equipment he had provided to GMF. Leon, McDonald said, used the innocent reimbursement to accuse him of stealing from the company.

After the firing, Dick McDonald went his way. However, he later learned that Ron Getty had leveraged his way into Zenon and then, McDonald suggested, put so much pressure on Ralph Hogue, Hogue suffered a fatal heart attack. Getty, McDonald stated, took control of Zenon, transferring the assets to his wholly owned corporation and opening a plant in the San Fernando Valley. McDonald, who was still a shareholder in Zenon, filed a $140 million lawsuit. The evening after the suit was filed, Getty, McDonald asserts, went to the Zenon

---

198 The film, a World War I thriller starring Michael York and Elke Sommer, involved the use of an actual blimp. In addition to technical difficulties with the airship, such as the gondola becoming detached, tragedy struck when a helicopter that was being used to shoot aerial scenes collided with a biplane killing four people.

warehouse and smashed all of the equipment so there would be nothing of value for McDonald to go after.

GMF, which had shrunk into Getty-Fromkess Productions, made a total of five pictures and was the final, inglorious chapter of my grandfather's filmmaking career. Ron Getty wound up with the company and all of its holdings.

Dick McDonald recently recalled his impressions of my grandparents and my mother from those days:

"Rita seemed like a lady who was very powerful at one time and was still trying to exert her power but didn't have any...Leon was a very powerful guy and he took advantage of it from time to time... [The] first time I went into Chasen's, which of course was a big deal, he insisted that we have the head table, the table that everybody walked by to get into the place, and he got it. He was *powerful!*" "I didn't really get to know Maxine. I just remember that she seemed to be deeply dependent on her parents, and troubled."

Remarkably, despite having been "stabbed in the back by Leon," Dick McDonald still remembers my grandfather with fondness and refers to him as "a decent guy."

McDonald's story and his lack of acrimony pretty well sums up the dichotomy that was my grandfather.

But was it dichotomy, or was it deceit?

In contrast to Richard McDonald, Gregory Amsterdam remains remarkably bitter about his three-year stint working for my grandfather, his father's good friend. In fact, when I first contacted him Gregory did not want to speak of his experiences: "...to be truthful, your grandfather screwed up my life really great, and I really don't want to talk to you about him or anything to do with those people."

But after explaining my background and a little of the family history, Gregory opened up. Recalling the relationship between my grandfather and Ron Getty, here's what he had to say: "He didn't care how bad Getty was, or what Getty would do, or how he would louse people up...he was just gonna go ahead and do his thing." As an example, Gregory related the following anecdote: "...it was the second or third day that I was working with him. Getty came into town and we were walking down one of the corridors at Goldwyn and Getty comes out with this anti-Semitic remark, I just couldn't believe it, your grandfather, it just never fazed him a bit, he just kept right on walking, just ignored it...whatever [Getty] wanted, no matter what the heck he said, no matter how it worked, your grandfather went along with it."

Gregory observed that my grandfather was a *"really good"* producer who knew his business, and for that reason wondered why he was involved with people who knew nothing about making motion pictures. He surmised at the time that it was probably because it was "[Leon's] last hurrah" in the industry.

Remembering Rita and the relationship between her and Leon, Gregory offered an intriguing analysis: "Your grandmother was a great benefit in making people feel sympathy toward your grandfather. When she came on like gangbusters—*she got into just about everything*—everybody would say, 'Oh, poor Leon.' I think he used that for years and years. I think it was a real benefit, like having a linebacker block for you," "Manipulation?" I asked. Amsterdam laughed, "Absolutely! He was spectacular at that."

In February of 1963, Allied Artists published a mini biography of my grandfather. It was part of a publicity campaign prior to the release of *Shock Corridor,* the initial product of F&F productions, and it contains some interesting "facts" about Leon Fromkess:

1. "He came to Hollywood as a Wall Street Financier." (Not true. He was a stock salesman who became a film salesman/treasurer who became a producer.)
2. "He graduated from Columbia University, where he majored in Corporation Finance." (His Columbia University transcript indicates that he took only one course.)
3. "He became a general office man for an import-export firm..." (Not quite true. He was a traveling dish salesman.)
4. "...he went into the brokerage business for himself, with a seat on the American Stock Exchange." (No such record could be located with the NYSE/AMEX archivist. According to my father, as well as Henry Magnin, Rabbi Magnin's son, who worked as a broker alongside my father, my grandfather traded stocks from a first floor window at a time when the nascent AMEX was known as "the Curb.")
5. He became President of PRC in "1939." (1942 would have been more accurate.)
6. He formed "his own TV company...It was Television Programs of America..." (No, he sold *his* co-owned television company to TPA, where he headed production.)
7. He sold TPA for $11 million. (At least the amount was correct.)
8. He retired and then "took his wife around the world, and they lived in England for a while before his return to movie-making." (Not unless touring Santa Monica Boulevard is like rounding the globe and England was a subdivision of Los Angeles at the time.)

9. "And he has had the same wife, his first, for 35 years. She was Rita Minton, a brilliant soprano whose accompanist was Giuseppe Bamboscheck..." (The same wife, yes, but hardly his only female companion, and who, according to the New York Times, performed a mediocre recital in 1927 at Aeolian Hall. There is no one named "Giuseppe Bamboscheck" mentioned in the review.)

10. He was financing his own pictures. (Yes, but with Sam Firks' money.)

11. "[Leon and Rita] have a daughter, Maxine, wife of Los Angeles stock broker Mark Bennett, and two grandchildren, Leon, Jr., 7, and Michael, 5." (Finally something that was true.)

My grandfather had no reason to lie and embellish. He had a remarkable and prolific career and was held in high esteem by his colleagues in the industry. Sadly, it wasn't enough; he needed a false legend.

In addition to all of the deceptions, which I had sensed since I was a child, it turned out that the man who had been squeezing his grandson for ten dollars a month for phone calls to his mother from college had also disinherited him for having loved and been loyal to his father.

Lastly, winning Bozo the Clown's Treasure Chest of Toys was a setup and Iron Eyes Cody was really an Italian.

After he marginally recovered from his first heart attack, my grandfather suffered cardiac arrest while at the racetrack at Hollywood Park. He was found with about fifteen hundred dollars in his pocket. At the time of his death, his estate was worth a little over $71,000, which included a block of Columbia Pictures Corporation debentures; ironically almost his same net worth and holdings after engineering the Columbia Pictures' public stock offering in 1929.

In the end, his more than forty-year career in motion pictures and television brought him no blessings where they mattered most—with his family. Instead, the morally bankrupt and ethically corrupt culture of Hollywood caused him only sorrow and tragedy. He became a slave to his passions. His life and the life of his family would have been better served had he remained a traveling dish salesman.

LF With PRC 1940

...with Goldwyn 1946

...on location 1970

The one question remaining was not so much why but how my mother became addicted to drugs? Was Dr. Oucest the only medical villain in that part of the story?

In her diary, during the period from January 5, 1945 until May 15, 1949, my mother noted two hundred and forty-three office visits to one doctor alone: a well-known, Beverly Hills otolaryngologist who frequently used two controversial techniques for ostensibly treating sinus conditions: one involved puncturing and draining people's sinuses, the other, briefly implanting metal capsules of the radioactive mineral radium in their sinus cavities. The doctor was not only draining for dollars, and in so doing creating an opening for chronic sinus infections, which then had to be treated with antibiotics and pain medication, he was exposing his patients to a known cancer-causing agent. Both my mother and my grandmother, who also frequented the same doctor, predictably developed thyroid cancer and eventually lost all of their teeth. My grandmother, according to family legend, was also addicted to prescription drugs.

And there were other doctors mentioned in my mother's diary; doctors who were known in Hollywood as "studio docs," or "script doctors," and who also made house calls.

While my mother's hypochondria may very well have been caused by the pain her parents inflicted on her through their selfishness and being destructive role models, doctors who debased their profession and abrogated their sacred duty in order to ingratiate themselves into the entertainment industry and the society pages were responsible for getting her hooked on drugs and then perpetuating her addiction. It's a Hollywood custom that continues to this very day.

Leon and Rita Fromkess' only child, who was clearly a loving, caring, sensitive, and compassionate human being, and who would have made a wonderful mother and proud grandmother, never had a chance.

When the Maskilim abandoned their incomparable heritage of sacred values, wisdom, and Holiness, and engaged in their campaign of assimilation and shameful disparaging of the irreproachable rabbis, they effectively robbed generations of Jews of their identities, indeed their very lifeblood, dooming them to blindly chasing after dreams that were little more than noxious vapors...dreams such as Hollywood.

"I call to testify against you this day the heavens and the earth; life and death I place before you, the blessing and the curse; and you shall choose life, so that you will live, you and your seed."

— Deuteronomy 30:19

Acknowledgments

Agood friend warned me that writing a book is like rowing across the ocean...alone. I appreciate the simile. But while I did the rowing, I was not really alone; I had the generous help of many people. In no particular order, here are but some:

To my cousins, Wayne and Yvone Rowe, who spent days reading and reviewing the manuscript, answering my endless emails and phone calls, offering expert advice, suggestions, and so much more: Wayne and Yvone, if there's polish, you helped add it. I could not imagine better advisors. I am deeply indebted. Thank you barely scratches the surface. You have my eternal gratitude.

With profound gratitude to Sharen Hogarth, who reconstructed a long lost family history: The hours of phone calls and your dogged persistence in trying to uncover and reconnect with Dora's family history, and therefore our family history, were essential in returning us a long-lost identity: thank you from all of us, Sharen.

To the late Hyman Bogen for relating to me his experiences in the HOA and for writing his book, *The*

646

Luckiest Orphans: Thank you, Hy. You preserved an important history.

To Seymour Siegel, a former "inmate" of the HOA, for the many hours of phone conversations and his insights as a veteran therapist, not to mention his book, *An Orphan in New York City*: Thank you from the heart, Sy.

To Leona M. Ferrer who lovingly delivered on the goods when it came to my father's Hebrew Orphan Asylum records, as well as the staff of the Jewish Childcare Association: Thank you all.

And a hardy thank you to Gunnar Berg, archivist at the Yivo Institute in New York, for digging through the dusty boxes of National Desertion Bureau records in a New Jersey warehouse.

My appreciation also goes to Dr. Virginia Keiser for her expertise on the Rockland State Hospital.

A special debt of gratitude is owed to Sherman Grancell and Bernard "Bud" Rowe (Uncle Bud). Thank you both. At one hundred years young, you guys are remarkable treasures.

Thanks also go out to Professor Fred Viehe for sharing his encyclopedic knowledge of California's corrupt political history.

When it came to researching early Hollywood and my grandfather's career, I was fortunate to have the assistance of the following: Samuel Goldwyn Jr., Adele Nadel, Ann Rutherford, the late Virginia Gray, the late Virginia Mayo, Gregory Amsterdam, the late Kay Amsterdam, Arianne Ulmer, the late Shirley Ulmer, the late Peter Graves, Alex Kogan Jr., the late Sidney Salkow, Pat Salkow, Emanuel Wolf and Barry Efson from Allied Artists, the late Leon Kaplan, Herb Baerwitz, the late Joseph H. Lewis, Stan Neufeld, Max Seligman, A.C. Lyles of Paramount, the staff of the Margaret Herrick Library, the late Ann Savage, the late Lionel Hampton,

Professor Malvin Wald, Marc Wannamaker, Michael Kahn (film editor extraordinaire), the late Leon Chooluck, the late Jackson Dube, Mrs. Ralph Hogue, the late Eddie Dean, Marvin Gluck, Patrick Curtis, Peter Breck, Gerri Firks Brawerman, Dale Robertson, The Producers Guild, Michael York, Stanley Sherdorf, and Constance Towers.

For their personal recollections of my mother and grandparents, my sincere appreciation goes to Adele Nadel, Rhoda Hyman, the late Monroe Sachson, Bernie Roth, Stan Neufeld, Arianne Ulmer, the late Shirley Ulmer, Perry Maltz, and Justice Joan Dempsey Klein.

A huge thank you goes to Richard McDonald who, for years, answered my questions with good cheer and has never kept a chip on his shoulder. Thank you Dick!

Gratitude is also due to Geoffrey Doughty for sharing his knowledge of Robert Young.

To Roger Mobley: There are not enough words, Roger. So please just accept an insufficient thank you. My father made the right choice!

To Charlene Mobley and the late Lance Mobley: My sincere thanks for sharing your fond memories of my father. He held the same for you.

When it came to deciphering military jargon and guiding me through my father's military career and those terrible war years, I was privileged to have Lieutenant General James Vaught (U.S. Army, Ret) by my side. General, you are a patriot, a worthy commander, and, I'm proud to say, a friend. Thank you and I salute you.

And an additional salute goes to Major General Maurice Edmonds (U.S. Army, Ret) for helping as well and encouraging me to follow through on the project.

To our wonderful neighbor, Truman Hamrick, a proud American and the greatest liberal redneck who ever lived: Thank you Truman for your friendship, support, and for turning me on to General Vaught and General Edmonds.

In his 90s and more than sixty-five years after the event occurred, Major Jerold Wilwerding (U.S. Army, Ret) still laughs at the incident that almost got my father court-martialed; thank you, Major.

Joe Rodimak may not have been thrilled about having to serve at the 21st. Replacement Depot, but he did so with competence and determination, just like he did when he spoke with me about the 21st. I'm grateful, Joe.

To John Lauless and the late Orill Mack and the late Joe Chartrand for relating their experiences at the Los Negros landing: You are owed much gratitude and are worthy of being among "The Greatest Generation."

Thaddeus "Ted" Majusick has nothing to be ashamed of for not shooting that enemy infiltrator at the beach on Los Negros. On the contrary, we all owe him a salute of respect. Thanks Ted for all of the help and sharing the painful memories.

Albert Anthony Pinto gave his life so that Americans could remain free. His brother, Tommy Pinto, has spent the last sixty-seven years with the heartache of going through life without a brother. And he has kept his brother's memory alive and afforded him the honor he deserves. Thank you for your recollections Tommy.

When Troy McGill defended his position and then charged the oncoming enemy at the Momote airstrip, he made the ultimate sacrifice so that his fellow soldiers would live. General MacArthur made the right decision in awarding him the Congressional Medal of Honor. Wesley McGill has kept the flame of his Uncle Troy's memory burning bright. Thank you, Wesley, for your assistance and kindness.

Much appreciation goes to the 1st. Cavalry Division and 5th Cavalry Regiment Associations for their help and the respect they have afforded my father's memory.

The competent and remarkably congenial staff at the National Archives and Records Administration in College Park, Maryland (a true national treasure) pointed me again and again in the right direction to finding the files on the 5th Cavalry Regiment. Thanks to their assistance I was able to accurately reconstruct my father's combat experience, although I often had to hold back tears while reading the documents.

Much appreciation goes out to James Zobel, chief archivist for the Douglas MacArthur Memorial and Library in Norfolk, Virginia for his assistance in researching my father's service with SWPA General Headquarters and more.

Although it is now peaceful, with the exception of things like Nike sneakers and digital cameras, not much has changed on Los Negros. Malaria remains a serious problem and war munitions still occasionally injure natives. Special gratitude goes out to David Ulg Ketepa from New Guinea who graciously sought out a contact for me on Los Negros, and to Rhoda Kolopen, the fruit of David's effort, who walked off distances and photographed locations on the island in response to my requests. David and Rhoda, you are both gems. My father must be smiling.

To Sheila and Liz Weller for their thoughts and comments about the house on Elm Drive where they grew up and their impressions of Dr. Federico Oucest (the pseudonym): Thank you Sheila and Liz, we've all somehow managed to survive growing up in the toxic haze of Hollywood.

And my appreciation goes to Steven Kopald for his recollections of Richie Mark.

Thank you to Dr. Sharon Buck and Dr. Mayer Liebman for their expert psychological insights.

Dear Gus Russo: Thank you for your sage advice, and for writing *SUPERMOB*. Your work has helped to bring to light the corruption that infected the lives of so many.

Thanks are also due to Janet Linde, the archivist for the NYSE who eagerly searched the voluminous files for me, only to find nothing.

To my cousin, Dennis Rowe, who made himself available and was willing to delve into the recesses of his memory and embrace a not always pleasant past: Thank you, Den; I still look up to you for your kind and elegant ways. You have inherited much of that naturally aristocratic aura possessed by your mom as well as my father and Uncle Phil.

Richard Bennett embodies the same love, compassion, and sensitivity of his father, my Uncle Phil. Thanks for everything, Rick. You'll always be in my heart.

To Barb K., Bill K., AG, GM, AH, BJ, BF, AK, BF, MB, RL, LM, LG, PH, JH, LM, DN, MM, MAJ, and all the rest who dwell in the ranks of the anonymous: Your assistance in helping me fight for my father by fighting for others is hereby recognized and, as always, very deeply appreciated.

And to David Wildberger, who stood stalwart by me through the fight and always offered sound advice and trustworthy counsel: As you would say, David, thank you my friend.

A special thank you goes to the journalists and others who took my father's story to heart and expertly presented it to the public so that others may not have to suffer. They include: Mary Claude Foster, Terry Moran, Tisha Thompson, Lisa Fletcher, David Snyder, Bob Langreth, Melanie Alnwick, Jane Akre, Bruce Leshan, Michael Berens, Judith Graham, Coco Ballantyne, Jonathan Rockoff, Dennis O'Brien, Arthur Allen; as well as the staff at ABC, CBS, FOX, Scientific American, Forbes Magazine, The Baltimore Sun, The Washington Times, The Washington Post, Infection Control Today,

The Townsend Letter, Resources For The Future (RFF), Extending The Cure (ETC), and the Robert Wood Johnson Foundation, to name a few.

My longtime friend, Ed. Ritenour (Chief of Police, Ret), who took the time to review the manuscript and offer his comments and suggestions: That's what friends are for. Thank you, Ed.

Resounding applause are due to Bill Hackney of Staiman Designs for taking a personal interest and expertly performing computer wizardry to translate a cover concept into meaningful and striking artwork. And thanks to Jeremy Staiman for having rachmonis on my budget.

To my brother Leon: Lee, what can I say. You came through when dad needed you most and you provided me with much big-brother support. You also weathered my incessant questions over the last three years. You're a good son and brother. Dad loved you and was proud of you, and so am I.

And to my mother-in-law, Ruth Leibowitz: Thank you, Bubby, for the love you showed to my father, and the chicken soup.

To our wonderful children, Meira, Yair, Yehuda, Amitai, and Yoni: You are fortunate to have had such a special grandfather, and his soul remains fortunate to have all of you. You are his blessings, and the blessings of your parents.

To my wife Sharon: Besides all of your gorgeous qualities and the amazing things that you do, including keeping our family firmly anchored in the often turbulent sea of life, you treated my father with unbounded love and consideration. He loved you immensely, and so do I.

Author's Note

Federico Ousest, Jerold Maisef, Carmen Vietik, Helga von Flancelaut, Bruce Orko, Ralph Leslie Mudd, Fanny Bergoine, Linda Bland, Louise, Janet, Darla, and Bernie, are all pseudonyms. Any similarities between these names and the physical descriptions of the characters in this book and real people are coincidental.

Rabbi Dov Hesed is a pseudonym.

In consideration of the families of these brave men who were killed in the service of their country, Major Frank Fordleigh and Captain John Strong are also pseudonyms.

In addition to other devices of obfuscation, Beauford, Pleasantville, and Sunnyside are pseudonyms. The reader is encouraged *not* to attempt to identify which hospitals these represent. Because these institutions have taken significant steps to reduce their infection rates since the events that took place in this book, it would be unfair to associate the facts of my father's case with them now. Furthermore, infection control failures are problems that exist in facilities across the country.

Therefore, it serves no purpose to point an accusing finger at merely a few hospitals.

Similarly, although this book details many of the failures of the American medical system, it would be irresponsible to leave the reader with the impression that medical care or medical science is mainly about harm. On the contrary, the majority of doctors and nurses are caring, competent professionals who utilize their skill and talents to deliver often lifesaving care to those in need and most medical procedures do exactly that. Nevertheless, there remains far too much on the other side of the scale, which in addition to the injuries and deaths has eroded the relationship between patients and caregivers that once existed. Hopefully this book will contribute in some way to reducing preventable harm and re-establishing mutual respect by encouraging *true* leadership.

All photographs contained in this book are from the author's collection and/or are in public domain. The maps of Los Negros Island and Leyte Island are from the Center for Military History.

17687627R00395

Made in the USA
Middletown, DE
04 February 2015